Peter H. Solomon Jr., Kaja Gadowska (Eds.)

LEGAL CHANGE IN POST-COMMUNIST STATES
Progress, Reversions, Explanations

Bibliografische Information der Deutschen Nationalbibliothek
Die Deutsche Nationalbibliothek verzeichnet diese Publikation in der Deutschen Nationalbibliografie; detaillierte bibliografische Daten sind im Internet über http://dnb.d-nb.de abrufbar.

Bibliographic information published by the Deutsche Nationalbibliothek
Die Deutsche Nationalbibliothek lists this publication in the Deutsche Nationalbibliografie; detailed bibliographic data are available in the Internet at http://dnb.d-nb.de.

Cover picture: ID 39446908 © Vecarla | Dreamstime.com

ISBN-13: 978-3-8382-1312-5
© *ibidem*-Verlag, Stuttgart 2019
Alle Rechte vorbehalten

Das Werk einschließlich aller seiner Teile ist urheberrechtlich geschützt. Jede Verwertung außerhalb der engen Grenzen des Urheberrechtsgesetzes ist ohne Zustimmung des Verlages unzulässig und strafbar. Dies gilt insbesondere für Vervielfältigungen, Übersetzungen, Mikroverfilmungen und elektronische Speicherformen sowie die Einspeicherung und Verarbeitung in elektronischen Systemen.

All rights reserved. No part of this publication may be reproduced, stored in or introduced into a retrieval system, or transmitted, in any form, or by any means (electronic, mechanical, photocopying, recording or otherwise) without the prior written permission of the publisher. Any person who does any unauthorized act in relation to this publication may be liable to criminal prosecution and civil claims for damages.

Printed in the EU

Soviet and Post-Soviet Politics and Society (SPPS) Vol. 208
ISSN 1614-3515

General Editor: Andreas Umland,
Institute for Euro-Atlantic Cooperation, Kyiv, umland@stanfordalumni.org

Commissioning Editor: Max Jakob Horstmann,
London, mjh@ibidem.eu

EDITORIAL COMMITTEE*

DOMESTIC & COMPARATIVE POLITICS
Prof. **Ellen Bos**, *Andrássy University of Budapest*
Dr. **Gergana Dimova**, *University of Winchester*
Dr. **Andrey Kazantsev**, *MGIMO (U) MID RF, Moscow*
Prof. **Heiko Pleines**, *University of Bremen*
Prof. **Richard Sakwa**, *University of Kent at Canterbury*
Dr. **Sarah Whitmore**, *Oxford Brookes University*
Dr. **Harald Wydra**, *University of Cambridge*

SOCIETY, CLASS & ETHNICITY
Col. **David Glantz**, *"Journal of Slavic Military Studies"*
Dr. **Marlène Laruelle**, *George Washington University*
Dr. **Stephen Shulman**, *Southern Illinois University*
Prof. **Stefan Troebst**, *University of Leipzig*

POLITICAL ECONOMY & PUBLIC POLICY
Dr. **Andreas Goldthau**, *Central European University*
Dr. **Robert Kravchuk**, *University of North Carolina*
Dr. **David Lane**, *University of Cambridge*
Dr. **Carol Leonard**, *Higher School of Economics, Moscow*
Dr. **Maria Popova**, *McGill University, Montreal*

FOREIGN POLICY & INTERNATIONAL AFFAIRS
Dr. **Peter Duncan**, *University College London*
Prof. **Andreas Heinemann-Grüder**, *University of Bonn*
Prof. **Gerhard Mangott**, *University of Innsbruck*
Dr. **Diana Schmidt-Pfister**, *University of Konstanz*
Dr. **Lisbeth Tarlow**, *Harvard University, Cambridge*
Dr. **Christian Wipperfürth**, *N-Ost Network, Berlin*
Dr. **William Zimmerman**, *University of Michigan*

HISTORY, CULTURE & THOUGHT
Dr. **Catherine Andreyev**, *University of Oxford*
Prof. **Mark Bassin**, *Södertörn University*
Prof. **Karsten Brüggemann**, *Tallinn University*
Dr. **Alexander Etkind**, *University of Cambridge*
Dr. **Gasan Gusejnov**, *Moscow State University*
Prof. **Leonid Luks**, *Catholic University of Eichstaett*
Dr. **Olga Malinova**, *Russian Academy of Sciences*
Dr. **Richard Mole**, *University College London*
Prof. **Andrei Rogatchevski**, *University of Tromsø*
Dr. **Mark Tauger**, *West Virginia University*

ADVISORY BOARD*

Prof. **Dominique Arel**, *University of Ottawa*
Prof. **Jörg Baberowski**, *Humboldt University of Berlin*
Prof. **Margarita Balmaceda**, *Seton Hall University*
Dr. **John Barber**, *University of Cambridge*
Prof. **Timm Beichelt**, *European University Viadrina*
Dr. **Katrin Boeckh**, *University of Munich*
Prof. em. **Archie Brown**, *University of Oxford*
Dr. **Vyacheslav Bryukhovetsky**, *Kyiv-Mohyla Academy*
Prof. **Timothy Colton**, *Harvard University, Cambridge*
Prof. **Paul D'Anieri**, *University of Florida*
Dr. **Heike Dörrenbächer**, *Friedrich Naumann Foundation*
Dr. **John Dunlop**, *Hoover Institution, Stanford, California*
Dr. **Sabine Fischer**, *SWP, Berlin*
Dr. **Geir Flikke**, *NUPI, Oslo*
Prof. **David Galbreath**, *University of Aberdeen*
Prof. **Alexander Galkin**, *Russian Academy of Sciences*
Prof. **Frank Golczewski**, *University of Hamburg*
Dr. **Nikolas Gvosdev**, *Naval War College, Newport, RI*
Prof. **Mark von Hagen**, *Arizona State University*
Dr. **Guido Hausmann**, *University of Munich*
Prof. **Dale Herspring**, *Kansas State University*
Dr. **Stefani Hoffman**, *Hebrew University of Jerusalem*
Prof. **Mikhail Ilyin**, *MGIMO (U) MID RF, Moscow*
Prof. **Vladimir Kantor**, *Higher School of Economics*
Dr. **Ivan Katchanovski**, *University of Ottawa*
Prof. em. **Andrzej Korbonski**, *University of California*
Dr. **Iris Kempe**, *"Caucasus Analytical Digest"*
Prof. **Herbert Küpper**, *Institut für Ostrecht Regensburg*
Dr. **Rainer Lindner**, *CEEER, Berlin*
Dr. **Vladimir Malakhov**, *Russian Academy of Sciences*

Dr. **Luke March**, *University of Edinburgh*
Prof. **Michael McFaul**, *Stanford University, Palo Alto*
Prof. **Birgit Menzel**, *University of Mainz-Germersheim*
Prof. **Valery Mikhailenko**, *The Urals State University*
Prof. **Emil Pain**, *Higher School of Economics, Moscow*
Dr. **Oleg Podvintsev**, *Russian Academy of Sciences*
Prof. **Olga Popova**, *St. Petersburg State University*
Dr. **Alex Pravda**, *University of Oxford*
Dr. **Erik van Ree**, *University of Amsterdam*
Dr. **Joachim Rogall**, *Robert Bosch Foundation Stuttgart*
Prof. **Peter Rutland**, *Wesleyan University, Middletown*
Prof. **Marat Salikov**, *The Urals State Law Academy*
Dr. **Gwendolyn Sasse**, *University of Oxford*
Prof. **Jutta Scherrer**, *EHESS, Paris*
Prof. **Robert Service**, *University of Oxford*
Mr. **James Sherr**, *RIIA Chatham House London*
Dr. **Oxana Shevel**, *Tufts University, Medford*
Prof. **Eberhard Schneider**, *University of Siegen*
Prof. **Olexander Shnyrkov**, *Shevchenko University, Kyiv*
Prof. **Hans-Henning Schröder**, *SWP, Berlin*
Prof. **Yuri Shapoval**, *Ukrainian Academy of Sciences*
Prof. **Viktor Shnirelman**, *Russian Academy of Sciences*
Dr. **Lisa Sundstrom**, *University of British Columbia*
Dr. **Philip Walters**, *"Religion, State and Society", Oxford*
Prof. **Zenon Wasyliw**, *Ithaca College, New York State*
Dr. **Lucan Way**, *University of Toronto*
Dr. **Markus Wehner**, *"Frankfurter Allgemeine Zeitung"*
Dr. **Andrew Wilson**, *University College London*
Prof. **Jan Zielonka**, *University of Oxford*
Prof. **Andrei Zorin**, *University of Oxford*

* While the Editorial Committee and Advisory Board support the General Editor in the choice and improvement of manuscripts for publication, responsibility for remaining errors and misinterpretations in the series' volumes lies with the books' authors.

Soviet and Post-Soviet Politics and Society (SPPS)
ISSN 1614-3515

Founded in 2004 and refereed since 2007, SPPS makes available affordable English-, German-, and Russian-language studies on the history of the countries of the former Soviet bloc from the late Tsarist period to today. It publishes between 5 and 20 volumes per year and focuses on issues in transitions to and from democracy such as economic crisis, identity formation, civil society development, and constitutional reform in CEE and the NIS. SPPS also aims to highlight so far understudied themes in East European studies such as right-wing radicalism, religious life, higher education, or human rights protection. The authors and titles of all previously published volumes are listed at the end of this book. For a full description of the series and reviews of its books, see www.ibidem-verlag.de/red/spps.

Editorial correspondence & manuscripts should be sent to: Dr. Andreas Umland, Institute for Euro-Atlantic Cooperation, vul. Volodymyrska 42, off. 21, UA-01030 Kyiv, Ukraine

Business correspondence & review copy requests should be sent to: *ibidem* Press, Leuschnerstr. 40, 30457 Hannover, Germany; tel.: +49 511 2622200; fax: +49 511 2622201; spps@ibidem.eu.

Authors, reviewers, referees, and editors for (as well as all other persons sympathetic to) SPPS are invited to join its networks at
www.facebook.com/group.php?gid=52638198614
www.linkedin.com/groups?about=&gid=103012
www.xing.com/net/spps-ibidem-verlag/

Recent Volumes

206 *Michal Vít*
The EU's Impact on Identity Formation in East-Central Europe between 2004 and 2013
Perceptions of the Nation and Europe in Political Parties of the Czech Republic, Poland, and Slovakia
With a foreword by Andrea Pető
ISBN 978-3-8382-1275-3

207 *Per A. Rudling*
Tarnished Heroes
The Organization of Ukrainian Nationalists in the Memory Politics of Post-Soviet Ukraine
ISBN 978-3-8382-0999-9

208 *Peter H. Solomon Jr., Kaja Gadowska (Eds.)*
Legal Change in Post-Communist States
Progress, Reversions, Explanations
ISBN 978-3-8382-1312-5

209 *Paweł Kowal, Georges Mink, Iwona Reichardt (Eds.)*
Three Revolutions: Mobilization and Change in Contemporary Ukraine I
Theoretical Aspects and Analyses on Religion, Memory, and Identity
ISBN 978-3-8382-1321-7

210 *Paweł Kowal, Georges Mink, Iwona Reichardt (Eds.)*
Three Revolutions: Mobilization and Change in Contemporary Ukraine II
An Oral History of the Revolution on Granite, Orange Revolution, and Revolution of Dignity
ISBN 978-3-8382-1323-1

211 *Li Bennich-Björkman; Sergiy Kurbatov (Eds.)*
When the Future Came
The Collapse of the USSR and the Emergence of National Memory in Post-Soviet History Textbooks
ISBN 978-3-8382-1335-4

212 *Olga R. Gulina*
Migration as a (Geo-)Political Challenge in the Post-Soviet Space
Border Regimes, Policy Choices, Visa Agendas
With a foreword by Nils Muižnieks
ISBN 978-3-8382-1338-5

213 *Sanna Turoma; Kaarina Aitamurto; Slobodanka Vladiv-Glover (Eds.)*
Religion, Expression, and Patriotism in Russia
Essays on Post-Soviet Society and the State
ISBN 978-3-8382-1346-0

Table of Contents

Peter H. Solomon Jr., Kaja Gadowska
Legal Change in Post-Communist States:
Contradictions and Explanations 9

I. Legal Institutions

Mihaela Şerban
Stemming the Tide of Illiberalism? Legal Mobilization
and Adversarial Legalism in Central and Eastern Europe .. 23

Kriszta Kovács, Kim Lane Scheppele
The Fragility of an Independent Judiciary: Lessons from
Hungary and Poland — and the European Union 55

Alexei Trochev, Peter H. Solomon Jr.
Authoritarian Constitutionalism in Putin's Russia:
A Pragmatic Constitutional Court in a Dual State 97

Olga Semukhina
The Evolution of Policing in Post-Soviet Russia:
Paternalism versus Service in Police Officers'
Understanding of their Role 139

II. Legal Accountability in Public Administration

Maria Popova, Vincent Post
Prosecuting High Level Corruption
in Eastern Europe 183

Marina Zaloznaya, William M. Reisinger, Vicki Hesli Claypool
When Civil Engagement is Part of the Problem:
Flawed Anti-Corruptionism in Russia and Ukraine 221

Kaja Gadowska
  Constitutional Values and Civil Servant Recruitment:
  The Principles for Filling Revenue Service Positions
  in Poland 253

Elena Bogdanova
  Obtaining Redress for Abuse of Office in Russia:
  The Soviet Legacy and the Long Road to
  Administrative Justice 297

Acknowledgements

This book began its life as a special issue of the journal *Communist and Post-Communist Studies*, designed and proposed by us, its coeditors Peter Solomon and Kaja Gadowska. In bringing this publication to fruition, we benefited immeasurably from professional, devoted and even inspired help of the journal's managing editor Lucy Kerner. We are pleased to acknowledge her role in nurturing and improving the various contributions. We are also grateful to the editors of the journal for granting permission for the publication of the issue's contents as a book.

The idea for the book came from Andreas Umland, who proposed publishing it in the distinguished series he edits at ***ibidem***-Verlag, "Soviet and Post-Soviet Politics and Society". The book's editors and contributors readily accepted the proposal, agreeing that the subject of their special issue—legal change in post- communist states-- deserved the added visibility and coherence that the book form would provide.

Working with the publisher ***ibidem*** has also been a very positive experience, and we are grateful to its editor Valerie Lange for her role in improving individual chapters and seeing to the publication and marketing of the book.

Legal Change in Post-Communist States: Contradictions and Explanations

Peter H. Solomon Jr., Kaja Gadowska
Munk School of Global Affairs, University of Toronto, Canada,
and Jagiellonian University, Krakow, Poland

Reformers had high hopes that the end of communism in Eastern Europe and the former Soviet Union would lead to significant improvements in legal institutions and the role of law in public administration. However, the cumulative experience of 25 years of legal change since communism has been mixed, marked by achievements and failures, advances and moves backward. This volume documents the nuances of this process and starts the process of explaining them. This introductory essay draws on the findings of the articles in this issue to explore the impact of three potential explanatory factors: regime type, international influences, and legal (or political) culture. Regime type matters, but allows for considerable variation within authoritarian and democratic states alike and the possibility of reversals. The influence of international organizations (like the European Union) is also far from predictable, especially once states have joined the organization. Finally, legal cultures and political traditions play a large role in explaining developments in individual countries, but there is nothing inevitable about their impact.

Keywords: Post-communist legal change, Legal reform, Authoritarian law, Democracy and judicial power, The European Union and legal reform, Legal culture and tradition

In the quarter century since the collapse of communist regimes in Eastern Europe and the USSR almost every country in the region has tried to reform its legal institutions and enhance the role of law in public administration. According to conventional wisdom, both democratization and the creation of market economies required the creation of law-based states (or *Rechtsstaat*), which assured that government officials (including politicians) would be subject to legal restraints, and that citizens could defend their rights and interests in impartial and effective courts (Linz and Stepan, 1996). Accordingly, most countries did make efforts to produce independent and empowered courts and police that served society (Seibert-Fohr, 2012; Kuhn, 2011; Solomon and Foglesong, 2000); and struggled to make public administration more rule-based and less corrupt (Inkina, 2018; Dmitrova, 2009; Meyer-Sahling, 2009; Gadowska, 2018). Before long it became clear that the goals of reformers were fulfilled only in part, in some countries more, others less, and that some achievements had proven short-lived and subject to reversal (Solomon, 2007, 2015b; Hendley, 2017). Differences emerged between authoritarian regimes in the post-Soviet space and democratic ones in central Europe that were part of the European Union. But events of recent years have shown that empowered and independent judiciaries could be threatened even in the countries that had apparently made successful legal transitions—Hungary and Poland, for example (Bugaric, 2015; Bugaric and Ginsburg, 2016; von Bogdandy and Sonnevend, 2015; Scheppele, 2018).

The cumulative experience of post-communist legal change within Eastern Europe has turned out to be mixed, marked by achievements and failures, advances and moves backward. The challenge to be addressed in this special issue of Communist and Post-Communist Studies is determining and documenting the nuances of these developments and starting to explain them. The contributors to this issue are all scholars who pursue socio-legal research on Eastern European countries—political scientists and sociologists—who are also members of a new collaborative research network of scholars who share an interest in this subject. We, the co-editors, should stress that the papers are not the product of a conference or directed inquiry but represent the ongoing research of the several contributors. We are pleased that the topics cohere, and that the sum of them will likely prove greater than their parts.

The paper topics range across the region and focus on both the former Soviet Union and Eastern Europe proper. The topics fall nicely into two groups—papers that deal with legal institutions, especially courts but also police; and papers that address law and legal accountability in public administration, including efforts to fight corruption and complaint mechanisms. The extent to which legal reform has improved the accountability of government officials is one broad concern that unites all the papers, including those on legal institutions. Two of these papers deal at least in part with administrative justice (holding individual officials to account) and other two with the accountability of police and the role of supranational tribunals in holding domestic officials to account.

The authors of the articles share a concern with the role and impact on their findings of at least three potential explanatory factors: regime type, international influences, and legal (or political) culture. Most observers assume that the achievement of independent and empowered courts is easier in democratic than in authoritarian regimes. Probably so, but it may well be that democratic government is a necessary but insufficient condition. The impact of political competition also turns out to be variable (Finkel, 2008; Popova, 2012). Just what can be achieved within authoritarian states is another open question (Ginsburg and Moustafa, 2008; Solomon, 2015a). International influence, especially through the processes of linkage and leverage may make a difference (Levitsky and Way, 2006). A prime example is the impact of the European Union and its demands, whether addressed to would-be members or actual ones. It turns out, however, that there have been limits to the impact of the EU, whether in the shaping of legal institutions or the struggle with corruption (Kochenov, 2008; Gadowska, 2010; Boerzel et al., 2012; European Commission, 2016). Finally, as one country or another moves backward and counter-reforms prevail, observers increasingly turn to cultural explanations (Krygier, 1999; Kurkchiyan, 2003; Bobek, 2008). One country lacks a legal tradition or a strong role for law in public life, perhaps because informal relations trump formal institutions; another country has a long heritage of illiberal impulses, which facilitate attempts by leaders to curtail legal accountability.

In the first article Mihaela Serban documents the extraordinary growth of the use of courts in post-communist Eastern Europe, for both litigating conflicts and pursuing rights claims, what she calls a process of legal mobilization. She explores the sources of this mobilization, including the opportunities provided by new courts on the domestic and international levels, and goes on to probe its consequences. While paying special attention to developments in Romania and with the European Court of Human Rights, she demonstrates that the expanded use of the law has involved all the countries of the region. Finally, she argues that the explosion in litigation and the version of an adversarial culture that it represented may temper the effects of the rejection of liberalism that has affected the seemingly most developed democracies, Hungary and Poland, which has resulted in the subjugation of their judiciaries including their constitutional courts.

In their contribution Kriszta Kovács and Kim Lane Scheppele analyze the process and consequences of the illiberal turn for the courts of Hungary and Poland. They start by analyzing and comparing the legal mechanisms used to subjugate the judiciary (including the constitutional courts). These turn out to have been tools that are available to many autocrats. But what distinguishes the situation in Hungary and Poland is the presence of an external check in the form of the European Union. Sadly, the EU failed to take the appropriate measures, and in the process signaled that it would tolerate the changes. In so doing, it conveyed a message that there is such a thing as "autocratic constitutionalism", which it would not oppose.

The terms "autocratic" or "authoritarian" constitutionalism may sound ominous when used to characterize developments within the context of democracies like Hungary and Poland, but they carry a more positive valence when characterizing a constitutional court within an authentic authoritarian state. Alexei Trochev and Peter H. Solomon Jr. see the Russian Constitutional court operating in a dual state, where for some matters the needs of the political leaders have priority and on other issues the Court is free to exercise its discretion. Both the Court and its Chairman Valerii Zorkin have succeeded in making the right choices and following a pragmatic approach. The authors demonstrate that this pattern has been in place for a long time and that loyalty of judges has become the norm where expected. Moreover, by asserting Russia's autonomy from the ECHR in Strasbourg, Zorkin has made the Court even more useful to the regime. At the same time, in the past decade the Court has decided many cases on the merits, gained more respect, and does much better than before in getting its decisions implemented. In short, by adapting to the needs of leaders the Court has gained autonomy and power on some matters.

Not only courts but also police in Russia have had to adjust to changing political priorities and dispositions. Olga Semukhina uses interviews with police officials to track the ups and downs in their self-conception and confidence, which reflected their attitudes toward different rounds of reform. In the 1990s organizational changes, decreased funding, corruption, rising crime rates, and a new emphasis on service led to demoralization. But in the 2000s the situation gradually changed, first with new funding, then with a further round of reforms, which did not achieve most of its goals but did foster a return to paternalistic values. The revived mission of protecting society on behalf of the state gave police officers a renewed sense of value and self-respect. For the short run at least, continuity trumped change.

To what extent prosecutors and judges succeed in holding politicians to legal standards of conduct represents another important aspect of the post-communist legal order. In their contribution Maria Popova and Vincent Post examine the prosecution of government ministers across Eastern Europe, drawing on a data-based that they constructed. This enabled them to uncover significant variations in both levels of corruption and rates of conviction. However, explaining these variations did not prove easy, as none of the likely factors had had a consistent effect — not EU conditionality or membership, party politics, or the existence of specialized anticorruption prosecution or a relatively independent judiciary.

Holding leaders to account is also a concern in the post-Soviet world, and in both Russia and Ukraine special anticorruption programs are a staple. The Marina Zaloznaya, William B. Reisinger and Vicki Hesli Claypool's article uses interviews with anti-corruption practitioners in these countries to ascertain the role of the participation of civil society members. While conventional wisdom assumes that this involvement is positive, the authors discovered that this need not be the case. Their findings about Russia and Ukraine suggest two models of civic engagement in the struggle against corruption that produce negative outcomes — what they call false collaboration and a non-collaborative presence.

At least in democracies the role of law in public administration should extend beyond accountability of leaders to the mode of operation of the bureaucracy itself. Weberian standards of recruitment and promotion of officials, that is, the manifestations of legal rationality, are near universal goals for post-communist efforts to create politically neutral civil services. In her article Kaja Gadowska examines the theory and practice of the filling of key positions in the tax administration of Poland. She chronicles an evolving process that starts with promising legal regulations, to be sure with loopholes that politicians in power increasingly utilized, and culminates in new laws that effectively undermine competitive and non-partisan recruitment. In so doing, she illuminates another domain (besides judicial power) where political considerations trump legal principles in the post-communist world, even in democracies.

Ideally, law and legal institutions not only hold leaders accountable but also provide ways that members of the public can find redress for illegal actions on the part of government officials. The availability of courts or quasi-judicial tribunals is the norm in Western democracies and not surprisingly the development or expansion of administrative justice became central to judicial reform in many post-communist countries, including the Russian Federation. But, according to Elena Bogdanova's research, Russia continues to rely on a variety of alternatives to courts, especially mechanisms of complaint. In the Soviet period, when the possibilities of challenging official actions in court were limited, complaints (for example to party bodies like the Central Committee) were the primary means for obtaining redress and holding officials accountable. In post-Soviet Russia complaints to the President and other centers of power remain commonplace, the establishment of administrative justice notwithstanding.

What insights come to light from a reading of these eight articles as a group? To begin, these studies confirm the generalization that states embarking on a transition from authoritarian (and communist) regimes have not had an easy time creating modern legal order (*Rechtsstaat* or rule of law) and with it courts that are autonomous and powerful. But the papers do more than this. They also shed light on the influence of the three potential explanatory variables that we identified earlier—regime type, international influences, and culture.

The relevance of regime type for the state of law and courts is self-evident, but the relationship is not a simple one. Many of the countries of the former Soviet Union sooner or later ended up with authoritarian states, and the nature of their law and legal institutions reflects this. In the case of the Russian Federation a constitutional court was established at a time of democratic expectations. That it managed to adjust to an increasingly authoritarian context, and find a pragmatic approach that enabled it to satisfy political leaders while maintaining integrity and self-respect is remarkable. It may supply a model for one variety of authoritarian constitutionalism.

At the same time, some countries of the former Soviet Bloc did succeed in creating democracies, at least for a generation, and most of them also became members of the European Union. While these facts may have helped the role of law and legal institutions in the short run, they proved insufficient to prevent a serious backsliding to the point where courts in both Hungary and Poland were no longer independent and their formerly progressive constitutional courts lost much of their power (through loss of jurisdiction and discretion). At the same time, at least in Poland, efforts to entrench recruitment of government officials handling taxes on a non-partisan basis also failed as politicians manipulated loopholes and gained the confidence to restore a system of patronage.

The role of international influences in promoting law and legal institutions also turns out to be variable. The European Union did exercise influence over legislation in some countries during the accession phase, but evidently its influence on member states has been less predictable. The growth of illiberalism in some countries and the failure of the EU to punish countries that departed from what were previously thought to be pan-European norms left some member states without adequate legal institutions. Few observers had anticipated the emergence of authoritarian leaders through elections and their aspirations to cripple the role of courts as alternative centers of power. Perhaps, the actions of transnational courts like the European Court of Human Rights will continue to temper the sharp edge of the domestic trampling on rights, but it is unlikely that such bodies can compel national leaders to change their ways.

When all is said and done, cultures (legal and political) and traditions end up playing a large role in explaining the limited development of law and legal institutions in the post-communist world. Russia has a long tradition of law serving the interests of the state more than the individual or society, and this was reflected in not only the pragmatism of the Constitutional Court but also the evolution of policing and its reform. Moreover, many members of the public feel more comfortable complaining to state leaders about misconduct of lower officials than to the courts. Hungary and Poland had multiple periods of authoritarian rule where the role of courts was limited. Of course, these countries and others also had more positive forerunners, and there was nothing inevitable about the revival of a one tradition or another. Contemporary actors draw on and foster traditions to suit their purposes, but it is helpful when useful ones are available.

Finally, the failure of anti-corruption activities in most countries of the former communist world may also be overdetermined. With some exceptions authoritarian states of today feature corruption; international influences rarely reduce it; and the political cultures even of new democracies may support it. The studies of anti-corruption activities in this issue say more about the ways politicians can manipulate the corruption fight than documenting (or explaining) its impact.

References

Bobek, M., 2008. The fortress of judicial independence and the mental transitions of central European judiciaries. Eur. Publ. Law 14 (1), 100–127.

Boerzel, T.A., Stahn, A., Pamuk, Y., 2012. The European union and the fight against corruption in its near abroad: can it make a diffe7rence. In: Moroff, H., Schmidt-Pfister, D. (Eds.), Fighting Corruption in Eastern Europe. A Multilevel Perspective. Routledge, Taylor & Francis Group, London and N.Y, pp. 34–56.

Bugaric, B., 2015. The rule of law derailed: lessons from post-communist word. Hague J. Rule. Law 7 (2), 175–197.

Bugaric, B., Ginsburg, T., 2016. The assault on post-communist courts. J. Democr. 27 (3), 69–81.

Dimitrova, A.L., 2009. Administrative reform in central and Eastern Europe: extracting civil services from communist bureaucracies. In: Simons, W. (Ed.), Private and Civil Law in the Russian Federation. Brill, pp. 279–295.

European Commission, 2016. Rule of law: commission issues recommendation to Poland. Press Release, 27 July 2016, on-line. http://europa.eu/rapid/pressrelease_IP-16-2643_en.htm.

Finkel, J.S., 2008. Judicial Reform as Political Insurance: Argentina, Peru and Mexico in the 1990s. University of Notre Dame Press, Evanston.

Gadowska, K., 2010. National and international anti-corruption efforts. The case of Poland. Global Crime 11 (2), 178–209.

Gadowska, K., 2018. The process of creating civil service in Poland in the perspective of the new institutionalism. In: Itrich-Drabarek, J., Mazur, S., Wiśniewska-Grzelak (Eds.), The Transformations of the Civil Service in Poland in Comparison with International Experience. Peter Lang, Berlin, pp. 77–108 et al.

Ginsburg, T., Moustafa, T., 2008. Rule by Law: the Politics of Courts in Authoritarian Regimes. Cambridge University Press, Cambridge.

Hendley, K., 2017. Everyday Law in Russia. Cornell University Press, Ithaca.

Inkina, S., 2018. Making Sense of Russian Civil Service Reform: what Matters in Explaining Policy Implementation Process. National Research University Higher School of Economics (Basic Research program, Working Papers. Series: Political Science).

Kochenov, D., 2008. EU Enlargement and the Failure of Conditionality: Pre-accession Conditionality in the Fields of Democracy and the Rule of Law. Kluwer, Dordrecht.

Krygier, M., 1999. Institutional optimism, cultural pessimism and the rule of law. In: Krygier, M., Czarnota, A. (Eds.), The Rule of Law after Communism. Problems and Prospects in East-Central Europe. Ashgate, Aldershot, pp. 7–105.

Kuhn, Z., 2011. The Judiciary in Central and Eastern Europe: Mechanical Jurisprudence in Transformation? Nijhoff (Leiden).

Kurkchiyan, M., 2003. The illegitimacy of Law in post-soviet societies. In: Galligan, D., Kurkchiyan, M. (Eds.), Law and Informal Practices: the postcommunist Experience. Oxford University Press, Oxford.

Levitsky, S., Way, L.A., 2006. Linkage versus leverage. Rethinking the international dimension of regime change. Comp. Polit. 38 (4), 379–409.

Linz, J., Stepan, A., 1996. Problems of Democratic Transition and Consolidation: South America, Southern Europe and post-communist Europe. John's Hopkins Press, Baltimore.

Meyer-Sahling, J.H., 2009. Varieties of legacies: a critical review of legacy explanations of public administration reform in East Central Europe. Int. Rev. Adm. Sci. 75/3, 529–528.

Popova, M., 2012. Politicized Justice in Emerging Democracies. A Study of Courts in Russia and Ukraine. Cambridge University Press, Cambridge. Scheppele, Lane, Kim, 2018. Autocratic Legalism, 2. University of Chicago Law Review 85, pp. 545–583.

Solomon, P.H., 2007. Threats of judicial counterreform in Putin's Russia. In: Hendley, K. (Ed.), Remaking the Role of Law: Commercial Law in Russia and the CIS, pp. 1–40. Juris, Huntington, N.Y.

Solomon, P.H., 2015a. Law and courts in authoritarian states. In: Wright, J.D. (Ed.), International Encyclopedia of Social and Behavioral Sciences, second ed. Elsevier, Oxford.

Solomon, P.H., 2015b. Post-soviet criminal justice: the persistence of distorted neo-inquisitorialism. Theor. Criminol. 19 (2), 159–178.

Solomon, P.H., Foglesong, T., 2000. Courts and Transition in Russia: the Challenge of Judicial Reform. Westview, Boulder.

Seibert-Fohr, A. (Ed.), 2012. Judicial Independence in Transition. Springer, Heidelberg et al.

von Bogdandy, A., Sonnevend, P. (Eds.), 2015. Constitutional Crisis in the European Constitutional Area: Theory, Law and Politics in Hungary and Romania. Hart Publishing, Oxford.

I. Legal Institutions

1 Legal Institutions

Stemming the Tide of Illiberalism? Legal Mobilization and Adversarial Legalism in Central and Eastern Europe

Mihaela Şerban
Ramapo College of New Jersey, School of Social Science and Human Services, USA

This paper explores the rise of rights-based regulation through litigation as a distinctive feature of legal culture in Central and Eastern Europe post-1989. This type of adversarial legalism was born at the intersection of post-communist, European integration, and neoliberal discourses, and is characterized by legal mobilization at national and supra-national levels, selective adaptation of adversarial mechanisms, and the growth of rights consciousness. The paper distinguishes Eastern European developments from both American and Western European types of adversarial legalism, assesses the first quarter century of post-communism and represents a first step towards constructing a genealogy of the region's legal culture post-1989.

Keywords: Legal mobilization, Eastern Europe, Public interest law, Rights

1. Introduction

A populist billionaire with authoritarian tendencies is the current prime minister of the Czech Republic, Poland's Law and Justice Party has been steadily chipping away at the rule of law and human rights since 2015, and Hungary has become the poster child of illiberal democracy under Prime Minister Viktor Orban. In both Poland and Hungary, the ruling parties have targeted the judiciary at all levels. In Poland, the battle over controlling the membership, internal functioning, and powers of the Constitutional Tribunal has been ongoing since 2015 (Human Rights Watch, 2017), while in Hungary the government essentially gutted the Constitutional Court's powers with the 2012 Constitution and the 2013 amendment. Both Poland and Hungary have also attacked civil society and human rights, and have refused to comply with the EU requests to restore the rule of law. Both countries stand now as warnings of emerging global authoritarianisms.

And yet not all is lost. I argue in this paper that the groundwork for countering authoritarianism has been laid out since 1989 and the outcomes, specifically a growth in legal mobilization and adversarial legalism, have been valuable for fighting current rule of law and human rights battles. The explosion of litigation in Central and Eastern Europe (CEE) post-1989 is a clear indicator and striking development, even when considering the low 1989 baseline. Since its establishment in 1959, for example, more than half of the judgments delivered by the European Court of Human Rights (ECtHR) concerned only six states: Turkey, Italy, the Russian Federation, Romania, Poland, and Ukraine, four of them from Eastern Europe (European Court of Human Rights Overview 1959-2016, 2017). Their litigiousness stands out even more considering that they became members of the European Convention on Human Rights (ECHR) only after the fall of the Berlin Wall. The Court, in return, has both opened its doors more widely to claimants (in 1994) and has become increasingly more involved in policy-making for these countries and the region at large,[1] most recently through the creation of pilot judgments (addressing repetitive cases arising from structural problems at the national level). Across the board, we see citizens who are willing to defend their rights and challenge their states, and courts, whether domestic (national) or supranational (at the European level), eager and willing to take on the challenge.

This litigiousness is indicative of broader trends in the legal culture(s) of the newest members of the European Union, one that is distinctive compared to Western European trends and European legal mobilization (Conant et al., 2017). This rise in litigation is also visible at national levels and contributes to a significantly more adversarial legal culture compared to pre1989. Courts and litigation have become central to policy-making in CEE countries in ways

---

1 "Region" refers to countries of Central and Eastern Europe.

that are reminiscent of Kagan's argument about adversarial legalism — regulation through law and litigation in the US (Kagan, 2001). Nonetheless, CEE trends are distinct from both the US and Western European countries.

If American adversarial legalism is driven by commerce, individualism, egalitarianism and anti-statism (Kagan, 2001), and Western European developments are driven endogenously by political fragmentation and neoliberal deregulation and reregulation (Kelemen, 2011), the adversarial legal culture in CEE is fueled by the massive expansion of its legal mobilization infrastructure over the past twenty-five years in a post-communist neoliberal context. The result is a specific type of adversarial legal culture and regulation through litigation characterized by active and politicized courts (in particular constitutional courts), mobilization of supranational courts (such as the ECtHR), selective adaptation of adversarial mechanisms (such as public interest law litigation), and the growth of litigation and rights consciousness at domestic levels. These key features have risen in a discursive terrain dominated by neoliberal, post-communist, and European integration discourses, which partially converge (primarily in a rights-based discourse), as well as backlash to them, evident most recently in post-recession illiberal developments in Poland and Hungary.

I focus here primarily on CEE countries that are also EU members, as well as signatories of the ECHR: Bulgaria, Croatia, the Czech Republic, Hungary, Poland, Romania, Slovenia and Slovakia. I chose countries that belong to different accession waves, from the earliest — Hungary, Poland, Czech Republic, Slovakia, Slovenia in 2004, to the latest — Romania, Bulgaria in 2007, and Croatia in 2013. There are significant differences among CEE countries both pre-1989 and since then, but for the purposes of this paper I consider the commonalities are stronger than the differences. The paper takes 1989 as its starting point. I do not aim to compare specific countries here, but rather to identify and explore common patterns at a regional level (individual countries therefore serve here as illustrations of broader developments).

The paper uses a legal mobilization framework to introduce the emerging adversarial legal culture in the region and the factors that contributed to it. The next section presents some key indicators and causes of this adversarial legalism, while the third section discusses building the legal mobilization infrastructure over the past quarter century, focusing on discourses, resources, institutions, expertise, and public interest litigation. The last two sections explore some consequences, primarily the rise of rights-based regulation through litigation at the national and supranational levels. I conclude by touching upon the recent anti-judicial and anti-democratic backlash in some of the CEE countries.

2. Legal mobilization in Central and Eastern Europe

Almost two decades ago Charles Epp, focusing on common law countries, argued that their recent "rights revolutions" were less a matter of judicial activism and more of broadened access to justice and increasing legal mobilization, in particular highlighting the role and importance of material support and resources. Legal mobilization refers to the process by which individuals claim their rights and pursue those claims in court (Epp, 1998). Since then, legal mobilization theory, drawing from law and society, political science, and sociology, has both de-emphasized litigation and underscored the importance of other factors, such as material, legal, and political resources, promises of rights and rights consciousness, support networks, and broader politics and opportunities for mobilizing law through litigation and otherwise, towards eventually achieving social change (McCann, 1994; Cichowski, 2016; Vanhala, 2012).

From this broadly defined legal mobilization perspective, the legal opportunity structure (LOS) approach emphasizes the extent to which legal systems are open and accessible for both individual and collective actors along various dimensions, such as procedural variables (for example, standing, costs, time limits), material resources, legal resources and existing legal stock, judicial receptivity, cultural frames, presence of allies or counter-mobilizing forces

(Vanhala, 2012). Obstacles include in particular blocking or limiting access to justice (for example, funding) — what can be litigated, by whom, where, when, and how.

The legal mobilization theory and legal opportunity structure approach help frame CEE developments by identifying key factors that contribute to its specific adversarial legal culture. There are four factors that shape the legal opportunity structure in the region studied: political and ideological changes, resources and expertise, a new institutional landscape, and a litigation-friendly environment. Political and ideological changes include four distinct types and phases: the fall of communism, the European Union accession process, the EU integration (positives and disenchantment), and the post-recession fragmentation of the region and shifts to illiberalism. Second, the creation of a new institutional landscape includes not only the establishment of constitutional courts, but also of other types of institutions that play a role in legal mobilization, from Ombudsmen to anti-corruption agencies (I am setting aside for now their effectiveness or capture). Third, there was massive outpouring of resources from external sources, both the US and the EU, from funding to expertise. The fourth and final key factor is the creation of an overall litigation-favorable environment, consisting primarily in expanding access to justice rules and resources at all levels, judicial attitudes (for example, how constitutional judges understand their role), explicit expectations that higher courts play a policy-making role, and the numbers and roles of legal experts and support networks.

3. Indicators of legal mobilization and adversarial legalism in the region

Clear signs of mobilization and adversarial legalism in the countries studied are high rates of litigation at supranational and national levels. Low levels of trust in domestic courts compared to Western European countries partially explain the turn to supranational courts (although CEE citizens truly mobilize at both domestic and supranational levels). Despite variations both on north-south and east-west axes among European countries, three-quarters of Western countries trust their justice systems, with Finland and Denmark as high as 85-percent. The exceptions are Italy, Spain, Cyprus, and Portugal, but even there, Italy with 33-percent is still more trustful than the last four countries, all from CEE. By contrast, less than half of the population in all CEE countries studied here trust their courts, with Slovakia and Slovenia as low as 25 and 24-percent, respectively (Flash Eurobarometer, 2013). The distrust of national courts is at the heart of the specifically post-communist context across the region. While there are differences among these countries, there are also some common trends: state capture or attempted capture of judiciaries (for example, Hungary), corruption (for example, Romania and Bulgaria), path dependency at the institutional level, and questions about judicial independence have all fueled the turn to the supranational. CEE countries have thus flooded the ECtHR with applications, entrusting it to regulate key areas where national courts failed (See Chart 1).

Chart 1. Claims by country and year.

Sources: Data compiled from ECtHR Annual Reports.

The years 2010–2013 recorded the highest number of applications before the ECtHR in general (65,800 in 2013), but Croatia is the only country here that mirrors that broader trend. Only Bulgaria and Slovakia overall show a somewhat even path, while the spike in

Hungary's numbers is sharp and correlated with its turn towards authoritarianism. The number of decisions over time tell a more interesting story, as the number of decisions per country has been levelling off as the ECtHR increased using pilot judgments (See Chart 2):

Chart 2. Number of judgments per country, 1998–2016.

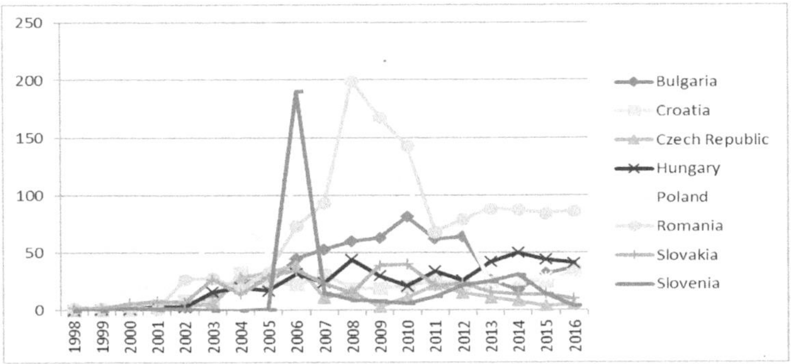

Sources: Data compiled from ECtHR Country Statistics and Annual Reports.

Romania and Poland have the highest number of applications and judgments overall, not surprisingly given their populations (although Poland is twice the size of Romania). The top areas of litigation before the ECtHR for the eight countries include liberty and security, length of proceedings, effective remedy, privacy, and, for Romania only, property.

At the national level, there is significant variation among constitutional courts from a caseload perspective, and there is some correlation between the moment a country joined the EU and a decrease in its constitutional court's caseload. The Romanian Constitutional Court, for example, has been increasingly active. At its lowest, the Court issued 49 decisions in its first year (1992), and at its highest 1,751, a year before joining the European Union. Since its inception, the Court issued 18,071 decisions, finding a constitutional violation in 631 cases. The overall number of petitions before the Court is 40,450, and 97percent of them were raised in concrete review (Romanian Constitutional Court, 2017). The Court's load dropped significantly after 2011, with changes in procedure allowing for the continuation of regular court proceedings while the constitutional complaint was before the Court.

From a caseload perspective and comparatively speaking, the Romanian Court has been very busy. Only the original Hungarian Court comes close to it (remember that Hungary has half the population of Romania). The Bulgarian Court, for example, averages only about ten decisions per year, and was particularly active in the 1990s in the area of privatization and especially restitution of agricultural land and urban property (Smilov, 2016). Examining the Hungarian Constitutional Court's caseload, we see a steady increase in the number of decisions (up to 631 in 2012), which is mirrored by a steady increase in the number of applications, before the 2012 restrictions on the Court's jurisdiction and powers (Venice Commission, 2013). Since 2012, the number of decisions has been falling to 258 decisions by 2016 (Hungarian Constitutional Court statistics, 2016; Solyom, 1994).

The trend of steep rises followed by a slight decline is also indicated by the number of new cases brought before constitutional courts. New cases before the Slovenian Constitutional Court, for example, have seen a steady increase after the country joined the EU, from 1271 new cases in 2004 to 1877 in 2005, 3053 in 2006, and 4354 in 2007 (Ribicic, 2008), followed by a decrease, but still showing a large number of complaints: 1324 in 2016 (Slovenian Constitutional Court, 2016). Slovenia is a country of 2 million people, so ten times smaller than Romania and five times smaller than Hungary.

Increases in applications and decisions are only one indicator of legal mobilization and adversarial legalism. Similar trends can be observed at national levels in terms of increased funding for legal services, litigation rates in non-criminal cases, and expanding numbers of lawyers, judges and mediators. Surprisingly perhaps, Romania is the most litigious EU country for civil and commercial cases, with almost 7 cases per 100 inhabitants and a significant jump from 2010 (5 cases per 100 inhabitants) to 2014. Not far behind are the Czech Republic (third most litigious), Croatia, and Poland— sixth and seventh, respectively (EU Justice Scoreboard, 2016). The clearance rates, moreover, are quite good across the board for non-criminal cases for most of these countries. Alternative dispute resolution mechanisms exist in all of these countries, and Hungary, Slovenia, Croatia, and Romania promote their use well above the European average.

While the budget dedicated to courts (per inhabitant) is not comparable to Western European countries, it has been slowly going up. Poland takes the lead here among the countries studied, with almost €60/inhabitant, while Romania is last, at half the amount. Luxembourg, for example, has the highest amount, at almost €180/inhabitant (EU Justice Scoreboard, 2016). As a percentage of the GDP, however, CEE countries have the highest rates on the continent, with Bulgaria first at almost 0.7-percent.

Other indicators of increased mobilization and litigation include increases in the number of lawyers, judges, and courts. In 1990, for example, the lower courts system in Poland included forty-four district and 282 lower level courts (Curtis, Library of Congress, 1994, p.196). By 2002, there were 705 courts, and by 2010, 827 courts (court reorganization can result in lower numbers, of course). With the exception of Romania, all of the CEE countries are above the EU average for number of judges per 100,000 inhabitants, with Slovenia leading by far at 47 judges per 100,000 inhabitants (compared to the EU average, at 21 judges). The number of judges in Romania is at the EU average as of 2014, having tripled from 1513 in 1990 to 4310 in 2012. Yet despite this substantial increase for a country whose population has slightly decreased since 1990, there is a constant backlog crisis in Romanian courts: in 2012, for example, there was a backlog of approximately 1 million case files. It took a year just to get a court date ... (Neacșu, 2013).

Interestingly, while the number of lawyers has also been going up steadily since 1990, all of the CEE countries are below the European average (166 lawyers per 100,000 inhabitants), with Bulgaria the closest at about 165 lawyers per 100,000 inhabitants. In absolute numbers, Poland stands out again, as it saw an increase from 29,469 lawyers in 2002 to 44,082 lawyers by 2010 (CEPEJ, 2008-2014) (See Chart 3).[2]

Chart 3. Increases in the numbers of lawyers per 100,000 inhabitants.

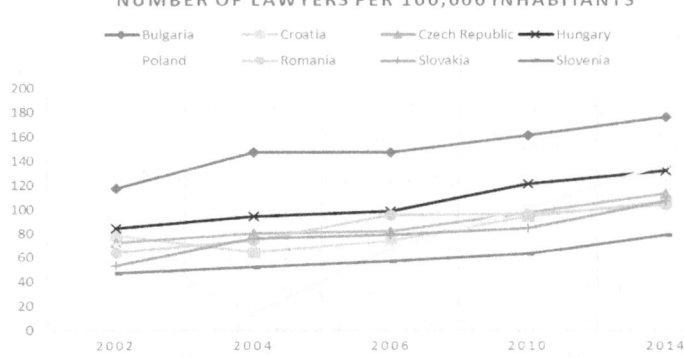

Source: Data compiled from CEPEJ, 2004-2016.

Other indicators of regulation through litigation, such as access to justice policies, procedures and institutions, including legal aid, litigation costs, litigation delays, enforcement of decisions, and harmonization of civil procedure (for example, the new code of civil procedure in Romania), show unmistakable upward trends. The litigation-favorable environment includes, inter alia, simplified procedures for small civil disputes (CEPEJ, 2014), and legal aid for criminal and non-criminal matters. In Romania, Slovakia, and the Czech Republic, for example, electronic submission of claims is permitted in all courts, while Poland, Hungary, and Slovenia allow for electronic submissions in about half the courts, and Bulgaria and Croatia in none (EU Justice Scoreboard, 2016).

Looking specifically at legal aid, while the CEE countries trail by far the rest of the continent in terms of resources, they all have a legal aid system in place. Led or initiated by the Open Society Insti-

---

2   The increase in Poland is largely due to the partial deregulation of the profession (CEPEJ, 2016). The increases in the numbers of lawyers generally do not necessarily reflect access to legal services.

tute (OSI), the national Helsinki Committees, and the Public Interest Law Initiative (PIL.net) over the years, legal aid discussions have been framed within a broader access to justice effort. In Bulgaria, for example, the Bulgarian Helsinki Committee and OSI documented for years the shortcomings of the justice system, which led to the Legal Aid Act of 2006, steady increases in funding and in the numbers of cases benefitting from legal aid—primarily criminal law (Cape and Namoradze, 2012). Croatia adopted a Free Legal Aid Act in 2009, Poland the Act on Free Legal Assistance and Legal Education in 2015, but Hungary still does not have a unified legal aid system. Less friendly measures are that all of these countries require court fees to start a non-criminal proceeding in a court of general jurisdiction, that lawyers' fees are freely negotiated (although there are differences in other respect), and that legal aid services are not necessarily fully functional.

4. Building the legal mobilization infrastructure in CEE

The emergence of adversarial legalism in CEE is a result of both endogenous and exogenous factors. The specificity of the region emerges from the juxtaposition (and partial success) of a neoliberal discourse in a post-communist context dominated by the European Union and its multidimensional system of dependence and disciplinary mechanisms (Böröcz, 2001). The ideal-type neoliberal model stresses the supremacy of the market logic and the rise of the disciplinary market-based state (Jessop, 2002). The neoliberal ideology, while dominant, has both competed with and taken advantage of other ideological discourses, such as the immediate post-1989 "return to normalcy" and "restoration" discourses, and more recently anti-globalization and anti-EU sentiments. Neoliberal policies supported unmaking state socialism, including reversing communist nationalizations and expropriations, which in turn prompted significant litigation. Civil society, the site of much rights-based resistance, has also been remade in a neoliberal image. Civil society in CEE post-1989 struggled initially with a legacy of 'anti-politics,' elitism, lack of resources, networks, and broader civic traditions. Nonetheless, civil society organizations have proliferated widely, if unevenly, in the post-communist space.

The consequences of CEE's neoliberal transition from communism for the rise of adversarial legalism have been twofold. On the one hand, law is a neutral, disciplinary mechanism in the new "good governance" paradigm focused on market-based structures for states that aim to gain and maintain the confidence of investors. Law, legal institutions and lawyers are thus crucial, ostensibly depoliticized instruments in achieving a new agenda of reform through law (Garth, 2003). In practice, this meant institutional reforms (for example, judiciary) and market-oriented legal reforms, as well as policy-making through law, particularly at the highest levels (constitutional courts).

The heavy, top down process of European integration is partially synergic with neoliberalism, yet also adds a distinct layer of regulation through bureaucracy, such as the expansive institutional and legal reforms aiming for conformity with the *acquis communitaire*. From an adversarial and legal mobilization perspective, European integration opened up new avenues for litigation and policy-making through supranational courts. Law's perceived neutrality both encourages high litigation rates and constructs the ECtHR as a key political player at the national level, reinforcing a culture of regulation through litigation.

On the other hand, in a complementary role, resistance to the market and the neoliberal paradigm takes place through civil society and rights-led development (Garth, 2003). Law is thus also a built-in space of resistance to neoliberalism through rights-based litigation and public interest law. This particular understanding of the role of law blends in seamlessly with the individualism and the focus on rights, in particular civil and political rights, that have been a key reason for the fall of communism. All these roads lead to a rights-based agenda, a new "myth of rights" perhaps (Scheingold, 2004), and contribute to the region's legal mobilization infrastructure.

The three discourses identified here—neoliberalism, European integration, and post-communism—are somewhat symbiotic, for example, in privileging rights and market-friendly institutions and norms, but there are also contradictory trends, for example when exploring national and supranational litigation patterns, or in terms of understanding the law-politics dynamic in different countries. Overall, however, they are key factors in the legal opportunity structure for the region as a whole and are constitutive of its specifically post-communist legal culture.

5. Resources, institutions, and expertise

Resources, institutions, and expertise are the foundation for building a legal mobilization infrastructure. Whether neoliberal or EU-accession oriented, post-communist reforms financed by the EU, the World Bank, and other state and private funders created material, political, and legal resources, as well as new institutions, overall a sturdy legal opportunity structure. The initial focus in the region post-1989 was overwhelmingly on institutional and market-oriented legal reforms, which in turn led to a heavy regulatory culture.

There are three key periods for most of the CEE countries studied here: the immediate post-1989 period lasting up until the moment of applying for EU accession, characterized by international and US-led involvement; the pre-EU accession period, when they were heavily monitored and pressured to fulfill various rule of law related criteria; and the post-EU accession period, which in some of these countries, such as Bulgaria and Romania, came with formal, but weak, EU monitoring focused on the reform of the justice system and anti-corruption mechanisms, and the corresponding ascendance of EU institutions, norms and culture. Early power players, like the US, receded in favor of the EU, while the presence of international organizations, like the World Bank and the IMF, remained somewhat constant, though their agendas, such as the World Bank's in the justice area, is purposely tailored to EU requirements.

Except for Croatia, whose situation was complicated by the Balkan wars, the period immediately following the fall of communism in 1989 lasted until 1993 to 1995, when these countries formally announced their intention of joining the European Union. The spotlight during this period was on establishing anti-authoritarian power structures through the adoption of new constitutions that included the principle of separation of powers, rights guarantees, and new institutions such as Constitutional Courts and Ombudsmen. Foreign activity in the region had a heavy law and development slant and was consequently focused on institutions and legal reform, particularly market oriented. This was a top-down process, with governments being the main focus of funding and attention, and only secondarily the promotion of civil and political rights and civil society.

As a result of these concerted efforts, all of the countries of the region overhauled their legal systems and institutions. Key pieces of legislation, such as civil codes, commercial codes, tax law and others, were significantly amended or newly adopted, and new institutions were created (See Table 1).

Table 1.   The new institutional landscape (entirely new or significantly revamped).

Country/ Institution	Bulgaria	Croatia	Czech Republic	Hungary	Poland	Romania	Slovakia	Slovenia
Constitutional Court	1991	1963 (1990)	1991, 1993	1989	1986	1992	1992	1991
Ombudsman	2003	1992	1999	1993	1988	1997	2001	1993
Central bank (independence)	1997	1990	1993	1991	1997	1991	1993	1991
Anti-corruption bodies	Yes, various	2001	2003	–	2006	2002 2008	2005	2002 2010
Competition authority	2008	1997	1991	1990	1990	1996	1991	1994
Supreme Judicial Council	1991	1990	–	2012	2001	1993	2001	1991
Supreme Administrative Court	1991		2003	–	1980 (1990)	–	–	–

For both governmental and private donors, broadly defined rule of law activities were a key concern, and donors both complemented each other and overlapped (for example, United States Agency for

International Development and the World Bank). Most donors were involved in law reform and institutional reform, albeit on different aspects of it. The World Bank's focus, for example, was initially on property rights, contract enforcement and the revision of commercial legislation, rather than institutions, and it was only in the mid-1990s that the Bank started putting more resources into strengthening courts and other legal institutions, such as modern facilities, case management practices, information sharing, training of judges and other court personnel, and stronger mechanisms to ensure transparency and accountability. Out of 239 projects supported by the Bank in the post-communist world between 1990 and 2001, only 40 targeted judicial reforms (there were none between 1990 and 1993) (Anderson et al., 2005, p. 14).

This regulatory neoliberal trend was reinforced during the process of EU integration. The Copenhagen criteria for the enlargement process included: (1) a functioning market economy; (2) stable institutions guaranteeing democracy, the rule of law, human rights, and respect for and protection of minorities, and market economy, and (3) the ability to implement the *acquis communautaire*. For most Eastern European countries, the EU pre-accession strategies focused on macro-economic progress and accession strategy, while underscoring the symbolic and aspirational aspects of these countries' desire to join the European Union. By contrast, once the formal accession process began, a stable rule of law, democracy and a rights-abiding culture took center stage alongside the region's capacity to absorb the *acquis communautaire*.

Significant amounts of external funding poured into the region throughout this period, with only a relatively small portion for legal activities. The major donors were the IMF, the World Bank, the European Bank for Reconstruction and Development, the European Investment Bank, European and American governments, the European Union and over sixty European, American and Japanese foundations (Quigley, 1997). Foreign governments, for the most part, provided assistance directly to the recipient governments and were mostly concerned with the regulatory frameworks of democracy and the market—issues such as free elections, separation of powers and an independent judiciary, support for privatization, and others (Spero, 2010).

Romania is a good example of building a legal infrastructure over the past twenty years, as outside funders and regulators focused on institutions, strengthening the state, and governing through bureaucracy. The World Bank consciously shifted its efforts to complement the EU requirements and developed cooperation mechanisms with EU bodies once the country was cleared for EU accession. Under the 2004 programmatic adjustment loan conditionality, the Romanian parliament adopted three organic laws on the judiciary—on the appointment of judges, judicial career development and court administration, and limiting the Prosecutor General's powers to interfere into the judicial process. World Bank funds also supported a comprehensive study on the rationalization of the courts. The single largest World Bank loan specifically designated for rule of law activities came only in 2005, and it totaled $130 million. In line with EU priorities, the loan was for judicial reform, and aimed to increase the efficiency of the courts and the accountability of the judiciary, specifically: court infrastructure rehabilitation, the administrative capacity of courts, court information system, and development of judicial institutions. Intermediate progress indicators included, inter alia, the adoption of new procedural codes, impact studies for the four key codes (civil and criminal), and embedding the LSAT into the magistrates' recruitment process (World Bank, 2011). A new, 2017 World Bank loan totals $72 million and similarly aims to improve the efficiency and accessibility of targeted justice institutions.

6. Public interest litigation

The neoliberal concept of law as a neutral, good governance mechanism helped build the legal infrastructure that bolstered rights in the post-communist world. The region has also moved more directly towards adversarial legalism anchored by a public interest law litigation system inspired by American models. This is neither coincidental, nor widespread across the rest of Europe. It is a specific post-1989 development fueled by private American and government funding, which took roots and has over time led to significant impact litigation. It also helped civil societies post-1989 to identify some spaces for themselves, primarily human rights, shoulder the social costs of the transition, and strengthen their infrastructure and overall position.

Initially, money and support came from both American and European foundations. American foundations, for example, committed over $60 million in the region between 1990 and 1994, with the total jumping to $307 million by 2008 (Spero, 2010). Data from the Foundation Center and the Council on Foundations show that the key private funders were the Soros Network (providing approximately $43 million in 1994 alone for the entire region), the Ford Foundation (approximately $112 million between 1989 and 2001), Pew Charitable Trusts ($35 million), Rockefeller Brothers Fund, and the C.S. Mott Foundation. Their leading priorities were development, international affairs, human rights and civil society. By the late 1990s, however, most foreign foundations in the region had significantly scaled back their activities (Anheier and Hammack, 2010), or created autonomous funds, such as the Trust for Civil Society in Central and Eastern Europe (a $75-million dollar sinking fund that disbursed all its funds by 2013).

Private donors prioritized resources (material, legal, and others) and support networks, key elements in creating the legal opportunity structure of today. The funders worked to strengthen civil society, human rights, public interest law, legal reform and access to justice, primarily by creating and supporting NGOs and think tanks working on human rights, strategic litigation, legal services, clinical legal education, and legal literacy programs, for example, the European Roma Rights Center and the Public Interest Law Initiative on a regional basis, and the Helsinki Committees in various countries. A long-term activist from the region noted in an interview that there was "unusual experimentation in Central and Eastern Europe during the beginning of the transition in particular, a lot of hybrid models, a little bit of everything, for example very strong legal advocacy oriented NGOs, more American style teaching in law schools, [...] skills oriented education, legal clinics, interactive teaching techniques, pro bono work—a lot started to be developed in Central and Eastern Europe and only later in Western Europe."

The American model of adversarial legalism also came directly to the region. CEELI—the American Bar Association's Central and Eastern European Law Initiative, funded by USAID, was one of the most active foreign actors until the EU accession. CEELI had country offices in many countries of the region for extended periods of time. The Romania office, for example, closed in 2008, and overall had over 5000 foreign lawyers involved in its activities in the region, from constitutional drafting to prison reform (Rule of Law Symposium, 2009). As one of the lawyers involved described in an interview, the organization was initially criticized for amateurism and serving as a conduit for American lawyers "sent over as beachheads from law firms," with no interest in the country, its legal system and overall a very American-centric approach. The flipside of a lack of a coherent strategy, however, was the relative freedom of the staff (which by the end of CEELI's tenure in Romania was overwhelmingly Romanian) to try out diverse projects, some of which included cultivating a rule of law culture, and "trying to get people to think differently" by bringing together, for example, judges and prosecutors, and using hypothetical examples during training seminars.

Training lawyers with a rights-oriented approach was also not neglected. The Global Network for Public Interest Law (PIL. net), for example, was created as the Public Interest Law Initiative in Transitional Societies at Columbia University in 1997 to train lawyers in the public interest (with seed money from the Ford Foundation). PIL.net has had offices in Budapest (2002), Russia (2004), and China (2008), and over time has worked to create a global network of public interest lawyers, strengthen access to justice and legal aid, and legal education. Its network includes 130 lawyers from around the world, whose work and influence over time has grown exponentially. Law schools around the region established legal clinics or street law projects (such as Jagiellonian University in Poland), while organizations such as the Open Society Foundation have offered advice, trainings, and workshops on human rights and strategic litigation (Cichowski, 2016).

7. Domestic mobilization and rights-based regulation through litigation

These efforts have been paying off, at both national and supranational levels. At the national level, constitutional courts in particular have become active legal and political actors, and some of them have consequently seen a backlash. Unlike the American Supreme Court, post-1989 CEE constitutional courts were not particularly concerned with an anti-democratic deficit, but rather found themselves placed at the heart of the transition. The existence of a constitutional court was taken as an absolute constitutional insurance, and the lack of one (or at least other means of constitutional adjudication) cast long shadows of suspicion over the democratic character of the country in question (Schwartz, 2000).

CEE constitutional courts have been quite active, dealing with a vast range of issues, from separation of powers to transitional justice (dealing with the past writ large) and defending constitutional rights. The Bulgarian Constitutional Court, for example, positioned itself as the sole institution with the authority to interpret the constitution and as the arbiter in all separation of powers disputes by the mid-1990s (in the Pirinski dispute, the Court effectively disqualified Pirinski, who was the candidate of the most powerful party, from running for the presidency) (Ganev, 2007). The reputation of the new Courts overall ranges from occasionally very activist (the Hungarian Court) to very restrained (the Romanian or Bulgarian Courts). The extent of their activism—understood here broadly in terms of caseloads, rates of overturning legislation or regulation, and degree of involvement in politics—is heavily dependent on their powers, which vary quite a bit throughout the region.

Courts' powers that explicitly make them into policy-makers include abstract a priori review,[3] and checking the constitutionality of referenda or the legality of elections (See Table 2).

Table 2.   Select East European Constitutional Court powers.

Country	Bulgaria	Croatia	Czech Republic	Hungary	Poland	Romania	Slovakia	Slovenia
Preventive review	✓			✓	✓	✓		✓
A posteriori abstract review	✓	✓	✓	✓		✓	✓	✓
Concrete review		✓	✓	✓	✓	✓	✓	
Statutory interpretation				✓				
Constitutional interpretation	✓		✓	✓		✓		
Judicial review of legislative initiative						✓		
Jurisdictional disputes		✓	✓		✓		✓	✓
Constitutional complaint (human rights protection)		✓	✓	✓	✓		✓	✓
Referendum				✓			✓	✓
Impeachments	✓		✓	✓			✓	✓
Elections	✓		✓			✓	✓	✓

Source: Arne Mavcic, www.concourts.net.

Five out of the eight countries have a priori abstract review, and all but one have a posteriori abstract review. Regulation through litigation, in other words, is expressly part of many East European systems. With higher caseloads over time, many have also seen relatively high rates of findings of unconstitutionality.

Some constitutional courts, like the Hungarian one, were initially propelled by extensive powers, almost limitless standing rules, and no discretion to refuse cases, as well as activist judicial philosophies (under Chief Justice Sólyom, 1990–1998). The new constitution (Fundamental Law of Hungary, 2012), however, limited the Court's jurisdiction over budget legislation, while 2013's Fourth Amendment bans the Court from referring to decisions it made before January 1, 2012 (Scheppele, 2015; Lambert, 2018). The Court, at least for now, has been "packed" (almost all its members have been appointed by FIDESZ) and tamed.

---

3   A core power of constitutional courts is judicial review, which means checking the constitutionality of various legal acts against the constitution. Different types of judicial review include reviewing constitutionality in the abstract, without a concrete case, of either a bill (a priori), or a statute (a posteriori), or as applied to a case or controversy (concrete review).

The Romanian Constitutional Court, by contrast, has very narrow powers, and even narrower standing rules. Thus, its restraint is delineated from the very beginning. The Romanian Constitutional Court found totally or partially unconstitutional 638 claims (out of the total number of decisions). Out of this, 43-percent of decisions on abstract preventive review were declared partially or totally unconstitutional, a clear indication of regulation through constitutional review. The Court also found unconstitutional five out of eight initiatives to revise the constitution, and 42-percent of parliamentary regulations. Decisions of unconstitutionality for concrete review amount to only 2.6-percent of the total number of decisions, which is close to the numbers of other Constitutional Courts, such as Germany, albeit lower than others (Italy) (Federal Constitutional Court, 2017), but misleadingly low, as the Court consolidates dozens or even hundreds of similar claims in its decisions (Decision 1238/2009 consolidated 404 identical referrals) (Gâdiuță, 2010).

Substantively, the Romanian Court has issued decisions on highly controversial topics, such as property, nationalization, expropriation and compensation, has been at the center of separation of powers fights, and has become increasingly active regarding restrictions of rights, due process, and equality before the law, among others (Șerban, 2000), yet has not been particularly embracing rights across the board. The Coman case, before the European Court of Justice (ECJ) this past year, has attracted widespread national and international attention (*Coman and Others*, Case C-673/16). The case involves a Romanian-American gay couple whose marriage, officiated in Belgium, was not recognized by Romania. After lengthy proceedings, the Romanian Constitutional Court decided to dodge the issue and instead asked the ECJ for a preliminary ruling. The ECJ ruled in favor of Coman in June 2018, and the decision impacts the entire EU. All EU countries must now recognize same-sex marriage when freedom of movement is involved and at least one spouse is an EU citizen, regardless of individual countries' position on same-sex marriage.

Yet the paradigm of adversarial legalism initially was the Hungarian Constitutional Court during its first nine years, both in terms of expanding its jurisdiction and interpretive practice ("the invisible constitution") (Sájó, 1995). It established the right to life and human dignity as a foundational right, similarly to Germany, and it was not afraid to tackle deeply controversial issues from abortion, to freedom of information, restitution and compensation (Schwartz, 2000). In its early landmark decisions, for example, the Court declared the death penalty unconstitutional (1990) and went on to develop various other rights, such as the right to know one's blood origin, litigation rights, the right to a personal name, and the freedom of marriage (Szente, 2013).

What sets apart the CEE constitutional courts, even those not particularly active, from other high courts is the explicit expectation that they play a policy-making role. The constitutional courts' protection of individual rights gathers various threads together: anti-communism, market economy, top (European) and bottom-up (citizens) pressures. Many of the region's constitutional courts have come to the defense of social and economic rights against neoliberal encroaching, clearly playing a policy-making role. One of the best-known examples is the 1995 austerity package decisions of the Hungarian Constitutional Court. The Court unanimously struck down twenty-six provisions of the austerity package reducing welfare benefits; among the areas affected were sick leave benefits and long-term maternity and child care benefits (Schwartz, 2000). The plan struck down by the Court was important for a new loan from the IMF, and the Court's aggressive stance caused enormous controversy in Hungary.

8. Mobilization and rights-based regulation through litigation at the supranational level

The most striking exemplification of today's adversarial legal culture in CEE comes from the levels of mobilization before European courts, with the focus here on the ECtHR. The infusion of resources and expertise, and the institutional groundwork laid out over the past two decades bear fruit today, as leading NGOs in the region consistently bring cases or intervene in cases before both domestic and international courts. The number of amicus briefs before the ECtHR has been steadily going up, and among the top amici and repeat players is the Polish Helsinki Foundation for Human Rights, which intervened in 25 cases (Cichowski, 2016). The Foundation is highly organized and strategic in its work, which includes impact litigation, antidiscrimination litigation, legal assistance for refugees and migrants, monitoring the legislative process, and a broad defense of rights and liberties.

Its Hungarian counter-part, the Hungarian Helsinki Committee, has similar areas of activity, and has been consistently holding Hungary's illiberal government to account, such as through reports documenting the practices of Orban's illiberal state (most recently in January 2019). PIL.net network has also had a multiplier effect. As an example, Romanița Iordache, a 1999 fellow, has chaired the board of the Romanian Helsinki Committee, is a committee board member for Accept (the main NGO fighting for LGBT rights in Romania), and developed a project to establish a human rights legal clinic at the University of Bucharest. One of her students was the lead lawyer in the Coman case mentioned above.

Anti-discrimination efforts across the continent, and Roma rights more specifically, have been spearheaded by public interest litigators from the region. In the landmark case *D.H. and Others v. Czech Republic* (2007), which concerned discrimination against Romani children in the Czech Republic's schools, the ECtHR not only found that the Czech Republic had discriminated against the 18 Roma students who brought the case, but also established a number of key principles in the area of discrimination. The Court stressed that the ECHR addresses systemic practices, not just specific discriminatory acts, that segregation is discrimination, and that equal access to education for Roma is a persistent problem throughout Europe. The Court also found that intent to discriminate is not required for discrimination to occur, that unequal impact of policies can amount to indirect discrimination, and that the

Roma are a specific type of disadvantaged group who require special protection.

The case was brought before the Court by the European Roma Rights Center (ERRC), an international public interest law group founded in 1996 and heavily supported initially by American funders (Open Society, Ford Foundation). Since then, it has established itself as the most visible NGO working for Roma rights through strategic litigation, advocacy at national, regional and international levels, policy and research, and training of Roma activists. The ERRC explicitly models their fight for Roma rights in Europe on the civil rights movement in the United States and have brought over 500 court cases in 15 countries and at the supranational level. The ERRC helped establish groundbreaking European precedents in the areas of school segregation (Czech Republic), the state's obligation to investigate racial motivation in crimes committed by non-state actors (Croatia, Bulgaria), police brutality (Bulgaria, Macedonia), housing rights and forced eviction issues (Montenegro, Slovakia, Greece, Italy, Bulgaria), compensation to victimized community and implementation of anti-racism and non-discrimination programs (Romania), and coerced sterilization of Romani women (Hungary). The organization won the Justice Prize from the Gruber Foundation (2009), the Stockholm Human Rights Prize (2012), and the Raoul Wallenberg Prize (2018).

Landmark decisions such as *D.H. and Others* are paradigmatic of the CEE adversarial legal culture and matter more broadly in at least three ways: first, for their contribution to a European constitution-making culture from a vantage point that is non-EU and non-Western European (albeit aligning with EU case law); second, for making discrimination against the Roma a legal and policy-making subject across the continent and inserting the Court, a supranational body, into national policy-making; and third, for pointing out that American-style public interest litigation has been a success on the Eastern part of the continent.

Other CEE claimants pushed the ECtHR to become a policy-maker for Europe in areas as diverse as property and procedural due process, and even to revise its own procedures in order to respond more efficiently to rights-based claims. Romania has been unable to resolve in a satisfactory manner its post-communist property issues in terms of dealing with the property (land and urban housing in particular) nationalized and expropriated by the communist regime. Consequently, Romanians sued the Romanian state before the ECtHR by the thousands, and the Court effectively became a policy-maker for the country with its landmark decisions. In *Maria Atanasiu and Others v. Romania* (2010), the Court noted that it already found over 150 violations of the Convention in cases concerning the restitution of properties nationalized under communism, and that it had several hundred other similar cases pending. The Court issued a pilot judgment (one of the first of this kind), adjourned the cases concerning properties nationalized during the communist era in Romania pending general measures at national level, and gave the Romanian government a new deadline for the implementation of general measures to resolve shortcomings in the system of restitution or compensation.

In *Vlad and Others v. Romania* (2013), which concerned the length of legal proceedings and remedy available for the three applicants, the Court found that the length of proceedings had exceeded a reasonable length and there appeared to be no effective remedy such as compensation available to litigants whose cases had taken too long. Since there were 500 similar cases against Romania pending before the ECtHR concerning excessive length of criminal and civil proceedings, the Court held there was a systemic problem which required further reforms of the legal system in order for the right to a fair trial within a reasonable time to be secured in Romania.

Hungarians have been pushing back against their illiberal government, and the Court responded. In *Magyar Helsinki Bizztosag v. Hungary* [Hungarian Helsinki Committee v. Hungarian Constitutional Court (2016), the Committee challenged the refusal by two Hungarian police stations of an access to information request regarding the manner of appointment of public defenders in Hungary. Not only did the Court find in favor of the Committee, but it also consolidated, for the first time, its principles and jurisprudence on access to information and tied it to freedom of expression (Uitz, 2016). Symbolically, this is also a clear rebuke to Hungary's trampling of rights. The ECtHR was even clearer in *Baka v. Hungary* (2016), where it found Hungary in violation of András Baka's right of access to a court and freedom of expression when it prematurely removed him from the presidency of the Hungarian Supreme Court without any possibility of judicial review.

In *Hagyó v. Hungary* (2013), the Court found unanimously that Hungary violated the Convention articles banning inhuman treatment, right to liberty, respect for private and family life, and right to an effective remedy. The Hagyó affair is instructive for understanding both the encroaching of politics on law in Hungary, and the possibilities and limits of resistance. The petitioner, former deputy mayor of Budapest, was at the center of a corruption investigation that involved fourteen others, and widely believed to be a witch trial conducted by FIDESZ for political purposes. He was arrested the moment he lost his parliamentary immunity and spent nine months in jail and later time under house arrest (Balogh, 2015).

Rates of litigation before the ECtHR and landmark decisions are key indicators of the growing importance of the Court as a policy-maker at national levels and of its role in CEE's adversarial legal culture. The Court developed the legal mechanism of pilot judgments to correct systemic problems in specific countries. Pilot judgments are perhaps the clearest indicator of the emerging type of European-style adversarial legalism in the former communist countries. Of the approximately 89,000 cases pending before the ECtHR, many are "repetitive cases" deriving from a common dysfunction at the national level. The Court developed the pilot judgment procedure not only to identify violations of the Convention, but also "to identify the systemic problem and to give the Government clear indications of the type of remedial measures needed to resolve it" (ECtHR, 2017). As of 2017, the Court issued 26 pilot judgments. Seventy-percent (18 out of 26) of the pilot judgments are against post-communist countries, and eleven against the countries specifically discussed in this chapter. Substantively, the pilot judgments mostly cover inhuman conditions of detention, excessive length of proceedings and prolonged non-implementation of court decisions, and property rights. With the exception of Russia, Ukraine, and possibly Albania, there is at least partial compliance from all post-communist countries. Despite sometimes significant delays, such as Romania and Hungary, so far countries have altered their domestic legislation and adopted the measures required by the Court.

9. Conclusion

This paper makes a cautious argument that legal structures build since the fall of communism have provided a relatively robust and for now functioning opportunity for legal mobilization and rights-based regulation through litigation. Under liberal democratic conditions, they strengthen the rule of law and defend rights in the region, while under illiberal conditions, they could serve as a counterpoint (up to a point). Altogether, they indicate a rapid shift from heavily bureaucratized socialist states pre-1989 to contemporary neoliberal states characterized by adversarial legalism. Initially the impetus was exogenous, and altogether changes in institutions, resources, and expertise were fairly comprehensive and for now lasting.

The East European trajectory looks markedly different from the Western European one. Starting from a point of overregulation, bureaucratization, low rights protection, and minimal levels of adversarial legalism, there was nowhere to go but up post-1989. The extent to which the EU is fragmented, under-staffed and bureaucratized, which is a main cause of adversarial legalism in Western Europe, is overshadowed by formal, top down EU requirements with a neo-colonial flavor in Eastern Europe. Brussels is still farther away from Bucharest than from Paris.

The backlash against the courts and the weakening of constitutional democracies in CEE is particularly visible in Poland and Hungary at the moment, but over the past two decades most of these countries have attempted to capture their judiciaries, and many (Bulgaria and Romania most prominently) have struggled with systemic corruption. In Poland and Hungary, the governments targeted the Constitutional Tribunal and Court, respectively, precisely because of their activism and defense of rights. Between 2010 and 2013, the Hungarian Court struck down legislation that allowed state employees to be fired with no reason, legislation reducing the mandatory retirement age for judges to 62 years old, and criminalizing homelessness, among others.

Reasons for concern in both countries at the moment include not just attacks on courts and judicial independence, but concerted efforts to dismantle the legal mobilization infrastructure built since 1990, specifically current attacks against civil society organizations that have been at the forefront of legal mobilization and litigation. The Hungarian government has been on a rampage against George Soros, Central European University (which it has successfully pushed out of Hungary), and NGOs. Hungary's intelligence services have been instructed to investigate "the Soros network," and Hungary adopted in 2017 a Russian look-alike statute that stipulates that any foundation or association that receives foreign funding in excess of $26,000 must register as a foreign-supported organization. Polish authorities have ransacked in early fall 2017 the offices of NGOs that work on women's rights and changed funding rules for NGOs to secure their control and weaken their autonomy (Dempsey, 2017). The EU must step in more forcefully. In the meantime, it may be time to look east and learn how Russian civil society and lawyers have adapted their tactics in the shadow of its new authoritarianism (Van der Vet and Lyyttikäinen, 2015).

References

Anderson, J.H., Bernstein, D., Gray, C.W., 2005. Judicial Systems in Transition Economies: Assessing the Past, Looking to the Future. World Bank, Washington, DC available at: https://openknowledge.world bank.org/handle/10986/7351. License: CC BY 3.0 IGO, Accessed 20 March 2018.

Anheier, H., Hammack, D., 2010. American Foundations: Roles and Contributions. Brookings Institution Press.

Balogh, E., 2015. One of many of FIDESZ-inspired show trials: the Hagyó case [online]. Available at: http://hungarianspectrum.org/tag/miklos-hagyo/. (Accessed 20 October 2017).

Böröcz, J., 2001. Empire and coloniality in the 'eastern enlargement' of the European Union. In: Böröcz, J., Kovacs, M. (Eds.), Empire's New Clothes. Unveiling EU Enlargement. Central Europe Review, pp. 15–18 [online]. Available at: www.ce-review.org. (Accessed 13 September 2014).

Cape, E., Namoradze, Z., 2012. Effective criminal defence in Eastern Europe. Legal aid reformers' network [online]. Available at: https://www.opensocietyfoundations.org/. (Accessed 30 May 2018).

European Commission for the Efficiency of Justice (CEPEJ), 2004-2016. Evaluation of judicial systems [online] Available at: www.coe.int/cepej. (Accessed 5 May 2018).

European Commission for the Efficiency of Justice (CEPEJ), 2008-2014. European judicial systems [online] Available at: www.coe.int/cepej. (Accessed 4 November 2016).

Cichowski, R., 2016. The European Court of Human Rights, amicus curiae, and violence against women. Law Soc. Rev. 50 (4), 890-919.

Conant, L., Hofmann, A., Soennecken, D., Vanhala, L., 2017. Mobilizing European law. J. Eur. Publ. Pol. 1: 14.

Curtis, Glenn E., 1994. Poland: A Country Study. Federal Research Division, Library of Congress, Washington, D.C [online] Available at: www.loc.gov/item/ 93046235/. (Accessed 25 May 2018).

Dempsey, J., 2017. Shrinking spaces in Hungary and Poland. Carnegie Europe [online] Available at: http://carnegieeurope.eu/strategiceurope/74581. (Accessed 4 November 2017).

European Court of Human Rights, 2017. Pilot Judgments [online] Available at: http://www.echr.coe.int/documents/fs_pilot_judgments_eng.pdf. (Accessed 4 November 2017).

Epp, C., 1998. The Rights Revolution. The University of Chicago Press.

European Court of Human Rights, 2000-2016. Annual reports [online] Available at: http://www.echr.coe.int/. (Accessed 4 November 2017).

European Court of Human Rights Overview 1959-2016 (2017). [online] Available at: http://www.echr.coe.int/[Accessed 4 November. 2017].

European Union, 2016. Justice Scoreboard [online] Available at: http://ec.europa.eu/. (Accessed 10 October 2017).

Federal Constitutional Court, 2017. Annual statistics 2017 [online] Available at: http://www.bundesverfassungsgericht.de. (Accessed 23 May 2018).

Flash Eurobarometer 385, 2013. Justice in the EU [online] Available at: http://ec.europa.eu/public_opinion/flash/fl_385_en.pdf. (Accessed 16 November 2015).

Fundamental Law of Hungary (2012). [online] Available at: http://www.kormany.hu/en/news/the-new-fundamental-law-of-hungary [Accessed 30 May 2018].

Gâdiuță, F., 2010. The Romanian Constitutional Court: Some Causes of the High Caseload [online] Available at: http://ssrn.com/abstract¼1653848. (Accessed September 2014).

Ganev, V., 2007. Preying on the State: The Transformation of Bulgaria after 1989. Cornell University Press.

Garth, B., 2003. Law and society as law and development. Law Soc. Rev. 37 (2).

Human Rights Watch, 2017. Eroding checks and balances. In: Rule of Law and Human Rights Under Attack in Poland [online] Available at: https://www.hrw. org/. (Accessed 4 November 2017).

Hungarian Constitutional Court, 2016. Statistics [online] Available at: http://www.mkab.hu/constitutional-court/statistics. (Accessed 4 November 2017). Jessop, B., 2002. The Future of the Capitalist State. Polity Press.

Kagan, R., 2001. Adversarial Legalism: the American Way of Law. Harvard University Press.

Kelemen, D., 2011. Eurolegalism. The Transformation of Law and Regulation in the European Union. Harvard University Press.

Lambert, S., 2018. The Constitutional Court [online] Available at: https://theorangefiles.hu/the-constitutional-court/. (Accessed 4 November 2017).

McCann, M., 1994. Rights at Work: Pay Equity Reform and the Politics of Legal Mobilization. University of Chicago Press.

Neacșu, T., 2013. Are Romania prea puțini judecători? [online] Available at: http://www.magistrati.ro/s674-are-romania-prea-putini-judecatori-.html [Accessed 2015].

Quigley, K., 1997. For Democracy's Sake. Johns Hopkins University Press.

Ribicic, C., 2008. Strengthening constitutional democracy [online] Available at: http://www.venice.coe.int/wccj/papers/slo_ribicic_e.pdf. (Accessed 13 August 2012).

Romanian Constitutional Court, 2017. Statistics [online] Available at: https://www.ccr.ro/Statistici-periodice. (Accessed 4 November 2017).

Rule of Law Symposium, 2009. The history of CEELI, the ABA's rule of law initiative, and the rule of law movement going forward. Minn. J. Int. Law 18, 304.

Sajo, A., 1995. Reading the invisible constitution: judicial review in Hungary. Oxf. J. Leg. Stud. 15 (2).

Scheingold, S., 2004. The Politics of Rights. University of Michigan Press.

Scheppele, K.L., 2015. Kim Lane Scheppele Analyzes the Present Situation in Hungary. Available at: https://lapa.princeton.edu/. (Accessed 4 November 2017).

Schwartz, H., 2000. The Struggle for Constitutional Justice in Post-Communist Europe. University of Chicago Press.

Şerban, M., 2000. Judicial Activism and the Romanian Constitutional Court. SJD. Central European University.

Slovenian Constitutional Court, 2016. Annual Report [online] Available at: http://www.us-rs.si/. (Accessed 4 November 2017).

Smilov, D., 2016. Bulgaria [online] Available at: http://emuchoices.eu/. (Accessed 4 November 2017).

Solyóm, L., 1994. The Hungarian Constitutional Court and social change. Yale J. Int. Law 19, 223.

Spero, J., 2010. The Global Role of US Foundations. The Foundation Center.

Szente, Z., 2013. The interpretive practice of the Hungarian constitutional court: a critical view. German Law Journal 14 (8).

Uitz, R., 2016. MHB v Hungary Judgment on Access to information. [Blog] ECHR blog. Available at: http://echrblog.blogspot.nl. (Accessed 4 November 2017).

Vanhala, L., 2012. Legal opportunity structures and the paradox of legal mobilization by the environmental movement in the UK. Law Soc. Rev. 46 (3), 523-556.

Venice Commission, 2013. Opinion on the fourth amendment to the fundamental law, June 17, 2013 [online] Available at: http://www.venice.coe.int. (Accessed 14 October 2015).

Van der Vet, F., Lyyttikäinen, 2015. Violence and human rights in Russia: how human rights defenders develop their tactics in the face of danger 2005-2013. Int. J. Hum. Right. 19 (7), 979-998.

World Bank, 2011. Implementation status and results. In: Romania Judicial Reform Project. Report No. ISR5628 [online] Available at: www.worldbank.org. (Accessed 30 October 2012).

The Fragility of an Independent Judiciary: Lessons from Hungary and Poland — and the European Union[1]

Kriszta Kovács, Kim Lane Scheppele
Eötvös Loránd University, Budapest, Hungary,
and WZB Center for Global Constitutionalism, Berlin, Germany
Woodrow Wilson School and Department of Sociology,
Princeton University, Princeton, USA

When the European Union was founded, it was assumed that all Member States admitted as consolidated democracies would maintain their constitutional commitments. In recent years, Hungary and Poland have challenged this premise as elected autocratic governments in those countries have captured independent institutions and threatened long-term democracy. The judiciaries of these countries have been hard hit. In this paper, we trace what has happened to the judiciaries in Hungary and Poland, showing how first the constitutional courts and then the ordinary judiciary have been brought under the control of political forces so that there is no longer a separation of law and politics. We also explore why the European Union has so far not been able to stop this process. In the end, the European judiciary, particularly the Court of Justice, is attempting a rescue of national judiciaries, but the results are so far unclear.

Keywords: Comparative constitutional law, Judicial independence, Hungary, Poland, European Union, Democratic decline

1. Introduction

By the time of the "big bang" accession in 2004, when ten new Member States entered the European Union, it seemed that the fate of East-Central Europe was settled. From that time forward, the westward states of post-communist Europe were certified as democracies in good standing, ready for membership in the most

---

[1] The events we describe in this chapter are fast moving. The chapter is current as of June 2019 and events after that date could not be taken into account here.

exclusive club in the world. At the time, political scientists spoke of "consolidated democracies" (Linz and Stepan, 1996), defined as countries in which democracy was the "only game in town" because there were no realistic alternatives. A country whose democracy was consolidated would stay a democracy forever. Or so the experts thought.

Before the first decade was out on the big bang accession, however, it became painfully clear that a consolidated democracy could come unraveled. Hungary's constitutional system began imploding shortly after 2010 so that by 2015, Freedom House lowered its assessment of Hungary from a consolidated to semi-consolidated democracy (Freedom House, 2015), the first time a consolidated democracy had officially fallen from grace. Shortly thereafter, Poland began a short, sharp slide toward autocracy, with Freedom House reducing its overall democracy score for 2018 to a level where Poland just barely hung onto consolidated democratic status (Freedom House, 2018). Since that score appeared, things have not improved. When it came to democratic consolidation, it turned out that what went up could also go down.

What happened? In both Hungary and Poland, parties with autocratically inclined leaders were voted into power with unprecedented majorities. The Fidesz party in Hungary won two-thirds of the parliamentary seats in the 2010 election, giving the party a constitutional majority, which it has largely retained to the present day.[2] The Law and Justice party (PiS in its Polish acronym) in Poland won an absolute majority of seats in the lower house of Parliament in 2015, governing as a single party alone for

---

2   Between 2010 and 2014 the election system had been restructured (László 2016) so the party's relative lead in the general elections (44,87 % in 2014 and 49,27 % in 2018) was translated into a qualified majority in Parliament. Furthermore, a study documents electoral clientelism in rural Hungary which played a role in the enduring success of Fidesz party in the 2014 elections and in the 2018 general elections (Mares and Lauren, 2019). For two years between its second and third consecutive elections, Fidesz lost its two-thirds majority in two by-elections but sometimes managed to pass laws requiring "relative" two-thirds majorities (two-thirds of those present and voting). Constitutional amendments require an "absolute" two-thirds (two-thirds of all MPs).

the first time in the country's modern democratic history, while simultaneously capturing the presidency and the upper house of the parliament. In both cases, the elections could be seen as ordinary rotations of parties away from those that had already been in power for too long (Scheppele, 2018). But in both cases, these pivotal elections, which gave full legislative and executive power to a single party, spelled the beginning of the end of consolidated democracy in East-Central Europe.

It was each country's bad luck that the leaders of these successful parties—Viktor Orbán in Hungary and Jarosław Kaczyński in Poland—lied about their revolutionary ambitions before they were elected. Had these leaders been honest about their autocratic plans, it is unclear whether either could have won. Once in office, however, both Orbán and Kaczyński began attacking key independent public institutions in order to eliminate them as veto points. The first institutions to be attacked were the constitutional judiciaries which were poised to hold Orbán and Kaczyński to account under the democratic constitutions they inherited. Once the constitutional courts were neutralized, the ordinary judiciaries were dismembered when they held out the possibility for individuals and opposition groups to challenge through law what these new autocratic governments were doing. Judicial independence, once quite strong in both Poland and Hungary, is now a thing of the past.

Perhaps no one was more surprised at democratic backsliding in East-Central Europe than the leaders of EU institutions, who—along with the academic consensus—had believed that consolidated democracy was irreversible. They had had faith that national institutions in general—and judiciaries in particular—could contain any values-based threat that might arise. The EU had carried out a thorough check of countries on their way in the door but made no provision for ongoing monitoring of the democratic health of Member States once they were admitted. Consolidated democracies were supposed to stay consolidated, so there seemed to be no need for monitoring mechanisms. At EU level, however, the deconsolidation of democratic governments not only posed a threat of contagion, as we have already seen with the uptake of autocratic tactics now in Poland, but deconsolidation also threatened the operation of the EU as such. The Member State judiciaries are the institutions through which EU law is enforced throughout the Union. If they are disabled, the Member States are not the only ones to suffer, but the whole EU suffers too because its writ does not run throughout the EU if the national courts do not ensure uniform compliance with EU law.

It did not help that the European Union believed it had few tools to prevent democratic backsliding because the EU was designed to protect Member States from an overreaching Union instead of protecting the Union from failing Member States. Treaty change requires unanimous agreement among the Member States; even ordinary legislation cannot be passed without qualified majority approval of the Member States. Without the Member States supporting in force what the EU does, the EU can do very little. And the Member States do not contemplate being seriously sanctioned themselves. In the basic design of the EU, Member States largely protected themselves from sanction from the center. Member States can quit (hence, Brexit) but they cannot be thrown out.

The primary sanctions mechanism for values-based non-compliance with EU law is a political process identified in Article 7 of the Treaty on European Union (TEU) that requires supermajority agreement of the other Member States to identify a *risk* of non-compliance. It requires a *unanimous* judgment of all other Member States except the offender to determine that EU values have *in fact* been breached. With even one other fellow-traveler state supporting an offender, Article 7 TEU has been thought impossible to use for levying sanctions. Now the EU has two. As we will see, the other legal process for ensuring the uniform enforcement of EU law, the infringement procedure, allows the European Commission to bring Member States to the European Court of Justice if the Member State violates EU law. But infringement procedures to date have been used for relatively technical violations—nothing so big as a threat to European values or the deconsolidation of a democratic state.

The attack on national judiciaries is the most important element in the EU's democratic backsliding story because, with disabled judiciaries, no one can be assured of fair treatment once they challenge the government. If courts will not neutrally enforce the law—whether national or EU law—then it becomes impossible for those inside or outside the state to counter the autocratic state through legal means. For that reason, we will concentrate in this article on the methods and results of the attacks on the judiciaries in Hungary and Poland, focusing on the interventions that the European Union attempted to make as the judiciaries were politically captured. First we will explain what happened in Hungary and then we will turn to Poland. We will conclude by explaining why the European Union has been so powerless (so far) to arrest the capture of the courts and what it could still do now.

2. Judicial independence in Hungary

Hungary's national parliamentary election of 2010 occurred at a bad time for the country. Hungary had been hit hard by the global financial crisis when a housing bubble fueled by foreign-currency-denominated mortgages burst just as the government's debt itself became unsustainable. The IMF, the lender of last resort, bailed Hungary out in 2008, insisting on a program of radical austerity. Forced to make draconian cuts to the state budget causing more pain all around, the Socialist government of the day was clearly going to lose the upcoming election in 2010. Besides, the Socialists had been in power for eight years, longer than any other post-communist Hungarian government. It had presided over a moral crisis in which much of the Hungarian public believed that the sitting government was both corrupt and mendacious. As a result, voters in 2010 voted to elect the main opposition party at that time, Fidesz (which ran in coalition with a tiny almost non-existent party, the Christian Democrats).

The Fidesz-Christian Democratic coalition won a landslide victory in the general elections in 2010, which opened the way for a profound shift in the direction of the state even though the victorious parties did not campaign on a platform of constitutional reform. The lightly entrenched 1989 democratic constitution, still in force at that time, could be amended by a single two-thirds vote of the Parliament, and the new government, headed by Prime Minister Viktor Orbán, had 68 per cent of the seats. This numerical reality gave Fidesz the possibility of changing the constitution at will. One year into its term, after the governing coalition had amended the constitution it inherited 12 times, it adopted a wholly new constitution without the support of any other party. This new "Fundamental Law," as it was called, signaled that the constitutional transformation had begun.

The Fundamental Law changed the core characteristics of Hungarian constitutionalism. Instead of the universal principles of liberty, equality and democracy that had animated the old constitution, the new Fundamental Law now has its foundation in the contentious, nationalistic, historical and religious narrative of the preamble (Kovács and Tóth, 2011: 198ff). Moreover, the Fundamental Law aims at consolidating the power of the ruling parliamentary majority by restricting the competitive political process (Arato et al., 2012: 483). In the Hungarian system of government, a two-thirds governing majority is the supreme and constitutionally unlimited organ of state power because this majority can amend the constitution at will.

In its first few years, the Fundamental Law was supplemented by more than 800 new laws, changing the whole legal system established after the democratic transition of 1989. The new legal order rapidly removed virtually all of the checks on executive power that the first democratic constitution of 1989–1990 had managed to install (Bánkuti et al., 2012). Previously, the judiciary and the Constitutional Court were the institutions that served as main checks on the power of governmental majorities. But already in 2011, European bodies called the attention to the fact that the independence of neither the Constitutional Court nor the judiciary were expressly guaranteed in the Fundamental Law (Venice Commission, 2011: para 102; 2012b: para 10). The European Parliament expressed concern about "the weakening of the system of checks and balances" (European Parliament, 2011: para F). Similar concerns were raised by the Group of States against Corruption (GRECO, 2015). But the Hungarian government did not respond. The critics were proven correct in their warnings.

In Hungary's unicameral parliamentary system after 1990, the Constitutional Court was the strongest check in the constitutional structure. But immediately after its election in 2010, the Fidesz government attacked the independence and the competencies of the Constitutional Court. First, an early constitutional amendment of July 5, 2010 changed the selection procedure for the justices of the Constitutional Court and the election rules for the Court's President. Since then, the President of the Court has been elected by a two-third vote of the Parliament while Constitutional Court judges have been nominated by a parliamentary committee that the governing party dominates, followed by a two-thirds vote of the Parliament. Thus, only governing party votes are needed to select new judges (European Parliament, 2011: para Q). Later, through another constitutional amendment (Act LXI/2011), the parliamentary majority, noting that jurisdictional changes it had made under the new constitution, increased the Court's workloads, changed the number of judges on the Constitutional Court from 11 to 15 so the government could select more judges for the Court without gaining support of any other parliamentary party.

As the Court was being packed, however, it fought back. When it nullified a 98% retroactive tax on severance bonuses for those who had served in the last (non-Fidesz) government,[3] the governing coalition amended the old constitution (Act CXX of 2010) to restrict the competencies of the Constitutional Court so that the Court could no longer review the constitutionality of certain financial measures. The Venice Commission criticized this restriction (Venice Commission, 2012b: para 38), and reiterated this criticism with growing urgency in repeated opinions (Venice

---

3   Hungarian Constitutional Court Decision 184/2010 struck down the tax, a judgment that the European Court of Human Rights later upheld when it found that the former public servants had property rights in their bonuses which could not be taken away retroactively. N.K.M. v. Hungary, Judgment of 14 May 2013.

Commission, 2013: para 113). But the government did not back down, instead eventually entrenching this restriction on constitutional review in Art. 37.4 of the Fundamental Law with the new constitution's Fourth Amendment in 2013.

The Fourth Amendment, which marked the final capture of the Constitutional Court by the governing coalition, also nullified the entire case law of the Constitutional Court from 1990 to 2011, so none of the decisions of the Court from before the enactment of the new constitution could be relied on as legal authority. The Fourth Amendment also inserted directly into the constitution nearly all of the legal provisions that the once-independent Constitutional Court had found unconstitutional after the Fidesz government took office (European Parliament, 2013: paras AM-AR). The entire activity of the Constitutional Court between its founding and the date of the Fourth Amendment was therefore destroyed as a matter of law by this amendment. To complete the government domination of the Court, the Fourth Amendment also prevented the Court from reviewing all constitutional amendments for their compliance with the basic principles of the Fundamental Law. This applied first and foremost to the Fourth Amendment itself.

By spring 2013, the Constitutional Court was effectively neutralized as a check on government because the governing coalition had named a majority of the judges who in turn refused to nullify almost any law that the government supported.

While the Fundamental Law formally retained the Constitutional Court on paper, the changes in its functioning were considerable in practice. The Fundamental Law abolished the primary vehicle for constitutional challenges before that time: the *actio popularis* petition, through which anyone could turn to the Constitutional Court to request review of the constitutionality of laws. There are now three ways that laws and normative acts can come before the Constitutional Court.

First, certain identified parties may ask for abstract constitutional review. The government itself, one-fourth of the MPs, the President of the Kúria (newly renamed Supreme Court), the Prosecutor General or the Ombudsperson for Fundamental Rights can initiate this procedure (Sec. 24.1 of Act CLI/2011 on the Constitutional Court). The government is unlikely to ask for review of its own legal acts, and the current President of the Kúria, the Prosecutor General and the Ombudsperson were all chosen by this government from among those friendly to their party. From this group, only the Ombudsperson has ever brought cases to the Constitutional Court and he has said that he only brings cases that he deems to be not "political" (IBAHRI, 2015: 35). While the parliamentary opposition might be expected to bring abstract review cases, the current parliamentary opposition, less than one-third of the MPs, is divided almost equally between fragmented parties of the left and a party of the far right. Given this configuration, it happens very rarely that one-quarter of the MPs agree on constitutional challenges. Abstract review has therefore virtually disappeared when it was once the most common form of constitutional procedure. In 2017, only about 1 per cent of the Constitutional Court's caseload (4 cases out of 461) were based on abstract review petitions (Constitutional Court of Hungary, 2017). In 2018 even less, only 2 new cases out of 391, were based on abstract review petitions (Constitutional Court of Hungary, 2018).

A second way that cases can now come to the Constitutional Court is through the judicial initiative. If a judge is bound to apply a legal rule that he or she perceives to be unconstitutional, the judge shall suspend the proceedings and submit a petition to the Constitutional Court for its determination of the constitutionality of the law (Sec 25.1 of Act CLI/2011). But judges use this option rarely. In 2017, only about 10 per cent of the Constitutional Court's caseload, 48 out of 461 were judicial initiatives (Constitutional Court of Hungary, 2017). Similarly, in 2018, 44 cases out of 391 were judicial initiatives (Constitutional Court of Hungary, 2018).

The third possibility for bringing cases to the Constitutional Court, and by far the largest contributor to the Court's docket now, is the newly enacted constitutional complaint. By introducing a constitutional complaint against court decisions the Fundamental Law cleverly shifted the focus of the review from the law itself to its application. Now it is no longer possible to challenge directly the constitutionality of the laws themselves or the decisions of the government; only the court decisions that rule on these matters can be reviewed. In 2017, most of the petitions before the Constitutional Court (330 out of 461) challenged other court decisions (Constitutional Court of Hungary, 2017) and not the underlying state action or the underlying law itself. In 2018, 288 petitions out of 391 challenged court decisions (Constitutional Court of Hungary, 2018).

From once having been the key check on executive and legislative power in the constitutional order, the Hungarian Constitutional Court has now both been packed with political allies and also had its wings clipped. The constitutionality of laws and of government actions can therefore not be guaranteed.[4]

Capturing and neutralizing the Constitutional Court was just the beginning, however. The ordinary judiciary has been attacked as well. Beginning with Act CLXII/2011 on the Status and Remuneration of Judges, the independence of the ordinary courts has been threatened. This law lowered the age-limit for compulsory retirement from 70 to 62–65 years according to a graduated system depending on the date of birth of judges. The vast majority of senior judges—between 10 and 15% of all judges in the country, and disproportionately including judges in the leadership of the courts—were forced to leave the bench almost immediately. The not-yet-packed Hungarian Constitutional Court in its decision 33/2012 found that lowering the judicial retirement age as applied to sitting judges was unconstitutional because it violated the principle of judicial irremovability. In response, the government inserted the already annulled provision on the retirement age into

---

[4] The already packed Constitutional Court upheld the ban on protesting in front of the Prime Minister's house (Decision 13/2016), declared that national identity entrenched by the Fundamental Law is a basic principle of constitutional interpretation (Decision 22/2016), upheld the so-called Stop Soros legislation which criminalized the support of "illegal immigration" in Hungary (Decision 3/2019) and ruled that collecting signatures in support of Viktor Orbán's anti-immigration program during EP election campaign was in harmony with EP election campaign rules (Decision in case IV/747/2019).

the Fundamental Law as an amendment (now Art 26.2 of the Fundamental Law). The Venice Commission strongly criticized the move and did not see "a material justification for the forced retirement of judges, including many holders of senior court positions" (Venice Commission, 2012a: para 104). The European Commission and the European Parliament also raised concerns about Hungary's decision to reduce suddenly the retirement age of judges (European Commission, 2012; European Parliament, 2012: para G). The Commission brought an infringement action to the European Court of Justice (ECJ) which in turn held that premature judicial retirements were a violation of EU law on age discrimination (Commission v. Hungary, Case C-286/12, 6 November 2012). Hungary paid compensation but was able to avoid restoring the most important judges to their prior posts (IBAHRI, 2015). Though the Commission took rapid action to challenge this firing of judges and ECJ condemned the practice, the Hungarian government won the facts on the ground by keeping all of its newly appointed judges when the case (that they lost) was over.

At the same time as judges were being fired *en masse*, a unique system of judicial administration—existing in no other European country—was introduced through the abolition of the previous structure of judicial self-governance and the creation of a new National Judicial Office (Act CLXI/2011 on the Organization and Administration of Courts of Hungary). The president of the new National Judicial Office has the power to exercise the "central responsibilities of the administration of the courts" (Fundamental Law, Art. 25.5), which also includes the power to appoint new judges conditioned only on the countersignature of the President of the Republic. This lone official is, therefore, the "crucial decision-maker in practically every aspect of the organization of the judicial system" (Venice Commission, 2012a: para 118). The current incumbent, elected by the parliamentary supermajority for a term of nine years, has complete discretionary power to promote and demote judges as well as to transfer and reassign them, and she has a role in initiating and organizing judicial discipline. Her sweeping powers give her control over every aspect of a judge's career and, according to the Venice Commission, "the essential elements of the reform not only contradict European standards for the organization of the judiciary, especially its independence, but are also problematic as concerns the right to a fair trial under Article 6 ECHR" (Venice Commission, 2012a: para 117). Although a so-called National Judicial *Council* composed of judges is also part of the system, and recently it has been critical of National Judicial Office,[5] it plays only a negligible role in the administration of the judiciary. Given the new system, judges cannot enjoy true autonomy and independence from the National Judicial Office (Venice Commission, 2012c, European Parliament, 2013: paras AV-BC).

The new system of political control over the courts also changed the qualifications for the presidency of the Supreme Court. These new qualifications had the effect of removing the incumbent President before the end of his lawful term. The European Court of Human Rights found that the premature termination of the President's mandate had violated the right of access to a court and the right to freedom of expression (Baka v. Hungary, ECtHR Judgment of 27 May 2014), but here too, the remedy was compensation and not reinstatement. It was hard to reach the principle of judicial independence through a human rights convention when the violation did not occur in the form of an unfair trial. As with the judicial retirement case at the ECJ, the Hungarian government lost the case but it got the new court President it wanted.

In 2011, the government began floating the idea of establishing a separate system of administrative courts. For years, however, the administrative court proposal was stalled because it proved surprisingly controversial among Fidesz loyalists. Unlike the other court-capturing laws which were forwarded with rationales that one might believe were connected to reasonable reform (for ex-

---

[5] On May 8, 2019 the National Judicial Council proposed to deprive the President of the National Judicial Office of her office arguing that the President did not comply with the law when appointing judges, court leaders and when transferring judges to another court. The resolution was sent to Parliament and Fidesz's two-thirds parliamentary majority voted to keep the President in place.

ample, getting rid of judges trained in the communist time, adding judges to a system that would now have more cases), this one seemed too obviously aimed at creating a separate court system for politically sensitive cases in which the government would always win by design. But in 2016, Parliament passed two laws, Act CL/2016 on Administrative Procedure and T/12234 Act on Administrative Court Procedure, laws that would have created a parallel judiciary of administrative courts. The latter not yet promulgated Act was referred by the President of Hungary to the Constitutional Court for a preliminary review. In its Decision 1/2017, the Court declared the Act unconstitutional because the creation of new courts outside the regular judiciary required a constitutional majority of a two-thirds vote in the Parliament. But these laws had passed during a period when Fidesz had lost its two-thirds majority in two by-elections, so it had counted on getting these laws through on a simple majority, which the Constitutional Court blocked. But the government proceeded as far as it could anyway; in February 2017, Parliament adopted Act I/2017 on Administrative Court Procedure without the contested provisions and both statutes entered into force on January 1, 2018. The government could not create totally new courts but it could create administrative chambers within already existing courts.

Since then eight specialized administrative regional centers within the general judiciary have been tasked with a whole range of politically sensitive cases. They have the sole jurisdiction to rule in appeals against the administrative decisions of those public bodies that are supposed to be most independent of the government, like the Hungarian National Bank or the Hungarian Academy of Sciences. In these cases, politically aligned judicial review could reverse decisions that the government was otherwise not able to control. These regional courts also have unusual jurisdiction in two types of individual rights cases with political implications: "right to assembly" cases that involve permits for public demonstrations and freedom of information cases that would expose the internal workings of the government if requests were granted (Sec. 12 of Act I/2017). These administrative chambers also hear appeals against the decisions of the county governments. But, operating as they have within the general judiciary, they have not ensured the degree of control over these cases that the governing party apparently wanted.

After the ruling coalition regained its two-thirds majority in the 2018 general election, it almost immediately pushed through the Parliament yet another amendment to the Fundamental Law, circling back to its earlier reforms that had been blocked. The Seventh Amendment to the Fundamental Law passed in July 2018 now permits the creation of a wholly separate public administration court system, including an Administrative Supreme Court that is separate from other public courts but with the same legal status as the Kúria. The task of the Administrative Supreme Court will be to review the application of the law by the administrative courts, and to make "uniformity decisions" guiding interpretation of the law which are binding on the administrative courts. The constitutional amendment has brought significant changes to the system of public administration which required further lawmaking to fill in. Act CXXX/2018 on Administrative Courts and Act CXXXI/2018 on the Entry into Force of the Act on Administrative Courts set up a new administrative court system that deals in politically sensitive matters like electoral law, asylum, freedom of information, media and the right to assembly. The National Judicial Office opposed splitting up the court system (Hungarian Helsinki Committee, 2018: 2), hence, the appointment and disciplinary procedure of administrative judges and court Presidents run through the Minister of Justice and not through the National Judicial Office. Although the Administrative Judicial Council is established and it has some say in judicial applications, ultimately, the Minister decides on the nomination of the new judges and court Presidents. The Venice Commission's report stressed that "the broad powers reserved for the Minister by the law as regards the appointment and career of judges, promotion to positions of responsibility, salary increases and so on raise questions over the lack of real review procedures" and that the Minister "is vested with extensive powers including in the areas of recruitment and appointments to posts of head of court, without adequate criteria and principles being established to provide a framework for the Minister's decisions (particularly when establishing the final ranking of candidates) or any express provision for remedies for challenging those decisions" (Venice Commission, 2019: para 114). And although some changes were made on the text after the Venice Commission's report, the laws still do not comply with international standards (Hungarian Helsinki Committee, 2019). Persons without any experience as a judge can be appointed as a "judge" or elected as the President of the Supreme Administrative Court and the Minister decides who becomes a judge or a court President. Furthermore, there is no possibility for appeal from the Supreme Administrative Court to the Supreme Court, so the purpose of the new administrative courts seems to be to wall off administrative action from serious judicial scrutiny. Recently, the governing majority has postponed the creation of the parallel court system, but insisted that "the administrative court system has a longstanding historical precedent" in Hungary (Viktor Orbán's letter to EPP).

As these attacks on the independence of the judiciary continued over nine long years, some of the European Union institutions took note, made repeated criticisms, but ultimately did not succeed in altering the course of events substantially. The most aggressive action taken by the European Commission was the expedited infringement procedure brought against Hungary as the government fired judges *en masse* by lowering their retirement ages. But the Commission did not feel it could call what was happening by its proper name—interference with the independence of the judiciary. The Treaties presume that all states will have independent judiciaries; there was, as the Commission saw it then, no black-letter legal provision either in the Treaties or in the rest of EU law that would have permitted the Commission to charge Hungary with destruction of something whose existence was not explicitly legally mandated but only presupposed. So the Commission did the next best thing: charge Hungary with violating the prohibition on age discrimination. Though the Commission won the case, the government got to keep its captured judiciary (Scheppele, 2016). It was clear that the tools the European Commission felt it had were not up to the task.

The European Parliament was more active as the Hungarian government consolidated its control over the judiciary, passing resolution after resolution, most prominently on July 3, 2013 in the "Tavares Report," named after its tenacious rapporteur who drafted a full-scale indictment of Hungary's slide into autocracy (European Parliament, 2013). But the other EU institutions—namely the Commission and the Council—largely ignored the parliamentary resolutions. The European Parliament may have been calling Hungary out on each move in its fall from European norms, but no one appeared to be listening. Throughout Hungary's long slide into autocracy, the Council failed to say a critical word.

As the European Commission was nearing the end of its term in 2014, Vice President Viviane Reding proposed, and the Commission adopted, a new "Rule of Law Framework." Designed to allow the Commission to enter a dialogue with a backsliding Member State and to permit the Commission to give concrete warnings and specific recommendations as the Commission considered whether Article 7 TEU should be launched, the Rule of Law Framework became available for use by the Commission just as new European elections meant that all those who had worked on the case against Hungary left office. The new Commission that came into office in 2014 did not pick up where the old Commission left off. When the European Parliament later called on the European Commission to invoke its Rule of Law Framework for Hungary, the Commission did not find it necessary to do so. It has filed some infringement procedures against Hungary for offenses against EU law unrelated to the autocratic consolidation of power in the country[6] but there has been no talk of using the Rule of Law

---

[6] For instance, the Commission opened infringement procedure on rights of cross-border investors to use agricultural land (No. 20142246) and referred to the Court for failing to transpose the Energy Efficiency Directive (No. 20142257).

Framework to assess whether Hungary should be subjected to a warning under Article 7 TEU. Instead, Poland has occupied all of their energy, as we will see in the next section.

On September 12, 2018, however, the European Parliament adopted a new comprehensive condemnatory report authored by rapporteur Judith Sargentini for the Parliament's Civil Liberties Committee. The "Sargentini report" (European Parliament, 2018; Hungarian Government, 2018),passed the whole European Parliament by the requisite supermajority triggered Article 7(1) with regard to Hungary.

In generating the Sargentini report, neither the Commission nor the Council has been of much assistance and the Council would have to vote by a four-fifths majority to agree with the Parliament before a warning to the government of Hungary can issue. Many believe that the Council will never consent despite the fact that since the adoption of the Sargenti report Hungary has further increased the government's control over the judiciary by setting up a parallel administrative court system.

3. Judicial independence in Poland[7]

Politics in Poland, as in Hungary, had become very polarized by the time of the 2015 national elections. The Civic-Platform-led government of the center-left had been in power for eight years, and its popular leader, Donald Tusk, had been drafted to Brussels to serve as the first new accession-state President of the Council of the European Union. Headless and running out of ideas, with its national support slipping, Civic Platform was bound to lose. To make matters worse for the left, their supporters split their votes in the 2015 elections between Civic Platform and an upstart party called Modern Poland while the right voted *en bloc* for the PiS party. With only half the voters turning out, and the victorious PiS party winning only 37.5% of the vote of that participating half, PiS

---

[7] The narrative in this section is drawn from Wojciech Sadurski, 2018a and 2018b; European Commission, 2017a, 2017b, 2017c, 2017d and 2018; Venice Commission 2016a, 2016b and 2017.

gained an absolute majority of seats in both chambers of the Parliament, after having just won the Presidency in an election earlier in the year. With half-hearted support from half the population, an autocratic government was born.

Civic Platform committed the first constitutional offense on its way out of the office, however. Seeing an opportunity to pack the Constitutional Tribunal itself before suffering an election defeat, the Civic Platform government had changed the law under which constitutional judges were elected (25 June 2015 amendment to the Act on the Constitutional Tribunal). The old rule had been that the Parliament in power on the day that a judge's term ended had the legal authority to fill that seat, but under the new rule, the Parliament could elect judges months ahead of an actual opening on the court. Three judgeships came open under the old rule on Civic Platform's watch but the outgoing Parliament elected five judges under the new rule—filling two openings that had not yet materialized but that would open up soon after the new PiS Parliament was seated.

Given this unconstitutional maneuver (as the Constitutional Tribunal would later confirm in its judgment on 3 December 2015), PiS came to power with an "own goal" legal violation by Civil Platform from which PiS was determined to benefit. None of the Civic Platform judges had been sworn in by PiS President of the Republic Andrzej Duda, so technically the seats that had not been filled before the election were still open. The PiS Parliament therefore cancelled the election of all five Civic Platform judges, even though only two had been illegally elected (19 November 2015 amendment to the Act on the Constitutional Tribunal). Instead, PiS elected five of its own judges to fill all of the open seats. The Constitutional Tribunal, pulled into the political fight because it had to assess the legality of the election of all of these judges as well as the constitutionality of the laws under which they were all elected, properly found that three of the judges elected by Civic Platform should be sworn in by the President along with two of the judges PiS had elected (Sadurski, 2018a). But President Duda refused to publish the decisions of the Tribunal and also refused to swear in any of the Civic Platform judges. Instead, President Duda swore in all five of the PiS judges. The President of the Constitutional Tribunal then refused to seat the three illegally elected PiS judges and the stand-off was on.

Unlike in the Hungarian case, where the European Commission watched nervously but did little as the judiciary was captured, European Commission this time got involved quite quickly. In December 2015, just as the stand-off between the Constitutional Tribunal and the government became serious, the Commission wrote to the Polish government, asking it to follow the decisions of the Constitutional Tribunal and to hold off on passing pending new legislation affecting the Tribunal until the Venice Commission could weigh in on the proposed bills. When the Polish government went ahead and passed the worrisome laws anyway without waiting for the Venice Commission report, the European Commission invoked its Rule of Law Framework—originally designed for but never used in the case of Hungary. Poland became the first target of this new tool on January 13, 2016. The PiS government had only been in office for a few months, but already the European Commission had acted decisively to bring EU oversight to bear.

The European Commission's intervention made no difference, however. During the whole of 2016, while the Constitutional Tribunal blocked the illegally elected PiS judges from taking their seats and the government refused to recognize the legal election of the Civic Platform judges, the PiS government bombarded the court with restrictive legislation. No fewer than six laws affecting the Constitutional Tribunal's procedures and powers were passed and signed into law during the stand-off. One new restriction required a two-thirds majority on the Tribunal before a vote of the judges could nullify a law (despite the fact that the Constitution itself required only a simple majority decision). Given that the court was working at less than full strength while the controversy was going on, no such two-thirds vote was possible. The situation was made worse by a new legal provision that allowed any three judges on the court to require that any case be heard *en banc* with all of the judges present, which meant that no case could be decided that PiS friendly judges wanted to avoid as long as the stand-off over the judges continued. To this was added a new requirement that the Prosecutor General be present for all cases of a full bench, so that the Prosecutor's absence would mean that a case could not proceed. (Shortly before this, the government had given the Justice Minister the Prosecutor General's portfolio, so this conditioned the Tribunal's ability to hold a hearing in a case on the specific presence of a particular member of the government.) Another restriction limited the court's review of laws to those that had been already in effect for six months, which in turn created a sort of constitutional vacuum around all new laws which could not be challenged before they went into effect. Yet another required the Tribunal to decide cases in the order in which they came in, which meant that any cases involving the new PiS government would go to the back of the queue. In the meantime, the government refused to publish many of the opinions of the court.

Throughout this legal blitz, European institutions were active in criticizing these developments. In March, an opinion of the Venice Commission condemned the first major law restricting the Constitutional Tribunal's functioning (Venice Commission, 2016a). In April, the European Parliament passed a resolution supporting the decisions of the Constitutional Tribunal against the government (European Commission, 2016a,b). Emboldened by this European support, the General Assembly of the Supreme Court of Poland, consisting of all of the judges of the Supreme Court, passed a resolution stating that it would take the unpublished decisions of the Constitutional Tribunal as binding. In the meantime, the European Commission met with the Polish government on numerous occasions to persuade it to end the stand-off and follow the Tribunal's decisions.

When the government refused to bend, the Commission in June 2016 issued a Rule of Law Opinion, a formal document that recorded the Commission's objections, which—when it was met with no positive response from the Polish government—turned into a Rule of Law Recommendation in July (European Commission, 2016a). (Opinions and Recommendations are terms of art in the Rule of Law Framework, indicating increasing levels of seriousness and concern.) The Recommendation stated that Poland in fact already suffered from a systemic threat to the rule of law and it demanded that Poland change its ways. The Polish government refused to comply—and instead barreled ahead with new legislation designed to cripple the Constitutional Tribunal further (2 August 2016 Act on the Constitutional Tribunal). The European Parliament adopted another critical resolution in September; the Venice Commission produced another critical report on the new law restricting the Constitutional Tribunal in October (Venice Commission, 2016b). And the stand-off between the government and the Constitutional Tribunal continued for a whole year, despite all of the European criticism.

The Constitutional Tribunal's stand-off with the government ended with the close of 2016. In December 2016, the term of the President of the court, Andrzej Rzepliński, came to its normal end. He, supported by the other "legal" judges elected before 2015, had kept the illegal judges off the court to that point, but once Rzepliński stepped down, the court was quickly captured by the government. European institutions were again active through this process. Just as President Rzepliński's term ended, the European Commission adopted a second Recommendation asking the Polish government to delay the process for selecting his successor (European Commission, 2016b). But one of the legally elected PiS judges, Julia Przyłębska, was made "interim President" of the Tribunal (a completely new position) by a hastily passed statute, even though the pre-existing rules of the court specified that the sitting vice-president (a judge who had been elected prior to 2015) should preside over the selection of the next President. Interim President Przyłębska was almost immediately then called for the election of the President of the Tribunal in a highly questionable process over which she herself presided and from which she emerged as the new President herself. Her election involved the violation of black-letter rules about how a new President of the Constitutional Tribunal should be selected (since she held only one vote of the other judges instead of two as required by law). And her election resulted from an illegally constituted vote. Interim President Przyłębska simply did not count the eight judges who refused to recognize her legal right to convene the proceedings as an "interim" President and who boycotted the proceedings. But, to gain sufficient votes, she admitted all three of the illegally elected PiS judges to the bench just in time to vote for her.

With these tricks, she narrowly won the election over which she presided to become President of the Tribunal. Several new vacancies on the Tribunal after that were engineered by her through the government's retroactive challenge to the legitimacy of the election of three non-PiS judges, who were then replaced before their terms expired in moves that allowed PiS to capture the court's majority by late spring 2017, less than two years into the PiS government's term.

As soon as the government gained a comfortable majority on the Tribunal, government's attempts to tie the Tribunal's hands through nuisance regulation stopped. As Wojciech Sadurski wrote: "All of these legislative attacks on the Tribunal [CT] only continued up to the point when PiS acquired a majority on the CT (8 out of 15) — at which time all these innovations were miraculously forgotten because they had become unnecessary" (Sadurski, 2018a). Instead, once the Tribunal could be considered friendly, the government then sent it numerous petitions to legitimate the government's various rule-of-law challenging activities. In short order, the Constitutional Tribunal declared the 2011 statute regulating the National Judicial Council (Polish acronym: KRS) to be unconstitutional (Decision K5/17) and also nullified the law regarding the selection process for the President of the Supreme Court (Decision K3/17). Both of these decisions opened the way for new legislation that would later gut the independence of the ordinary judiciary. On top of that, Przyłębska, as the new President of the Constitutional Tribunal, publicly blessed *ex cathedra* a number of laws promoted by the PiS government, laws designed to hobble the ordinary judiciary. She announced, with no case before her, that these laws were fully compatible with the separation of powers. The opaque assignment of cases depends on the president alone and the "most important decisions are taken by the one-man team of Judge Przyłębska who (...) become the most trusted guardian of the new constitutional order" (Koncewicz, 2019).

As this was going on in violation of repeated efforts to get the PiS government to stop, the European Commission for the first time engaged the Council, which until then had been completely silent on both the Hungarian and Polish cases. The General Affairs Council broadly endorsed the actions of the Commission with regard to Poland in a meeting on May 17, 2017, but did not take action of its own. Instead, the Council endorsed the Commission engaging in "dialogue" with the government of Poland, dialogue that had, to that point, not been notably successful.

After the destruction of the independence of the Constitutional Tribunal, the ordinary judiciary came next. In summer 2017, the government brought forward three new laws, all of which were designed to make the courts politically dependent and all of which were passed by the PiS-dominated Parliament. One law would have allowed the KRS, the National Judicial Council which makes judicial appointments, to be captured by the PiS party through a new system for appointing its members. Another law would have fired all judges on the Supreme Court, subject to discretionary retention upon application to the Justice Minister. Finally, the third law permitted the Justice Minister to fire without giving any reasons for their dismissal all sitting court Presidents throughout the judiciary within six months of the passage of the law. In a move reminiscent of Hungary's strategy for judicial capture, this third law also lowered the judicial retirement age from 67 to 65 for men and 60 for women for all courts below the Supreme Court, thereby opening many new senior appointments to the bench that the newly renovated KRS would get to fill. But in the face of massive public demonstrations and critical responses from the European Union, President Duda vetoed the first two laws. He signed the third.

Immediately thereafter, in July 2017, European Commission issued a third Recommendation under the Rule of Law Framework, this time both noting that the constitutionality of laws could not be assured given the disabling of the Constitutional Tribunal and expressing concern about the laws on the ordinary judiciary (European Commission, 2017a). In addition, the Commission launched an infringement procedure on the laws on the ordinary judiciary (European Commission, 2017b). The two vetoed laws had been referred back to the Parliament for further consideration, indicating that the government had not given up, but instead intended to move forward with different versions of the same laws. Not only was there a systemic threat to the rule of law, the Commission concluded, but the situation had seriously deteriorated. The Polish government still refused to cave in.

Protestors in the streets of Polish cities may have celebrated their victory in getting President Duda to veto two of the three offending laws in summer 2017, but the one that allowed the court Presidents to be fired with no reason and judges to be subjected to a new retirement age took effect and removed key judges from the ordinary courts. The Presidents of the ordinary courts assign judges to different divisions of the courts, which could in turn guarantee that judges not favored by the government would never get politically sensitive cases. In addition, court Presidents can assign and replace certain judges hearing particular cases specifically in criminal matters, which means that politically dependent court Presidents could ensure that cases came out as the government might want. This law also created a hierarchy of supervision among court Presidents, with lower court Presidents being reviewable by the Presidents of the courts above them and so on up the chain until the hierarchy stopped at the Justice Minister who could review the performance of all court Presidents, providing an ultimate political check on the operation of the judiciary.

Many judges were dismissed soon after this law went into effect. But because the law on the KRS was vetoed so the old KRS members were still in place, the government delayed appointments to these positions, pending a newly packed KRS to be entrusted with the task of packing the courts. Before this occurred, nearly 10% of all of the judgeships in the country were vacant at once, waiting for PiS-friendly KRS members to name their replacements.

In fall 2017, President Duda emerged with draft laws to replace the two he had vetoed. Though these new draft laws were slightly less brutal than the prior laws, the effect was similar.

Under the new law on the KRS that makes appointments to the judiciary, the KRS was to be filled by judges approved by the governing party and its parliamentary majority—as before. The old members of the KRS, whose four year terms of office were guaranteed in the Constitution, would be immediately dismissed without completing their terms. As a result of these developments, on September 17, 2018 the European Networks of Councils for the Judiciary suspended the membership of KRS for its lack of independence of the executive and legislature. The law might well have been deemed unconstitutional because it transferred from judges to politicians the decision on the judicial members of the KRS (Sadurski, 2017) and it fired judges from positions that had constitutionally guaranteed terms of office. But on March 25, 2019 a five-judge chamber of the Constitutional Tribunal consisting exclusively judges appointed by PiS held the manner of appointing judges to the KRS constitutional and declared that the KRS does not have to be independent (K 12/18 and K 2/19). The other law on the Supreme Court did not fire all of the judges, as the summer law would have done, but instead subjected all of the judges to a newly set retirement age of 65. Given the civil-service career paths of most judges in Poland, where judges advance into the more important positions only with advancing age, this new retirement age meant that nearly 40% of the Supreme Court judges would be dismissed (Sadurski, 2017). Of course, this was the same trick used by the Hungarians, and that the European Court of Justice had said was contrary to EU law on age discrimination, but given that the Hungarian government only had to pay compensation to the fired judges but otherwise got to keep their captured judiciary, why not try it?

As these new laws were going through the legislative pipeline, a number of international actors chimed in that these laws spelled the destruction of independence of the Polish judiciary. Between October and December 2017, the United Nations Special Rapporteur for the Independence of Judges and Lawyers, the Consultative Council of European Judges, the Office of Democratic Institutions and Human Rights of the OSCE, the Council of Bars and Law Societies of Europe, the European Network of Councils for the Judiciary and the Council of Europe Commissioner for Human Rights condemned the new laws (European Commission, 2017c: 53-54). In November, the European Parliament passed another resolution against Poland's assault of the judiciary (European Parliament, 2017d) and in December, the Venice Commission issued another critical report about these new laws affecting the judiciary (Venice Commission, 2017), which the lower house of the Polish Parliament nonetheless passed without modification on the very same day that the Venice Commission's report was published. The Polish government didn't even appear to adjust its strategy for capturing the courts in the face of this new criticism. It barreled ahead, unchecked.

The European Commission, which had been repeatedly threatening, all without result, by that time looked completely ineffective. Finally, on December 17, 2017, faced with a *fait accompli* as the Polish government enacted the laws that all outside observers had told them not to pass, the European Commission issued a "reasoned proposal" to the Council asking the Council to invoke Article 7(1) TEU against Poland (European Commission, 2017c). Never mind that Article 7(1) TEU only finds that there is a risk of a breach of European values, while Poland's independent judiciary would already be long gone by the time the procedure was invoked. Even invoking Article 7(1) TEU, with its four-fifths vote of Member States and two-thirds vote of the European Parliament, was a political heavy lift, given that the Council had never seen fit to publicly condemn either Hungary or Poland for failing Europe's basic constitutional commitments. Throughout the winter, through the spring and into the summer, the Council merely urged the Commission to keep talking to the government of Poland, while in the meantime, the new laws took effect. The Parliament has passed resolutions (European Parliament, 2016a, 2016b, 2017a, 2017d), but nothing can happen without the Council. Even if Article 7(1) could be invoked, it would simply issue a warning without sanctions of any sort. Poland clearly knew that it could get away with almost anything.

And so the Polish government tried. The new law on the Supreme Court did not just permit the premature removal of nearly one third of the Court's judges (27 out of 72 judges), but it also created a new form of judicial review for previously issued final and binding judgments: the extraordinary appeal. This new procedure permits almost any decision made by the Polish courts in the last 20 years to be re-opened upon petition by either the Prosecutor General (a.k.a. the Justice Minister) or by the Ombudsperson. A special new chamber of the Supreme Court, in which new judges appointed under the new PiS-dominated system will sit, may then decide the old case in a new way. Suddenly the legal settlement of issues in the decades since the end of communism will be up for grabs again. No legal judgment could be considered to be final any longer. And all of these new decisions about old legal questions will be made by judges who will have been appointed by agents put in place by the heavy hand of the PiS party.

New disciplinary procedures for judges on the Polish courts have been enacted as well. The new laws establish the position of special disciplinary officer directly appointed from among the judges in each court by the President of the Republic, a key PiS figure himself, to bring charges against judges thought guilty of disciplinary infractions. The Minister of Justice can inform the President about the need to appoint a disciplinary officer, so the process is even more overtly political than it might seem at first. Disciplinary proceedings against judges can use evidence that would be otherwise inadmissible in court in normal cases, and judges can be tried in absentia. There are no deadlines for these procedures, which means that judges charged with disciplinary offenses could be held in limbo for long periods of time without a resolution of the charges against them. Not surprisingly, all appeals from these disciplinary proceedings in the ordinary courts must go to another new chamber at the Supreme Court set up precisely to handle disciplinary cases against judges. It, too, will be filled with the new judges appointed with the special influence of the governing party.

Since the start of the new disciplinary system in April 2018, disciplinary proceedings against dozens of justices have been launched (Strzelecki and Bodoni, 2019). The report of the umbrella organization KOS consisting of 12 civil organizations lists plenty disciplinary proceedings launched to intimidate and compromise judges and to obtain the ability to influence judges and their decisions (Justice Defence Committee/KOS, 2019).

To make these reforms even more political and less legal, these two new Supreme Court chambers—the one to handle cases from the past that have been newly reopened and the one to handle disciplinary actions against judges—will have lay judges as part of the mix. The lay judges—who do not have to have any formal legal training—will be appointed by the upper chamber of the Parliament (currently dominated by PiS). While many legal systems have lay judges participating in factfinding and judgment at the trial level, it is highly unusual to introduce decision-makers without any legal training at the final stage of appeal only. The fact that these two chambers handle the politically most sensitive issues increases suspicion that the governing party is trying to isolate those cases so that they can be handled outside the law as such. Both chambers are effectively above all Supreme Court chambers, which creates a risk that the whole judicial system is dominated by them (Venice Commission 2017, para 92).

The combined effect of all of these changes—achieved with breathtaking speed in just three years with the European Commission in hot pursuit—is that the government has captured the Constitutional Tribunal so that it now is a mouthpiece of the government. The PiS government has also put the judges in the ordinary courts under the control of politically appointed court Presidents with a draconian and arbitrary disciplinary procedure run by PiS-vetted judges. Judicial independence from the governing party is not to be tolerated. All of this is occurring in a context in which any decision from the past 20 years could be reopened on a political petition and re-decided as the new government dictates. Judicial independence in Poland is well and truly dead. The irony of this situation was not lost on the Venice Commission:

> While the Memorandum [from the Polish government to the Venice Commission explaining the rationale for the changes] speaks of the 'de-communization' of the Polish judicial system, some elements of the reform have a striking resemblance with the institutions which existed in the Soviet Union and its satellites [Venice Commission, 2017: para 89].

The European Commission, in recommending to the Council that Article 7(1) TEU be invoked, had a similarly dire assessment of the state of judicial independence in Poland:

> The Commission considers that as a result of laws adopted in 2016 and the developments following the appointment of the acting President [of the Constitutional Tribunal], the independence and legitimacy of the Constitutional Tribunal is seriously undermined and the constitutionality of Polish laws can no longer be guaranteed [European Commission, 2017b: para 109].

And more recently, the European Commission has made it clear that the common pattern of the changes affecting the judiciary "is that the executive and legislative powers now can interfere throughout the entire structure and output of the justice system." (European Commission, 2019a: 42)

As we write, Article 7(1) TEU still hangs in the air in the EU institutions. The Commission has urged the Council to trigger this warning and the European Parliament has indicated its readiness to support Council action. But the other Member States that sit on the Council have dragged their feet, lest they be seen to criticize the government of a fellow Member State. Article 7(1) comes with no sanctions; it is merely a warning. But the time when warnings might have made a difference is already over.

4. Why is the EU so powerless?

Both Hungary and Poland now no longer have reliably independent judiciaries. The pattern of government capture first of the constitutional courts and then of the ordinary judiciaries was relentless in both cases. The Polish courts stood up for themselves and each other (both at the Constitutional Tribunal and at the Supreme Court) while the Hungarian courts resisted very little. Resistance mattered little in the final outcome in any event. Autocratic governments have learned that if they strike fast and eliminate resistance quickly, they will win facts on the ground—new judges already in place willing to do the government's bidding. When that happens, the autocratic governments have won and there is little that outsiders can do to dislodge the new judges or turn the situation around.

All of these attacks on judges in both countries occurred in plain sight, were reported in real time and were carried out on the basis of laws that were translated quickly for a broader audience. Officials at the European institutions knew what was happening every step of the way; the Venice Commission performed pedantic assessments of each major legal change quickly and professionally. No one paying attention could say that they did not know. The institutions of the European Union that could have sanctioned these countries simply took no effective steps to make the destruction stop.

Even now, after the judiciaries have been captured—with political officials ousting the regular judges and replacing them with politically compliant ones, with new rules and procedures being enacted on a regular basis that guarantee the dominance of the government over the judiciary, and with newly redesigned judicial institutions designed to cement this partisan control for a long time—the European Union has yet to do a single thing that would save the independent judiciaries of its Member States. Why is the EU so powerless?

One reason—frequently offered by officials in the Barroso Commission that served from 2009 to 2014 when Hungary's autocratic consolidation occurred—was that the European Commission simply did not have the tools to intervene. To its credit, the Barroso Commission, after its experience with Hungary, created the Rule of Law Framework to give itself the leverage to act the next time a Member State started attacking basic European values. But as we can see with Poland, the Rule of Law Framework has so far made no difference even when it has been used promptly and aggressively. The Rule of Law Framework is not attached to sanctions or real consequences, and so Poland has felt free to ignore it.

Another reason—in our view, more persuasive—is that Member States simply do not want to judge each other lest they be judged themselves. While the Commission and the Parliament have both been relatively active in criticizing the decline of both Hungary and Poland, the Council—where Member States are represented *as* Member States—has remained completely silent. It has neither criticized along the way nor voted to censure when called upon by other institutions to do so. When the Hungarian government was capturing the judiciary, some have claimed it was protected by the European People's Party (Kelemen, 2017), the party to which Fidesz belonged at European level until very recently. (On March 20, 2019 EPP suspended Fidesz—in part because of the new system of administrative courts—and on May 7, 2019 Viktor Orbán announced that "Fidesz is unable to envisage itself in an EPP in which pro-immigration forces are in the majority" (Cabinet Office of the Prime Minister, 2019). Still, after the EP elections Orbán seeks to keep Fidesz in the EPP in the new European Parliament.) But PiS is a member of the European Reformers and Conservatives Group, a marginal party at EU level that has the British Tories as its main anchor. Not a lot of political capital there. And still the Council has so far done nothing. Member States will simply not act against other Member States on matters that look like purely internal affairs. No serious sanctions can be issued as long as the Council remains uninvolved.

But perhaps an even more obvious reason is attributable to the way that the EU has been designed as a legal matter. Member States delegate competencies to the EU institutions; the EU institutions may only act within the competencies that they have been delegated. And the national constitutional structure of Member States is not one of those competencies that has been delegated to EU level. Rather the opposite: national constitutional structures are protected from EU interference by the Treaty on European Union itself:

> Article 4(2) TEU: The Union shall respect the equality of Member States before the Treaties as well as their national identities, inherent in their fundamental structures, political and constitutional, inclusive of regional and local self-government ...

Unlike federal systems in which a federal constitution is typically supreme and contains principles that must be honored down through the regional governments, the EU is definitely not a federation. Instead it operates like two parallel polities. A sharp partition divides two parallel legal systems that are effective on the same territory but that have completely separate normative origins. EU law is supreme with regard to the subjects it has been delegated; national law is supreme on the subjects it retains. Constitutional rule-of-law Member States of the EU will have values that harmonize with those at EU level, making the partition between the two systems nearly invisible, but the Member States that have turned illiberal and no longer respect the system of checks and balances at national level harden the partition so that the EU cannot reach national competencies from its side of the divide.

However, any two legal systems operating on the same territory have inevitable overlaps that will eventually give each system some leverage over the other. Parallel systems on the same territory are inherently unstable when their underlying values clash. The EU can be rightly concerned that illiberal governments in Hungary and Poland will eventually have an effect on the quality of life and law in the EU just as these illiberal governments realize that the EU may eventually figure out how to fight back when its values are violated.

As it turns out, the European Court of Justice started to cut through the partition. The ECJ has recently held that national judiciaries are dual-use institutions. While national judiciaries have a place in national constitutional systems for which independence from EU law is guaranteed in the treaties, national judiciaries also have a central role in the operation of the EU and must be bound by EU law. The EU courts handle a relatively small slice of EU-law cases; the vast majority goes through the national courts for resolution. When those with legal claims believe that their EU law rights have been violated, 99% of the time they must go to the national courts, not to the EU courts, for an effective remedy. National judiciaries are, therefore, also EU judiciaries.

In its decision in *Associaçao Sindical dos Juízes Portugueses v Tribunal de Contas* (C-64/16, 27 February 2018), the European Court of Justice threw out a lifeline to the other European institutions seeking to fight the destruction of judicial independence in Hungary and Poland. The case before the ECJ turned on a wholly different issue: the reduction in salaries of the Portuguese judiciary caused by austerity measures imposed during the Euro-crisis. Dispensing easily with the claim that a small across-the-board cut to all public employees threatened the judiciary in particular (it did not), the ECJ then went on to explain that all Member States were obligated by Article 19(1) TEU ("Member States shall provide remedies sufficient to ensure effective legal protection in the fields covered by Union law") to have an independent judiciary. As the Court helpfully elaborated:

> The concept of independence presupposes, in particular, that the body concerned exercises its judicial functions wholly autonomously, without being subject to any hierarchical constraint or subordinated to any other body and without taking orders or instructions from any source whatsoever, and that it is thus protected against external interventions or pressure liable to impair the independent judgment of its members and to influence their decisions. ... (Case-64/16, para. 44).

All national courts in the EU must be independent in this way because national judiciaries have a role in both EU law and national law. Independence means no political control – even from, or perhaps especially from, national leaders.

For instance, even with the Commission's "reasoned proposal to the Council" pending to trigger Article 7(1) TEU, and an already launched second infringement action to maintain an independent judiciary (European Commission, 2018), the Polish government was undeterred. On July 3, 2018, the Polish government prematurely terminated the mandate of the President of the Supreme Court of Poland and 26 other Supreme Court judges. The most prominent of those judges, President of the Supreme Court Małgorzata Gersdorf, refused to leave office, because she thought that the law was unconstitutional. A month later, the Supreme Court referred three sets of questions (in cases III PO 4/18, 5/18, 6/18, IV Uzp 4/18, and III PO 8/18, 9/18) to the ECJ for a preliminary ruling asking the Court whether under the EU law Member States can lower the retirement age of Supreme Court judges and apply it to judges currently in office. The Polish government then made some concessions, e.g. Parliament passed a law that "reinstated" the judges of the Supreme Court, but the situation concerning the judicial independence on the ground was getting worse, not better. Spectacular nationwide billboard campaigns defame judges (Mazur, 2019) and the new disciplinary regime allows for judges to be subject to disciplinary proceedings for their judicial decisions, first and foremost, for referring questions to the ECJ (Biernat and Kawczyńska, 2018, Pech and Wachowiec, 2019). Consequently, on April 3, 2019 the Commission launched the third infringement procedure with respect to the new disciplinary regime for judges (European Commission, 2019b).

Currently, there are three infringement actions pending against Poland in which the Commission is raising a violation of Article 19(1) TEU. In one of these cases the ECJ issued an interim order calling Poland to immediately suspend the application of the contested provisions of the Act on the Supreme Court (Case C-619/18 R Commission V Poland). The ECJ in its interim order announced that Poland has a treaty obligation to maintain independent judiciary. It was an important step to avoid what had already happened in Hungary: the completed reshuffling of the judiciary with judges forced into early retirement and with newly appointed judges remaining in the bench. Advocate General Tanchev suggests in his opinion that the Court should take into account the whole structure within which judicial appointments are made and the Court should declare that by lowering the retirement age of judges Poland failed to fulfil its obligations under EU law (Opinion of Advocate General Tanchev, 2019). The case will give the ECJ the opportunity to elaborate its stance on the principle of judicial independence.

If these pending cases are not settled with an effective climbdown on Poland's part, the ECJ can use the Portuguese judges case to find against Poland. And if Poland fails to comply with the decision, the Commission can ask the Court to levy large fines for every day that Poland remains in non-compliance. That's how infringement actions work, the humble tool of the European Commission to police day to day legal violation on the part of Member States. Infringement actions have real consequences, unlike the warnings of Article 7(1) TEU. And while infringement actions have not so far been used effectively to challenge autocratic consolidation of a Member State, the ECJ has strongly hinted that it would be open to such a challenge.

With the ECJ elevating the infringement action so that it can be used to enforce constitutional-level values of the EU, the European Commission has been given a way to save the independent judiciaries in Hungary and Poland that does not rely on the courage of the Member States to challenge each other. Of course, the European Commission would have to be courageous to challenge Poland, and equally committed to pursuing Hungary as well through a similar infringement action. But perhaps if the Commission can win a strong judgment in the Polish case, it will be emboldened to try.

References

Arato, A., Halmai, G., Kis, J., 2012. Opinion on the Fundamental Law of Hungary (amicus brief). In: Tóth, G.A. (Ed.), Constitution for a Disunited Nation, on Hungary's 2011 Fundamental Law. CEU Press, New York-Budapest, pp. 455-490.

Bánkuti, M., Halmai, G., Scheppele, K.L., 2012. From separation of powers to a government without checks: Hungary's old and new constitutions. In: Tóth, G.A. (Ed.), Constitution for a Disunited Nation, On Hungary's 2011 Fundamental Law. CEU Press, New York-Budapest, pp. 237-268.

Biernat, S., Kawczyńska, M., 2018. Though this be Madness, yet there's Method in't: Pitting the Polish Constitutional Tribunal against the Luxembourg Court, VerfBlog, 2018/10/26.

Cabinet Office of the Prime Minister, 2019. On its southern border section Hungary also protects Austria's borders, Available at http://www.miniszterelnok.hu/on-its-southern-border-section-hungary-also-protects-austrias-borders/

Constitutional Court of Hungary, 2017. Statistics of Cases of the Constitutional Court of Hungary 2017. Available from https://hunconcourt.hu/uploads/sites/3/2018/07/2017_12_31_ab_stat_en.pdf (Accessed 13 June 2019).

Constitutional Court of Hungary, 2018. Statistics of Cases of the Constitutional Court of Hungary 2018. Available from https://alkotmanybirosag.hu/uploads/2019/01/2018_12_31_ab_ugyforgalom.pdf (Accessed 13 May 2019).

European Commission, 2012. Press release: European Commission launches accelerated infringement proceedings against Hungary over the independence of its central bank and data protection authorities as well as over measures affecting the judiciary. 17 January 2012. Available from http://europa.eu/ rapid/press-release_IP-12-24_en.htm. (Accessed 13 June 2019).

European Commission, 2016a. Commission Recommendation (EU) 2016/1374 of 27 July 2016 regarding the rule of law in Poland (OJ L 217, 12.8.2016, p. 53).

European Commission, 2016b. Commission Recommendation (EU) 2017/146 of 21 December 2016 regarding the rule of law in Poland (OJ L 22, 27.1.2017, p. 65).

European Commission, 2017a. Commission Recommendation (EU) 2017/1520 of 26 July 2017 regarding the rule of law in Poland complementary to Recommendation (EU) 2016/1374 and (EU) 2017/146 (OJ L 228, 2.9.2017, p. 19).

European Commission, 2017b. Press release: European Commission launches infringement against Poland over measures affecting the judiciary, 29 July 2017. europa.eu/rapid/press-release_IP-17-2205_en.pdf

European Commission, 2017c. Reasoned proposal in accordance with Article 7(1) of the Treaty on European Union regarding the rule of law in Poland. Brussels, 20 December 2017, 2017/360(APP).

European Commission, 2017d. Commission Recommendation (EU) 2018/2013 of 20 December 2017 regarding the rule of law in Poland complementary to Recommendations (EU) 2016/1374, (EU) 2017/146 and (EU) 2017/1520 (OJ L 17, 23.1.2018, p. 50).

European Commission, 2018. Press release: Rule of Law: European Commission launches infringement procedure to protect the independence of the Polish Supreme Court, 2 July 2018. Available from http://europa.eu/rapid/press-release_IP-18-4341_en.htm

European Commission, 2019a. European semester report for Poland, 27 February 2019, SWD(2019)1020 final.

European Commission, 2019b. Press release: Rule of Law: European Commission launches infringement procedure to protect judges in Poland from political control, 3 April 2019. Available from http://europa.eu/rapid/press-release_IP-19-1957_en.htm

European Parliament, 2011. Resolution of 5 July 2011 on the revised Hungarian constitution, P7_TA (2011)0315. Available from http://www.europarl.europa.eu/sides/getDoc.do?pubRef¼-//EP//TEXTþTAþP7-TA-2011-0315þ0þDOCþXMLþV0//EN. (Accessed 13 June 2019).

European Parliament, 2012. Resolution of 16 February 2012 on recent political developments in Hungary, P7_TA (2012)0053. Available from http://www.europarl.europa.eu/sides/getDoc.do?pubRef¼-//EP//TEXTþTAþP7-TA-2012-0053þ0þDOCþXMLþV0//EN. (Accessed 13 June 2019).

European Parliament, 2013. Resolution of 3 July 2013 on the situation of fundamental rights: standards and practices in Hungary (pursuant to the European Parliament Resolution of 16 February 2012) [the Tavares report], (2012/2130(INI)), P7_TA(2013)0315, A7-0229/2013. Available from http://www.europarl.europa.eu/sides/getDoc.do?pubRef¼-//EP//TEXTþTAþP7-TA-2013-0315þ0þDOCþXMLþV0//EN. (Accessed 13 June 2019).

European Parliament, 2016. Resolution of 14 September 2016 on the recent developments in Poland and their impact on fundamental rights as laid down in the Charter of Fundamental Rights of the European Union (2016/2774(RSP).

European Parliament, 2017. Resolution of 15 November 2017 on the situation of the rule of law and democracy in Poland (2017/2931 (RSP).

European Parliament, 2018. Resolution of 12 September on a proposal calling on the Council to determine, pursuant to Article 7(1) of the Treaty on European Union, the existence of a clear risk of a serious breach by Hungary of the values on which the Union is founded (2017/2131(INL)) [the Sargentini Report]. Available from http://www.europarl.europa.eu/doceo/document/TA-8-2018-0340_EN.html . (Accessed 13 June 2019).

Freedom House, 2015. Nations in transit 2015. Archived at http://perma.cc/SJ7F-QCJR. (Accessed 13 June 2019).

Freedom House, 2018. Nations in transit 2018: Poland. Available at https://freedomhouse.org/report/nations-transit/2018/poland. (Accessed 13 June 2019).

GRECO (Council of Europe, Group of States against Corruption), 2015. Fourth evaluation round: Corruption prevention in respect of members of parliament, judges and prosecutors, Evaluation report: Hungary, adopted by GRECO at its 67th plenary meeting 23-27 March 2015, publication 22 July 2015, Grevo Eval IV Rep (2014) 10E. Available from https://rm.coe.int/CoERMPublicCommonSearchServices/DisplayDCTMContent?documentId¼09000016806c6b9e. (Accessed 13 June 2019).

Hungarian Government, 2018. Information sheet of the Hungarian Government on the issues raised by the draft report of Judith Sargentini on "A proposal calling on the Council to determine, pursuant to Article 7(1) of the Treaty on European Union, the existence of a clear risk of a serious breach by Hungary of the values on which the Union is founded". Available from http://abouthungary.hu/media/DocumentsModell-file/1536582679-information-sheetsargentini-report.pdf (Accessed 13 June 2019).

Hungarian Helsinki Committee, 2018. Blurring the Boundaries. New Laws on Administrative Courts Undermine Judicial Independence, Available from https://www.helsinki.hu/en/blurring-the-boundaries-new-laws-on-administrative-courts-undermine-judicial-independence/ (Accessed 13 June 2019).

Hungarian Helsinki Committee, 2019. Hungary's Laws on Administrative Courts Comply with only 30 % of Venice Commission Recommendations, Available from, https://www.helsinki.hu/en/hungarys-laws-on-administrative-courts-comply-with-only-30-of-venice-commission-recommendations/ (Accessed 13 June 2019).

IBAHRI (International Bar Association Human Rights Initiative), 2015. Still under threat: the independence of the judiciary in Hungary, October 2015. Available from https://www.ibanet.org/Document/Default.aspx?DocumentUid¼a00b5f64-4b05-4b25-81c6-5e507c45cc74. (Accessed 13 June 2019).

Justice Defence Committee (KOS), 2019. A country that punishes. Pressure and repression of Polish judges and prosecutors, KOS.

Kelemen, R.D., 2017. Europe's Authoritarian Equilibrium. Foreign affairs, December 22, 2017. Available from https://www.foreignaffairs.com/articles/hungary/2017-12-22/europes-authoritarian-equilibrium (Accessed 13 June 2019).

Koncewicz, Tomasz Tadeusz, 2019. From Constitutional to Political Justice: The Tragic Trajectories of the Polish Constitutional Court, VerfBlog, 2019/2/27. DOI: https://doi.org/10.17176/20190324-205438-0.

Kovács, K., Scheppele, K.L., 2017. Hungary's post-socialist administrative law regimes. In: Rose-Ackerman, S., Lindseth, P.L., Emerson, B. (Eds.), Comparative Administrative Law, 2d Ed. Elgar, Cheltenham, UK, pp. 119-136.

Kovács, K., Tóth, G.A., 2011. Hungary's constitutional transformation. Eur. Constitut. Law Rev. 7 (2), 183-203.

László, R., 2016. The new Hungarian election system's beneficiaries, http://cens.ceu.edu/sites/cens.ceu.edu/files/attachment/article/579/laszlo-thenewhungarianelectionsystemsbeneficiaries.pdf (Accessed 13 June 2019).

Linz, J.L., Stepan, A., 1996. Problems of Democratic Transition and Consolidation: Southern Europe, South America, and Post-Communist Europe. Johns Hopkins University Press, Baltimore.

Mares, I., Young, L., 2019. Varieties of Clientelism in Hungarian Elections Comparative Politics Vol 51, No 3, April 2019, pp. 449-480.

Mazur, D., 2019. Judges under special supervision, that is "the great reform" of the Polish justice system, 5 March. Available at https://komitetobronysprawiedliwosci.pl/app/uploads/2019/03/Judges_under_special_supervision_-first-publication-pdf.pdf

Opinion of Advocate General Tanchev, 2019. Delivered on 11 April 2019 in case C-619/18, European Commission v Republic of Poland.

Pech, L., Wachowiecz, P., 2019. 1095 Days Later: From Bad to Worse Regarding the Rule of Law in Poland (Part II), VerfBlog, 2019/1/17, DOI: https://doi.org/10.17176/20190211-221846-0.

Sadurski, W., 2017. Judicial "Reform" in Poland: The President's Bills are as Unconstitutional as the Ones He Vetoed, VerfBlog, 2017/11/28, DOI: https://dx.doi.org/10.17176/20171128-122808.

Sadurski, W., 2018a. Polish Constitutional Tribunal Under PiS: From an Activist Court, to a Paralysed Tribunal, to a Governmental Enabler. Hague Journal on the Rule of Law. Online publication 13 June 2018 at. https://doi.org/10.1007/s40803-018-0078-1. (Accessed 13 June 2019).

Sadurski, W., 2018b. How Democracy Dies (in Poland): A Case Study of Anti-Constitutional Populist Backsliding. University of Sydney Law School, Legal Studies Research Paper No. 18/01. January 2018, at. https://papers.ssrn.com/sol3/papers.cfm?abstract_id¼3103491. (Accessed 13 June 2019).

Scheppele, K.L., 2016. Enforcing the basic principles of EU law through systemic infringement procedures. In: Kochenov, D., Closa, C. (Eds.), Reinforcing the Rule of Law Oversight in the European Union. Cambridge University Press, Cambridge, pp. 105-132.

Scheppele, K.L., 2018. The Party's over. In: Graber, M., Levinson, S., Tushnet, M. (Eds.), Constitutional Democracy in Crisis? Oxford University Press, New York.

Strzelecki, M., Bodoni, S., 2019. Polish Judges Intimidated as Judicial Clash With EU Rages, Bloomberg, March 20. Available at https://www.bloomberg.com/news/articles/2019-03-20/censure-and-intimidation-for-polish-judges-as-eu-clash-revives

Venice Commission, 2011. Hungary, Opinion on the New Constitution of Hungary [CDL-AD(2011)016].

Venice Commission, 2012a. Hungary, Opinion on Act CLXII of 2011 on the Legal Status and Remuneration of Judges and Act CLXI of 2011 on the Organisation and Administration of Courts of Hungary [CDL-AD(2012)001].

Venice Commission, 2012b. Hungary, Opinion on Act CLI of 2011 on the Constitutional Court of Hungary [CDL- AD(2012)009].

Venice Commission, 2012c. Hungary, Opinion on the Cardinal Acts on the Judiciary that Were Amended Following the Adoption of Opinion CDL-AD(2012) 001 [CDL-AD(2012)020].

Venice Commission, 2013. Hungary, Opinion on the Fourth Amendment to the Fundamental Law of Hungary [CDL-AD(2013)012].

Venice Commission, 2016a. Poland: Opinion on Amendments to the Act of 25 June 2015 on the Constitutional Tribunal of Poland [CDL-AD(2016)001].

Venice Commission, 2016b. Poland: Opinion on the Act on the Constitutional Tribunal [CDL-AD(2016)026].

Venice Commission, 2017. Poland: Opinion on the Draft Act Amending the Act on the National Council of the Judiciary; on the Draft Act Amending the Act on the Supreme Court, Proposed by the President of Poland, and on the Act on the Organisation of Ordinary Courts [CDL-AD(2017)031].

Venice Commission, 2019. Hungary: Opinion on the Law on Administrative Courts and on the Law on the Entry into Force of the Law on Administrative Courts and Certain Transitional Rules [CDL-AD(2019)004].

Authoritarian Constitutionalism in Putin's Russia: A Pragmatic Constitutional Court in a Dual State

Alexei Trochev, Peter H. Solomon Jr.
School of Humanities and Social Sciences, Nazarbayev University, Nur-Sultan, Kazakhstan and Munk School of Global Affairs, University of Toronto, Toronto, Canada

This chapter analyzes the successful adaptation of the Russian Constitutional Court (RCC) to an increasingly authoritarian regime under President Vladimir Putin. It argues that the key to its success lay in its pragmatic approach, whereby the Court decides cases that matter to the regime in a politically expedient way, while giving priority to legal and constitutional considerations in other cases, thereby recognizing the reality of a dual state. Over the years the RCC has taken a pragmatic approach in its reaction to changes in the rules of its operations, in its personnel, and in the policies of the popular political leader, including reducing the country's subordination of European legal norms. In so doing, the Court and its skillful chairman Valerii Zorkin achieved considerable autonomy in pursuing its own legal vision on many issues and even improved the implementation of its decisions by other judges and political bodies alike (previously a big problem). In short, the RCC developed its own version of "authoritarian constitutionalism", which may serve as a model for constitutional judicial bodies in other authoritarian states.

Keywords: Constitutional courts, Constitutional Court of the Russian Federation, Authoritarian constitutionalism, Judicial pragmatism, Dual state, Valerii Zorkin, Courts in Russia

In 2016 and 2017, the Constitutional Court of the Russian Federation (RCC) failed to support the constitutionality of a single challenged law. Three quarters of its judgments on the merits in both years either required the legislature to issue new laws or pronounced new constitutional interpretations of existing laws. In the past, other courts tended to ignore such interpretations but the 2016 amendments to the Law on the Russian Constitutional Court (CC) — a product of successful lobbying by the RCC — made these interpretations binding on the rest of the judiciary. Moreover, in 2017 RCC justices, some of them Vladimir Putin appointees, wrote 19 dissenting opinions, in contrast to the absence of dissenting opinions by the Russian Supreme Court justices. Despite the objections from Vladimir Putin's lawyers, the RCC requested in politically sensitive cases amicus curiae submissions from NGOs that the Russian government had earlier declared to be "foreign agents" in an effort to force them out of political life. Further, in November 2016, after its Chief Justice publicly slammed the Western-style gender equality as anti-Christian and anti-humanity, the Court declared that European human rights were fundamental to the Russian legal order. And in May 2018, following the violent crackdown against those protesting against Vladimir Putin's inauguration, the Chief Justice had to remind Russian authorities that ordinary citizens had a constitutional right to protest against government actions (Zorkin, 2018). How could such an activist constitutional review tribunal, which resembles a powerful debate club more often than a rubber-stamping robot, survive in an authoritarian regime that does not tolerate dissent?

As we show below, 2016 and 2017 were not unique in the life of the 25-year-old RCC. This increasingly pragmatic (Vaipan, 2014; Antonov, 2017a; Trochev, 2017) tribunal was established in 1991 during the dying days of Soviet power. At that time, rule by the communist party had ended, and the Court began its operation at a time of struggle to create a workable democracy. Importantly, the RCC was created as a democracy-promotion institution and not as a "Potemkin village" or a golden parachute for important individuals. Many RCC judges embraced this democratic accountability role and supported the efforts of their first Chief Justice to save democratic Russia from power-hungry politicians at the center and in the regions. As a former vice-Chairman of the RCC Tamara Morshchakova put it a few years after the bloody confrontation between President Yeltsin and the Russian Parliament, her court was not 'a decorative bow in Russian democracy' (Maslennikov, 1996).

Still, over the course of the Court's life thus far, especially in the Putin era, Russia's political regime became less democratic and more authoritarian. The Court has been forced to adjust to the new political realities, and that adjustment has reflected both the uncertainties in the political situation and how members of the court understand its role. Adjusting to the needs of an authoritarian regime intensifies the challenge that is faced by any constitutional court of balancing the conflicting demands of law and of politics.

Moreover, the duality of the Russian state complicates this balancing act (Sakwa, 2011; Hendley, 2017). This duality (Fraenkel, 1969) refers to the contradictory co-existence of two governance regimes, what we call the constitutional and the politically expedient, the co-existence of which can be observed in not only Russia but also to varying degrees in Ukraine (Kyselova, 2014), Turkey (Soyler, 2013), Thailand (Merieau, 2016), and even the United States (Wilson, 2016). In the Russian context, the constitutional regime refers to the operation of formal constitutional rules and rules of European human rights law, which both constrain and guide Russia's leaders in ruling their country. The regime of political expediency, in contrast, refers to the unrestrained rule of the powerful, whose strategies, tactics and whims bypass constitutional restraints and prevail over constitutional values. As the Russian CC Justice Gadis Gadzhiev (2012: 55) put it at the time of Vladimir Putin's return to presidency in 2012, "Russia faces a choice: either use archaic forms of realpolitik, under which one lives according to a cynical realism that privileges momentary success, or turn to a morally based realism" that is based on constitutional values constraining the state. The latter, he contends, "is better for Russia in the long term".

To put it simply, this duality means that "the same court - even the same judge - can follow the law to the letter or openly disregard it, depending on the context" (Hendley, 2017: 4). The political leaders expect that the Russian Constitutional Court will do both and by so doing take part in the operation of both regimes. At the same time, like any large hierarchical organization, the RCC has its own internal autonomy, mechanisms of decision-making, and lines of accountability (Dzmitryieva, 2017; Grigoriev, 2018), all of which influence the operation of both governance regimes.

To be sure, over the years Russia's leaders have limited the court's autonomy through changes in the system of selecting its leaders and lowered its prestige through moving the Court from the capital city Moscow to St. Petersburg. But what mattered most for the Court's longevity was its demonstration of enhanced sensitivity to the needs of the regime in particular cases. At the same time, the Court became a trusted ally of the regime in its defense of national prerogatives against decisions of the European Court of Human Rights that seemed to threaten Russian national interests. That these things happened without open conflict (as in the 1993 constitutional crisis) or a diminution of the Court's role (as in Egypt) is significant, especially as some actors had even contemplated the absorption of the CC into the Supreme Court (the fate of the Higher *Arbitrazh* court). The stability of the RCC today was due in large part to the pragmatic behavior, and shifting intellectual predispositions, of its chairman Valerii Zorkin (Antonov, 2014; 2017b), who managed to fend off attacks on the tribunal through his interactions with Russia's leaders.

This article analyzes the conduct of the RCC (and its chairman), in an effort to explain its institutional health and longevity. It starts by outlining three key characteristics of an institutionalized constitutional review tribunal - access and jurisdiction, decision-making autonomy in handling cases and managing the Court's internal operations, and authoritativeness. Then, it specifies the patterns of conduct that each of the two regimes — constitutional and political expediency — anticipates, and explores the pragmatism of the RCC as reflected in its loyalty to a popular President and in its resilience and activism. This involves consideration of the formal and informal rules of court operation (Solomon, 2007), the court's handling of ordinary cases, and its reaction to politically salient ones, including its defense of Russian interests against the ECtHR and the requirements of international law. From all this we conclude that the Constitutional Court's standing in the Russian political system depends on its skill in catering to the political needs of Russia's rulers.

1. Defining the power of the constitutional court

Scholars who study supreme, constitutional, and supranational courts have identified three key dimensions of the power of these tribunals, which may even help them constrain the conduct of leaders: 1) jurisdiction and rules of standing, 2) autonomy in deciding cases and managing internal operations, and 3) authoritativeness that encourages implementation of decisions (Solomon, 2004). These variables are not dichotomous but rather present a spectrum of possibilities.

The first aspect of power is the accessibility of a tribunal for social groups and the range of state actions subject to review by the courts. Often, constitutional tribunals actually expand their jurisdiction through decisions in particular cases, and they sometimes lobby the political branches to enshrine this expansion in enabling legislation. Arguably, increases in formal access to a tribunal indicate a powerful tribunal, especially when they are realized in practice.

The second characteristic of a powerful tribunal is a high degree of autonomy in both deciding cases and arranging its own internal operations. Judicial autonomy refers to both the institutional autonomy of the tribunal and the individual autonomy of its members. We deliberately use the word autonomy instead of independence because of the realistic expectation that top level tribunals are usually constrained courts (Moustafa, 2014). For they operate in a modern state marked by overlapping networks of public and private institutions, which cannot be independent from each other (Rubin, 2002). Moreover, top judges are usually not random people who happen to occupy the bench, but persons who know what is expected of them and of their tribunal. They are scrutinized by the rulers prior to their appointments, they are socialized within the legal profession, and they may also be integrated as clients within the governing network of patronage (Dressel et al., 2017). Constitutional courts are institutionally autonomous when they are free to decide on the key aspects of their organization: including how to handle cases, the identity and powers of their court's leaders, the court's institutional roles, the structure of its budget, and the discipline of its members. Constitutional court judges are individually autonomous when they are free to decide cases impartially and announce dissenting and concurrent opinions (Popova, 2012). Autonomous constitutional courts are free to rule against the powerful, even to declare government decisions unconstitutional. But they may also act strategically (let's avoid political questions), pursue change incrementally (let's decide one case at a time) and issue principled judgments (the law made me do it). All of these may reflect the agency of individual judges and constitute products of an autonomous tribunal. What matters is the extent to which these judgments constrain the discretion of the powerful or protect the interests of the weaker social groups.

Finally, powerful tribunals are authoritative institutions that see their decisions implemented on the ground. Most judges want their decisions to make a difference yet they often lack the means to secure their implementation. As Stephen Breyer (2010: 2010), the US Supreme Court Justice, told a Russian paratroop general Aleksandr Lebed, to have judgments carried out, "judges and paratroopers must be friends." A high proportion of implemented constitutional court decisions — decisions that require the powerful to do something-indicates an authoritative tribunal. In contrast, constitutional court decisions that are forgotten or ignored, are signs of a marginalized tribunal. Moreover, implementation of non-binding advisory opinions that are unfavorable to the rulers, suggests that key actors think that they have a duty to respect constitutionality, itself a reflection of an authoritative tribunal. Authoritativeness also depends on the tribunal's reputation among judges, other government officials and the general public (Garoupa and Ginsburg, 2015). A good reputation may create diffuse institutional support that protects the tribunal against backlash for issuing unpopular decision.

In sum, powerful constitutional courts have broad jurisdiction over politically sensitive cases, have wide discretion in handling these cases as well as managing their internal organization, and enjoy respect that allows them to issue unpopular decisions and get them implemented.

2. Tension between political expediency and constitutionalism: what are constitutional courts expected to do?

Both of the governing regimes in Russia — the constitutional and the regime of political expediency have a use for an activist and viable constitutional court, one that actually reviews the constitutionality of government decisions. To function effectively both regimes need legal hierarchy that works and a situation where bureaucrats at all rungs of the state apparatus obey the rules issued by the central authorities, for which endorsement by the Constitutional Court can help. Both regimes value highly trusted institutions, including constitutional courts, because high levels of public support make governing easier, especially when it involves unpopular decisions. Finally, both regimes can work pragmatically and value "living law" as interpreted by (activist) judges but for different reasons. A constitutional regime requires flexibility in achieving substantive equality (so that following judicial procedures does not result in actual injustice), while political expediency privileges the capacity of the powerful to disregard due process to achieve favorable outcomes. A constitutional regime accepts and encourages litigation to protect human rights, giving voice to politically active citizens and constraining state officials. But the regime of political expediency also needs accessible and friendly judicial tribunals, to provide well-paid employment to cronies and endorse, not to speak of legitimate, rulers' unrestrained exercise of power.

A constitutional regime requires judicial efficiency ("justice delayed is justice denied") and it does so to bring constitutional values — such as fairness, law and order, a competitive market economy, and an accountable political system, into state-society relations. But a regime of political expediency also demands that judges quickly and favorably handle the cases that matter to the rulers, involving for example oppressing political opponents, redistributing property to the rulers and their cronies, and maintaining discipline within the governing coalition (Moustafa, 2014: 281). Moreover, both regimes may welcome activist courts but again for different reasons. A constitutional regime needs judges to decide cases impartially and hold the rulers accountable. In contrast, the political expediency regime requires favorable judgments only, judgments that confirm the legality and/or constitutionality of decisions made by the powerful.

For both constitutionalism and political expediency, the visibility of individual opinions of judges may be useful. A constitutional regime favors the independence of individual judges and public availability of their dissenting opinions as a source of dialogue about constitutional ideas, a form of legal argumentation, and a check against arbitrariness during deliberations of judges (Drigo, 2016). Meanwhile, the regime of political expediency values only judge-made dissents that are aligned with the interests of the rulers and does not tolerate dissents where judges criticize rulers' decisions. In this regime an ideal judge is politically mature: s/he works hard and learns quickly to sense the direction of political winds, which can change suddenly and unexpectedly, and to find legal cover for the arbitrary or expedient decisions made from above (Trochev and Solomon, 2004: 98–99). This definition of judicial role is based on the 1923 statement of Nikolay Krylenko, later the Russian Commissar of Justice, "Our judge is above all a politician, a worker in the political field" (Berman, 1963: 36). Note that some post-Soviet presidents (Yeltsin in 1993, Lukashenka in 1994, Nazarbayev in 1995, and Yushchenko in 2007) used dissenting opinions and splits among judges of their constitutional courts as pretexts to abolish or paralyze these tribunals.

Finally, both constitutionalism and political expediency call for effective constitutional review that makes a difference on the ground. Both regimes need lower officials to follow orders from the top and they find acceptance in society as well. Both regimes anticipate that judges and paratroopers will cooperate, to echo Justice Breyer's concern. Constitutionalism requires that judges have the power to issue marching orders while political expediency gives it to paratroopers. Constitutionalism requires that decisions of the constitutional court be respected and implemented so that constitutionally protected values matter for ordinary people and in the functioning of the state. Political expediency also needs a respected yet loyal constitutional court in order to reduce the use of coercion and ensure that the orders from the top of the power vertical are carried out at the bottom (Sanchez-Urribarri, 2011).

3. Judicial pragmatism through adaptation to institutional changes

Before illustrating the pragmatic tactics of the RCC in Putin's Russia, let us briefly explain what we mean by legal pragmatism. According to William James (1975: 31), the pragmatist "turns away from abstraction and insufficiency, from verbal solutions, from bad a priori reasons, from fixed principles, closed systems, and pretended absolutes and origins. He turns towards concreteness and adequacy, towards facts, towards action, and towards power." Pragmatists focus on "fruits, consequences, and facts" instead of principles and categories (James, 1975: 32). Pragmatism is an instrumental forward-looking and activist approach that values continuity with the past as long as it helps handle the problems of the present and of the future (Posner, 1995: 4). Thus, pragmatic courts may conveniently "forget" their previous judgments and reject "the idea that law is something grounded in permanent principles and realized in logical manipulation of those principles" (Posner, 1995: 405). This approach facilitates the work of a judge in a dual state who needs the flexibility to 'follow the law to the letter or openly disregard it, depending on the context" (Hendley, 2017). Article 73 of the 1994 RCC Act, which was written by a group of RCC judges, provided explicitly that the Court could change its legal opinions. Moreover, a pragmatic court is activist in the sense that its judges believe that their judgments can change reality on the ground. But activism does not mean that pragmatic judges always maintain a high profile (Posner, 1995: 5). RCC judges do not hide the fact that their judgments are often serious compromises, in which they try to balance the political needs of the rulers against constitutional values (Trochev, 2008: 184; Pilipchuk, 2014). The RCC judges learned a lot about pragmatism from the 1993 constitutional crisis, in which rival political leaders asked the Court to intervene and judges obliged, provoking the near closing down of their tribunal. As veteran RCC judge Gadis Gadzhiev put it bluntly (in 2004): "the Constitutional Court will cease to exist, if its judges fail to pay attention to the political realities of the day" (Trochev, 2008: 49). None of the sitting RCC judges would wish to be blamed for the demise of their court.

In Russia under Putin, the Constitutional Court chose to pursue a pragmatic approach in order to satisfy the demands for loyalty and resilience from the highly popular President and his regime of political expediency, which has tended to prevail over constitutionalism since the early 2000s. In this section, we discuss the Court's pursuit of judicial pragmatism in maintaining and displaying loyalty in exchange for concrete personal and organizational rewards — a typical kind of interaction in clientelist regimes, in which authoritarian rulers as patrons have frequently changing preferences and "have a lawful power to alter constitutional provisions at will" (Tushnet, 2015: 425). As Maria Popova (2017: 65) argues, use of the law by the President in Russia "tends to be arbitrary, expedient, and instrumental, rather than predictable and principled." Indeed, her diagnosis confirms the alarm raised by the RCC judge Vladimir Yaroslavtsev in 2009 that "nobody knows what the authorities will decide tomorrow. They do not consult anyone and do not debate with anyone" (Bonet, 2009). According to Yaroslavtsev, President Medvedev acted in the way described by the Roman poet Juvenal: "I want it this way, I command it, and my will suffices as a reason" (Bonet, 2009).

In contrast to the absence of changes made to the 1994 RCC Act under Yeltsin, who did to be sure, face a recalcitrant Parliament, presidents Putin and Medvedev amended the 1994 RCC Act seventeen times between 2001 and 2018. Some of these amendments (see Table 1) reflected the desire of the both rulers to make the tribunal more dependent on them, in the process giving RCC judges generous pay raises, perks and benefits. Indeed, lucrative salaries for RCC judges—between 10 and 13 million rubles ($170,000 - $220,000) in 2017, which is much higher than those of any other judges, strengthened clientelist relations between the tribunal and President instead of promoting judicial independence. Even though none of the RCC judges wished to relocate to Saint-Petersburg (Vedomosti, 2005; Sobesednik, 2009), and (Chairman Zorkin's agreement with the plan notwithstanding), all of them "pragmatically" made the move after Chairman Zorkin secured promises of generous relocation benefits (NewsRu.Com, 2006).

Even though the June 2009 amendments abolished the election of the RCC leaders by judges themselves by transferring this power to President and the Federation Council, both Putin and Medvedev kept and extended the length of tenure of Valerii Zorkin as the RCC Chairman and judges Mavrin and Khokhriakova as the RCC Vice-Chairs—choices that satisfied most of the judges. As one RCC judge put it anonymously, the changes made both Zorkin and Mavrin more accountable to their external patrons rather than to their peers on the bench, so that now: "Someone may want to demonstrate that he is more Catholic than the Pope" (Kommersant, 2009: 1). This remark followed the RCC meeting in October 2009, in which the judges as a group threatened to impose sanctions on judges Kononov and Yaroslavtsev for criticizing Putin and Medvedev and allegedly destroying judicial independence in the media (Bonet, 2009; Sobesednik, 2009). RCC leaders then made a point of informing President Medvedev that judge Kononov chose to resign at the end of 2009 and judge Yaroslavtsev had recused himself from representing the RCC at the Council of the Russian Judges (Kommersant, 2009).

Table 1. Key changes in regulating the RCC, 2000-2018.

Date of changes	Summary of changes	Goals and impact of changes
FEB. 7, 2000	Acting President Putin matched perks and benefits of judges with those of ministers and of the RCC Chairman to those of the Prime Minister	Accountability — presidential administration is responsible for providing generous perks and benefits to the RCC. Still, the RCC Chairman Zorkin complained in 2005 that he incessantly lobbied for 2 years to obtain housing for newly appointed judges.
FEB. 8, 2001	Term of judges appointed in 1994-2000 extended from 12 to 15 years and age limit removed	Accountability — aimed at keeping Chairman Marat Baglai in office yet removing Vice-Chairman Tamara Morshchakova from the bench
DEC. 15, 2001	Brought back age limit of 70 to judges appointed in 1994-2004 — to be in force from 2005 onward	Simplification - same age limit as for judges in other courts
	Established disciplinary sanctions on the RCC judges - warning and dismissal from the bench - for violating the Judicial Ethics Code and for an opinion that resulted from criminal abuse of office. RCC approval for launching a criminal case against the RCC judge is no longer required	Accountability & Simplification - aimed at making the RCC judges accountable on par with judges of other courts. In 2009, the RCC threatened to issue warnings against judges Kononov, who chose to resign immediately, and Yaroslavtsev, who recused himself, for criticizing Putin and Medvedev in the media.
	Clarified duties of government bodies in carrying out RCC decisions	Strengthened the binding power of the RCC decisions
APR. 5, 2005	Removed 15-year term and applied age limit of 70 to all RCC judges	Simplification - all sitting RCC judges are subject to the same age limit after the outspoken judges Nikolai Vitruk and Viktor Luchin had retired reaching the age of 65
FEB. 5, 2007	Relocated the RCC from Moscow to Saint-Petersburg	Accountability - test for loyalty of the RCC judges to the Kremlin, soft purge of the RCC apparatus who did not agree to relocate, lucrative contracts for trusted construction companies, displeasure of local residents

Date of changes	Summary of changes	Goals and impact of changes
DEC. 23, 2007	President Putin offered generous relocation benefits to judges and clerks	Accountability—aimed at rewarding the RCC judges and clerks, who had agreed to relocate to Saint-Petersburg
JUN. 2, 2009	Abolished election of the RCC Chairman and Vice-Chairman by the RCC judges for 3-year term and dismissal of these RCC officers by the RCC judges. Instead, President nominates the RCC Chairman and two Vice-Chairmen from among the RCC judges, and the Federation Council approves them for a 6-year renewable term. President also proposes to the Federation Council to dismiss these RCC officers from office.	Dependence & Simplification - aimed at making the RCC leaders accountable to the President the same procedure as the chairmen and vice-chairmen of other courts.
NOV. 3, 2010	Abolished the age of 70 term limit of the RCC Chairman	Accountability - aimed at keeping Chairman Valerii Zorkin in office. This age limit has also been removed for the Russian Supreme Court Chairman Viacheslav Lebedev, who has been in office since 1989
	Abolished both chambers of the RCC. The RCC as a whole hears and decides cases and can decide individual complaints without hearing oral arguments. The RCC is no longer allowed interpret statutes while dismissing the cases.	Simplification - aimed at improving the unity of judicial opinions on the bench, speeding up disposition of cases brought by citizens, and interpreting statutes only in decisions on the merits
DEC. 25, 2012	Authorized President to set the salary of the RCC Chairman and to use this figure for calculating salaries of all other judges	Dependence—aimed at reducing the power of Prime Minister in setting judicial salaries in favor of President's power to set them
MAR. 19, 2013	President Putin set the salary of the RCC Chairman at 32,752 rubles	Dependence
APR. 5, 2013	Set the 6-month deadline for the Cabinet to introduce law to fill the gap in the law, as identified by the RCC	Strengthened the binding power of the RCC decisions
JUN. 4, 2014	Authorized the RCC to check constitutionality of proposed referendum question	Expanded the power of the RCC beyond the letter of the Russian Constitution
	Lowered the quorum for making decisions from 3/4 of the total number of judges to 2/3 of the actual number of judges	Simplification - aimed at enabling the RCC to function with a smaller number of judges: 13 instead of 16 for a 19-member tribunal, and easing the control of the Chairman over the RCC judges
	Authorized the RCC to check constitutionality of the ECtHR judgments at the request of courts	Expanded the power of the RCC beyond the letter of the Russian Constitution

Date of changes	Summary of changes	Goals and impact of changes
JUN. 8, 2015	Authorized the RCC to accept petitions via Internet page of the RCC	Expanded access to the RCC and enhanced monitoring of submitted petitions within the RCC
DEC. 14, 2015	Authorized the RCC to check the possibility of implementing the ECtHR judgment at the request of the Justice Ministry in the proceedings without oral hearings	Expanded the power of the RCC beyond the letter of the Russian Constitution and gave a formal pretext to Russia not to implement the unfavorable ECtHR judgment
	Authorized the RCC to issue official interpretation of the Constitution at the request of President and Prime-Minister after the RCC confirmation about the impossibility of implementing the ECtHR judgment	Expanded the power of the RCC beyond the letter of the Russian Constitution and gave a formal pretext to Russia not to implement the unfavorable ECtHR judgment
DEC. 28, 2016	Authorized the RCC in a single decision on the merits - to declare the law constitutional, issue binding interpretation of a law and order to reopen a case of complainant. Set the deadlines for government bodies in implementing such RCC decisions	Strengthened the binding power of the RCC decisions and overcame the resistance of the rest of the judiciary that refused to reopen cases in the absence of declaration of unconstitutionality
JUL. 29, 2018	Age limit of the Vice-Chairs of the RCC extended to 76	Accountability—aimed at keeping sitting Vice-Chairs of the RCC in office

Source: composed by Alexei Trochev

Meanwhile, other changes to the 1994 RCC Act listed in Table 1 formalize practices that the RCC has developed without prior legislative approval, such as deciding cases without oral arguments, making binding statutory interpretations, and reviewing the constitutionality of the ECtHR judgments. This judicial self-empowerment does not seem to bother Russia's rulers. Finally, a small group of amendments, actively promoted by RCC judges, aimed at improving compliance of Russian state officials with RCC judgments, as an answer to the long-standing pattern of the Russian leaders implementing only those court decisions that suited their current needs. Clearly, the changes made to the RCC by both Putin and Medvedev were products of exchanges of personal and organizational rewards for loyalty to the Kremlin's wishes, rather than products of pressure or blackmail.

4. Judicial pragmatism through adaptation to personnel changes

Like their predecessor Yeltsin, presidents Putin and Medvedev expected to have loyal judges and courts in exchange for generous funding. But as insurance they also tried to make the composition of the Court congenial. As Table 2 shows, together Putin and Medvedev made the total of 9 appointments to the RCC, and Vladimir Putin will have a chance to make 5 appointments during his fourth (2018–2024) term. All but one of their appointees had taught law at prestigious universities and faced the prospect of long terms on the court. In contrast to the appointees of Yeltsin era, none of them came from Moscow (known for its cosmopolitanism). Instead, they came from teaching posts on the law faculties in four cities: Saint-Petersburg—alma mater of Putin and Medvedev, Ekaterinburg, Vladivostok, and Rostov on the Don.

Table 2. Composition of the RCC, June 2016.

Judge	Background	Appointed	President	Reaches 70	Status
Zorkin (no age limit)	Constitutional law professor, MVD Academy, Moscow	1991	Yeltsin	2013	Chairman, 1991–93, 2003–present
Gadzhiev	Civil law professor, Dagestan State Univ., Dagestan Council of Ministers, Makhachkala	1991	Yeltsin	2023	Judge
Rudkin	Law lecturer, Supreme Soviet Deputy, Yaroslavl	1991	Yeltsin	2021	Judge-Secretary, 1995-98
Khokhriakova (until 76)	Social security law researcher, Moscow	1994	Yeltsin	2019	Vice-Chairwoman, 2008-present
Danilov	Justice Ministry, State Anti-Monopoly Committee, Moscow	1994	Yeltsin	2020	Judge-Secretary, 2001-2009
Yaroslavtsev	Judge, Saint-Petersburg	1994	Yeltsin	2022	Judge
Zharkova	Vice-Minister of Justice of the Republic of Karelia, Petrozavodsk	1997	Yeltsin	2025	Judge
Bondar	Municipal law professor, Rostov State Univ., Rostov-Don	2000	Putin	2020	Judge
Kazantsev	Legal history professor, St-Petersburg State Univ., St-Petersburg	2002	Putin	2025	Judge
Krasavchikova	Civil law professor, Ural State Law Academy, Ekaterinburg	2003	Putin	2025	Judge
Mavrin (until 76)	Labor law professor, St-Petersburg State Univ., St-Petersburg	2005	Putin	2021	Vice-Chairman, 2009-present
Melnikov	Procurator, Rostov-Don and Yakutsk	2005	Putin	2025	Judge
Kniazev	Administrative law professor, Far East State Univ., Chair of Election Commission, Vladivostok	2008	Medvedev	2029	Judge
Aranovskii	Constitutional law professor, Far East State Univ., Chair of Election Commission, Vladivostok	2010	Medvedev	2034	Judge
Kokotov	Constitutional law professor, Ural State Law Academy, Ekaterinburg	2010	Medvedev	2031	Judge
Boitsov	Criminal law professor, St-Petersburg State Univ., St-Petersburg	2010	Medvedev	2020	Judge

Source: Russian Constitutional Court (2016).

This may reflect both the lack of interest of Muscovites in relocating to the banks of Neva and the efforts of sitting RCC judges in bringing their former colleagues to the bench. Moreover, at least three relatives of a RCC judges work in the RCC apparatus. RCC judge Nikolai Bondar criticized the life tenure of RCC judges (up to the age of retirement) for its potential to produce conservatism on the bench. In contrast to Putin's initial presidential terms (2000–2008), when he filled the vacancies on the bench in a timely way, since his return to Kremlin in 2012, Vladimir Putin has failed to fill vacancies on the bench and, instead, extended the tenure of the Court's vice-chairpersons to the age of 76. From fall 2016 there were three vacancies, none of which had been filled as of early 2018, in stark contrast to the timely re-appointment of Chairman Zorkin in January 2018. As we will show below, these unfilled judgeships did not harm judicial efficiency. On the contrary, they make it easier for judges to deliberate the growing number of cases in plenary meetings — it is easier to reach an agreement among 16 than 19 members. Vacancies on the bench also help the RCC Chairman to manage the tribunal and to redistribute the unspent funds among the judges. Finally, Prime-Minister Dmitry Medvedev, who reportedly said that he would not mind heading the RCC and is rumored to be in line to succeed Zorkin as its Chairman, may also be interested in keeping judgeships vacant for now so that he can fill them later on with his loyalists.

The regime's expectation of loyalty has been made clear to top judges in Russia through rewards for favorable judgments, as in the YUKOS case, and punishments for the opposite (Trochev, 2016). Moreover, in 2003, when the RCC judges contrary to the Kremlin's wishes elected Valerii Zorkin as a chairman of their tribunal, it produced "shock" and "panic" in the Kremlin's corridors, according to one insider in Putin's administration. However, the Kremlin accepted Zorkin after an informal conversation between him and Putin's aides and having received assurances that he would not cause problems (Vedomosti, 2018). In December 2005, the Speaker of the State Duma announced that he had spoken with Chairman Zorkin about the move of the Court to St. Petersburg and Zorkin had approved it. Moreover, in early 2011, Chairman Zorkin reportedly fired an adviser after a complaint on the phone from the head of the presidential administration Sergei Naryshkin, who had been outraged at the advisor's public criticism of Dmitrii Medvedev's criminal justice reform (Svobodnaia Pressa, 2011). This concession came at a time when the RCC faced threats to its survival, according to another of Zorkin's advisers (Polit.Ru, 2011).

Some RCC judges have resented this expectation of judicial loyalty. Thus, Judge Yaroslavtsev complained in 2009, that the "security services can do anything they want, while judges are left with the task of confirming their decisions" (Bonet, 2009). The former chief justice of the disbanded Higher *Arbitrazh* Court of Russia Anton Ivanov bitterly characterized the Kremlin's approach to judicial decisions: "State bodies are so built that the skill of a lawyer in dealing with them does not matter. You can be an excellent expert and speaker, but if there is an order [from above] to decide the case not according to law, you cannot overcome this [order]" (Merkacheva, 2017). The regime of political expediency means that the rulers are sure that they can obtain any judgment in their favor, and this strikes them as natural. Vladimir Putin reportedly could not believe that in 2003 Tony Blair was unable to influence London judges to extradite to Russia maverick millionaire Boris Berezovskii and the Chechen leader Akhmed Zakayev (Zygar, 2016: 300). In Russia, transmitting orders to judges is not difficult. In 2011, even Vladislav Surkov, then deputy head of the presidential administration, who, according to Bill Bowring (2013: 7), "strongly influenced senior figures in the judiciary, especially Valery Zorkin," had a direct phone line to the chairmen of both the Russian Supreme Court and the RCC (Kommersant-Vlast, 2011: 24).

Still, the expectation of judicial loyalty does not lead to automatic obedience from the bench. RCC judges themselves sometimes criticize their Court. The RCC has been allowed to publish dissenting and concurring opinions since the start of its operation in 1992. Since then, of the 32 judges who have served on the bench of the RCC only four have never written a dissent or concurring opinion. Instead, most RCC judges, including Putin's appointees, do so and treat this act as a normal and essential aspect of their individual independence. In 2016, the RCC began publishing dissenting and concurring opinions on the RCC website together with its decisions. By 2017, RCC judges had written a total of 351 dissents and concurring opinions, including 101 during the previous 5 years (see Table 3). This is a sign of frequent disagreements among the judges despite a growing authoritarian milieu and the efforts by Chief Justice Zorkin to encourage unanimity.

Table 3. Dissenting and concurring opinions in the Russian constitutional court, 2012–2017.

Year	Dissenting opinions	Concurring opinions	Total
2012	6	18	34
2013	12	16	28
2014	4	7	11
2015	7	12	19
2016	4	5	9
2017	7	12	19

Sources: Drigo (2016) and authors' own calculations for 2016 and 2017.

The continuation of dissents and concurrences in recent years indicates that political leaders accept that the credibility of RCC judges (and the value of their support) depends upon their appearing autonomous as individual judges This indicator of their authenticity as judges stands in stark contrast to fraudulent elections and the regime's disdain for and punishment of dissent in the Russian Parliament in the last decade (Ledeneva, 2013). Moreover, the phenomenon of judge-reporters sometimes publishing dissents or concurring opinions (37 between 1992 and 2016) distinguishes the RCC from the Supreme Court, where a judge-reporter who can't convince the majority of her peers must re-write his draft judgment and support the new version (Drigo, 2016: 91).

At the same time, since 2014, coincidentally a year of authoritarian consolidation outside the Court, there has been a marked decline in the number of dissenting and concurring opinions (see Table 3). This may reflect the fact that most RCC judges engage in pragmatic self-censorship, something that RCC judge Anatolii Kononov, the author of 53 dissents, who "prioritized fair resolution of constitutional cases" (Drigo, 2016: 90), could not tolerate. He resigned from the bench at the end of 2009. But his case is unusual because all but one of the RCC judges from his day have remained on the bench for the whole of their tenure.

5. Judicial pragmatism through adaptation to a popular leader

Facing these expectations of loyalty, as well as occasional threats to its very existence, the RCC transformed itself into a friendly executor of Kremlin's needs, a vocal supporter of Kremlin's agenda, and a vehicle for lobbyists trying to change the hastily adopted laws. By defending and approving the decisions made by Putin and Medvedev the RCC so far has been able to fend off proposals for its emasculation or abolition, proposals that have circulated in Moscow since the early 1990s and even led in 2016 to a draft law that would merge the RCC with the Supreme Court (Vedomosti, 2016; Gaaze, 2017). Consider as an example of responsiveness the following change of heart of the RCC leadership. In 2000, then Chairman Marat Baglai, to whom Boris Yeltsin had openly complained about the lack of cooperation with the tribunal, actually praised the existence of political opposition and freedom of speech in the country as a check against authoritarianism and warned the executive branch not to threaten individual rights. But in 2013, his successor, Valerii Zorkin, who had in 1993 engineered the green light for Yeltsin's impeachment, bitterly complained that political opposition itself had become a threat to the Russian state (Iskenderov, 2000; Kommersant, 2013).

The RCC skillfully managed to convince the powers that constitutional review could help them achieve the politically expedient goal of governance without constraints. For example, in 2005, a few months after the Kremlin had significantly raised the salaries of RCC judges, the Court received 58 constitutional complaints against Putin's decision to abolish gubernatorial elections and assertion of presidential power to fire governors. At first, the two judge-reporters—Nikolay Bondar and Boris Ebzeev—proposed ducking this "hot potato" to avoid public criticism of the reform by the Court (Katanian, 2005). However, the majority of judges overruled their attempt to bury the dispute and, in a matter of six months, upheld the constitutionality of the abolition, reversing a 1996 decision, in which the RCC had declared that governors had to be directly elected and its 2002 decision that President could fire governors only after three judicial decisions against them. One long-term observer of the Court called this reversal "Solomonic" (Katanian, 2005), while the RCC critics including dissenters on the bench slammed the reversal as unconstitutional. Boris Strashun (2008), one of the original Constitution-writers and the head of the RCC Analytical Center, complained that this "argumentation of the Constitutional Court, if one may call this, totally changes public understanding of the supremacy of the Constitution, of its relationship to legislation and about legal opinions of the Constitutional Court, which may freely change according to "the spirit of time." Using this approach, one can justify anything but this goes beyond the boundaries of jus." Chairman Zorkin, however, rebuked the opposition for criticizing his tribunal and insisted that the RCC had to take into account both "the spirit of the Constitution and the spirit of life," meaning a political milieu led by a popular President (Kommersant, 2013). This lively dispute confirms Hendley's (2017) observation that with legal duality judges can issue contradictory decisions and supports our contention that pragmatic activist judges may disregard their previous decisions (Zagretdinov, 2015) to serve the political needs of the regime. Ordinary Russians, however, failed to notice this dispute among top jurists. According to one public opinion poll, which was conducted at that time, 62% of those polled knew nothing about the RCC and 95% failed to name any RCC decision (VTsIOM, 2006).

But issuing friendly verdicts, which very few people read and even fewer understand, was not enough to justify keeping a separate constitutional review tribunal. The RCC has also supported the Kremlin by supplying legal justifications for governance reforms in advance of their adoption. As Vladimir Putin publicly admitted in December 2016, "I can reveal that when the government or individual ministries and departments are about to take decisions, the question is often raised whether the new rule will be consistent with the Constitution. Here, Valery Dmitrievich [Zorkin] knows that from time to time I phone and ask him how this or that rule will look, when it is being prepared for adoption either in the Parliament or in the Cabinet." (Kremlin.Ru, 2016) Such advance private consultation about proposed laws stands in a stark contrast to the routine refusal of the RCC judges to comment on proposed laws in public—which is forbidden by the RCC Act. Moreover, as we shall see below, this consultation between the Chief Justice and President parallels an increase in the number of statutes declared unconstitutional. More recently, the RCC offered support for the Kremlin's foreign policy decisions. For example, until 2008, the RCC repeatedly ignored petitions related to the relations between Russia and South Ossetia's breakaway region as well as the Black Sea fleet. However, in the wake of the 2008 war with Georgia, Chief Justice Valerii Zorkin spoke and wrote in defense of that war and later of the annexation of Crimea as well, accusing the West and the US of spreading terrorism and fueling an anti-Russian information war (Antonov, 2017b). These public actions of Zorkin probably helped to maintain his name recognition among ordinary Russians—9% of them identified him as belonging to the judiciary, according to the May 2018 public opinion poll, a very low figure as compared to his high public approval during the 1993 constitutional crisis (VTsIOM, 2018).

While many ridiculed Zorkin's rhetoric, it sent an important signal to Russia's *siloviki* (security leaders) that the RCC was on their side, a signal that is much easier understood than actual RCC decisions. Zorkin seems to have convinced Vladimir Putin that his tribunal would make an effective mediator between Russian and the European Court of Human Rights, the tribunal that has become the most popular court among Russians and has increasingly decided politically salient cases against Russia (Trochev, 2009). RCC judges predicted the avalanche of the Russia-related cases in the Strasbourg-based tribunal and insisted from the early 2000s that no other institution in Russia knows the ECtHR better. Indeed, the quality of jurists representing Russia at the ECtHR has not improved in the last decade, a fact that gives the RCC an unrivalled advantage among government jurists who deal with international human rights. This is why the RCC could be so bold yet direct in denying the binding force of those ECtHR judgments on Russia. The Court proceeded to develop a mechanism for checking their binding force, inserted itself in this mechanism, had it adopted in 2015, and promptly used it in confirming, at the request of the Russian government, the non-binding force of two ECtHR judgments that were particularly controversial in Russia: prisoner voting rights and the YUKOS compensation (Mälksoo and Benedek, 2017). This is why Putin chose to engage the RCC in dealing with unfavorable judgments of the Strasbourg-based tribunal instead of simply defying them. In sum, to address Justice Breyer's call for judges and paratroopers to be friends, Russia's top judges have become friends with paratroopers and allowed the latter to issue marching orders at home and abroad and rely on efficient constitutional review when needed.

Still, the RCC pragmatically realized that it should not hedge its bets on the Kremlin alone. Instead, it presents itself as a tribunal that is friendly to many groups. As Valerii Zorkin quipped: "On paper the Constitutional Court is mighty. But in reality, it exists insofar as society needs it" (Kommersant, 2011). At that time, the RCC was highly trusted, according to a 2010 Levada public opinion survey of 2000 Russians (Gudkov et al., 2010: 15). The Court has accepted complaints from and ruled in favor of many litigants who are not mentioned in the 1994 RCC statute, such as local self-government bodies and other actors not affiliated with government. The RCC clerks publish all RCC decisions on the easily searchable RCC website and issue clear instructions for complainants who have lost at the RCC about how to resubmit their complaints (Sivitskii, 2015). The RCC has started to accept amicus curiae briefs — expert opinions from various think-tanks and NGOs, including those labeled as "foreign agents" by the Russian government. The RCC justices did so over objections of Putin's representative at the hearings and eventually inserted the practice of amicus curiae into the Court By-Laws in October 2017. As Chairman Zorkin told journalists, "the court chooses its friends on its own" (Kommersant, 2017). A well-informed insider, former State Duma representative at the RCC Valerii Lazarev (2014), argues that the RCC is used by lobbying groups who had previously lost their battles in the political branches of government or courts. For example, in January 2011, the RCC ruled against state-owned oil giant Rosneft, when it had found that as a minority shareholder Alexei Navalny had a right to demand copies of the minutes of meetings of Rosneft's board of directors (Rossiiskaia gazeta, 2011). In February 2017, the RCC ruled that the recently adopted Article 212.1 of the Criminal Code criminalizing repeated participation in street protests was too harsh and had to be changed and the convictions of repeat rioter Ilya Dadin re-visited (Mednikov, 2017).

To be sure, the RCC pragmatically avoids some politically divisive issues, deferring their resolution to the Parliament or to the Supreme Court. But not all. Thus, in 2014, the RCC confirmed the constitutionality of the merger of the Higher Arbitrazh Court (HAC) with the Supreme Court, after 100 Duma members contested its constitutionality and dozens of the HAC judges lost their jobs, justifying the merger as a "unique case" and hoping that a similar merger would not happen to itself (Rossiiskaia gazeta, 2014). A year later, in July 2015, the RCC ruled that the Duma elections may be moved to an earlier date as an exception for the sake of "constitutional goals", which the Court failed to enumerate (Rossiiskaia gazeta, 2015). But even when the Court defers to the political branches, in essence, playing in bureaucratic ping-pong, the tribunal may make paradoxically unbureaucratic pronouncements. For example, in December 2012, the RCC ruled, at the request of 116 State Duma members from the Fair Russia party, that while the Duma member Gudkov, who was expelled by the vote of simple majority of the Duma, loses his mandate, he gets to keep his immunity from criminal prosecution 'until there has been a decision of the Supreme Court' on the legality of his expulsion, a decision that could be reviewed by the RCC. The RCC also ruled, that the Duma majority should adopt a clear procedure on expelling the Duma members inter alia allowing the parliamentary opposition to challenge the majority's refusal to expel in the Supreme Court. While Gudkov and his lawyers slammed the RCC decision as allowing the ruling party to punish the opposition and change the will of the voters, Chairman Zorkin defended the verdict by arguing that "We live not in a political refrigerator but in a global world and common European legal space where various mechanisms of resolving such conflicts are practiced" (Kommersant, 2012).

In short, while the growing significance of political expediency, the weakening constitutionalism, and the threat of merger of the RCC with the Supreme Court reduced the RCC's policy space and autonomy, they failed to eliminate it. The Court was effectively forced to decide politically sensitive matters favorably to the Kremlin and provide unconditional support of Putin's key policies, including the Court's own exile to Saint-Petersburg. But in matters where the Kremlin does not have a clear interest, the RCC has been able to involve other actors and decide cases impartially.

6. Judicial pragmatism through resilience: a busy and activist RCC

Quantitative analysis of the overall work of the RCC—all its cases, not just those with political coloration—reveals remarkable continuity in the operation of tribunal despite the growing authoritarian trends. As Table 4 shows, the total number of complaints received in the last two years was 40% higher than in the 1990s, when the RCC received about 10,000 complaints annually, and is about the same as in 2002 (14,472 petitions). As in the past, citizens or their associations submit 99% of petitions, even though the overall number of their complaints has declined in the past seven years by 30%. This decline is much smaller than the halving of the number of complaints against Russia in the European Court of Human Rights—the tribunal with which the RCC tries to compare itself - in the past four years—from 12,328 to 5591 (ECHR, 2017). Importantly, the number of petitions to the Court from government bodies in the last decade has remained the same (the RCC receives one a week) a sign of their utility to government actors. The petitions from government involve policing local judges and bureaucrats and legitimating policies of the ruling regime, two well-documented functions of authoritarian judiciary that connect to political expediency (Moustafa, 2014).

Table 4. Complaints and petitions to the Russian constitutional court, 1995–2018.

Year	Citizen complaints	Petitions by government bodies and courts	Total
1995–2007	166160	1432	167572
2008	16551	41	16592
2009	20573	56	20629
2010	18178	36	18214
2011	19099	43	19142
2012	18694	51	18745
2013	15062	39	15101
2014	15969	36	16005
2015	14570	52	14622
2016	14000	31	14031
2017	14604	34	14638
2018	15125	24	15149

Source: Russian Constitutional Court (2018).

While the demand for constitutional review in Russia has been stable despite its shift to authoritarianism, the number of cases that RCC judges handled - has roughly doubled in the last decade (Dzmitryieva, 2017; Grigoriev, 2018). Moreover in 90% of the cases it hears, the RCC takes decisive actions. It declares laws unconstitutional, interprets statutes in a new constitutionally acceptable way, asks for contested legislation to be changed, and orders the cases of successful complainants to be re-opened and decided according to the Constitution (see Table 5). One can add to this a handful of the RCC rulings in which the tribunal orders the case of the complainant be re-tried according to an existing RCC interpretation of contested statute. The overall result was that in 2016 (see Table 5), for the first time in its history, the RCC found not a single reviewed law to be constitutional!

This expanding judicial activism in the context of the Russia's authoritarianism is striking, but it is also compatible with both constitutionalism and political expediency. Both governance regimes value efficient judicial tribunals but for different reasons. At the request of top government officials, the RCC promptly moved the case up and unanimously approved the incorporation of Crimea into the Russian Federation, as Chairman Zorkin reminded Vladimir Putin in December 2016 (Kremlin.Ru, 2016), prompting criminal charges with aiding and abetting in Crimea's annexation against the tribunal by Ukraine's Prosecutor General (112.Ua, 2018). The Court also promptly approved the claim of the Justice Ministry that it was impossible to enforce two judgments of the European Court of Human Rights lost by Russia. And in a matter of days, the RCC announced that it would not consider Alexei Navalny's complaint against the federal law that bars individuals with a criminal record from participating in presidential elections albeit the Constitution barred convicts only. To be sure, both the Russian Parliament, which has been labeled a "mad printer" for its fast passage of barely considered legislation (Johnson, 2016: 649), and the Cabinet of Ministers have sped up the adoption of laws on issues prioritized by the Kremlin. It appears that Zorkin does not want his tribunal to be perceived by the Kremlin as slow or inefficient. As he confessed to President Putin in December 2016, "it was possible to double the number of judgments" (Kremlin.Ru, 2016). Indeed, in 2017, the RCC issued the record high 40 judgments on the merits (see Table 5), including 23 issued in the written procedure without holding a full-blown hearing.

Table 5. Outcomes of the Russian constitutional court decisions on the merits, 2004–2017.

Year	Issued decisions on the merits	Declared constitutional	Declared new constitutional meaning	Declared unconstitutional	Ordered to amend the law	Ordered to reopen the case of complainant
2004	19					
2005	14					
2006	10					
2007	14					
2008	11					
2009	20					
2010	22	1	16	7	7	
2011	30	1	17	15	12	20
2012	34	1	22	18	18	23
2013	30	2	13	26	18	20
2014	33	1	20	20	16	24
2015	34	1	17	19	14	27
2016	28	0	20	19	21	17
2017	40	0	29	14	16	32

Source: Russian Constitutional Court (2017).

By now an observant reader may point out that this increase in RCC activity touches mainly upon marginal issues of politics in Putin's Russia and avoids criticizing, not to speak of rejecting actions that solidified his non-democratic rule. To be sure, the pragmatic RCC has skillfully refused to decide some politically sensitive matters under both Yeltsin and Putin (Trochev, 2008). Yet the quantitative analysis of the RCC decisions on the merits does not show drastic changes in its decisions involving political rights. This category of rights comprised but a small share of the human rights jurisprudence under both Yeltsin and Putin (see Table 6). Chairman Zorkin told Vladimir Putin that his Court received only 59 complaints regarding political rights in 2017 and confessed that it was "difficult, of course, to reach decisions when they touch upon a delicate sphere of political rights" (Kremlin.Ru, 2017). Of course, the path of political expediency favors this judge-made avoidance of sensitive political issues. Yet the RCC still manages to decide many of these cases impartially as the regime of constitutionalism requires it to do. While the number of decisions on the merits in such cases has slightly declined, the success rate for appellants has never fallen below 45%, a figure that some would take as an indicator of an impartial court. In contrast, RCC decisions on the merits in personal and social rights cases have doubled in the last five years, yet the success rate in these cases is like the success rate in decisions over political rights, including voting rights and rights to protest in public (see Table 6).

Table 6. Rates of success in constitutional rights litigation in the Russian constitutional court, 1995–2015.

Period	Decisions on personal rights	Won by complainant	Decisions on political rights	Won by complainant	Decisions on social rights	Won by complainant
1995–1999	35	30	23	**17**	31	26
2000–2004	31	18	14	**10**	40	18
2005–2009	26	17	11	**5**	32	15
2010–2015	50	30	19	**12**	70	39

Bold indicates success rate in the political rights cases Source: Karasev (2017).

To be sure, some critics of the RCC accuse it of producing narrow, formalistic and wrong-headed human rights jurisprudence (Blankenagel and Levin, 2015; Sheinis, 2016). But such criticism is normal for any rights tribunal, especially when it comes to balancing one right against another.

7. Judicial pragmatism through tolerating disobedience with judgments

Overall, the record of the compliance with RCC decisions improved somewhat under consolidated authoritarianism — a consequence of intensified cooperation of the Court with the Parliament and the Cabinet. The Court now faces little or no open defiance from the regions, thanks to the concentration of law-making powers and gubernatorial appointments at the federal center and monitoring of the regional laws by the Procuracy. In November 2012, Prime-Minister Medvedev scolded the Cabinet "over its failure to implement 58 decisions issued by the country's Constitutional Court and to adopt over 200 government edicts" and called this failure "outrageous" and "unacceptable" (Sputnik News, 2012). For example, in drafting the Customs Code of the Russia-led Customs Union with Belarus and Kazakhstan, the Cabinet copied word for word provisions of the Russian Customs Code, which the RCC had earlier declared unconstitutional, and eventually had them adopted. Yet the RCC chose not to slam this defiance by the executive while insisting in a series of unpublished rulings that its declarations of unconstitutionality remained valid (Ispolinov, 2014). As Table 7 shows, the Russian Parliament has also become more efficient in complying with the growing number of the RCC orders to change federal laws. In fact, since 2010 the number of non-implemented RCC decisions has shrunk, while the number of federal statutes implementing RCC decisions has grown. This moderate improvement should not come as a surprise, for it is expedient for both the RCC and the Parliament to please the popular ruler. The change on the part of the parliament was intentional. In 2012 the Federation Council held a full-blown hearing on the implementation of RCC decisions and in 2013 published a 130-page monitoring report.

Table 7. Implementation of the Russian Constitutional Court decisions, 2010-2017.

Year	RCC orders to amend the federal statute	RCC decisions not implemented by the russian parliament	Number of federal statutes implementing the RCC decisions	RCC orders to reopen case of complainant	Complaints about non-implementation of the RCC decisions
2010	7		10		374
2011	12	47	13	20	418
2012	18	44	17	23	145
2013	18	39	20	20	55
2014	16	36	19	24	61
2015	14	45	13	27	52
2016	21	35	19	17	53
2017	16	28	19	32	No data

Source: Russian Constitutional Court (2017).

Still, this improvement is only partial, and there remain RCC decisions that get ignored, because either they are not a priority or the absence of a mechanism for their implementation. A case in point is the saga of the abolition, reinstatement and repeat abolition of early voting, in which the RCC played its part but was ignored in a policy reversal. Early voting, that is a turnout-increasing measure that allows those who cannot come to their designated polling station on election day to vote earlier, was a common practice in elections at all levels in Russia in the 1990s (Bader, 2016). However, similar to other democratic mechanisms adapted to authoritarian rule, early voting facilitated the manipulation of the outcome of the elections, through such devices as violations of ballot secrecy, coercion of voters and fixing and counting the votes of people who would not vote regardless, such as labor migrants or conscripts (Bader, 2016: 99). All these machinations associated with early voting were present in the 2009 municipal elections and generated electoral fraud scandals in Astrakhan, Sochi, Irkutsk, and Moscow, scandals that the Kremlin could no longer ignore (Ross, 2010). At the end of 2009, President Medvedev proposed banning early voting because of the irregularities perpetrated by the authorities, and in May 2010 the State Duma approved the ban.

An early voting ban that tied the hands of the local authorities and relieved the federal center of the burden of monitoring local officials is compatible with both authoritarian law that is supposed to regulate discipline of local agents and democratic law that constrains incumbents from using administrative resources against opposition candidates. Indeed, the September 2013 elections of Moscow Mayor, which were held without early voting and had a low 30% turnout, gave 52% to the incumbent Mayor Sergei Sobianin and 27% to the opposition candidate Alexei Navalny. This risky election result did not bode well with the Central Election Commission Chief Vladimir Churov, who promptly proposed reinstating early voting. Then, the legislature of the Vladimir Province asked the RCC to declare the early voting ban unconstitutional on the grounds that it deprived the right to vote for 35,000 residents of the province who worked in Moscow. The RCC promptly accepted this case and at the end of March 2014 held a hearing at which representatives of President Putin, State Duma, the Central Election Commission and the Procuracy supported lifting the ban, while the representatives of the Federation Council, the upper chamber of the Parliament formally representing interests of the regions, Prime-Minister Medvedev and the Justice Ministry defended the ban (Garant, 2014). On April 15, the Court, in a 14–2 vote, declared the early voting ban unconstitutional, expanded the grounds for allowing early voting, and ordered that this voting procedure be allowed immediately. Moreover, it took just three weeks for the Russian Parliament to amend the election law to comply with the RCC orders.

Not surprisingly, the provincial elections held in September 2014 witnessed active manipulation through early voting by local authorities (Zagretdinov, 2015: 117). Yet in 2016 President Putin banned early voting in Duma and local elections once again, and the head of the Central Election Commission Ella Pamfilova, a Putin appointee, slammed early voting as a cause of violations and irregularities in elections (RIA Novosti, 2016). Neither Putin nor Pamfilova had a problem with the fact that the RCC had ruled the earlier ban unconstitutional.

Moreover, the RCC is often dissatisfied with the quality of the compliance with its decisions. In its annual reports it accuses Duma deputies of hastily copying and pasting the wording of the RCC pronouncements into amended or newly adopted statutes. The RCC insists that the Parliament should instead amend the unconstitutional statutes in a systematic way, together with other relevant statutes in order to implement constitutional values. However, the Justice Ministry, which has been authorized to monitor implementation of the RCC decisions since 2011, insists that Russia lacks a mechanism for changing once again laws that have already been adopted or amended in accordance with the RCC decisions. In practice the Justice Ministry rubber-stamps the hasty decisions of the Duma without looking at the substance of the newly adopted laws and their actual match with constitutional values, as interpreted by the RCC. This is a typical bureaucratic approach to rulemaking that prioritizes reporting about changes made on paper and discourages actual monitoring of impact of the laws on the ground. This means that the RCC has to review the constitutionality of these hastily adopted laws all over again in order to make Constitution work. Moreover, the staff of the Justice Ministry sometimes defends these hastily adopted laws and disagrees with the RCC over the state of implementation of the Court's decisions. This happened with three decisions in 2011, four in 2012, seven in 2013, six in 2014, six in 2015, and three in 2016, according the RCC annual implementation reports. To overcome such bureaucratic sabotage and agreeing with the criticism of Russia's penitentiary system by the ECtHR, the RCC in November 2016 directly ordered prison authorities to allow long meetings between prisoners serving for life and their relatives (Rossiiskaia gazeta, 2016). Similarly, in May 2017, the RCC ordered courts to conduct a mandatory judicial review of deportation orders of stateless persons held in custody for longer than 3 months – a requirement in line with the ECtHR jurisprudence (Rossiiskaia gazeta, 2017).

More surprising is another trend reflected in Table 7. Since 2012, the RCC has been receiving substantially fewer complaints about non-implementation of its decisions by the rest of the judiciary. These complaints are typically sent to the Court by litigants when judges ignore the RCC orders to reopen their court cases. In the 1990s, other Russian courts ignored most RCC decisions, and the RCC went to great efforts to persuade the Supreme Court and the Higher Arbitrazh Court to get their subordinated judges to comply (Burnham and Trochev, 2007; Trochev, 2008). In 2011, the Supreme Court did establish a special department for supervising the enforcement of the ECtHR judgments and RCC decisions in the wake of the legislative changes establishing that RCC decisions invalidating statutes constituted legal grounds for reopening civil and criminal cases. With this provision most judges complied, but the courts routinely refused to reopen other cases in which the RCC provided a new constitutionally acceptable interpretation of the federal law without declaring the particular law unconstitutional. At the end of 2016, the RCC Act was amended yet again, authorizing the RCC to issue such decisions and requiring the rest of the judiciary to obey them, effectively codifying RCC-made practice. Yet it is far from clear that rank-and-file judges understand the language of the RCC decisions.

8. Conclusion

As a constrained court the RCC has not been able to stem the rise of non-democratic tendencies in Putin's Russia. Yet, by performing the roles that courts in authoritarian regimes do (Solomon, 2007, 2015) and adapting to heightened responsiveness demanded by political leaders, the RCC has been able to preserve a degree of autonomy for its judges and space for the opponents of the ruling regime. Authoritarian constitutionalism Russian style does involve compromise, but the overall result is encouraging.[1]

Under Putin as before the RCC has been pragmatically navigating the tension between constitutionalism and political expediency–by displaying loyalty to the rulers in public, allowing criticism of them in the courtroom, and resisting any merger of their tribunal with the Supreme Court in private. Most RCC judges see their Court as a policymaker rather than a rubber-stamping tool, and they see themselves as pragmatic forward-looking individuals deciding the future of Russia – who may also be forced at times to behave like bureaucrats or politicians.

In line with its 'judges' self-image, the RCC of today displays many positive features, including: the generation of a stable demand the constitutional review; growing efficiency; high rates of declaring statutes unconstitutional including in rights cases; vibrant exchanges of opinions among its judges, who serve their terms without interruption; and slight improvements in the implementation of its judgments. Despite the Court's pragmatic responsiveness to political demands, it remains a viable and active(ist) constitutional review tribunal. Assuming the RCC survives Vladimir Putin's fourth term, its place in Russian politics will be shaped

---

[1] Maria Popova (2017) recently argued that Russia does not have "authoritarian constitutionalism", precisely because of the RCC's deference to the political leadership in the cases that matter to it (that is its pursuit of political expediency). But with such a demanding understanding of "authoritarian constitutionalism", based on Tushnet's analysis of Singapore (Tushnet, 2015), there would be little place for constitutional protection of rights or constitutional courts in most authoritarian states, let alone Russia.

in part by his nominees, including a new chairman. By 2024 it will become truly Putin's court.

References

112 Ua, 2018. Ukraine charges Russia's Constitution Court with Conniving Crimea's Annexation. 112. Ua. March 12. https://112.international/politics/ukraine-charges-russias-constitution-court-with-conniving-crimeas-annexation-26475.html.

Antonov, M., 2014. Conservatism in Russia and sovereignty in human rights. Rev. Cent. East Eur. Law 39 (1), 1-40.

Antonov, M., 2017a. Law and economics, judicial pragmatism and their limits on both sides of the Atlantic. Rev. Cent. East Eur. Law 42 (1), 73-94.

Antonov, M., 2017b. Philosophy behind human rights: Valery Zorkin vs. the West. In: Mälksoo, L., Benedek, W. (Eds.), Russia and the European Court of Human Rights: the Strasbourg Effect. Cambridge University Press, New York, pp. 150-187.

Bader, M., 2016. The Reintroduction of early voting in Russian elections: a tool for electoral manipulation? Russ. Polit. 1 (1), 95-111.

Berman, H.J., 1963. Justice in the U.S.S.R.: an Interpretation of Soviet Law, Rev. Harvard University Press, Cambridge, MA.

Blankenagel, A., Levin, I., 2015. In principle, no but yes, it is possible! The Russian Constitutional Court and the binding power of decisions of the European Court of Human Rights. Sravnitelnoe konstitutsionnoe obozrenie (5), 152-162.

Bonet, P., 2009. En Rusia mandan los organos de seguridad, como en la epoca sovietica. El Pais. August 31. https://elpais.com/diario/2009/08/31/internacional/1251669606_850215.html.

Bowring, B., 2013. Laws, Rights and Ideology in Russia. Landmarks in the Destiny of a Great Power. Routledge, London.

Breyer, S., 2010. Making our democracy work: the Yale lectures. Yale Law J. 120, 1999-2026.

Burnham, W., Trochev, A., 2007. Russia's war between the courts: the struggle over the jurisdictional boundary between the Constitutional Court and regular courts. Am. J. Comp. Law 55 (3), 381-452.

Dressel, B., Sanchez-Urribarri, R., Stroh, A., 2017. The informal dimension of judicial politics: a relational perspective. Annu. Rev. Law Soc. Sci. 13, 413-430.

Drigo, E., 2016. Institut osobogo mneniia sudi Konstitutsionnogo Suda Rossiiskoi Federatsii: regulirovanie i praktika primeneniia. Sravnitelnoe konstitutsionnoe obozrenie (3), 79-93.

Dzmitryieva, A., 2017. Case selection in the Russian Constitutional Court: the role of legal assistants. Laws 6 (3), 12. http://www.mdpi.com/20 75-471X/6/3/12/htm.

ECHR, 2017. Analysis of Statistics 2016. January. https://www.echr.coe.int /Documents/Stats_analysis_2016_ENG.pdf.

Fraenkel, E., 1969. The Dual State: a Contribution to the Study of Dictatorship. Octagon Books, New York.

Gaaze, K., 2017. Premer-ministr i ego sotsialnyi sloi. CHto ne tak s Dmitriem Medvedevym. Carnegie Moscow Center. March 30. https://carnegie.ru/commentary/68447.

Gadzhiev, G., 2012. Realpolitik, eskobarstvo, konstitutsionnaia politika i russkaia kulturno-etnicheskaia traditsiia [Realpolitik, Escobarism, Constitutional Policy and Russian Culture-Ethnic Tradition]. In: Zapesotskii, A. (Ed.), Dialog Kultur V Usloviiakh Globalizatsii: XII Mezhdunarodnye Likhachevskie Nauchnye Chteniia, 17−18 Maia 2012 G. Tom 1. Sankt-peterburgskii Gumanitarnyi Universitet Profsoiuzov, Saint_Petersburg, pp. 55-58. https://publications.hse. ru/chapters/98074536.

Garant, 2014. Pravo na dosrochnoe golosovanie mogut vernut' vsem grazhdanam RF. Garant. March 31. http://www.garant.ru/news/53 4360.

Garoupa, N., Ginsburg, T., 2015. Judicial Reputation: a Comparative Theory. University of Chicago Press, Chicago.

Grigoriev, I., 2018. Law clerks as an instrument of courtegovernment accommodation under autocracy: the case of the Russian Constitutional Court. Post Sov. Aff. 34 (1), 17-34.

Gudkov, L., Dubin, B., Zorkaia, N., 2010. Rossiiskaia sudebnaia sistema v mneniiakh obshchestva. Vestnik obshchestvennogo mneniia. Dannye. Analiz. Diskusii 4 (106), 7-43.

Hendley, K., 2017. Everyday Law in Russia. Cornell University Press, Ithaca.

Iskenderov, F., 2000. Ravnenie na Konstitutsiiu. Senator. https://www.se nat.org/Russia/RuNova-2.html.

Ispolinov, A., 2014. Trebuiutsia pragmatiki: konstitutsionnyi sud Rossii i evraziiskii pravoporiadok. [Pragmatics requred: the Russian constitutional court and the eurasian legal order]. Sravnitelnoe konstitutsionnoe obozrenie 5, 14-20.

James, W., 1975. Pragmatism and the Meaning of Truth. Harvard University Press, Cambridge, MA. As quoted in Tamanaha, B., 2017. A Realistic Theory of Law. Cambridge University Press, New York.

Johnson, J.E., 2016. Fast-tracked or boxed in? Informal politics, gender, and women's representation in Putin's Russia. Perspect. Polit. 14 (3), 643-659.

Karasev, R., 2017. Osushchestvlenie Konstitutsionnym Sudom Rossiiskoi Federatsii zashchity prav i svobod cheloveka i grazhdanina. dissertation. Tiumen State University. https://search.rsl.ru/ru/record/01 008810006.

Katanian, K., 2005. Delo 'Kreml e gubernatory,'. Konstitutsionnyi sud ne sviazan prezhnimi resheniiami, no obrechen na "solomonovo" [case "KremlinGovernors." constitutional court is not bound by previous judgments but is doomed to "Solomon's" one"]. Politicheskii zhurnal 24 (July), 80-84.

Kommersant, 2009. Konstitutsionnyi Sud teriaet osobye mneniia. Kommersant. December 2. https://www.kommersant.ru/doc/1284828.

Kommersant, 2011. Poumnet nikogda ne pozdno. Kommersant. October 26. https://www.kommersant.ru/doc/1802908.

Kommersant, 2012. Konstitutsionnyi Sud otklonil zhaloby oppozitsii po "delu Gudkova." Kommersant. December 27. https://www.kommersant.ru/doc/ 2099204.

Kommersant, 2013. Valerii Zorkin sveriaet pozitsii Konstitutsionnogo Suda s "dukhom zhizni." Kommersant. March 23. https://www.kommers ant.ru/doc/2153284.

Kommersant, 2017. Konstitutsionnyi Sud vybiraet druzei. Kommersant. October 19. https://www.kommersant.ru/doc/3442458.

Kommersant-Vlast, 2011. Surkov i koreshki [Surkov and spines]. Kommersant-Vlast, January 31, 2011. http://kommersant.ru/doc/1573537.

Kremlin.Ru, 2016. Vstrecha s sudiami Konstitutsionnogo Suda. Kremlin.Ru. December 6. http://kremlin.ru/events/president/news/53421.

Kremlin.Ru, 2017. Vstrecha s sudiami Konstitutsionnogo Suda. Kremlin.Ru. December 12. http://kremlin.ru/catalog/persons/170/event s/56366.

Kyselova, T., 2014. Dualism of Ukrainian commercial courts: exploratory study. Hague Journal on the Rule of Law 6 (2), 178-201.

Lazarev, V., 2014. Lobbirovanie pravotvorcheskikh reshenii. Iuridicheskaia tekhnika 8, 216-223.

Ledeneva, A.V., 2013. Can Russia Modernise?: Sistema, Power Networks and Informal Governance. Cambridge University Press, New York.

Mälksoo, L., Benedek, W., 2017. Russia and the European Court of Human Rights: the Strasbourg Effect. Cambridge University Press, New York.

Maslennikov, V., 1996. Konstitutsionnyi Sud—ne dekorativnyi bantik v rossiiskoi demokratii Rossiiskaia Gazeta. August 2.

Mednikov, D., 2017. Taking Some Human Rights Back: the Case of Ildar Dadin. OxHRH Blog, 22 May 22. http://ohrh.law.ox.ac.uk/taking-some-human-rightsback-the-case-of-ildar-dadin.

Merieau, E., 2016. Thailand's deep state, royal power and the constitutional court, 1997-2015. J. Contemp. Asia 46 (3), 445-466.

Merkacheva, E., 2017. Eks-glava Arbitrazha Ivanov "vzorval bombu" na iuridicheskom forume. Moskovskii Komsomolets. May 19. http://www.mk.ru/social/2017/05/18/eksglava-arbitrazha-ivanov-vzorval-bombu-na-yuridicheskom-forume.html.

Moustafa, T., 2014. Law and courts in authoritarian regimes. Annu. Rev. Law Soc. Sci. 10, 281-299.

NewsRu.Com, 2006. Zorkin peredumal: Glava Konstiutsionnogo Suda ne khochet pereezzhat v Peterburg. NewsRu.Com. May 2. http://www.newsru.com/ russia/02may2006/ks.html.

Novosti, R.I.A., 2016. Pamfilova: Dosrochnoe golosovanie privodit k narusheniiam na vyborakh. RIA Novosti. April 21. https://ria.ru/so ciety/20160421/ 1416660844.html.

Pilipchuk, A., 2014. Pravila zhizni Nikolaia Bondaria. Pravo.Ru, December 2. https://pravo.ru/story/view/112919/.

Polit.Ru, 2011. Vladimir Pastukhov o rossiiskom pravosudii. January 20. http://polit.ru/article/2011/03/01/russianlaw.

Popova, M., 2012. Politicized Justice in Emerging Democracies: a Study of Courts in Russia and Ukraine. Cambridge University Press, New York. Popova, M., 2017. Putin-style "rule of law" & the prospects for change. Daedalus 146 (2), 64–75.

Posner, R.A., 1995. Overcoming Law. Harvard University Press, Cambridge, MA.

Svobodnaia Pressa, 2011. General Ovchinskii: Menia «ushli» za kitaiskuiu kontrabandu [General Ovchinsky: I Was "let Go" for Chinese Smuggling]. Svobodnaia Pressa. March 15. http://www.tks.ru/reviews /2011/03/15/02.

Ross, C., 2010. Sub-national elections and the development of semi-authoritarian regimes. In: Cameron Ross, C., Gelman, V. (Eds.), The Politics of Subnational Authoritarianism in Russia. Routledge, London, pp. 189–208.

Rossiiskaia gazeta, 2011. Opredelenie Konstitutsionnogo Suda Rossiiskoi Federatsii 8-O-P of January 18, 2011. Rossiiskaia Gazeta. February 24. https://rg.ru/ 2011/02/24/ks-opredelenie-dok.html.

Rossiiskaia gazeta, 2014. Opredelenie Konstitutsionnogo Suda Rossiiskoi Federatsii 1567-O of July 17, 2014. Rossiiskaia Gazeta. August 1. https://rg.ru/2014/ 08/01/opredelenie-dok.html.

Rossiiskaia gazeta, 2015. Postanovlenie Konstitutsionnogo Suda Rossiiskoi Federatsii 18-P of July 1, 2015. Rossiiskaia Gazeta. July 8. https://rg.ru/2015/07/08/ postanovlenie-dok.html.

Rossiiskaia gazeta, 2016. Postanovlenie Konstitutsionnogo Suda Rossiiskoi Federatsii 24-P of November 15, 2016. Rossiiskaia Gazeta. November 24. https:// rg.ru/2016/11/24/ konstsud-dok.html.

Rossiiskaia gazeta, 2017. Postanovlenie Konstitutsionnogo Suda Rossiiskoi Federatsii 14-P of May 23, 2017. Rossiiskaia Gazeta. June 2. https://rg.ru/2017/06/ 02/sud14-P-dok.html.

Rubin, E., 2002. Independence as a governance mechanism. In: Burbank, S.B., Friedman, B. (Eds.), Judicial Independence at the Crossroads: an Interdisciplinary Approach. SAGE Publications, Inc., Thousand Oaks, CA, pp. 56-100.

Russian Constitutional Court, 2016. Sud'i Konstitutsionnogo Suda Rossiiskii Federatsii (Judges of the Russian Constitutional Court of the Russian Federation). http://www.ksrf.ru/ru/Info/Judges/Pages/default.aspx.

Russian Constitutional Court, 2017. Informatsionno-analisticheskii otchet ob ispolnenii reshenii Konstitutsionnogo Suda RF v 2017 godu (Informationalanalytical Report on the Implementation of the Decisions of the Constitutional Court of the Russian Federation). http://www.ksrf.ru/ru/Info/Maintenance/Informationks/Pages/default.aspx.

Russian Constitutional Court, 2018. Statistika po obrashcheniiam v Konstitutsionnyi Sud Rossiiskoi Federatsii (Statistics on Petitions to the Constitutional Court of the Russian Federation). http://www.ksrf.ru/ru/Petition/Pages/StatisticDef.aspx.

Sakwa, R., 2011. The Crisis of Russian Democracy: the Dual State, Factionalism, and the Medvedev Succession. Cambridge University Press, New York.

Sanchez-Urribarri, R.A., 2011. Courts between democracy and hybrid authoritarianism: evidence from the Venezuelan Supreme Court. Law Soc. Inq. 36 (4), 854–884.

Sheinis, V., 2016. Konstitutsionnyi sud v politiko-pravovoi sisteme Rossiiskogo gosudarstva. Vestnik obshchestvennogo mneniia. Dannye. Analiz. Diskussii 1-2 (122), 15–32.

Sivitskii, V., 2015. Vozvrashchenie Konstitutsionnogo Suda Rossiiskoi Federatsii k otsenke konstitutsionnosti normy. Zhurnal konstitutsionnogo pravosudiia 2, 10–15.

Sobesednik, 2009. Sudia Kononov: Nezavisimykh sudei v Rossii net. Sobesednik. October 27. https://sobesednik.ru/politics/kononov-sb-41-09.

Solomon Jr., P.H., 2004. Judicial power in Russia: through the prism of administrative justice. Law Soc. Rev. 38 (3), 549–582.

Solomon Jr., P.H., 2007. Courts and judges in authoritarian regimes. World Polit. 60 (1), 122-145.

Solomon Jr., P.H., 2015. Law and courts in authoritarian states. In: Wright, J.D. (Ed.), International Encyclopedia of the Social and Behaivoral Sciences, second ed., 13. Elsevier, Oxford, pp. 427–434.

Soyler, M., 2013. Informal institutions, forms of state and democracy: the Turkish deep state. Democratization 20 (2), 310–334.

Sputnik News, 2012. Medvedev scolds government for inaction on court rulings. Sputnik News. November 19. https://sputniknews.com/russia/20121119177585630/.

Strashun, B., 2008. Problemy realizatsii konstitutsii. Konstitutsionnyi vestnik 1 (19), 57–61, 2008.

Trochev, A., 2008. Judging Russia: the Role of the Constitutional Court in Russian Politics 1990–2006. Cambridge University Press, New York.

Trochev, A., 2009. All appeals lead to Strasbourg? Unpacking the impact of the european court of human rights on Russia. Demokratizatsiya 17 (2), 145–178.

Trochev, A., 2016. Regulating judges in Russia's dual state: between constitutional and administrative regimes. In: Devlin, R., Dodek, A. (Eds.), Regulating Judges: beyond Independence and Accountability. Edward Elgar Publishing, Cheltenham, UK, pp. 349–371.

Trochev, A., 2017. The Russian constitutional court and the Strasbourg court: judicial pragmatism in a dual state. In: M€alksoo, L., Benedek, W. (Eds.), Russia and the European Court of Human Rights: the Strasbourg Effect. Cambridge University Press, Cambridge, pp. 125–149.

Trochev, A., Solomon, P.H., 2004. Courts and federalism in Putin's Russia. In: Reddaway, P., Orttung, R.W. (Eds.), Dynamics of Russian Politics: Putin's Reform of Federal-regional Relations, 2. Rowman & Littlefield, Lanham, MD, pp. 91–122.

Tushnet, M., 2015. Authoritarian constitutionalism. Cornell Law Rev. 100 (2), 391–461.

Vaipan, G., 2014. Acquiescence affirmed, its limits left undefined: the markin judgment and the pragmatism of the Russian constitutional court vis-a-vis the european court of human rights. Russian Law Journal 2 (3), 130–140.

Vedomosti, 2005. Peterburgskaia ssylka: Konstitutsionnym Sudom ukrepiat prestizh vtoroi stolitsy. Vedomosti. December 21. http://www.ksrf.ru/RU/PRESS-SRV/SMI/Pages/ViewItem.aspx?ParamId¼1127.

Vedomosti, 2016. Zorkin vystupaet protiv obedineniia Konstitutsionnogo Suda s Verkhovnym. Vedomosti. December 6. https://www.vedomosti.ru/politics/news/2016/12/06/668391-predsedatel-konstitutsionnogo.

Vedomosti, 2018. Zorkin stal nezamenimym dlia Kremlia. Vedomosti. January 31. https://www.vedomosti.ru/politics/articles/2018/01/31/749494-zorkinstal-nezamenimim-dlya-kremlya.

VTsIOM, 2006. Konstitutionnyi Sud: organ vazhnyi, no maloizvestnyi. VTsIOM, 395. February 16. https://wciom.ru/index.php?id¼236&uid¼2722.

VTsIOM, 2018. Pravookhranitelnye i sudebnye organy: reiting zashchitnikov prav i svobod. VTsIOM, 3667. May 22. https://wciom.ru/index.php?id=236&uid=9110.

Wilson, E. (Ed.), 2016. The Dual State: Parapolitics, Carl Schmitt and the National Security Complex. Routledge, London.

Zagretdinov, V., 2015. Konstitutsionnoe orudie politicheskoi borby. Sravnitelnoe Konstitutsionnoe Obozrenie 5, 104–119.

Zorkin, V., 2018. Pravo v tsifrovom mire. Rossiiskaia Gazeta. 29 May. https://rg.ru/2018/05/29/zorkin-zadacha-gosudarstva-priznavat-i-zashchishchatcifrovye-prava-grazhdan.html.

Zygar, M., 2016. All the Kremlin's Men: inside the Court of Vladimir Putin. Public Affairs, New York.

The Evolution of Policing in Post-Soviet Russia: Paternalism versus Service in Police Officers' Understanding of their Role

Olga Semukhina
Department of Criminal Justice, Tarleton State University, USA

This paper examines two interrelated issues: the role of police as an institution of Russian society and their role during the past 25 years. This research is based on a series of in-depth interviews conducted by the author in 2014–2016 with former and current police officers in three Russian cities. The paper traces changes in the perceived institutional roles of the Russian police by comparing police officers' views during three periods: early through mid-1990s, late-1990s through mid-2000s, and mid-2000s through 2010s. The study reports that, during the early period, Russian police were disfranchised from the state and this abandonment was a source of institutional identity crisis for law enforcement officers who remained on the job. This process was coupled with high levels of job dissatisfaction and the overall feeling of "abandonment" of police by the state. At the same time, it was during this post-Soviet period, when ideas of policing as a service to the society were introduced and sometimes entertained among the professional circles of police officers and other government officials. Furthermore, this period was marked by continuous, though often sporadic, institutional reforms and anti-corruption measures. In the second period, the Russian police were slowly engaging back into the state-building process, which caused increased job satisfaction and better retention rates. At the same time, the second period signified a decline of the "police as service" ideology and the comeback of paternalistic views on policing. During this time, the government's efforts to reform police and anti-corruption measures became systemic and better organized. Also, in the second period, members of the civil society became more active in demanding public accountability and transparency from the Russian police. Finally, the modern period of police development presents a case in which the institutional identity of the Russian police has been clearly connected to the state's capacity. This process is coupled with increased paternalistic views among police officers and a failure of "police as a service" doctrine. In such an environment, the efforts by a maturing civil society to demand public transparency and accountability of the police are often met with hostility and anger. The paper concludes that further development of the Russian police depends on the role that they will play within the modern Russian state.

Keywords: Post-soviet police, Police occupation identity, Russian law enforcement, Evolution of policing

1. Introduction and research question

Over[1] the past 25 years, Russia has experienced tremendous political, economic, and social changes. A political transformation began in the early 1990s with the dismantling of the autocratic Soviet state and continued into the late 1990s and early 2000s with the creation of a hybrid political regime that combined elements of democracy and authoritarianism. The mid-2000s to 2010s saw the progressive decay of democratic elements when Russia's political development took a turn toward "competitive authoritarianism." The current political regime is often described as a stable political configuration in which "democratic institutions are viewed as the principle means of obtaining and exercising political authority, but incumbents violate democratic rules so often and to such an extent, that the regime fails to meet conventional minimum standards for democracy" (Levitsky and Way, 2002).

The introduction of free-market elements into the Soviet-planned economy in the early 1990s created tremendous opportunities for the Communist Party nomenclature and its affiliates to misappropriate and aggregate state-owned assets to create a new social class of "oligarchs" (Favarel-Garrigues, 2002; Volkov et al., 2012).

The 1990s in Russia were marked by a violent redistribution of these assets among competing oligarchs, while the country's

---

1   In this article "paternalistic view" refers to the officers' views that society is incapable of any crime reduction on its own and needs to be supervised and protected by police from dangerous offenders.

economy experienced a lack of real economic gains, hyperinflation, growing internal and external debts, and budget deficits (IMF, 2011; Rutkevitch, 1998).[2] At this time, the life savings of most Soviet citizens were lost through the significant depreciation of the currency. As a result, over one-third of the Russian population (33.5%) in 1992 was living below the poverty level. These numbers remained at an average of 25.0% through the 1990s (GKS, 2018c).[3]

In 1998, the Russian economy experienced a serious financial crisis resulting in a dramatic devaluation of Russian currency and the government's defaulting on its debt, which further exacerbated the impoverishment of the Russian population (Pinto et al., 2005). However, by the early 2000s, Russia posted a stable increase in annual GDP rates, which was associated with continuous growth in the industry sector, healthy levels of foreign investments, and growing internal consumption. Much of this growth was attributed to the sharp increase in crude oil prices in the early 2000s and the "stabilization" of the political regime under newly elected President Putin (Cooper, 2009). Russian economic growth was interrupted by the global financial crisis of 2008 and the consequent sharp decline in crude oil prices.

The 2008–2009 period was marked by a significant loss of foreign investments and a dramatic decline in the annual GDP growth[4] (Aganbegyan, 2010). Further increase in oil prices during 2010–2013 provided Russia with some opportunities for economic recovery and modest growth of GDP. However, the new decline in oil prices in 2014 impeded further economic growth and caused further devaluation of the currency (Gurvich, 2017). Economic sanctions imposed by the U.S. and European Union since 2014 placed an additional burden on Russia's economic development (Gurvich and

---

2   According to the International Monetary Fund, gross domestic product based on purchasing-power-parity (PPP) valuation of country GDP in current international dollars constituted $900 billion in 1998, compared with almost $1200 billion in 1992.
3   GKS is an abbreviation for Russian State Statistics Committee; or Государственный Комитет Статистики
4   In 2008–2009, Russia lost over $250 billion in foreign investments, and the average annual GDP growth for 2009–2013 is estimated at 1% based on World Bank's data (World Bank, 2018).

Prilepskiy, 2016). Since 2014, the Russian economy has been described in terms of recession or even as "stagflation" with a modest outlook of future recovery and growth (Russell, 2015; WorldBank, 2018).

1.1. Research questions and theoretical framework

The dramatic economic and political changes had a direct impact on Russian society, including the police, as represented by the Ministry of Internal Affairs (MVD). Some of these institutional changes within the Russian police have been documented in the extant literature. A growing body of literature focuses on the issues related to the organizational changes within the MVD associated with various "reforms" of law enforcement in Russia (Beck, 2013; Beck and Robertson, 2009; Galeotti, 2012; Gall, 2011; Kosals, 2010; Paneyak et al., 2012). A number of researchers addressed the role that MVD plays in Russian politics and the state-building process (Galeotti, 2004; Gudkov et al., 2004; Taylor, 2014). A significant number of studies exists on the Russian police's struggles with abuse of power and corruption, and the effect on the police's ability to maintain public order (Borzov, 2006; Committee against Torture, 2006; Dubova and Kosals, 2012; Gilinskiy, 2011; INDEM, 2002).[5]

Finally, many studies explore the issues of public and police interactions and cooperation, public trust and satisfaction with the Russian police, and the role of media in public views on police (Andreev, 2005; Beck and Chistyakova, 2002; Bondarenko, 2006; Cherkasov, 2006; Dzutsev, 2010; Ermolaev, 2009; Reynolds et al., 2008; Uidriks and Reenen, 2005; Zernova, 2012).

What has been missing from the literature is the research on the evolution of the police's institutional identity and an understanding of whether the changes in the Russian political and economic landscape have affected the police officers' understanding of their role in Russian society and the role of police institutions. Most existing literature on police officers' views is focused on measuring the psychological fitness of these officers (Bobrova, 2005; Borisova,

---

5   INDEM stands for Information Science for Democracy Foundation.

1998; Borodavko, 2005; Brazhenskaya, 2011; Gavrilin, 2001), their views and experiences with corruption (Abdrashitov, 2009; Beck and Lee, 2001; Kolennikova et al., 2002), their knowledge and understanding of the rule of law (Berezin, 2011; Curfman, 1997; Korneeva, 2008; Novikova, 2005), and their views on job satisfaction and problems within the police service (Adyan, 2006; Bashkirova, 2008; Ermolaev and Verem'eva, 2007; Galkin, 2001; Gladarev, 2011).

This study examines police officers' occupational identity in Russia by looking at how the officers describe their duties and service in relation to three historic periods: early to late 1990s, late 1990s through late 2000s, and late 2000s through the current date. These selected time periods are one of the most common ways that Russian pro-government literature describes the development of law enforcement in the post-Soviet period (Grinenko, 2017; Polyakov, 2018; Sheparneva, 2015). This periodization is not without criticism. Many studies use different time periods that may be better justified by the development of Russian state, reforms of the Ministry of Internal Affairs, and changes in the nature of Russian police style (Semukhina and Reynolds, 2013; Taylor, 2014; Volkov et al., 2012). Because this paper is based on police officers' recollection of their service, I decided to use the official periodization that these officers are most familiar with, even though such classification is not consistent with some literature.

The study is based on Pino and Wiatrowski's research that defines the nature of policing through the relationship that police build with the community they serve and protect (2006). Pino and Wiatrowski emphasize that the main feature of democratic policing, especially in transitional societies, is the police's ability to build and sustain social capital in their partner community (2006). In contrast, the non-democratic police operate under the pre-determined mandate by the government where the community is treated as an object of its enforcement through both the benevolent paternalism and/or direct support of the political regime (Pino and Wiatrowski, 2006). This paper is also informed by Manning's (2003) phenomenological research on policing that brings together experiences that constitute democratic and non-democratic police practices. Manning's research warns us against a simplistic understanding of the police's occupational identity; instead, it proposes that officers' identification is a complex symbolic interaction of institutional and socio-cultural dimensions contextualized in the society it functions (Manning, 2010).

2. Methodology

The present study is based on 43 semi-structured, in-depth interviews with current and former police officers from three different cities in Russia conducted by the author in 2014–2017. These interviewees were chosen using a snowball convenience method that, considering the difficulties of getting information from Russian police (Mccarthy, 2015), is probably the best way to collect meaningful data on the subject. Nevertheless, because of this limitation, the findings of this paper cannot be extrapolated on the entire population of Russian police.

However, following the standards of qualitative research, these interviews were conducted until the point of saturation, such as the repetition of the same patterns, which ensures that findings represent independent and stable patterns of behavior and explore unique phenomenon (O'Reilly and Parker, 2013; Holstein and Gubrium, 1995). From 43 interviews, 10 officers spoke about the 1990s, 12 officers reported on the 2000s, and 21 officers were interviewed on the 2010s. For future research, it's important to increase the number of interviewees to provide nuanced and representative picture of police officers' identity in Russia.

The three cities are located in geographically distinct areas of Russia (central, southern, and Siberian regions), two cities represent large metropolitan areas with over one million residents, and one city is a midsized regional center. Interviewed police officers came from a variety of units within the Russian police and range in rank and experiences of service.[6] The choice of cities and police units was intentional to provide as much contextual variety as possible. This

---

6   See Appendix 1 for more information on the interviewees.

was done to avoid any patterns in data that are idiosyncratic of only one location or one specific police function. To preserve the anonymity of the interviewees, the locations are not named.

To understand the changing nature of the police's identity, the paper uses a retrospective interview method that asks the respondents to recall only one specific time period from their career (Freedman et al., 1988).[7] All interviews were conducted face to face with handwritten notes taken by the author verbatim when possible. A summary of the interviewed police officers' information is presented in Appendix 1.

The paper is organized as follows: the findings of each period are discussed in a separate section followed by implications and a conclusion.

2.1. Russian police institution during the 1990s

The period following the dissolution of the Soviet Union was arguably one of the most challenging times for police institutions in Russia. Starting in 1992, the Ministry of Interior Affairs (MVD) experienced significant delays in salary payments, with some regions reporting up to 12 months of delays to their rank and file officers (Gonyukhov and Gorobtsov, 2002).

Moreover, in the early 1990s, crime rates dramatically increased because of deteriorating economic conditions, which were exacerbated by further development of organized crime (Glinkina, 2002; Shelley, 2000). The number of registered crimes grew from 1243 per 100,000 residents in 1990 to 1886 per 100,000 residents in 1993 (GKS, 2018b) and then quadrupled between 1991 and 1996 (Association for Criminology, 1997). Serious crimes, violent crimes, and crimes committed by organized groups were leading offenses

---

[7] In most cases, the respondents were asked about a time period immediately preceding their departure from the service. Such a time anchor is known to provide more accurate recollections from the respondents. No respondents were asked to compare two or more time periods to avoid what is known as a "transfusion of memory effect," when recollections from one period of time are transferred to a different time period in the process of interview (Freedman et al., 1988). However, some respondents choose to provide comparisons on their own that I accepted.

in the 1990s (Association for Criminology, 1997). According to official statistics, the total number of serious crimes in Russia tripled from 513,910 in 1993 to 1,633,367 in 1995 (GKS, 2011c). The same upward trend could be observed for offenses committed by organized crime groups (GKS, 2018a), repeat offenders (GKS, 2011a),[8] and drug-related crimes (GKS, 2011b).[9]

In addition, the 1990s were a time of constant organizational changes within the MVD system. New agencies were rapidly created, changed, renamed, and eliminated, as police institutions were trying to adjust to the changing social and economic landscape (Mulukaev et al., 2005). These changes included the creation of separate criminal and public-order police, which signified the division between federally funded and locally funded police units (President of Russia,1993b), the creation of an internal investigation department (MVD, 1994; MVD, 1996), and the re-naming and revising of the passport service functions (Cabinet of Ministers, 1993), the juvenile delinquency service (President of Russia, 1993a), and the traffic police service (Gonyukhov and Gorobtsov, 2002; MVD, 1998).

Deteriorating conditions of police services and increasing crime rates caused a massive exodus of qualified cadres from police institutions. Up to 20% of all police job openings remained vacant by 1998 (Galkin, 2001), and over 70% of all police officers had less than five years of experience by 1996 (Adyan, 2006). Throughout the 1990s, police officers demonstrated low job satisfaction, with 41.6% officially saying they regretted becoming officers, and over 60% reported a desire to leave police service as soon as they could find another job (Kikot, 2002). Almost 50% of students of police academies and universities also reported no intent to enter the service despite their contractual obligations with MVD (Botov, 2001). Moreover, during the 1990s, Russian police gained a reputation for

---

8   According to the data provided by GKS, the number of offenses committed by repeat offenders grew by more than 1.5 times from 274,339 in 1991 to 459,602 in 1995.
9   According to the data provided by GKS, the number of drug-related crimes almost doubled from 53,169 in 1993 to 96,762 in 1995.

being corrupt and abusive, thus causing significant levels of public distrust and dissatisfaction (Reynolds et al., 2008).

2.2. Decoupling from the state in 1990s

Most interviewees remember the 1990s with sorrow, anger, and frustration. For those police officers who already served, the early 1990s were particularly painful, as they were dealing with the loss of their social status. An investigator who had worked in the Soviet police since 1984 described his feelings as follows: "It was very tough ... everything was changing ... most difficult part was to become a *ment* ... *musor*[10]... from respected Soviet militiamen to a hated by everyone and despised Russian police officer ... I did not sign up for that ... I left service in 1993 ... I couldn't be a ment anymore" (PO#22). The anger and frustration were often related to the lack of funding and deteriorating conditions of service: "They [government] stopped paying money ... I had to buy my own paper to record interrogations ... my grandma's pension was my only source of income for a good year or so ... luckily, I wasn't married yet ... I don't know how people with families survived" (PO#40). Much of the anger and frustration were targeted at perpetrators, victims, and growing crime rates

> New crimes were committed every day ... I didn't even heard of some of them when I was in the police academy ... racketeering ... kidnapping ... this staff did not exist in the Soviet Union ... and then in 1990s it was just coming and coming every day ... at some point I started telling victims to take their complaints back ... it was just impossible for me to keep up with this (PO#17).

Extreme conditions of service and heavy workloads created an incentive for massive violations, ranging from simple bribery to a full-blown participation in organized crime. Here is how a patrol policeman describes his typical "additional income " activity in 1990s: "We were 'supervising' a few hot spots (*tochki*) at the market ... every Sunday night, I would get some money from three of four vendors (*chelnoki*) ... and give it to my boss ... he will give me my

---

10 Pejorative term for soviet police officers used originally by convicted persons only but becoming a mainstream term in early 1990s.

share back " (PO#11). The poor service conditions and pervasive culture of corruption were often used by police officers to justify their violations of law. "I had my share of 'favors' ... it was easy to do since the system was in such a chaos ... I locked a guy for a few months [in preventive detention] because someone asked me to ... I had a number of cases where I terminated the investigation as a personal favor to someone ... everyone did it in the 1990s ... we had to survive in that mess ... I did it, too" (PO#3).

Though the lack of resources and corrupt practices were repeated themes among my interviewees, arguably more frustration came from what was often described as "neglect or abandonment by the state." Here is a good summary of this frustration by experienced police officer: "The state just left us ... we were left to die fighting with organized crime ... the government was busy building this new capitalism ... they forgot about us " (PO#22). The "neglect" described by the interviewees clearly indicates that a police officer's professional identity was tied closely to the Soviet police and Russian state, and dismantling of the state had a devastating effect on police self-assessment: "We are part of the state machine ... we are state people [*gosudartsvennye ludi*] ... in the 1990s, the old state was in shackles, and the new one was not built yet ... they [government] left us to die " (PO#9). The unclear identity of a new state reflected on the vague and often unexplainable purpose of police institutions at that time. "When I started service in Soviet times, I had a clear understanding of what I am doing ... we were protecting the Soviet state by fighting crimes ... when the new times came ... honestly, I did not know what my role was anymore ... what used to be a crime of speculation became a respectable business ... I wasn't sure what I was fighting against and more importantly why" (PO#4).

The lack of clear institutional purpose and identity was most frustrating for older police officers who served as Soviet police. This frustration caused many to leave the service (PO#25). Younger officers who entered the police force in the early 1990s were much less focused on the unclear institutional identity, as their motivations were mostly opportunistic or survival-oriented. Here is how an interviewee, who was a young investigator in 1990s, explains it: "Purpose of police ... you are kidding me ... I did not have time to think about it ... I had to survive in that nightmare ... feed my family and not get killed ... that was my purpose" (PO#13). Another police officer with a similar background elaborates on his experience: "I came to work for the police when there was no ideology, no asking why we are doing this job and who do we serve ... it was just a job that I could find after six years in the architecture school ... because nobody wanted to build anything, but people were still committing crimes" (PO#14).

Most of my interviewees acknowledged that the 1990s opened new channels of communication between police and society. Glasnost declared that perestroika provided some crime-related data and allowed police officers to communicate with media (Gonyukhov and Gorobtsov, 2002). In June 1988, after almost 50 years of prohibition, the Communist Party removed the ban on publication of crime-related statistics (Ivanov and Iliyina, 1991). The first official crime-related statistics was published in 1990 and contained almost 150 pages of data (MVD, 1990). Most regional MVD offices did not have units related to public communication but were prompted to create one in 1990–1991 as the requests for interviews and press-releases from media continued to mount (MVD, 2013).

Using provided data and new access to police officers, newspapers in the early 1990s began to publish frequent articles related to emerging crime trends.[11] These publications often contained harsh criticisms of police and their work (Luschai, 1990; Lukyanchenko and Binev, 1990).

These changes were not necessarily viewed as positive by the most of my interviewees. For many experienced officers, it was a source of frustration. For newly coming officers, it was mostly a source of income. An older police investigator, who had eight years

---

11 A quick search of leading newspaper archive *Izvestiya* for 1987 returned only 3 articles for "crime." However, the number of articles in 1990 was 302, and it continued to grow in 1991 (495 articles) and 1992 (468 articles). Data retrieved from archive of newspaper *Izevestiya*.

of service in the Soviet police, explained: "It was unusual for me at first ... when I started in the 1980s, nobody talked to journalists about cases or communicated with anyone unless it was sanctioned by *partorg*[12]... then all of a sudden, the flood gates opened, and media was chasing officers for hot facts ... what good would it do ... they did not care about helping us ... they just wanted to make money" (PO#22). Another younger detective elaborated upon his opportunistic view of media at the time: "I had a deal with a couple of media outlets ... I will give them some details about juicy crimes ... they would pay me a small fee ... it wasn't often but I had some money from them" (PO#17).

The 1990s saw the proliferation of various NGOs, many of which were supported by larger international organizations. Some large foreign NGOs, such as Soros Foundation, McArthur Foundation, and Ford Foundation, attempted to build relations with the local police institutions in order to provide education and support. Most of such training was conducted by local branches of these international NGOs, for example, by Open Society Institute in Russia, Moscow branch of McArthur Foundation, and others. My interviewees did not find these interactions particularly interesting, as new information was presented by NGOs, including an idea of community policing and was often overshadowed by daily challenges or simply resisted as contradictory to the previous training. As in cases with media interaction, the contacts with NGOs were often met with either frustration or seen as an opportunity for personal gain. An officer in a leadership position at the time of service recalls

> It is hard to imagine now, but I actually went to a number of those trainings with some foundations ... I think they were sponsored by Ford or Soros ... we did not think about these meetings as being dangerous[13]... back then, it

---

12   Partorg is an acronym for a leader of a Communist Party primary organization imbedded in every company, enterprise and institution of the Soviet society.
13   Since 2015, many-foreign affiliated NGOs such as McArthur Foundation and National Endowment for Democracy have been branded "undesirable organizations " by a new law in Russia, and their local offices were forced to close. The Russian government argued that such organizations were "foreign spies" which try to undermine Russia's national security, defense and constitutional

was all new to us. I thought some ideas were good ... some bad ... honestly, it was all so abstract to me ... and what I had to deal with on the daily basis was so different ... I didn't really see how this can help me or my people (PO#9).

Another officer in a leadership role discussed his resistance of new ideas that challenged traditional roles of police institutions: "I was required by my command to go to some of these meetings ... they wanted to talk about some garbage ... like police being a service ... maybe it worked in other countries ... I don't know how these ideas would work here ... I know I was there to help the government to fight crime ... that is what police is for" (PO#37).

A younger police officer provides his sobering account on motivation to participate in training: "I volunteered to go to some training with these NGOs because I heard they had nice food and took some people for a trip to Finland ... I didn't listen to what they said ... I was so sleepy after a double shift ... but I remember they had good tea and cookies, which was a big deal back then" (PO#30).

When asked about interactions with citizens and public–police cooperation, most interviewees described them in terms of fear, avoidance, and mutual alienation. One beat officer explains: "People did not want to help me ... I would walk for hours to find someone who wanted to help me ... nobody wanted to talk to police ... they were afraid of me, and it made my job so difficult ... I hated them for not helping" (PO#12). Another more experienced detective explains: "People were in survival mode, they had no time to help us, and honestly we weren't doing a great job helping them ... I don't blame people for trying to avoid us" (PO#5). Many interviewees highlighted the paternalistic expectations that police had when it came to public–police interactions: "People needed protection from crime, as a part of state we were fighting crime, so people will feel safe ... that's the type of cooperation ... people must cooperate by giving us information because we are there to protect them from danger" (PO#37).

---

order. It is generally understood that contact with these organizations by police officers nowadays will be threatening to the officer's future career (HRW, 2017).

In sum, the 1990s are marked by the abrupt and painful decoupling of the Russian police institution from the state. This process left the police with an unclear purpose and lack of professional values among new recruits. Poor conditions of service caused experienced officers to leave and then replacing them with more opportunistic and inexperienced cadres. These new police officers were facing tremendous challenges of skyrocketing crime rates and poor wages, which they used to justify abuses of power and corruption. The new civic society was immature and made a few attempts to shape the Russian institutional identity of the police. The sporadic interactions with the public were typified by mutual disrespect and alienation.

2.3. Police institutions during the 2000s

Russia in the 2000s is often described as a time of "stabilization", which usually refers to a slowdown of political changes and gradual economic recovery in the country (Kudrin and Gurvich, 2015). Despite these changes, until the mid-2000s, the crime rates continued to grow, with the highest crime rate per capita posted in 2006 at 2695 crimes per 100,000 residents (GKS, 2018b). However, in 2006–2010, registered crime rates started to decline with only 1566 crimes per capita registered in 2010. The proportion of serious crimes also decreased to 26% in 2010 compared with 58.8% in 2000. Dropping rates were also reported for crimes committed by organized groups (from 14.2% in 2000 to 5.5% in 2010), juvenile offenses (from 6.6% in 2000 to 3.0% in 2010), and crimes committed by intoxicated offenders (from 15.0% in 2000 to 9.0% in 2010). A slight increase in this period was registered only for crimes committed by immigrants (from 1.3% in 2000 to 1.9% in 2010). No changes were reported for crimes committed by repeated offenders, 21.0% in 2000 and 22.0% in 2010, and female offenders from 16.3% in 2000 to 15.5% in 2010 (GKS, 2011a; GKS, 2011c; GKS, 2018a).

The situation with police wages also improved; no delays in payments were reported starting in 2001 (Rybnikov and Aleksushin, 2008). During this decade, the budget for MVD increased by 30 times,[14] but so did the total number of police officers (Scherbak and Titaev, 2009). The growth in numbers was mainly due to the creation of departments at the federal district level and expansion of the central apparatus. Also, some of the budget increase was justified by newly acquired functions of MVD, for example, witness protection program and investigation of tax crimes. As a result, the average salary for rank-and-file police officers remained low with some regions reporting to pay only two minimum wages to their officers (Gladarev, 2011). The situation with job satisfaction and retention of qualified cadres remained troublesome until the mid2000s (Artem'ev, 2003).[15]

Starting from 2006, the data showed a modest increase in both job satisfaction and retention of experienced police officers (Berezin, 2011; Ermolaev and Verem'eva, 2007).

Law enforcement reforms conducted in the 1990s continued through the 2000s. One of the major legislative changes of this period was an adoption of the new Code of Criminal Procedure (CPC) in 2001 that heightened the expectations of quality investigations by the MVD providing for judicial approval of pre-trial detention decisions and increasing the rights of defense counsel (Fillipov, 2003). The 2000s also brought further bureaucratization of police work with a number of new detailed regulations mushrooming in the units of MVD, including instructions on employment conditions for police officers (MVD, 1999), work at juvenile delinquency

---

14 According to Ministry of Finances of Russia, in 2001, 35, 894, 526,500 rubles were allocated for the agencies of interior affairs. In 2012, the MVD budget was estimated at 1,103,000,000,000 rubles. (Ministry of Finances, 2012).
15 According to Artemev, the exodus of qualified cadres from MVD continued in 2002, whereas the numbers of employees with less than three years of experience grew from 21.5% in 2000 to 24.5% in 2002, and the numbers of employees with more up to 10 years of experience decreased from 50.9% in 2000 to 50.6% in 2002. However, the educational level of employees grew from 36.4% in 2000 to 41.3% of employees with higher legal education (not considering the low-rank police officers). 16
Though there are no absolute numbers, the International Crime Victimization Survey conducted by the United Nations Interregional Crime Research Institute, suggest that consistent levels of public trust and satisfaction measured below 50% are labeled as "low trust and satisfaction. "

agencies (MVD, 2000), work on the registration and review of citizens' complaints about crime (MVD, 2003a), the seizure of citizens and detention at the police precinct (MVD, 2003b), financial audit of businesses (MVD, 2005), issuing licenses for private detectives (MVD, 2006), and conducting internal investigations into the misbehavior of police officers (MVD, 2008).

Despite these organization and legal changes, the public trust and satisfaction with the police remained low in the 2000s.16 Independent representative studies found that public satisfaction was estimated at 24.5% in 2000 (ICVS, 2000) and 27% in

2010 (FOM, 2010). Similarly, independent researchers reported that only 11.5% of Russians trusted the police in 2001 (Andreev, 2005) and 24% trusted them in 2006 (Gudkov and Dubin, 2006). Government-affiliated research centers (WCIOM, FOM, RO-MIR) and authors employed by the Ministry of Interior Affairs published higher numbers for public trust and satisfaction of police (for example, 43% in 2005 (FOM, 2005), and 40% in 2007 (WCIOM, 2007)). However, these numbers need to be taken critically since pro-government poll organizations are known to manipulate their methodology to obtain desirable results (Public Verdict Fund, 2014; Masyuk, 2015). When various studies are examined in aggregate, there is no apparent improvement in public opinion of 2000s when compared with the 1990s (Semukhina and Reynolds, 2013).

As a result of low public trust, the majority of Russians continue to avoid contacts with police, including crime reporting (Semukhina, 2014). The public also reported continuous victimization by police from both physical abuse and solicitation of bribes (Gilinskiy, 2011; Gerber and Mendelson, 2008).

In the mid-2000s, MVD reported a decrease in the official crime rates; however, public fears of crime remained high (Mazaev et al., 2003). Many researchers argued that the actual crime rates continued to grow in Russia throughout the 2000s, while the decline in registered crime resulted from underreported crimes and unlawful practice by police to reject victims' criminal complaints (Inshakov, 2007).

2.4. Searching for new identity?

"Mild improvement" and "strengthening of the state" were repeated themes during my interviews regarding the 2000s. The changes were often framed in terms of police–state relations: Officers were looking for getting back some attention of the state and compared their experiences to the painful "abandonment" by the state in the 1990s.

This is how one police officer summarizes it: "The state all of a sudden remembered that they had the police ... somewhere in 2004–2005, I received my first decent salary ... they also gave me some money for extra hours that I worked ... it was first time in a long period when I finally was not ashamed to bring my salary back home" (PO#27). Another officer discussed the responsiveness of the state to the needs of police as an indicator of getting back the state's attention: "In 2006 I got my first computer, I asked for it for so long I could not believe it at first ... they [government] were no longer ignoring our requests for patrol cars and forensic equipment" (PO#10).

But not all the changes were related to improved funding and resource availability; some interviewees noticed nonmonetary signs of "the state's attention." One of the interviewees recalls: "When I saw President Putin thanking police officers during his end of the year speech, I felt things were getting better ... we were no longer ignored" (PO#6). Another officer explained a personal sign that showed "the state's respect": "After we closed a very difficult case in 2007, I and some other officers received personalized handguns ... it was signed by the minister ... and that had never happened before, though I investigated many difficult cases ... they put an article about me in the local newspaper, and I finally felt good about staying in the police service" (PO#31).

But the increased attention of the state in the 2000s came with a caveat: Limited attempts by government to curb police abuse of power and corruption. While the interviewees mostly agreed that such state oversight was needed and justified, many felt that anticorruption measures were applied arbitrarily and often were politically motivated. Here is how one of the officers explains the anti-corruption campaign in 2003: "This whole thing of 'werewolves in the epaulets'[16] was concocted by Gryzlov to show how our government fights police corruption ... what these officers did was the same as what all of us did back then ... but they were chosen as scapegoats ... many of us felt relief, it wasn't us" (PO#2).

Other less publicized attempts to curb corruption were often seen by interviewees as personal retaliation rather than a systematic government attempts to fight corruption: "We had a guy in my department who got publicly caught with some money ... it's not like he was the only one ... but since he got caught, they [internal affairs] wanted to make an example ... most of us believed he just did not share [the bribe] with his boss" (PO#15).

The decade of the 2000s also brought growing public attention to police work[17] and officers responded primarily with resentment and anger. Here is one typical example of such reaction: "

> All these activists, they started coming to me ... asking questions ... taking pictures of my officers on the streets ... implying that something illegal was going on ... who did they think they are ... we are state people ... we face the danger everyday ... what good would it make when some private person meddles with our police business ... there are appropriate government agencies that supervise us ... this is not a job for the dilettantes (PO#31).

As the civil society was developing (Uhlin, 2006), the 2000s saw a number of new NGOs that were actively trying to engage police in various community initiatives.[18] According to my interviews, the success or failure of these interactions depended primarily on the local conditions and persons involved; there was little government oversight or uniform guidelines as to what were the acceptable

---

16 This term was used first by the Minister of MVD Gryzlov to describe over 700 of Moscow police officers who took bribes and abused defendants in order to manipulate statistical reports.
17 For example, see the project "Open Police" by the Committee on Civil Initiatives or Report by Russian NGOs on monitoring police violations of Convention against torture 2012 (Doklad, 2012).
18 Some examples include conferences with leaders of local communities, NGOs lawyers and police officers, public monitoring of police detention center, and publication of information on police violations and online consultations (Moscow Helsinki Group, 2018; Public Verdict, 2018).

forms of interaction and which were the organizations allowed for partnering. Taylor and Robertson in their research describe a few successful partnerships between members of civic society and local police (Robertson, 2005; Taylor, 2006).

> My interviewees also brought some examples: "I had a guy who came to me and said they wanted to volunteer when searching for missing people ... I thought, why not? ... we always needed more people when there was a missing person ... so we did work together for some time" (PO#15). The willingness of interaction with NGOs often depended on their ability to learn information that would otherwise remain unavailable to the public: "I had bunch of them [NGOs] showing up with various ideas, like they wanted to talk to the detained and observe the conditions of cells in the precinct ... I told them to forget about it ... then there were others who wanted to meet with beat police officers and discuss how to improve local safety in their yards ... I told them good ... this could help us" (PO#41).

Many NGOs active in 2000s were also involved in research on public-police relations, police corruption, and reforms.[19] These organizations conducted extensive empirical studies and published reports that often questioned the purpose and identity of Russian police. Findings from independent NGOs often included a discussion of community policing and examined police as a public good and service to the citizens (INDEM, 2007; Public Verdict Fund, 2010).

> These reports were strikingly different from the official research conducted by MVD and its affiliated organization, which tended to avoid uncomfortable question of police purpose and identity. Sadly, little of this independent research was ever known to my interviewees: "Ministry has its own surveys ... that's what mattered to us ... the boss will read these [reports] out laud, and we will learn what we needed ... who knows what these NGOs said and why " (PO#2). Crime-fighting paternalistic rhetoric appears to dominate the official police ideology at this time: "I went to some roundtable discussions with these people [NGOs] in 2006; they were talking about police offering services ... I told them we were not servants ... we represented the government ... we represented the president ... we fought the crime ... this idea of service was ridiculous" (PO#41).

In sum, the 2000s brought better funding and resources to the Russian police, which were often interpreted as drawing attention to

---

19 For example, these NGOs included INDEM, Public Verdict, and Committee against Torture.

what the state paid to its police institutions. This reconciliation was comforting for many officers not simply because it provided better working conditions but also because it gave police institutions at least some affiliation and identity. Though attention of the state was flattering, it came with a price of increasing state control over corruptive and abusive behavior. Nevertheless, the deterring effect of anticorruption measures was rather minimal because most police officers saw these attempts as politically motivated or simply arbitrary. The growing and maturing civic society attempted to engage police in various activities with some partial success, but these attempts were not consistent and carried little weight. Less successful were attempts of NGOs to enforce some measures of police accountability. Police officers were deeply troubled by this idea as they saw the civil society as an object of their surveillance rather than an equal partner, not to mention of being a society's servant.

2.5. Police institution in the 2010s

The 2010 decade began with yet another police reform conducted by President Medvedev in response to growing public demand for better police services and prompted by a massacre committed by Officer Evsyukov.[20] As a result of this reorganization, police received substantial increase in wages and benefits but lost 20% of their staff (Gall, 2011).

The reform called for a review of all police files to cleanse the "bad apples" and provided for further centralization of all police funding at the federal level. Medvedev's top-down reform of police was met with public skepticism with only 16%e19% of Russians believing in a positive outcome (Semukhina and Reynolds, 2013). Many researchers questioned whether the true purpose of reform had anything to do with corruption or changing the nature of policing in Russia (Solidarnost, 2010). Instead, it was precipitated from drastic public dissatisfaction with the police and the need of

---

20 Officer Evsyukov was the head of the district police precinct who, in 2009, walked into a supermarket and fired at the customers. He killed 2 people and injured 7. The massacre was captured by surveillance camera and publicly disseminated (Vesti, 2009).

political elites to reassure their control over the MVD security apparatus (Oxford Analytica, 2010). The police officers were rather skeptical about the outcomes of this reform (Savchenko, 2011).[21] Many NGOs and research centers, including Public Verdict Fund, Political movement Solidarity, the Institute of Rule of Law of European University and the Committee on Civil Initiatives, proposed alternative plans for police reform and most of them focused on decentralization of the police force and establishment of independent regional and municipal-funded police (Public Verdict Fund, 2010). Yet none of these measures were implemented by Medvedev's government. Despite economic recession and growing deficits in the federal budget, MVD continued to enjoy a stable increase in funding during 2014-2017. Though funding growth was modest when compared with 2011, it allowed MVD to provide rank-and-file officers with above-average wages and substantial benefits (RBC, 2017).

The registered crime rate remained stable throughout 2010-2016, with 1465 crimes per capita reported in 2010 and 1426 crimes registered in 2016. The proportion of crimes committed by organized groups averaged 6.5% during this period. Rates for crimes committed by juveniles and intoxicated offenders remained unchanged (GKS, 2018b). There was no change in rates of crimes committed by illegal immigrants, with 1.8% of crimes reported in 2011, and 2.0% of crimes committed by illegal immigrants in 2016. However, there were some changes in the structure of registered crimes. The number of homicides decreased from 15,563 in 2010 to 9738 in 2017 (Procuracy of Russia, 2018). At the same time, there was an increase in drug-possession crimes (by 10.9% from 2010 to 2016) and property-related crimes (thefts and fraud by 9.5% and 16% from 2010 to 2016, accordingly) (GKS, 2018b).

During the 2010s, for the first time in almost 20 years, some surveys showed an improvement in levels of public trust of police.

---

21 According to Savchenko (2011), 48% of police officers considered the new 2011 reform a "political intrigue " and 16% reported that it was just a "PRaction. " Only 28% of officers suggested that new law was intended as a true transformation of police.

In 2013, a study ordered to All-Union Center for the Study of Public Opinion (WCIOM) by MVD reported that 46% of Russians trust their police; however, in 2017 the number of those who trusted grew to 67% according to the same research organization (WCIOM, 2017). The data provided by Levada Center in 2017, an independent research center, demonstrate a modest increase, with 46% of Russians trusting police in 2017 (Levada, 2017b). Nevertheless, this number is also an improvement when compared with only 35% of those who trust the police in 2011, according to the same research center (Semukhina and Reynolds, 2013). The numbers presented by Levada are more likely to be trusted since WCIOM is a government affiliated organization and the study was funded by MVD. Some sociologists suggested that WCIOM numbers are likely to be inflated due to questionable survey instrument and methodology (Medizona, 2017)[22].

An increase of public trust in the Russian police during the mid-2010s is an interesting phenomenon, considering that crime rates had not changed significantly during this period. An official explanation credits the growth of public trust to Medvedev's reform of police undertaken in 2011 (MVD, 2018a). This conclusion contradicts some public surveys reporting that only 5% of Russians see the 2011 police reform as a success (Egorysheva, 2014). The researchers from Levada speculated that the modest increase in public trust of police is unlikely to be a response to an improved police work, since the number of those who were dissatisfied with dealing with police did not change in 2017, compared to 2007. Moreover, those who contacted with police were more likely to distrust the police compared to respondents with no such experience (Levada, 2017b). An alternative to the governments' explanation suggests that increased trust in police is a reflection on growing institutional trust in the president, army, and other agencies of executive branch

---

22 In WCIOM's study, the respondents were given an option to rank their trust of police as "average", which was counted towards 67% of trusting respondents. However, in Levada's survey, the respondents only had a choice between trust and distrust options.

caused by "patriotic mobilization" started in Russia after the annexation of Crimea (Levada, 2017a; Gudkov, 2017).

2.6. Police and the Russian state: Happy reunion?

Most interviewees describe the current state of Russian police in positive terms such as "improvement", "stable development." and "taking things under control." Similar to the previous periods, officers continue to frame these police institutions in terms of state-police relations. "The state does pay attention to what we do ... we are needed by the government ... things got much better nowadays" (PO#7). Just like in the previous periods, the terrifying experience of decoupling from the state in the 1990s is used as a reference point: "Things are different in police now than it was back in 1990s ... we are not abandoned ... the government wants strong police now" (PO#18). Surprisingly, the reference to the 1990s was also used by younger police officers who did not serve during this period, and in this regard the "awful 90s" have become a professional ethos within police culture: "I did not work in the 1990s but when I came I learned how bad things were back then when the state left us and I now know that what we have here is good" (PO#42).

A complete identification of police institutions with the state appears to have one important ramification that might give it a new goal for the current police institution in Russia. At least for some of my interviewees, the major function of the police in Russia nowadays relates strongly to protection of the state. While in the 2000s, police officers exhibited rather standard paternalistic language of "protecting the society from crime on behalf of state" in 2010s, some interviewees focused their crime-fighting rhetoric on state protection: "There are all these aggressive elements in our society ... they try to hurt us ... hurt the state ... we have to fight them to protect Russia in these difficult times" (PO#21).

Another police officer made it even clearer: "Fifth column,[23] traitors; they wanted our state to be weak; they enticed marginals to commit crimes ... we had to stop it ... Russia was tough ... we could get through it" (PO#43). This trend was more evident among younger respondents with fewer years of experience; older more experienced officers appeared to be more ambivalent about what the main function of police was or simply reiterated the standard crime-fighting rhetoric (PO#7). However, both experienced and new officers highlighted the duty of the police to maintain and assist a "strong state" at the times when Russia was challenged by "the outside, unfriendly forces" (PO#34, PO#39).

Unlike my interviewees who spoke about the 1990s and 2000s, officers who discussed the 2010s were familiar with the term "police services" and many of them were comfortable in describing police activities as services to citizens such as issuing passports or registering vehicles. But when it came to the topic of crime, younger and older officers alike were adamant in rejecting the service model and sticking with a traditional crime-fighting ideology: "The main purpose of the state is to make sure everyone is safe; we are the power arm of the state, and we supervise society to fight the crime; the state delegated to us the role to keep people safe by solving crime ... that's our function as police ... that what I tell my people every week when we meet" (PO#1). It is interesting to see a gendered context in understanding the police function, many officers were comfortable when describing the juvenile justice units of the police, (PDN)[24] as a service or a help to society. These units traditionally employed female officers, and their official purpose was not to reduce crime control but to provide delinquency prevention. "'PDN officers are there to help families; yes, they provide social services by alerting families about issues their children might have in school" (PO#8). Overall, female officers, regardless of their posi-

---

23 Fifth column is a degrading term applied in modern Russia to the liberal pro-Western individuals whose views are often seen as a way to undermine strong Russia.
24 Units for the juveniles' affairs (*podrazdeleniya po delam nesovershennoletnikh*, abbreviated as "PDN".

tion at MVD, were more likely to agree that service to the community is an important part of police function: "Yes, sometimes I see my job more as a service, assistance to the families ... than trying to fight the offenders ... in many cases this is more effective way of doing things" (PO#16). On the other hand, male police officers often looked down at the crime-preventive function and police work with the community even when it was an integral part of their official duties: "As a beat officer I have to deal with all these people ... yes sometimes I help them ... a lot of times I try to prevent crimes ... but most of the time I help officers to fight crime ... because I know all these areas well ... that's what the most important part of the police is" (PO#19).

Many of my interviewees actually knew about the ideas of community policing, public–police partnerships, and public–police interaction. Unlike in the 2000s, when these concepts were mostly discussed by independent NGOs, the ideas of public–police partnerships in the 2010s entered the official literature published by MVD (Andreeva, 2016; Belskyi, 2016; Stolyarenko et al., 2017). Moreover, most officers pointed out at the "public councils" created at each district, regional, and circuit levels of MVD as examples of successful public-police partnerships.[25] Many interviews referred to the newly adopted statute on public participation in policing as sufficient evidence that such interaction exists (PO#33).[26] Some interviewees suggested newly created auxiliary police units as examples of public-police cooperation.[27]

However, when prompted to explain what the police partnership with community entails, most officers reduced public participation to "providing information," "serving as eyewitnesses," or simply "getting informed about crime rates in their area" (PO#20).

---

25 Public councils (*Obschestvennye sovety*) were established by the Presidential Decree #668 issued on 5.23.2011.
26 Refers to the Statute #44 issued on 04.02.2014, "On participation of citizens in the public safety activity." The statute regulates activities of police volunteers or auxiliary police units, which are often abbreviated in Russia as DND.
27 DND existed in Soviet Union from 1957 to 1991. The members of DND were mostly active young members of the Communist Party. After the dissolution of USSR, auxiliary police units were terminated and officially reinstated only in 2014. (Semukhina, 2013).

In all these instances, society again was viewed as a passive subject acting in accordance with police needs or simply receiving information that police is willing to share. At least some interviewees recalled instances when members of NGOs groups and community activists were touring the police precinct to look at the conditions of detention cells, conditions of those who were arrested on administrative offense, and sent to juvenile detention centers.

As a part of these tours, they spoke to the detained and took complaints (PO#1). But it turned out that selection of NGOs and activists who could participate in such tours was conducted by the MVD and precincts were given advanced notice about their visits (PO#23). Most police officers agreed that complaints taken by activities and NGOs are not necessary for resolutions: "The boss [head of the precinct] will take a look at some of them, at the end it is his job to decide if there are any merits to these complaints ... from what I know most of them have no merits anyway" (PO#29).

In the 2010s, police in general became much more selective with the type of NGOs that would participate in any public–police partnerships. My interviewees explained that, unofficially, they need to make sure that organizations interacting with police are loyal and not in any cases tainted by connection with "foreign agents" or even "unwanted organizations."[28] The "safe organizations" for police to interact with typically included militarized units such as Cossacks and veterans or youth organizations affiliated with United Russia such as Nashi (PO#24). In explaining why the partnering with NGOs has to be preselected by police, the interviewees mostly invoke the "protection of the state" narrative: "If you let these liberals go, they will make sure to weaken the police and by doing so, they will try to weaken our Russian state ... in these difficult times we cannot allow our enemies to do this" (PO#26).

---

28 The statute on "unwanted organizations" #129-FZ issued on 05.23.2015 prohibits unwanted organization to operate on the territory of Russia.

3. Discussion and implications

This brief overview tracing police identity in Russia provides for a few interesting insights. First, a police identity, at any given period of its development, is closely related to the development of the Russian state as is personified in the president and the MVD minister. In this regard, the 1990s were viewed by police officers as "lost time" not only because of poor conditions of service but because of the loss of state identity and the officers' perceptions of Russia being a weak state. Police officers continue to carry this identity as "state people" throughout the 2000s and 2010s. This is why Putin's state-building efforts in the 2000s and direct inclusion of law enforcement in these efforts was viewed as a return to the true meaning of policing. The current period signifies even stronger identification of police with the Russian state in which police view its crime-fighting function as a way to protect state from hostile elements.

Second, in their close relationship with the state, the Russian police take a surprisingly immature position of a "state's child" — the officers generally refuse to take responsibility for their actions and attribute the failures to the state or to other outside forces, such as "the fifth column," "pro-Western liberals," or independent media. The literature repeatedly shows that police officers used a lack of funding and poor legal regulations as excuses for their own corruption and poor performance in the past (Bashkirova, 2008; Gudkov and Dubin, 2006). Moreover, in my interviews, even public dissatisfaction with the police is viewed mostly as "the state's fault" and as the consequence of poor support from the state (PO#28, PO#36). According to the officers, biased media and recently "the fifth column" are to be blamed for police underperformance (PO#32, PO#35, PO#38). In this long list of excuses, police officers refuse to accept any responsibility or any notion that police institutions can act independently in building relations with Russian society.

Third, Russian police inherited a strong tradition of crime-reduction philosophy from its Soviet predecessor. This view of police as primarily the crime fighter was logically combined with a predominant among officers' paternalistic view that society is incapable of any crime reduction and needs to be supervised and protected by police from dangerous offenders. The crime-fighting ideology was somewhat weakened by the collapse of the Soviet state in the 1990s, when the police institution found itself with an unclear purpose of whom and what to fight and why. Indeed, most experienced officers left the system in the early 1990s, which brought an opportunity for MVD to change the crime-fighting ideology of policing. However, this opportunity was lost in the turmoil of poor service conditions, skyrocketing crime rates, and rampaging corruption. The brief period of uncertainty in its institution identity was painful for police, and, in the absence of alternative input from the state or Russian civil society, the police institution throughout the 2000s returned to the comfortable ideology of crime-fighting paternalism.

Fourth, while Russian police appeared to have reverted to their Soviet roots, the modern Russian society exhibited significant changes. In the 1990s, public expectations of police were minimal, as little was known by the public about models of policing other than crime-fighting ideology. With the development and maturation of civic society during the 2010s, public demands for active interaction with police and its accountability increased, but they were met with anger and frustration by police officers. Officers did not see the developing civil society as a source of its legitimate power and equal partner; thus, these ideas directly contradicted the very nature of paternalistic crime-fighting ideology reinstated within the police institution by the 2000s. However, the rejection could not be a long-term strategy and in 2010s, the Russian government decided to change its tactics.

MVD has officially embraced the ideas of police accountability and community policing, that is, public councils and new auxiliary police units from volunteers were established to symbolize the participation of civil society. These concepts of community policing and public-police partnerships have been discussed and examined by faculty at MVD universities (Andreeva, 2016; Stolyarenko et al.,

2017). However, these efforts appear to be more of a façade then a real turn in police's ideology. Participating NGOs and activists appear to be carefully pre-selected to avoid any real scrutiny.[29] Moreover, the work of critical independent NGOs has been curtailed by a lack of funding as a result of new law on "foreign agents."[30] As such, the ideas of police accountability and public–police partnership are seriously devaluated in Russian society by MVD's effort to avoid any real external scrutiny.

Overall, despite significant political and economic changes that occurred in Russia over the past 25 years, the identity of the Russian police has not experienced a significant transformation. Police officers view themselves as a part of the state that they often personify as President Putin. This identification provides a safe haven for most police officers, as they refuse to take any responsibility for their failures to build better relations with Russian society. The current ideology of the Russian state in which Russia juxtaposes itself to the "collective West" allows officers to view crime-fighting as a means to protect the society and, more importantly, the state. In such a context, the dominant crime-fighting ideology is strengthened with this high-order value of state security. From 2013 to 2017, the Russian government skillfully hijacked the narrative of public–police partnership and accountability and gradually removed unwanted NGOs from public discourse on police. In doing so, the state secured full control of the police institution but effectively undermined attempts of Russian civil society to establish meaningful external control over law enforcement.

---

29   A closer look at the members of public councils reveals that they contain mostly former police officers, members of pro-government, and/or government-owned media such as "Russia Today" and members of pro-government organizations affiliated with United Russia such as "People's Front" and "Nashi" (MVD. 2018b).

30   For example, the amount and scope of studies conducted by INDEM, Public Verdict, Committee against Torture, and Sutyazhnik reduced significantly since 2013 when the new law on foreign agents was passed.

Appendix 1.
Demographic Information on Interviewees

Interviewee	Location	Age	Gender	Police unit/position*	Rank*
PO#1	Siberian Russia	52	Male	Head of district police precinct	Colonel
PO#2	Central Russia	58	Male	Senior detective	Senior lieutenant
PO#3	Siberian Russia	52	Male	Investigator	Senior lieutenant
PO#4	Southern Russia	76	Male	Head of investigative unit	Lieutenant colonel
PO#5	Southern Russia	49	Male	Senior detective	Major
PO#6	Central Russia	46	Male	Beat officer	Senior sergeant
PO#7	Southern Russia	38	Male	Investigator	Lieutenant
PO#8	Siberian Russia	48	Female	Head of juvenile affairs unit at regional level	Colonel
PO#9	Central Russia	71	Male	Head of detective unit	Major
PO#10	Siberian Russia	40	Female	Passport service	Junior lieutenant
PO#11	Southern Russia	46	Male	Patrol and post service	Private
PO#12	Siberian Russia	42	Male	Beat officer	Private
PO#13	Central Russia	47	Male	Investigator	Lieutenant
PO#14	Siberian Russia	46	Male	Investigator	Lieutenant
PO#15	Southern Russia	49	Male	Investigator	Lieutenant
PO#16	Siberian Russia	28	Female	Inquirer	Senior lieutenant
PO#17	Central Russia	42	Male	Detective	Junior lieutenant
PO#18	Siberian Russia	35	Female	Juvenile justice	Lieutenant
PO#19	Central Russia	26	Male	Beat office	Sergeant
PO#20	Southern Russia	34	Male	Investigator	Major
PO#21	Siberian Russia	24	Male	Detective	Junior lieutenant
PO#22	Central Russia	63	Male	Investigator	Lieutenant
PO#23	Southern Russia	49	Male	Head of detective unit	Lieutenant colonel
PO#24	Central Russia	51	Male	Head of beat officers' unit	Colonel
PO#25	Siberian Russia	67	Male	Head of detective unit	Major
PO#26	Southern Russia	47	Female	Head of juvenile justice unit	Lieutenant colonel
PO#27	Siberian Russia	54	Male	Detective	Junior lieutenant
PO#28	Central Russia	24	Male	Detective	Junior lieutenant
PO#29	Southern Russia	32	Female	Head of inquirers unit	Captain
PO#30	Southern Russia	51	Male	Traffic inspector	Sergeant
PO#31	Southern Russia	62	Male	Senior investigator	Major
PO#32	Siberian Russia	31	Female	Investigator	Senior lieutenant
PO#33	Southern Russia	28	Male	Senior investigator	Lieutenant
PO#34	Siberian Russia	33	Male	Detective	Captain
PO#35	Central Russia	28	Female	Inquirer	Lieutenant
PO#36	Central Russia	32	Female	Head of passport service	Colonel
PO#37	Siberian Russia	73	Male	Head of public safety police	Major
PO#38	Siberian Russia	24	Male	Traffic inspector	Junior lieutenant
PO#39	Central Russia	48	Male	Head of investigative unit	Lieutenant colonel
PO#40	Siberian Russia	45	Male	Patrol and post service	Private
PO#41	Southern Russia	61	Male	Head of district police precinct	Colonel
PO#42	Central Russia	25	Male	Patrol and post service	Private
PO#43	Siberian Russia	27	Male	Detective	Junior lieutenant

*During the time described at the interview.

References

Abdrashitov, E.E., 2009. Pravosoznanie sovremennogo sotrudnika militsii [Legal consciousness of modern police officer]. Soc. Res. 5, 146–152.

Adyan, A.O., 2006. Sovershenstvovanie sistemy stimulirovaniya truda sotrudnikov organov vnutrennikh del [Improving the system of job stimulation for the employees of the agencies of Interior Affairs]. Institute of State and Law, Russian Academy of Sciences.

Aganbegyan, A., 2010. Russian economy on the cross-roads. Choices. Post. Solu. Moscow (ACT).

Andreev, A.L., 2005. Pravovoi mentalitet i otnoshenie k militsii v Rossiskom obschestve: sotsiokulturnye aspekty [Legal mentality and public attitudes of police in Russian society: socio-cultural aspects]. Monit. Publ. Opin. 4, 26–37.

Andreeva, E., 2016. Vzaimodeistvie Gosudartvennykh Organov I Institutov Grazhdanskogo Obschestva Po Realizatzii Pravookhranitel'noi Funktsii Gosudratva [Ineraction of State Agencies and Institutes of Civil Society for Realization of Law Enforcement Fucntion of the State]. State and Law. Towards 300 Years of Russian Police. St. Petersburg: St. Petersburg MVD University.

1917–2015. Archive of newspaper "Izevestiya". Moscow: State Public Historic Library of Russia.

Artem'ev, A.M., 2003. Realizatsiya Kadrovoi Politiki MVD Rossii V Sfere Podgotovki Kadrov [Implementation of Personnel Policy in MVD of Russia in the Area of Training the Staff]. Zakon i Pravo, Moscow.

Association for Criminology, 1997. Prestupnost I Reformy V Rossii [Crime and Reforms in Russia]. Association for Criminology, Moscow.

Bashkirova, E.I., 2008. Pravookhranitelnye organy i rossiskoe obschestvo [Law enforcement agencies and Russian society]. Empir. Res. Civil. Soc (Moscow: Obschestvennaya Palata).

Beck, A., 2013. Police reform and building justice in Russia. In: Goodall, K., Malloch, M., Munro, B. (Eds.), Building Justice in Post-Transition Europe? Routledge, London and New York.

Beck, A., Chistyakova, Y., 2002. Crime and policing in Post-Soviet societies: briding the police-public divide. Polic. Soc. 12, 123.

Beck, A., Lee, R., 2001. Valeurs et pratiques professionnelles dans la police russe. Les Cahiers de la securite interiere 44, 115–142.

Beck, A., Robertson, A., 2009. Policing in the "new" Russia. In: Hinton, M.S., Newburn, T. (Eds.), Policing Developing Democracies. Routledge, London and New York.

Belskyi, V., 2016. Ligitimnost Politsii [Legitimacy of Police]. State and Law. Towards 300 Years of Russian Police. St. Petersburg: St. Petersburg MVD Academy.

Berezin, G.N., 2011. Organizatsionnaya kultura v rossiskoi politisii: problemy i perspektivy [Organizational culture in the Russian police: problems and prospects]. Bulletin of Adygei State University 4, 180–186.

Bobrova, I.A., 2005. Psikhologicheskie osobennosti lichnosti zhenschin-sotrudnikov organov vnutrennikh del MVD Rossii [Psychological features of female police officers employed by MVD]. St. Petersburg MVD University.

Bondarenko, T.A., 2006. Imidg organov vnutrennih del MVD v "militseiskih" teleserialah [The image of Agencies of Interior Affairs in the "police" soap operas]. Soc. Res. 9, 114–119.

Borisova, S.V., 1998. Professional'naya Defomatsiya Sotrudnikov Militsii I Ee Lichnostnye Determinanty [Professional Deformation of Police Officers and Their Personality]. Academy of Management of MVD.

Borodavko, L.T., 2005. Professional'noe Vospitanie Sotrudnikov Pravookhranitel'nykh Organov V Vuzakh MVD [Professional Education of Law Enforcement Personnel in the Universities of MVD System]. St. Petersburg MVD University.

Borzov, A.A., 2006. Korruptsia i dolzhnostnye prestuplenia v pravookhranitel'nykh organakh [Corruption in the law enforcement agencies]. Bulletin of St. Petersburg Academy of MVD 3, 239–243.

Botov, A.I., 2001. Organizatsiya I Pravovoe Regulirovanie Professional'noi Podgotovki Kadrov V Sisteme MVD [Organization and Legal Regulation of Professional Training within the MVD System]. Law Institute of MVD Russia.

Brazhenskaya, N.E., 2011. Sootnoshenie orientatsi na semyu i kareru u kursantov-devushek v vuze MVD Rossiii [The relationship between family and career values among female students of police academies of MVD of Russia]. Bulletin of St. Petersburg MVD University 2, 179–183.

Cabinet of Ministers, 1993. Decree "On Reorganization of Departments of Visas, Registration and Passport Work of Militia into Passport-visa Services of Agencies of interior affairs.".

Cherkasov, R.V., 2006. SMI o obschesvennoe menie o militsii (Mass media and public opinion about police). Soc. Res. 4, 85–88.

Committee against Torture, 2006. Sotsiologiya nasiliya. Proizvol pravookranitelnykh organov glazami grazhdan [Sociology of violence. Police abuse in the eyes of citizens]. Nizhniy Novgorod: Committee Against Torture.

Cooper, W.H., 2009. Russia's Economic Performance and Policies and Their Implications for the United States. Washington DC: CRS Report for Congress.

Curfman, R.S., 1997. Russian Police Transition to Democracy: Revising the Russian Police Attitude toward the Rule of Law. Naval Postgraduate School.

2012. Doklad nepravitelstvennykh organozatsiy po soblydeniyu Konvestii protiv pytok i drukhihzhestokih, beschelovechnyk i unizhayuzhih dostoinstov obrashcenii i nakazanii za 2006–2012 god [Report of nongovernment organization on complying with the Convention against torture and Other Cruel, Inhuman or Degrading Treatment or Punishment during 2006–2012]. Moscow.

Dubova, A., Kosals, L., 2012. Vkluchennost' Rossiskih politseiskoh v tenevuy ekonomiku (Inclusion of the Russian police officers in the "shadow economy"). Otechestvennye zapiski 2. Available: http://www.strana-oz.ru/2012/2/vklyuchennost-rossiyskih-policeyskih-v-tenevuyu-ekonomiku. Accessed 1.15. 2013.

Dzutsev, H., 2010. Sotsiologiya kriminogennosti v respublike Severnaya Osetiya-Alaniya [Sociology of crime in the republic of Ossetia]. Soc. Res. 12, 80–84.

Egorysheva, N., 2014. Reforma organov vnutrenikh del v kontekste pravovoi politki Rossiskogo gosudrtva [Police reform in the context of legal policy of Russian state]. Bulletin of Eastern Humanitarian Economic-Legal Academy 1, 36–43.

Ermolaev, V.V., 2009. Otnoshenie naseleniya k militsii kak proyavlenie stosialmykh predstavleniy on organizatsionnoi kulture i imidge organov vnutrennikh del [Public attitudes of police as measurement of organization and cultural image of police]. Bulletin of the Voronezh Institute of MVD 3, 46–50.

Ermolaev, V.V., Verem'eva, E.A., 2007. K problrme izucheniya organizatsionnoi kultury i imidga militsii [The problem of organizational culture and image of police]. Bulletin of the Voronezh Institute of MVD 2, 85–87.

Favarel-Garrigues, G., 2002. La bureacratie policiere et la chute du regime sovietique. Societe contemporaines 1, 63–81.

Fillipov, V.V., 2003. New Russian Code of Criminal Procedure: the next step on the path of Russia's democratization. Demokratizatsiya 11.

FOM, 2005. Naselenie i miltsiya [Population and police]. Available: http://bd.fom.ru/report/cat/power/powl/d082723. Accessed 11.24.2010.

FOM, 2010. Uroven' doveriya militsii [The level of trust of police]. Available: http://bd.fom.ru/report/cat/power/powl/d082723. Accessed 11.24.2010.

Freedman, D., Thornton, A., Camburn, D., Alwin, D., Young-Demarco, L., 1988. The life history calendar: a technique for collecting retrospective data. Socio. Meth. 18, 37–68.

Galeotti, M., 2004. The criminalization of Russian state security. Global Crime 7, 471–486.

Galeotti, M., 2012. Purges, power and purpose: Medvedev's 2011 police reforms. J. Power Inst. Post Sov. Soc. [Online], 13. Available: http://pipss.revues.org/ 3813.

Galkin, A.S., 2001. Pedagogicheskie osnovy kadrovoi raboty v organakh MVD [Pedagogical basis for human resources in MVD system]. Scientific Research Institute of MVD of Russia.

Gall, C., 2011. Das neue russische Polizeigesetz. Russland-analysen 219, 2–4.

Gavrilin, S.A., 2001. Formirovanie pravosoznaniya slushatelei vuzov MVD kak faktor sovershenstvovaniya ikh professional'noi podgotovki [Legal consciousness of MVD students as factor for improving their professional training]. Academy of management of MVD.

Gerber, T.P., Mendelson, S.E., 2008. Public experiences of police violence and corruption in contemporary Russia: a case of predatory policing? Law Soc. Rev. 42, 1–44.

Gilinskiy, Y., 2011. Torture by the Russian police: an empirical study. Police Pract. Res. 12, 163–171.

GKS, 2011a. Chislo povtornykh prestupleniy [Number of repeated offences]. Available: http://www.gks.ru/dbscripts/Cbsd/DBInet.cgi?pl¼2318014. Accessed 6.6.2011.

GKS, 2011b. Chislo prestupleniy svyzannykh s obortom narkotikov [Number of drug-related crimes]. Available: http://www.gks.ru/dbscripts/Cbsd/DBInet. cgi?pl¼2318012. Accessed 6.6.2011.

GKS, 2011c. Chislo tyazhkih i osob tyazhkih prestupleniy [The number of serious and very serious crimes]. Available: http://www.gks.ru/dbscripts/Cbsd/ DBInet.cgi?pl¼2318015. Accessed 6.6.2011.

GKS, 2018a. Chislo Prestuplneiy Sovershennykh V Gruppe [Number of Crimes Commited in the Group] [Online]. Moscow. Available: http://www.gks.ru/ freedoc/newsite/population/urov/urov51g.htm. Accessed 6.10.2018.

GKS, 2018b. Chislo zaregistrirovannykh prestupleni v raschete na 100 tysyach naseleniya [Number of registered crimes per 100,000 of population [. Available: http://cbsd.gks.ru/. Accessed 6.10.2018.

GKS, 2018c. Chisltennost Naseleniya S Denezhnymi Dohodami Nizhe Prozhitochnogo Minimuma [Proportion of Population Living below Minimum Wage]. Moscow. Available: http://www.gks.ru/freedoc/newsite/population/urov/urov51g.htm. Accessed 6.10.2018.

Gladarev, B., 2011. Professiya "rossioskiyi militsioner ": usloviya sluzhby i vnutri-institutsionnaya logika [Profession of Russian police officer: conditions of service and inter-institutional logic]. In: Romanov, P.V., Yuarskoi-Smirnov, E.R. (Eds.), Antropologiya Professii [Anthropology of Professions]. St. Petersburg: Variant.

Glinkina, S.P., 2002. Privatizatsiya and kriminalizatsiya: how organized crime is hijacking privatization? In: GALEOTTI, M. (Ed.), Russian and Post-Soviet Organized Crime. Dartmouth: Ashgate.

Gonyukhov, S.O., Gorobtsov, V.I., 2002. MVD Rossii [MVD of Russia] Moscow, Reitar.

Grinenko, A.V., 2017. Praookhranitelnye I Sudebnye Organy [Law Enforcement and Court Bodies]. Moscow Institute of International Relations, Moscow.

Gudkov, L., 2017. My vozvrschaemsya v pozdnesovetskie vremena [We are coming back to the late Soviet times] [Online]. Available: https://www.levada.ru/ 2017/10/13/my-vozvrashhaemsya-v-pozdnesovetskie-vremena/. Accessed 6.8.2018.

Gudkov, L., Dubin, B., 2006. Privatisatsiya politsii [Privatization of police]. Bulletin of Public Opinion 1, 58–71.

Gudkov, L., Dubin, B., Leonova, A., 2004. Militseiskoe nasilie i problema "politseiskogo gosudarstva " [Police violence and the problem of 'police state "]. Bulletin of Public Opinion 4, 31–47.

Gurvich, E., 2017. Junctions of the Russia's macroeconomic policy. Russian Academy of Sciences. Theoretical economy. 1, 40–54.

Gurvich, E., Prilepskiy, I., 2016. The impact of financial sanctions on the Russian economy. Scholar's Press.

Holstein, J.A., Gubrium, J.F., 1995. The Active Interview. Sage, Thousand Oaks, CA.

HRW, 2017. Russia: Punished over Hyperlinks. Russians Targeted for Links to Foreign 'Undesirable' Groups. Berlin. Available: https://www.hrw.org/news/ 2017/11/30/russia-punished-over-hyperlinks. Accessed 6.6.2018.

ICVS, 2000. Database. Cross-tabulations. [Online]. Available: http://www.unicri.it Accessed 8.04.2006.

IMF, 2011. World economic outlook database. Available: www.imf.org. Accessed 6.6.2011.

INDEM, 2002. Korruptsiya Na Dorogakh [Corruption on the Streets]. INDEM, Moscow.

INDEM, 2007. Opredelenie Faktorov Vliyayuschikh Na Effektivnost' Predostavleniya Uslug Po Bezopasnosti Ot Prestupnykh Posyagatel'stv [Determining the Factors Impacting the Effectiveness of protection Services from Crimes]. INDEM, Moscow.

Inshakov, S.M., 2007. Latentnya Prestupnost' V Rossiskoi Federatsii: 2001-2006 [Latent Crimes in Russian Federation, 2001-2006], Moscow, Unity. Statute and Law.

Ivanov, L.O., Iliyina, L.V., 1991. Puti I Sud'bi Otechestvennoi Kriminologii [The Paths and faith of Russian Criminology]. Nauka, Moscow.

Kikot, V.Y., 2002. Organizatsionno-pravovoe I Informatsionnoe Obespechenie Realizatsii Kadrovoi Politiki MVD Rossii V Sfere Podgotovko Kadrov [Organizational, Legal and Informational Support of Human Resource Policy of MVD of Russia]. Moscow University of MVD.

Kolennikova, O.A., Kosals, L., Ryvkina, R., Simagin, Y., 2002. Ekonomicheskaya Aktivnost' Rabotnikov Pravookhranitelnykh Organov V Postsovetskoi Rossii: Vidy, Masshtaby I Vliyanie Na Obschestvo [Economic Activities of Law Enforcement Agencies in post-Soviet-Russia: Types, Scope, and the Impact on the Society]. Open Society Institute, Moscow.

Korneeva, G.K., 2008. Sotrudnik pravookhranitel'nykh organov v rossiskom obschestve: suschnost' problemy pravovogo nigilisma [Staff Member of Law Enforcement Bodies on Russian Society: the Issues of Legal Nihilism]. An individual 4, 146-148.

Kosals, L., 2010. Police in Russia: reform or business restructuring? Russian analytical digest 84, 2-6.

Kudrin, A., Gurvich, E., 2015. A new growth model for the Russian economy. Russian Journal of Economics 1, 30-54.

Levada, 2017a. Institutsionalnoe doverie [Institutional trust [Online]. Available: https://www.levada.ru/2017/10/12/institutsionalnoe-doverie-3/. Accessed 6.6.2018.

Levada, 2017b. Otnoshenie k politsii [Online]. Available: https://www.levada.ru/2017/11/07/otnoshenie-k-politsii/. Accessed 6.6.2018.

Levitsky, S., Way, L., 2002. The rise of competitive authoritarianism. J. Democr. 13, 51–65.

Lukyanchenko, Y., Binev, A., 1990. S kazhdyaya tretyei ugolovnoi organizovannoi grupirovko sotrudnichaet sotrudnik pravoporyadka [Police officers cooperate with every third organized crime group]. Arguments and Facts, 09.01.1990.

Luschai, Y., 1990. Organizovanaya Prestupnost' [Organized Crime]. Arguments and Facts, 12.20.1990.

Manning, P., 2003. Police Contingencies. University of Chicago Press, Chicago.

Manning, P., 2010. Democratic Policing in a Changing World. Paradigm Publishers, Booulder, London.

Masyuk, E., 2015. Sociologist Victor Vornkov: surveys are always the manipulation of public consciousness. Novaya Gazeta, 04.29.2015.

Mazaev, Y.N., Yakovlev, O.V., Kamaev, B.G., 2003. Year. Sostoyanie vzaimootnoshei mezschdu militsiei i naseleniem i perspektivy ih sovershenstvovaniya [The state of relations between the public and police and the perspectives of its improvement]. In: Materials of the Round Table Discussion on 09.26. 2003. MVD Press, Moscow.

Mccarthy, L., 2015. Trafficking Justice. How Russian Police Enforce New Laws, from Crime to Courtroom. Cornell University Press. Itaca.

Medizona, 2017. 67% of Russians Said They Trust Police by Study from WCIOM. Medizona, 11.10.2017.

Minsitry of Finances, 2012. Federal budget for 2012 [Online]. Available: https://www.minfin.ru/ru/perfomance/budget/federal-budget/budgeti/. Accessed 4.12.2018.

Moscow Helsinki Group, 2018. Grazhdanin i poltsiya [Citizen and police] [Online]. Available: http://police.mhg.ru/. Accessed 6.8.2018.

Mulukaev, R.S., Malygin, A.Y., Epifanov, A.E., 2005. Istoriya otechestvennykh organov vnutrennikh del [History of agencies of interior affairs]. Nota Bene, Moscow.

MVD, 1990. Prestupnost' I Pravonarusheniya, 1989 [Crime and Delinquency]. Finance and Statistics, Moscow.

MVD, 1994. Decree "On Promulgation of the Structure and Number of Staff within the central Apparatus of MVD of Russia Federation.".

MVD, 1996. Decree "About Measures to Strengthen Legality in the Agencies of interior Affairs and Strengthening Internal Security. ". MVD, 1998. Decree "On Reforming the Activities of the State Automobile Inspection MVD of Russia".

MVD, 1999. Decree "On Police service.".

MVD, 2000. "The Instruction on the Work of Juvenile Delinquency units.".

MVD, 2003a. "The Instruction on Obtaining, Registering and Permitting Citizens Complaints about Crimes and Other information.". MVD, 2003b. "The Instruction on Organization of Short-term detention.".

MVD, 2005. "The Instruction on Conducting Audits and Revisions of Financial, Business and Other Trade activities.".

MVD, 2006. "The Instruction on Licensing and Controlling Private Detective activities.".

MVD, 2008. "The Instruction on Organization of Internal Reviews within Th Agencies of interior affairs.".

MVD, 2013. Proffesional [Professional]. Popular Legal Journal of MVD, 3.

MVD, 2018a. Rabota politsii. Doverie i otsenki [The work of police. Trust and assessment] [Online]. Available: https://Мвд.рф/publicopinion. Accessed 6.6. 2018.

MVD, 2018b. Sostav obschestvennogo soveta 2010-2017 [The members of public council] [Online]. Available: https://oc.Мвд. рф/SostavObshhestvennogo-soveta/Sostav. Accessed 6.8.2018.

Novikova, A., 2005. Social profile of rank and file police officers in the contemporary law enforcement system. Reforming law enforcement agencies: overcoming arbitrary work practices. Moscow Times: Demos Center.

O'Reilly, M., Parker, N., 2013. Unsatisfactory saturation: a critical exploration of the notion of saturated sample sizes in qualitative research. Qual. Res. J. 13, 190e197.

Oxford Analytica, 2010. Russia: Police Reform Fails to Address Key Challenges.

Paneyak, A., Pozdnyakov, M., Titaev, K.D., Chetverikova, I., Shlyaruk, M., 2012. Pravookhranitelnaya Deyatelnost' V Rossii: Struktura, Funktsionirovanie, Puti Reformirovaniya [Law Enforcement Activities in Russia: Structure, Function and the Path of Reform]. Committee of civil initiatives, Moscow.

Pino, N., Wiatrowski, M.D., 2006. Democratic Policing in Transitional and Developing Countries. Routledge, New York.

Pinto, B., Gurvich, E., Ulatov, S., 2005. Lessons from the Russian crisis of 1998 and recovery. In: Aizenman, J., Pinto, B. (Eds.), Managing Economic Volatility and Crises a Practitioner's Guide. Cambridge University Press.

PO#1 Personal interview with "Head of the district police precinct".

PO#2 Personal interview with "Senior detective".

PO#3 Personal interview with "Criminal investigator".

PO#4 Personal interview with "Head of the investigative unit".

PO#5 Personal interview with "Senior detective".

PO#6 Personal interview with "Beat officer".

PO#7 Personal interview with "Criminal investigator".

PO#8 Personal interview with "Head of juvenile affairs unit at regional level".

PO#9 Personal interview with "Head of detective unit".

PO#10 Personal interview with the "Officer of passport service".

PO#11 Personal interview with "Patrol and post servicemen".

PO#12 Personal interview with "Beat officer".

PO#13 Personal interview with "Investigator".

PO#14 Personal interview with "Investigator".

PO#15 Personal interview with "Investigator".

PO#16 Personal interview with "Inquirer".

PO#17 Personal interview with "Detective".

PO#18 Personal interview with "Officer of juvenile justice unit".

PO#19 Personal interview with "Beat police officer".

PO#20 Personal interview with "Investigator".

PO#21 Personal interview with "Detective".

PO#22 Personal interview with "Criminal investigator".

Personal interview with "Head of detective unit".

Personal interview with "Head of beat police unit".

Personal interview with "Head of detective unit".

Personal interview with "Head of juvenile justice unit".

Personal interview with "Detective".

Personal interview with "Detective".

PO#29 Personal interview with "Head of inquirers unit".

PO#30 Personal interview with "Traffic inspector".

PO#31 Personal interview with "Senior investigator".

PO#32Personal interview with "Investigator".
PO#33 Personal interview with "Senior investigator".
PO#34 Personal interview with "Detective".
PO#35 Personal interview with "Inquirer".
PO#36 Personal interview with "Head of passport service".
PO#37 Personal interview with "Head of public safety police".
PO#38 Personal interview with "Traffic inspector".
PO#39 Personal interview with "Head of investigative unit".
PO#40 Personal interview with "Patrol and pos servicemen".
PO#41 Personal interview with "Head of district police precinct".
PO#42 Personal interview with "Officers of patrol and post service".
PO#43 Personal interview with "Detective".
Polyakov, M.P., 2018. Pravokhranitelnye Organy [Law Enforcement Bodies], Nizhniy Novgorod, Nizhegorodskaya Academy of Ministry of Interior Affairs.
President of Russia, 1993a. Decree "On Prevention of Truancy and Juvenile Delinquency and protection of Their Rights. In: ". President of Russia, 1993b. Decree "On Promulgation of Decree on Militia of Public Security (Local Militia). ".
Procuracy of Russia, 2018. Portal of Legal Statistics.
Public Verdict Fund, 2014. Police Reform: Discussion and Comments by the Experts. Moscow.
Public Verdict Fund, 2018. Barometer reformy poltisii [Barometer of police reform] [Online]. Available: http://police-barometer.ru/. Accessed 6.7.2018.
Public Verdict Fund, 2010. Reforma Militisii: Otsenki I Ozhidaniya Grazhdan [Police Reform: Public Expectations and Assessment]. Public Verdict, Moscow.
RBC, 2017. Dopolnitelnye raskhody na MVD prevysyat v. 6 raz raskhody na zdravookhranenie [MVD funding is six time more than healthcare system]. RBC (Rev. Bras. Cir.), 5.29.2017.
Reynolds, K.M., Semukhina, O.B., Demidov, N.N., 2008. A longitudinal analysis of public satisfaction with the police in the Volgograd region of Russia: 1998e2005. Int. Crim. Justice Rev. 18, 158e189.
Robertson, A., 2005. Criminal justice policy transfer to post-soviet states: two case studies of police reform in Russia and Ukraine. Eur. J. Crim. Pol. Res. 11, 1–28.

Russell, M., 2015. The Russian economy. Will Russia ever catch up? European Parliamentary Research Service.

Rutkevitch, M.N., 1998. Protsessy sotsial'noi degradatsii v Rossiiskom obschestve [The processes of social degradation in Russian society]. Soc. Res. 6, 3–12.

Savchenko, I.A., 2011. Refroma MVD: vzglyad iz nutri [MVD reform: the internal view]. Monit. Publ. Opin. 2, 38–46.

Scherbak, A.N., Titaev, K.D., 2009. Chislennost' i finasirovanie pravookhranitelnykh organiv [Total numbers and funding of law enforcement agencies]. St. Petersburg: Institute of Legal Problems Implementation.

Semukhina, O., 2014. Unreported crimes, public dissatisfaction of police, and observed police misconduct in the Volgograd region, Russia: a research note. Int. J. Comp. Appl. Crim. Justice 38, 305–325.

Semukhina, O., Reynolds, K.M., 2013. Understanding the Modern Russian Police. CRC Press, Boca-Raton.

Shelley, L., 2000. Is the Russian state coping with organized crime and corruption? In: Sperling, V. (Ed.), Building the Russian State. Institutional Crisis and the Quest for Democratic Governance. Westview Press, Boulder.

Sheparneva, A.I., 2015. Istoriya organov vnutrennikh del [Hisotry of internal affair agencies], Orel, Orel Institute of Ministry of Interior Affairs.

Solidarnost, 2010. Perestroika MVD. Moscow.

Stolyarenko, A., Serdyuk, N., Filimonov, O., 2017. Sotsialno-pedagogicheskie fakotry pedagogiki partnerstva obschestva i politsii [Social and pedagogical factors of public-police partnership pedagogy]. Psychological Science and Education 22, 93–100.

Taylor, B.D., 2006. Law enforcement and civil society in Russia. Eur. Asia Stud. 58, 193–213.

Taylor, B.D., 2014. Police reform in Russia: the policy process in a hybrid regime. Post Sov. Aff. 30, 226–255.

Uhlin, A., 2006. Post-Soviet Civil Society. Routledge, London and New York.

Uidriks, N., Reenen, P., 2005. Police Reform and Human Rights. Intersentia. Open Society Institute, Antwerp, Oxford, New York.

Vesti, 2009. Evsyukov Denis Vikotorovich. 5.29.2009.

Volkov, V., Grigoriev, I., Dmitrieva, A., Moiseeva, E., 2012. Pravookhranitelnaya Deyatelnost' V Rossii: Struktura, Funktsionirovanie, Puti Reformirovaniya [Law Enforcement Activities in Russia: Structure, Function and the Path of Reform]. Committee of civil initiatives, Moscow.

WCIOM, 2007. Omnibus WCIOM Conducted on 02.04.2007 [Online]. Available: www.wciom.ru. Accessed 11/25/2010.

WCIOM, 2017. Rabota politsii: doverie i otsenki na maksimume [Police work: trust and assessment at maximum] [Online]. Available: https://wciom.ru/index.php?id¼236&uid¼116513. Accessed 6.5.2018.

World Bank, 2018. GDP PPP Data.

Zernova, M., 2012. The public image of the contemporary Russian police. Polic. An Int. J. Police Strategies Manag. 35, 216–230.

II. Legal Accountability in Public Administration

Prosecuting High Level Corruption in Eastern Europe

Maria Popova, Vincent Post
Department of Political Science, McGill University, Canada

Do Eastern European courts effectively constrain politicians and uphold the rule of law? Criminal prosecution of grand (high-level) corruption can further the central principle of equal responsibility under the law by demonstrating that even powerful political actors have to submit to the laws of the land. This article introduces the Eastern European Corruption Prosecution Database, *which contains entries for all cabinet ministers (927 in total) who served in a government that held office in one of seven post-Communist Eastern European countries since the late 1990s. The systematic data collection reveals that Bulgaria, Romania and Macedonia consistently indict more ministers than Croatia, the Czech Republic, and Poland; Slovakia has barely indicted anyone. We aim to start a research agenda by formulating hypotheses about which countries will see more corruption prosecutions and which ministers' characteristics would make them more likely to face the court. We use the database to begin testing these hypotheses and find some evidence for several associations. We find no strong evidence that EU conditionality or membership raises the profile of the grand corruption issue or leads to more indictments. Party politics seems to affect the frequency of corruption indictments more than the structure and behavior of legal institutions. Indictment rates are lower when a former Communist party controls the government and individual ministers from junior coalition partners are more vulnerable to indictment than other ministers. The existence of a specialized anti-corruption prosecution or a more independent judiciary do not seem to lead to the indictment of more ministers on corruption charges. Finally, we discuss avenues of future research that our database opens, both for the analysis of country-level and individual-level variation.*

Keywords: Corruption, Anti-Corruption agencies, Rule of law, Prosecutorial independence, Europeanization, Democratization, Central Europe, Balkans, Regression analysis

Do Eastern European courts effectively constrain politicians and uphold the rule of law? Have post-Communist states managed to build powerful and independent judiciaries? The growing literature on the topic has reached mixed conclusions. Some newly-established or emancipated Constitutional courts built enough power and legitimacy to prevent power grabs, reduce legislative overreach, and uphold constitutional rights (Schwartz, 2000; Smithey and Ishiyama, 2002; Herron and Randazzo, 2003; Ganev, 2003; Hanretty, 2014) to the point of becoming better at delivering and guarding democracy than elected institutions (Scheppele, 2005). Ordinary and administrative courts allow citizens to sue the state and protect their rights (Goldston, 2006). However, judicial power and independence can be fickle and have been rolled back by incumbents with strong popular mandates, as the weakening of Constitutional Courts in Hungary and Poland indicates (Bugaric, 2008; Bankuti et al., 2012 ; Bugaric and Ginsburg, 2016). Powerful and independent judiciaries do not always maximize the rule of law. Some post-Communist judiciaries became too powerful or too independent and created political dysfunction (Schonfelder, 2005; Popova 2010, 2012; Kosar, 2016); structural reforms, inspired and pushed by a combination of domestic champions and EU support, have produced major formal change and brought Eastern European judiciaries in line with international "best practices" (Coman and De Waele, 2007; Parau, 2012; Mendelski, 2012; Dallara, 2014; Bobek, 2015). But de facto judicial independence remains elusive, whether due to slower ideational or personnel change within the judiciary (Bobek, 2008, 2015; Kosar, 2016) or due to the failure of EU-mandated transplanted formal institutions to overcome domestic obstacles (Mendelski, 2015).

The quintessential manifestation of courts constraining politicians is the prosecution of grand political corruption. Criminal prosecution of high-level politicians demonstrates that even powerful political actors have to submit to the lawda development which upholds the central principle of equal responsibility under the law. Since most Eastern European states are blighted by high-level political corruption (Sajo, 1998; Karklins, 2016; Holmes, 2003;

Sandholtz and Taagepera, 2005; Mungiu, 2006; Kostadinova, 2012), electorates are highly concerned about it (Grigorescu, 2006), and mistrust political institutions because of it (Andersen and Tverdova, 2003), we can expect many corruption trials of high-level politicians in the region. There has been some research on the topic (Popova, 2012; Mendelski, 2015; Borzel and Schimmelfennig, 2017; Holmes, 2017; Elbasani and Šabić, 2018), but all studies we are aware of focus on single cases or on comparisons of two cases and discuss a few landmark illustrative cases, rather than the universe of cases or a selected sample.

To move the research agenda forward, we have created the first database that systematically tracks the prosecution of cabinet ministers on corruption charges. The Eastern European Corruption Prosecution Database contains entries for all cabinet ministers (927 in total) who served in a government that held office in one of seven post-Communist Eastern European countries (Bulgaria, Croatia, Czech Republic, Macedonia, Poland, Romania, and Slovakia) since the late 1990s. Table 1 contains an overview of the governments surveyed in this analysis (see Table 2).

Table 1: Cabinets included in the East European corruption prosecution data base.

Country	Cabinets
Bulgaria	Kostov (1997–2001), Sakskoburggotski (2001-5), Stanishev (2005-9), Borisov I (2009-13)
Croatia	Mateša (1995–2000), Račan I (2000-1), Račan II (2001-2), Račan III (2002-3), Sanader I (2003-6), Sanader II (2006-8), Sanader III (2008-9), Kosor I (2009-10), Kosor II (2010-11), Milanovič (2011-16)
Czech Republic	Zeman (1998–2002), Špidla (2002-4), Gross (2004-5), Paroubek (2005-6), Topolánek I (2006), Topolánek II (2006-10), Fischer (2009-10), Nečas (2010-13)
Macedonia	Georgievski (1998–2002), Crvenkovski (2002–2004), Bučkovski (2004–2006), Gruevski I (2006–2008), Gruevski II (2008–2011), Gruevski III (2011–2014)
Poland	Buzek I (1997–2000), Buzek II (2000-1), Miller I (2001-3), Miller II (2003-4), Belka (2004-5), Marcinkiewicz I (2005-6), Marcinkiewicz II (2006), Kaczyński (2006-7), Tusk I (2007-11), Tusk II (2011-14)
Romania	Isărescu (1999–2000), Năstase I (2000-3), Năstase II (2003-4), Popescu-Tăriceanu I (2004-6), Popescu-Tăriceanu (2006-7), Popescu-Tăriceanu (2007-8), Boc I (2008-9), Boc II (2009-10), Boc III (2010-12), Ungureanu (2012), Ponta I (2012), Ponta II (2012-14)
Slovakia	Dzurinda I (1998–2002), Dzurinda II (2002-6), Fico I (2006-10), Radičová (2010-12), Fico II (2012-16)

Source: East European Corruption Prosecutions (EECP) database.

Table 2: Overview of indictments (2000–2012).

Country	Total	Indictments	
		N	%
Bulgaria	107	11	10.3%
Croatia	135	7	5.2%
Czech Republic	126	5	4.0%
Macedonia	129	9	7.0%
Poland	167	7	4.2%
Romania	179	15	8.4%
Slovakia	84	2	2.4%
Total	927	56	6.0%

Source: EECP database.

For each minister, the database contains information about their portfolio, the beginning and end of their tenure in office, party membership and ideology, and their corruption prosecution experience, that is, whether a minister has been indicted on corruption-related criminal charges; if they have, when the indictment was filed in court; and whether and when the indictment has ended in an acquittal or a conviction. The database allows both individual-level and country-level analysis. The seven countries share a civil law judicial tradition and successful post-Communist era democratization, albeit with different pace and degree. They vary on the perceived level of corruption, the strength and timing of EU leverage, and the scope and success of judicial reform in the post-Communist period.

This chapter introduces the Eastern European Corruption Prosecution database by describing the variation in indictments for grand corruption in the region, both at the country level and at the individual level. The data demonstrates that more ministers get indicted for corruption in the Balkans than in Central Europe. We aim to start a research agenda by formulating a broad range of hypotheses that could explain variation in prosecutions of grand political corruption at the country level and at the individual level. We use the database to begin testing these hypotheses and find some evidence for several associations: 1) fewer ministers from cabinets that include a former Communist party get indicted for corruption; 2) countries with weaker democratic institutions indict more ministers for corruption; 3) ministers in portfolios with greater corruption opportunities get indicted more often; and 4) ministers from junior coalition partners are more vulnerable to a corruption indictment. Finally, we discuss avenues of future research that our database opens, both for the analysis of country-level and individual-level variation.

1. Introducing the Eastern European corruption prosecution (EECP) data base

When it is completed, the EECP Data Base will include all cabinet ministers from all cabinets that held office in Bulgaria, Croatia, Czech Republic, Macedonia, Poland, Romania and Slovakia between the late 1990s and the present. We chose the initial point of data collection as the beginning of "normal" democratic politics in the post-communist region, after "the triple transition" (Offe and Adler, 1991) from a command to a market economy, from a one-party to a multi-party system, and, in some cases, from a Communist federation to independent statehood and from interethnic war to peace was generally completed. We do not want to open the analytical can of worms that is defining and pinpointing the precise end of the transition. We only contend that politics in the 1990s was messier than in the 2000s. It seems that the nature of corruption opportunities for ministers in the 1990s may have been quite different due to the ongoing market transition, hyperinflation, and incomplete privatization. Comparing corruption prosecutions in the 1990s to those in the post-2000s may have an "apples and oranges" problem. In addition, there are significant data availability constraints for the early-mid-1990s. Our information about indictments comes from media coverage and online media archives before 2000 are much less reliable.

Creating the database is an ongoing effort. The team involved in this project is still collecting and coding data. In this chapter, we have restricted the analysis to ministers who have held office and (some of them) have been prosecuted on corruption charges between 1 January 2000 and 31 December 2012. The rationale is purely pragmatic-- the data for this period is complete and clean. The database could be expanded to the rest of the post-Communist country cases. For now, we have chosen cases from each sub-region of the non-Soviet post-Communist space:Central Europe (Poland, Czech Republic and Slovakia), former Yugoslavia (Macedonia and Croatia), and South Eastern Europe (Romania and Bulgaria).

Ministers are not the only perpetrators of grand political corruption, but they are a good starting point for this labor-intensive data collection process. A total of 927 individuals held office in one or more of the governments listed in Table 1 and we have collected extensive information on each of these individuals. Between 2000 and 2012, 56 of these ministers, including three former prime ministers, Adrian Năstase of Romania, Ivo Sanader of Croatia, and Vlado Bučkovski of Macedonia, were indicted for corruption and related offenses, such as abuse of office for corruption purposes.

This number represents the tip of an iceberg of corruption investigations. Currently, our database records the trial portion of the corruption prosecution experience: we record a corruption prosecution once prosecutors bring a case against a given minister to court, that is, the minister is indicted and becomes a defendant. The analysis does not record which ministers featured prominently in corruption scandals or which ministers were subject to pre-trial prosecutorial investigations that petered out without producing an indictment. This information could be added seamlessly to the data base and will enrich it. However, it is not essential for our present goal of assessing specifically the role of the judiciary in tackling high-level corruption. If a minister has not been indicted by the courts on corruption-related charges, it does not mean that he or she committed no corruption acts, while in office. It only means that the country's prosecution has not submitted an indictment to the country's courts against this individual. It is possible, and indeed highly probable, that some corrupt ministers have been never indicted. It is also possible that some of the indicted ministers did not actually commit corruption offenses. If our goal were to arrive at an assessment of the level of grand corruption in a given state at a given time, the indictment rate is a bad measure. If the judiciary is weak, many corrupt ministers could escape prosecution. If the law is weaponized for political competition purposes, some non-corrupt minister may end up indicted on trumped up charges. Our goal is to understand whether Eastern European judiciaries uphold the rule of law and tackle high-level corruption, so focusing our analysis on who the judiciary chooses to indict is appropriate. Our data base does not incorporate any criminal cases brought for criminal charges unrelated to corruption, such as drunk driving or assault, or administrative or civil cases brought against ministers. Lastly, indictments that occurred before 2000 or that have been brought outside the 2000–2012 time period we discuss here are not included in this analysis.

The main analytical advantage of the EECP data base is that it contains information on the entire universe of cases to be analyzed, not only a sample. It includes *each and every* one of the 927 ministers who served in cabinet. It also captures the entire universe of cases of prosecution indictments, rather than a sample. The 56 indicted ministers are all the ministers who faced corruption charges in court, rather than a sample. The data base then allows us to leverage the information on all ministers' corruption prosecution experience (whether they were indicted or not) to understand why some ministers feel the full brunt of the law and others are never prosecuted. The individual-level statistical analysis that we perform compares the characteristics of those indicted to those not indicted to reach conclusions about which characteristics increase or decrease the likelihood to be in one category or the other. The number of indictments (n=56) may appear to be small, given that we are analyzing the experience of 7 countries over 12 years. However, this kind of ratio (about 5% of the total number of observations) is common in statistical analyses. For example, in a survey study on vote choice with a sample of 1000 respondents, far-right voters might make only 5-6% of the sample, but we gain insight about who they are by comparing them to the other 95% who did not vote for the far-right. In our case, we can understand who is likely to get indicted by systematically comparing those who are indicted (56 people) to those who were not indicted (871 people). In sum, our conclusions are not based only on the analysis of the subgroup, but on the analysis of the entire universe of cases.

The region's leader in high profile corruption indictments is Bulgaria—more than 10 per cent of all cabinet ministers who served in Bulgarian governments that held office between 2000 and 2012 had been indicted by the end of 2012. In Slovakia, by contrast, only 2 out of 84 ministers (2.4 per cent) faced trial for corruption. The indictment rate is not related to the effectiveness of prosecutors in getting judges to side with them, as conviction rates vary throughout the region as well. While Bulgaria boasts the highest indictment rate, all the Bulgarian ministers who found themselves defendants in corruption cases between 2000 and 2012 were acquitted. Neighboring Romania presents a stark contrast, as nearly 80 per cent of the completed cases there have been converted into guilty verdicts, including jail time.

The prosecution of corruption varies over time as well, as the bulk of the cases are clustered in the 2006–2012 period. This is due in part to the simple fact that by the end of the research period, the pool of 'indictable' ministers in our sample is much greater than in the earlier years. In 2000, most of the individuals in our dataset had not yet held office, and any indictments before the time in office are not recorded. The three ministers indicted in 2000 were part of a much smaller group than the seven ministers indicted in 2012. Thus, the apparent increase in indictments can be misleading, and the absolute frequency of indictments is not appropriate for longitudinal analysis.

To accurately identify trends and to assess the impact of shifts in domestic politics and the institutions of the judiciary, it is necessary to calculate an annual indictment rate, which is the number of ministers indicted during a certain year as a proportion of the total number of 'indictable' individuals (see Fig. 1). This pool of 'indictable' ministers is restricted to those who 1) held office during or prior to a given year; 2) had not previously been indicted (we do not record additional indictments); 3) were still alive. This produces a time series that serves as the dependent variable in subsequent analysis. Fig. 2 (below) presents these annual indictment rates visually for each country.

As indicated by the sharp variation in both the frequency of indictments and the likelihood that those indictments are converted into a guilty verdict, the seven cases in this analysis do not share an approach towards battling corruption. The annual indictment rates reinforce this conclusion, as they show nothing resembling a common trend exhibited across the region. In Bulgaria and Macedonia, the likelihood of indictment appears to decline over time, while Romania and Croatia experienced a rise in indictments. Meanwhile, in Poland and the Czech Republic, indictments were most likely during the first few years after EU accession. In Slovakia, finally, no corruption indictments were brought against former or current cabinet officials until 2012.

2. Why do indictment rates vary from place to place and over time?

An obvious expectation is that more corrupt countries should have higher indictment rates. The pool of ministers who have engaged in corruption is going to be larger, so all things equal, the number of indicted ministers should be higher. All things equal is an essential caveat. Many other factors may affect the likelihood that acts of grand corruption will be uncovered in the first place, and subsequently investigated, prosecuted, and punished by the relevant law enforcement and judicial institutions.

Fig. 1. Frequency of indictments over time (2000–2012).

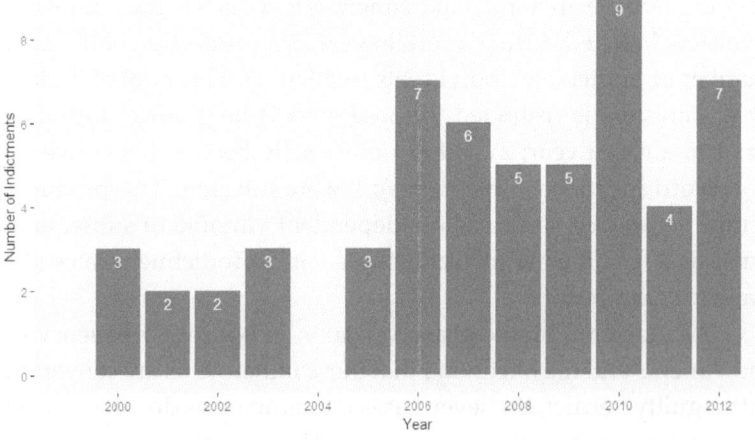

Fig. 2.   Annual indictments (2000-2012), 7 country cases.

Bulgaria

Croatia

Czech Republic

Macedonia

Poland

Romania

Slovakia

A growing literature on the sources of corruption finds that it flourishes when institutions and norms of democratic accountability are weaker. Electoral accountability, horizontal accountability through checks and balances between legislative, executive and judicial institutions, and transparency are linked with incidence of corruption (O'Donnell, 1998; Schedler, 1999; Treisman, 2000; Tavits, 2007). Lederman et al. (2005) find that corruption is, on average, lower in democratic regimes, especially if they are parliamentary systems and have a free press, than in authoritarian regimes.

Just as they fuel grand corruption, weak accountability institutions make uncovering corruption and prosecuting its perpetrators less likely. Corrupt politicians go to great lengths to cover up their abuse of office and the higher up they are on the political ladder, the more equipped they are to successfully hide their misdeeds. Strong democratic accountability institutions and norms are essential for uncovering, investigating, prosecuting and punishing grand political corruption. Thus, our first hypothesis is that, assuming a similar incidence of grand corruption, countries with stronger democratic institutions will be in a better position to tackle the problem through the legal process.

More specifically, we hypothesize that a developed investigative journalism sector within a thriving free press can contribute to a higher indictment rate of grand political corruption. Well-trained investigative journalists can disentangle grand corruption schemes and expose them to the public, which is often the first stage in any corruption prosecution. Frequent revelations of grand corruption by the press are likely to increase the salience of the issue with the electorate, which creates an incentive for institutions tasked with tackling corruption to get involved. The more corruption scandals the press breaks, the greater the pressure on the public prosecution to open an investigation and file an indictment in the courts.

A vibrant civil society sector dedicated to monitoring corruption processes can complement and enhance the work of investigative journalists. While investigative journalists tend to focus on uncovering the details of grand corruption schemes, anti-corruption civil society organizations (CSO) track the behavior of relevant institutions after the scandal has broken. As the sensation of a major corruption scandal starts to fade, journalists lose interest and move on to other stories. Pre-trial investigations usually move slowly and are too complicated and dry to cover. CSOs take a longer-term and broader view. They track and measure corruption opportunities and acts in different economic sectors and state institutions; they analyze, publicize and, occasionally, lobby for the adoption of specific anti-corruption policies; they train civil servants in detecting and counteracting corruption at their workplace and whistleblowing effectively; they monitor the movement of multiple cases throughout the legal process and signal if they see bottlenecks in the process. For example, the Southeast Europe Leadership for Development and Integrity (SELDI) unites 29 CSOs from 11 countries and regularly produces reports on the state of anticorruption efforts in the region. It is through the synergy of investigative journalists and anti-corruption CSOs that grand corruption stays on the public agenda, which boosts pressure on the relevant institutions to indict the perpetrators.

What happens if neither institution is independent from the political interests or clientelistic networks that sustain grand political corruption? Investigative journalists could be hired hands of one political machine, trying to collect dirt, or even fabricate a scandal about a political competitor. Anti-corruption CSOs could be set up in name only, perhaps in a tactical move by powerful political actors to claim ownership of the corruption fighting issue or to appear pro-European (Elbasani and Šabić, 2018). Or they could be politically biased and focus on uncovering corruption only in a certain sector of the political spectrum. Many of the anti-corruption CSOs in the region have received generous funding from the US and/or George Soros and their political opponents have accused them of catering to their benefactors' political agenda. Politically-engaged civil society institutions may or may not manipulate and decrease the transparency of anti-corruption discourse and even support the weaponization of corruption prosecutions against political opponents. But still their activity raises the salience of the grand political corruption issue and thus serves as a conduit for public pressure to indict perceived perpetrators, even if they are framed.

Hypothesis 1. Countries with stronger democratic institutions have a higher indictment rate.

Hypothesis 2. Countries with more investigative journalists have a higher indictment rate.

Hypothesis 3. Countries with a bigger anti-corruption CSO sector have a higher indictment rate.

Civil society may demand prosecutions of corruption within the higher echelons of power, but the legal process cannot move forward without a public prosecution office motivated to investigate corruption scandals and bring charges to court. A small portion of literature on specialized, centralized anti-corruption agencies argues that they could be an especially effective institutional mechanism for reducing corruption (Doig, 1995; Quah, 1999; Langseth, 2001; Meagher, 2005). The models for such agencies are Singapore's Corrupt Practices Investigation Bureau, created in 1952, and Hong Kong's Independent Commission Against Corruption, created in the 1960s. Both agencies are credited for the successful extrication of their countries from endemic corruption and restoring investor confidence (Quah,1999; Meagher, 2005). The success of these agencies has inspired nearly 40 countries around the world to establish similar institutions, including Croatia, Romania, and Macedonia in Eastern Europe. These agencies focus exclusively on corruption offenses, sometimes at all levels of the public administration, sometimes only at the highest echelons of power. They can be attached to the public prosecution or to the executive. They are most successful when they are given sufficient structural and fiscal independence from politicians, a strong mandate, and resources to investigate.

The literature implicitly assumes that specialized anti-corruption agencies reduce corruption largely by effectively prosecuting perpetrators of corruption. Why should such agencies be more effective than dedicated departments within the police or the general prosecution? An anti-corruption agency sees the task as its raison d'etre and its employees can be socialized into a stronger commitment to the anti-corruption cause. Employees in dedicated departments are less likely to develop a strong esprit de corps in their commitment to anti-corruption, because they would have competing professional identities: many of them will see themselves first and foremost as prosecutors or police, rather than as anti-corruption warriors. Specialized anti-corruption agencies that combine investigative and prosecutorial powers will also be more effective at disentangling complicated corruption schemes. They will develop greater expertise as they can dedicate themselves solely to the art of investigating corruption crimes. When investigative and prosecutorial powers are separated among departments in distinct law enforcement institutions, institutional rivalries may develop and jeopardize effective investigations. Finally, the leadership of specialized agencies does not have to compete with other prosecutorial or police departments for resources. When they have to compete, they often lose resources to departments that can close the most cases or deliver the most convictions with the least amount of resources.

There are, of course, dangers to the creation of a highly-motivated and specialized anti-corruption agency. They can become overzealous and trample civil rights in blind pursuit of corruption convictions. Critics of the Romanian Anti-Corruption National Directorate (DNA) have raised this objection to the DNA's flurry of activity over the past few years (Iancu, 2019). Specialized anti-corruption agencies which political independence gets compromised and come under the influence of a powerful political actor can seriously endanger justice and the rule of law if they become a political weapon in the hands of their principal. Macedonia's Special Prosecution Office (SJO), which in June 2017, filed charges against close to 100 politicians and functionaries from the main opposition, VMRO-DPMNE, including former prime minister Nikola Gruevski, have fended numerous attacks and accusations of political bias by the politicians they have investigated. But both dangers are consistent with the prediction that indictment rates will be higher in countries that have a specialized anti-corruption agency.

Hypothesis 4. Countries with specialized anti-corruption agencies that combine investigative and prosecutorial powers have higher indictment rates.

The absence of a specialized anti-corruption agency does not preclude frequent and/or effective prosecution of grand corruption. An empirical test by Van Aaken et al. (2010) shows that an independent public prosecution (both de jure and de facto) is strongly correlated with lower levels of perceived corruption, ostensibly because it prosecutes corruption crimes more often and thus decreases the expected utility of engaging in corruption for political actors. An independent judiciary should also enable the prosecution of grand corruption. Courts and a public prosecution that are dependent on politicians can go a long way towards sabotaging the work of any specialized anti-corruption agency. The prosecution can refuse to enter an indictment, even if investigators present well-documented cases. The courts can refuse to authorize various steps in the collection of evidence — temporary arrests, injunctions to prevent destruction of evidence, subpoenas for important witnesses, subpoenas to compel those under investigation to turn over evidence, and others.

This logic suggests that countries with higher levels of judicial and prosecutorial independence should have higher indictment rates, on average. Corruption indictments can be bona fide attempts by the prosecution and the courts to enforce anti-corruption laws. However, it is possible that politically captured judiciaries would also produce a high volume of corruption prosecutions. They can also be weaponized by various actors against their political opponents or competitors. Powerful political actors can lean on dependent prosecution and courts to indict opponents and competitors to get the upper hand in political competition. To complicate matters further, an independent prosecution can weaponize indictments and bring charges against more people than it should, to build up its own institutional power and legitimacy. In the countries that we examine, all these mechanisms could be plausibly at work. Corruption prosecutions could reflect good faith efforts to clean up grand corruption, or the weaponization of law by powerful political actors and/or a self-aggrandizing judiciary.

Hypothesis 5. The indictment rate is not correlated with the level of prosecutorial or judicial independence.

Even politicians without access to or leverage on the prosecution/courts can drive up the indictment rate. By leaking compromising materials (Balan, 2011) or by pushing forth investigations into wrong-doing by political opponents they can trigger major scandals and public outcry, which then put pressure on the prosecution to deliver an indictment. Thus, party politics can significantly influence indictment rates. In what ways, to be more specific?

Bågenholm and Charron (2014) identify the politicization of corruption as a growing electoral strategy in Europe and find that new parties and opposition parties make significant electoral gains when they take up the issue during electoral campaigns. They find that the strategy is particularly effective in Eastern European democracies. In a similar vein, Pop-Eleches (2010) argues that during the third electoral cycle in post-Communist democracies (in the early-mid-2000s) new parties successfully challenged the establishment, specifically by alleging widespread corruption.

Both theories imply that the growing salience and politicization of corruption during campaigns should be accompanied by spikes in the indictment rate. The spike could happen if a party running on an anti-corruption platform wins office and delivers on its promises to tackle corruption. New incumbents can do this without necessarily leaning on the prosecution and the courts, by starting focused investigations of the executive records of their predecessors. Enough digging into public procurement contracts often produces corruption allegations. If corruption-tackling is a salient enough issue with the public, the prosecution could feel obliged to indict someone. If the new incumbents have institutional levers that allow them to influence the prosecution, indicting some of their predecessors, even on paper-thin evidence, is easy enough. Even if the new party falls short of winning office, it can trigger corruption scandals involving its political competitors. The higher the volume of scandals, the more likely indictments will ensue.

Hypothesis 6. Countries with party systems that often produce new parties have a higher indictment rate.

Indictment rates should also be higher under "reformist", "pro-European" governments and lower under governments of Communist successor parties. Reformists are more likely to pursue anti-corruption as a strategy of bolstering the rule of law. Parties running on a pro-European platform may also pursue anti-corruption agendas either in earnest or as a tactic of demonstrating their commitment to Europeanization.

Communist successor parties would be less likely than average to pursue anti-corruption through prosecutions. Former communists and the "circles of companies" that surround them benefited the most from corrupt schemes during the transition to a market economy. They are less likely to embrace anti-corruption as an electoral or political competition tactic, because they would be afraid to open a can of worms.

Hypothesis 7. Indictment rates are higher under reformist or pro-European governments and lower under Communist successor party governments.

Curbing political corruption and bolstering the rule of law are essential goals promoted by the EU in its prospective and new members. Both are part of the Copenhagen criteria for accession. Since Bulgaria and Romania did not meet the benchmarks during the accession process, the EU instituted a Cooperation and Verification Mechanism (CVM), which involves monitoring both countries' progress towards controlling corruption through an independent and effective judiciary.

There is an intense debate on the relative success of European integration in the post-Communist members, especially when it comes to establishing the rule of law and tackling corruption. Some optimistic accounts (Noutcheva and Bechev, 2008; Levitz and Pop-Eleches, 2010) argue that even where domestic factors prevent quick or full reforms, EU leverage, both before and after accession, is a powerful tool for neutralizing domestic veto players and pushing reform forward. Pessimistic accounts (Mendelski, 2012; Spendzharova and Vachudova, 2012; Elbasani and Šabić, 2018) argue that EU leverage is the least powerful around judicial and anti-corruption reform, because the transfer of the acquis communautaire does not affect the de facto functioning of important institutions and does not preclude domestic elites from circumventing those institutions and preserving corruption rents. The most critical account of EU's role (Mendelski, 2012, 2015) even claims that EU's focus on increasing judicial capacity, but neglect for judicial impartiality has led to a vicious circle that exacerbates the political dependence of the judiciary.

What story do indictment rates support? Eastern Europeans have been getting a clear and consistent message from the EU that they need to put some corrupt politicians behind bars to prove that they are moving towards establishing the rule of law. During the pre-accession period, this message came with membership conditionality. We thus expect that indictment rates will be higher for pre-accession than for post-accession period for all countries, except for Romania and Bulgaria. For those two countries, EU pressure to prosecute political corruption only intensified after accession through the biannual monitoring missions carried out within the CVM framework. The carrot of membership was replaced by the stick of suspended structural and cohesion funds. In Bulgaria's case, the EU delivered on the threat in 2008 and suspended close to 1 billion euros in funds.

Hypothesis 8. For Bulgaria and Romania, indictment rates increase after accession in 2007; for Czech Republic, Poland, Slovakia and Croatia,[1] indictment rates are higher for pre-accession than for post-accession period.

---

[1] The database we use in this paper stops at the end of 2012, so for Croatia we cannot test the pre-/post-accession argument because the country entered the EU in 2013.

3. Individual-level variation: what puts ministers in legal jeopardy?

The database allows us to explore individual level variation in the likelihood of becoming the target of a corruption prosecution. The starting assumption is that individual ministers who have greater opportunities to benefit from a corruption scheme will be indicted more often than average. Ministers whose portfolios involve more discretionary spending than average, or conclusion of contracts in less competitive sectors, have greater opportunities to commit corruption-related offenses. We identify three main corruption-prone portfolios: defense, transportation/telecommunications, and energy/industry. These portfolios are listed in the Transparency International's Bribe Payers Index (2011) as the sectors of the economy most frequently cited by respondents as dominated by bribe-demanding bureaucrats and politicians and bribe-offering business actors (Hardoon and Hentich, 2011). Notably, the TI ranking of corruption-prone sectors is based on data from 28 countries around the world, among which only one post-Communist state (Russia). This distance from our cases means that when we estimate whether the availability of corruption opportunities is correlated with the probability of indictment, we are not following our data. In addition, we hypothesize that ministers who have spent longer time in office are more likely to become involved in corruption, because they would have more opportunities to identify a suitable corruption scheme.

Hypothesis 9. Ministers with corruption-prone portfolios are indicted more often.

Hypothesis 10. Ministers with longer tenure in office are indicted more often.

If prosecutions are good faith efforts to punish perpetrators of corruption, we can expect ministers from parties heavily involved in the privatization and marketization reforms of the 1990s to be prosecuted at higher rates. Those parties tended to build extensive networks of companies and bent the rules and syphoned state funds towards these companies. Communist successor parties were in a particularly privileged position to exploit these opportunities for amassing economic clout, so for them corrupt abuse of state office came close to becoming tacit party policy, rather than an unsanctioned aberration. We can expect the modus operandi from the 1990s to continue for older parties, and especially for communist successor parties, into the post-2000 period under study here. By contrast, reformist parties, especially those with a decidedly pro-European stance, as organizations usually take an anti-corruption stance and are thus more likely to monitor and actively discourage their ministers from engaging in corrupt acts. Standard principal-agent problems mean that some ministers from those parties will also attempt to enrich themselves from their office, but on average, we expect these individuals to engage in corruption at lower rates.

Hypothesis 11. Ministers from older and/or Communist successor parties are indicted more often. Ministers from newer, reformist and/or pro-European parties are indicted less often.

Party politics can also affect an individual minister's likelihood of indictment through the relative availability of political resources, which may help a minister elude legal repercussions. We hypothesize that ministers with more political resources at their disposal will be indicted less often. A minister's political resources stem from his/her incumbency status, from his/her position within a party, and from the party's relative political strength. Incumbent ministers have more resources to protect themselves from an indictment. They can use their control of the ministry to slow down, muddle, or even legally obstruct any investigation into their wrongdoing by withholding sharing of relevant documentation or discouraging cooperation by potential witnesses and whistleblowers. Ministers who are out of office, but are members of parliament also have significant political resources. Investigations against them cannot proceed towards an indictment without a formal majority vote by parliament to lift their immunity from prosecution. Ministers who have left office, but whose party is still in the government can benefit from protection by their co-partisans who are still incumbents. Their co-partisans drag out and obstruct (including in the legal sense) the prosecutorial investigation against them. The minister's position within their party will affect the probability that the party would go to bat to protect him or her from prosecution. The higher in the party hierarchy an individual is, the more political resources the party would be willing to expend. Individuals who have lost clout within their party may be thrown under the bus by their party in a parliamentary vote on the lifting of immunity from prosecution. Individuals who served in the executive as politically independent technocrats, who became politically unaffiliated at any point, or whose parties disappeared would be the most vulnerable to investigation and indictment because they would not have any political resources. In addition, an individual's level of political resource depends on his/her party's relative strength.

Ministers whose parties are in government will have greater opportunities to drag out and complicate the investigation and/or prevent an eventual indictment by blocking the immunity vote in parliament. Under coalition governments, the individuals belonging to the senior coalition partner will enjoy greater protection than their counterparts from the junior coalition partner. Finally, individuals whose party is in opposition will enjoy the lowest protection from prosecution.

Hypothesis 12. Incumbents, incumbent's co-partisans, and ministers from the senior coalition partner are indicted less often than ministers from the junior coalition partner, oppositionists, and independents.

Political resources are even more important if prosecutions are weapons used by powerful political actors against their competitors and opponents. Indicted politicians and their supporters regularly offer comments along the lines of Macedonia's VMRO party spokesman, who recently described the abuse of office investigation against former Prime Minister Nikola Gruevski as the creation of his political enemies, the Social Democrats: "The Special Public Prosecution is acting as a unit of the Social Democrats [...] It works only under political orders, and not on the basis of justice." (Okov, 2017).

If corruption prosecutions are indeed weaponized, the most vulnerable ministers will be those involved in close political competition with the political actors who control the investigation, the prosecution, and/or the courts. Politically unaffiliated or has-been individuals may also be more vulnerable as they are convenient scapegoats for incumbents who want to demonstrate that they are overseeing an effective fight against corruption or for prosecutorial institutions who want to demonstrate that they can catch "a big fish".

4. Hypothesis testing results

The country level hypotheses (numbers 1–8) are tested on the basis of a time-series cross-sectional dataset. This dataset includes thirteen annual observations (2000–2012) for each of the seven countries in our analysis, generating a total of 91 observations. The country-year data allow for a more fine-tuned measurement of our variables including the indictment rate, while also offering greater leverage for multivariate analysis. As the dependent variable, we take the annual indictment rate (presented above in Fig. 2) which is the percentage of the 'indictable' ministers who actually face charges during any given year. For our independent variables, we rely on a variety of data sources in addition to data collected specifically for this analysis.

First, to capture the strength of democratic institutions, we rely on the World Bank's Worldwide Governance Indicators, in particular the 'Voice and Accountability' index which gauges the extent to which policy making is subject to the informed democratic input of citizens (World Bank, 2018). Second, a robust investigative press is measured using the 'critical media' variable from the Varieties of Democracy Project (Coppedge et al., 2015). This variable is particularly suitable for testing the media hypothesis because it captures something about the behavior of news media by focusing on whether outlets are routinely critical of the government. Going beyond simply establishing what the theoretical constraints on freedom of the press are, this variable taps into whether there is tough and active journalism that takes advantage of those freedoms.

Third, the strength of the anti-corruption CSO sector is approximated using the broader Civil Society Index (again from the Varieties of Democracy Project) which reflects the strength of civil society more generally. This index combines characteristics of civil society organizations, including the extent to which they can operate independently from the state and the degree to which citizens are participating in them. Fourth, to gauge the role that specialized prosecutorial offices play, we construct a variable which is coded '1' for each year during which a country had such an office and '0' for every other year. Fifth, we rely on data generated by Linzer and Staton (2015) to estimate judicial independence. This source is particularly suitable for testing our hypothesis because it eschews the formal extent to which the judiciary should be independent of the executive according to constitutional rules, focusing instead on the degree of de facto independence that the judiciary enjoys given the practical balance of power in a country.

Sixth, to measure the political shifts that countries experience over time and that may create conditions under which prosecution of high-level officials becomes more likely, we calculate the number of seats that new parties occupy in the lower house of parliament of each country during each year. To be categorized as 'new', a party must not have been represented in parliament during the previous electoral cycle, and it cannot be the result of a merger, a party re-naming, or an ad hoc electoral coalition. This measure is different from ordinary electoral volatility insofar as it does not include the number of seats that changed hands between within the established party system. Because we intend to measure challenges to the party system, the focus on new parties is the most appropriate.

Seventh, to assess whether the legal successors to the communist regime that dominated politics in the region up the late 1980s affect the likelihood of prosecution in the 21st century, we construct a dummy variable that is coded '1' for each year a country's government included a successor party, and '0' for every other year. An additional measure that captures the nature of the incumbent government is the degree to which it supports EU integration. This variable draws on data compiled for the Chapel Hill Expert Survey during a series of waves starting in 2002 (Bakker et al., 2015). Where data was unavailable, we relied on Benoit and Laver (2006) or on separate Chapel Hill Surveys conducted in prospective EU member states in 2007 and 2014. On the basis of these sources, which rate party positions on EU integration, we construct a measure of the extent to which the incumbent government is pro-EU. We do so by taking the mean EU position of all parties included in the government coalition, weighted by the number of seats each party has in parliament. Finally, to estimate the impact of EU membership, we include a dummy variable that is coded '1' for each year a country was a member of the European Union. Table 4 summarizes the variables used in this analysis (see Table 3).

Table 3: Overview of convictions (2000–2012).

Country	Convicted	Acquitted	Conviction percentage
Bulgaria	0	11	0%
Croatia	5	2	71%
Czech Republic	0	4	0%
Macedonia	4	4	50%
Poland	2	2	50%
Romania	11	3	79%
Slovakia	0	0	N/A
Total	22	26	46%

As of June 2017. Eight cases are on-going at the time of writing.
Source: EECP database.

Table 4: Variable overview.

Variable	Scale	Min	Max	Mean	Source
Annual Indictment Rate	0–100	0	4.08	0.72	Authors' Calculation
Strength of Democracy	−2.5–2.5	−0.43	1.07	0.60	World Bank WGI
Critical Media	−5.0–5.0	−0.29	2.71	1.65	Varieties of Democracy
Civil Society Strength	0–1	0.75	0.94	0.89	Varieties of Democracy
Specialized Prosecution	0,1	0	1	0.25	Authors' Calculation
Judicial Independence	0–1	0.49	0.85	0.64	Linzer and Staton (2015)
New Party Seats	0–100	0	58.3	15.3	Authors' Calculation
Successor Party Incumbent	0,1	0	1	0.27	Authors' Calculation
Government Position on EU Integration	1–7	2.9	6.91	5.85	Chapel Hill Expert Survey; Benoit and Laver (2006)
EU Membership	0,1	0	1	0.43	Authors' Calculation

Note: Strength of Democracy and Critical Media are standardized variables with a mean of 0 and a standard deviation of 1. As a result of the standardization process, the lower and upper bounds are approximations that may be exceeded. Table 4 is generated by the authors through their statistical analysis.

A full analysis will involve analysis over time, but correlating long-term (2000-2012) averages can give a first sense of whether the data match the hypotheses. As a first step towards testing the hypotheses, the scatterplots in Fig. 3 present the correlation between average indictment rates and average values on selected independent variables for the seven countries. These plots offer initial confirmation for hypotheses 6 and 7, which both link party politics to indictments. The aggregate data show a positive link between the success of new parties in the most recent elections and the likelihood of indictment. In addition, between 2000 and 2012, pro-EU governments were likely to see more indictments than more euro-skeptic governments, in line with hypothesis 7. Finally, governments that included a successor party had a far lower average indictment rate than governments composed of parties without a communist-era heritage (0.42% vs. 0.83% - not displayed).

Fig. 3.   Indictment rate correlated with independent variables (2000-2012 averages).

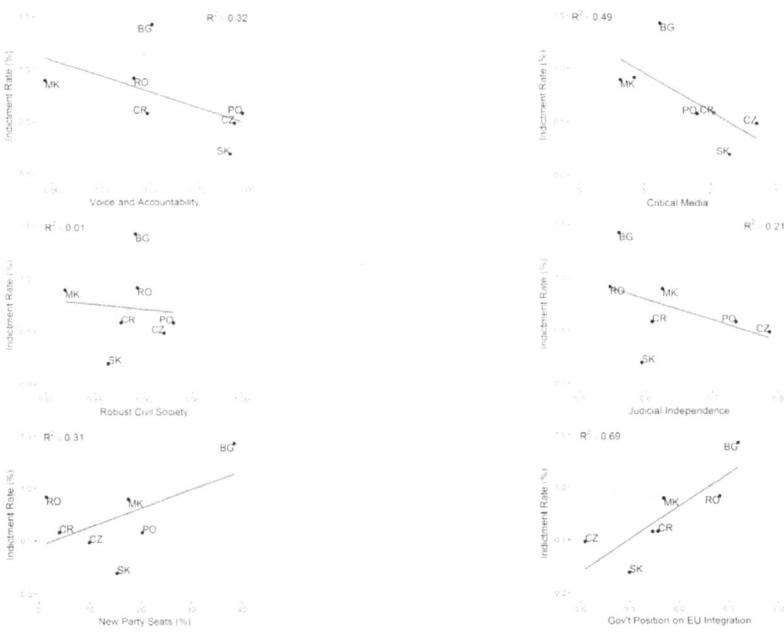

At the same time, the bivariate plots do not confirm hypotheses linking elements of democratic political culture to the likelihood of indictment. On the whole, indictments were most likely in the countries with weaker democracies and less critical journalism. Both these findings run counter to what we have hypothesized. The effect of civil society, expected to lead to a greater number of indictments, is also negligible. The bivariate analysis also does not find overwhelming support for the hypothesis that specialized prosecution offices increase the volume of corruption indictments. For years in which countries had such institutions, the average indictment rate was 0.77%; for all other years, the rate was 0.70%.

To fully test these hypotheses, it is necessary to go beyond the 2000-2012 averages and investigate the within-case variation over time as well. In addition, multivariate regression makes it possible to isolate the effect of individual variables while controlling for other causal factors. The fact that the observations in the pooled dataset (7 countries * 13 years) are not strictly independent does necessitate adjustments to the regression model—which otherwise follows the rules of standard OLS regression. In particular, it requires a more conservative way of estimating standard errors known as panel correction (Beck and Katz, 1995). In addition, to address the issue of repeated observations, we add a one-year lag of the dependent variable (indictment rate) to the predictive model, as well as country dummies, following Wilson and Butler (2007). The results of this regression analysis are presented in Table 5.

Table 5 reveals weak support for most hypotheses. The only expectation born out by the data is that fewer corruption indictments of cabinet ministers happen during the tenure of governments by Communist successor parties. The other part of Hypothesis 7 is not supported by the evidence, however. EU and reformist party tenure in government is not associated with a higher indictment rate. The combination of these results suggests that corruption indictments spike up whenever Communist successor parties are out of government. In other words, Communist successor parties are less likely to oversee many investigations into grand political corruption than their political opponents, whoever they are. This correlation may stem from the real or perceived involvement of Communist successor parties in grand corruption.

The most notable correlation is the negative relationship between the level of democracy and the indictment rate. Higher indictment rates are associated with weaker democratic institutions. Indictment rates are unaffected by the presence of a robust civil society, media that regularly challenges the government, and an independent judiciary. These results suggest that corruption prosecutions are more often weapons in political confrontations, rather than a cleansing mechanism in consolidating democracies.

The country-level analysis presented so far has been unable to include individual-level characteristics that might play a role in exposing some ministers to greater risk of indictment than others. Especially given the relatively poor performance of country-level variables in accounting for the varying indictment rates exhibited over time in each country, shifting our perspective to the individual level may provide useful insights that can help us understand the dynamics at play. We offer an initial test of two types of hypotheses on the sources of individual-level variation. One type (hypotheses 9 and 10) links the likelihood that a minister is indicted to his/her exposure to opportunities for corruption. We operationalize this by distinguishing between ministers on the basis of the portfolios they held, assuming that some ministries (defense, transportation, and economy, including telecommunications, energy and industry) give greater access to discretionary spending than others. The raw numbers (presented in Table 6) bear out this supposition, with those three portfolios all boasting above-average indictment rates.

Table 5:   Regression analysis of annual indictment rate.

Variable	Coefficient	Standard error
Strength of Democracy	-2.06	1.03*
Critical Media	0.15	0.41
Civil Society Strength	9.87	7.14
Specialized Prosecution	0.30	1.04
Judicial Independence	-1.79	6.00
New Party Seats	0.01	0.01
Successor Party Incumbent	-0.44	0.23*
Gov't Position on EU Integration	-0.05	0.13
EU Membership	0.29	0.28
Indictment Rate Previous Year	-0.17	0.13
Country Dummies	-0.75	
Croatia	-0.15	1.14 1.44
Czech Republic Macedonia	-0.24	0.77 1.26
Poland	-0.12	1.13
Romania	-0.46	0.78
Slovakia	-0.26	
Intercept	-2.06	1.03

Dependent variable is annual indictment rate.
Standard errors are panel corrected.
$R^2 = .31$ | N = 84 | *$p < 0.10$; **$p < .05$; ***$p < .01$.
Table 5 is generated by the authors through their statistical analysis.

Table 6: Indictments by cabinet portfolio (2000-2012).

Portfolio	Indicted Holders	Total Holders	Indictment rate
Defense	8	49	16.3%
Agriculture	6	52	11.5%
Economy	6	67	9.0%
Labour	4	48	8.3%
Deputy PM	9	123	7.3%
Transportation	4	57	7.0%
Prime Minister	2	33	6.1%
Health	4	66	6.1%
Interior	3	58	5.2%
Other	13	269	4.8%
Education	3	66	4.5%
Finance	2	47	4.3%
Environment	2	64	3.1%
Justice	1	58	1.7%
Foreign Affairs	0	43	0.0%
Culture	0	46	0.0%

Note: Totals exceed the total number of indictments and total number of cases in this analysis because different portfolios were held concurrently or in sequence by the same individual. Source: EECP database.

The second set of hypotheses (11 and 12) draws on the notion that indictments may be politically motivated, and that ministers vary in the extent to which they can use political resources to insulate themselves from legal jeopardy and avoid indictment. We operationalize this by distinguishing between the ministers whose party was the senior coalition partner and those whose party was the junior coalition partner. Of the 927 ministers in the data set, 435 belong to a major coalition party and 260 belong to a minor party; only 6.2 per cent of the former group was indicted, compared to 9.2 per cent of the latter group. Another implication of this hypothesis is that once ministers leave office and once their parties enter the opposition, they become more vulnerable and are more likely to be indicted. We have not collected data on incumbency status for all ministers, also because these factors vary over time and the individual-level data set is not set up to handle variation over time at this time. However, we can investigate the sub-sample of indicted ministers to see whether indictments are more likely to happen to ministers who have left office and whose parties are in the opposition. Table 7 shows that this is in fact the case, with the majority of indictments (54%) occurring at a time when the minister's party was in opposition, and an additional 26% coming after the minister left the government (while their party remained in government). Only a small proportion of the indictments happened to incumbent ministers. While this result is due in part to the fact that indictments take time to prepare and rely on information about wrong-doing to emerge over the months and years, they do suggest that the political position of a cabinet minister have an impact on their capacity to elude investigation and prosecution.

To further test these individual-level hypotheses, we conduct additional regression analysis. In this analysis, the dependent variable is whether an individual minister was indicted (1) or not (0). In addition to the portfolio variable (1 for a corruption-prone portfolio, 0 for all others) and the party status variable (1 for a junior coalition partner, 0 for all others), we include two controls. First, we assume that a greater time spent in office exposes the minister to greater opportunities for corruption and, in turn, makes an indictment more likely. Second, we assume that the greater time elapsed since a minister entered office makes indictment more likely, as prosecutors will have had more time to investigate and whistle-blowers will have had more time to expose wrong-doing. Both variables (time in office and time since first appointment) are measured in months. Finally, we include country dummies to account for country level variation in the likelihood of indictment. Table 8 presents our findings.

Table 7: Minister's political status at time of indictment (2000-2012).

Country	Minister in Office	Minister out of Office, Party Incumbent	Minister out of Office, Party in Opposition	Total
Bulgaria	1	1	9	11
Croatia	0	4	3	7
Czech Republic	1	3	1	5
Macedonia	2	3	4	9
Poland	1	0	6	7
Romania	6	4	5	15
Slovakia	0	0	2	2
Total	11	15	30	56

Source: EECP database.

Table 8: Logistic regression.

Variable	Coefficient	Standard Error
Party Status	0.040**	0.019
Portfolio	0.058***	0.021
Time in Office	–0.000	0.001
Time since Appointment	0.000**	0.000
Country Dummies		
Croatia		
Czech Republic	–0.062*	0.033 0.033
Macedonia	–0.058*	0.034
Poland	–0.065*	0.032
Romania	–0.074** 0.018	0.031
Slovakia	–0.103***	0.037
Intercept	0.07	0.03

Dependent variable is dichotomous (indictment ¼ 1, no indictment ¼ 0). Coefficients are logits.
*p < 0.10; **p < .05; ***p < .01.
Table 8 is generated by the authors through their statistical analysis.

Both hypotheses find confirmation in this analysis. The model predicts that of the ministers who belong to a senior coalition partner and who serve in a capacity that exposes them to few opportunities for corruption, 4.95% will be indicted. By contrast, cabinet ministers who belong to a junior partner and who hold a corruption-prone portfolio are three times more likely to be indicted (14.56%).

5. Conclusions and further research

This article introduced the East European Corruption Prosecution Database, proposed a series of hypotheses about the determinants of indictment rates across countries over time and the probability of indictment for individual ministers, and tested some of them by using the EECP database. The main conclusions we can draw is that Bulgaria, Romania and Macedonia consistently indict more ministers than Croatia, Czech Republic, and Poland; Slovakia has barely indicted anyone. We find no strong evidence that EU conditionality or membership raises the profile of the grand corruption issue or leads to more indictments. Party politics seems to affect the frequency of corruption indictments more than the structure and behavior of legal institutions. Indictment rates are lower when a former Communist party controls the government and individual ministers from junior coalition partners are more vulnerable to indictment than other ministers. The existence of a specialized anti-corruption prosecution or a more independent judiciary do not seem to lead to the indictment of more ministers on corruption charges.

Our initial empirical analysis reveals interesting results, but it also draws attention to the challenges of testing the hypotheses we have proposed here. Pooling the observations from different countries may not be the most fruitful empirical approach. It is possible that a variable has a powerful effect in one setting and a negligible or even negative effect elsewhere. Future research should start from the assumption that the hypotheses that we identified may hold in some places while they should be rejected elsewhere, and should ask what underlying processes account for the different functioning of such key variables as EU pressure and judicial reform. Crucially, future research should focus on how to determine reliably whether, where and when corruption prosecutions are a political weapon used against competitors or a bona fide effort of state institutions to root out grand corruption. The conflation of these two phenomena into the same observable event (an indictment or a verdict) complicate the analysis. Finally, future steps to systematically track and map out the phenomenon of tackling grand corruption through criminal prosecutions can include deputy ministers and heads of executive agencies, members of parliament, and elected and appointed heads of subnational administrative units (governors, mayors, municipal council chairs and members).

Acknowledgement

The authors would like to acknowledge generous grant support by Canada's Social Science and Humanities Research Council (SSHRC) (410-2011-1878) and the Fonds de Recherche du Quebec — Société et Culture (2012-NP-149492). We also thank all the research assistants who worked on data collection and data entry: Radu Parvulescu, Radu Giosan, David Dolibog, Sonja Solomun, Cristina Voicu, Ezster Sipos, Costin Ciobanu, Anabel Semerdjieva, and Juhi Sujan. Vincent Post thanks Maryanne Mutch for her support.

References

Anderson, C.J., Tverdova, Y.V., 2003. Corruption, political allegiances, and attitudes toward government in contemporary democracies. Am. J. Polit. Sci. 47(1), 91–109.

Bågenholm, A., Charron, N., 2014. Do politics in Europe benefit from politicising corruption? W. Eur. Polit. 37 (5), 903–931.

Bakker, R., De Vries, C., Edwards, E., Hooghe, L., Jolly, S., Marks, G., Polk, J., Rovny, J., Steenbergen, M., Vachudova, M.A., 2015. Measuring party positions in Europe: the Chapel Hill expert survey trend file, 1999–2010. Party Polit. 21 (1), 143–152.

Balan, M., 2011. Competition by denunciation: the political dynamics of corruption scandals in Argentina and Chile. Comp. Polit. 43 (4), 459–478.

Bankuti, M., Halmai, G., Scheppele, K.L., 2012. Disabling the constitution. J. Democr. 23 (3), 138–146.

Beck, N., Katz, J.N., 1995. What to do (and not to do) with time-series cross-section data. Am. Polit. Sci. Rev. 89 (3), 634–647.

Benoit, K., Laver, M., 2006. Party Policy in Modern Democracies. Routledge.

Bobek, M., 2008. Fortress of judicial independence and the mental transitions of the central European judiciaries. The. Eur. Pub. L. 14, 99.

Bobek, M. (Ed.), 2015. Selecting Europe's Judges: a Critical Review of the Appointment Procedures to the European Courts. Oxford University Press, USA.

Börzel, T.A., Schimmelfennig, F., 2017. Coming together or drifting apart? The EU's political integration capacity in Eastern Europe. J. Eur. Publ. Pol. 24 (2), 278–296.

Bugaric, B., 2008. Populism, liberal democracy, and the rule of law in Central and Eastern Europe. Commun. Post Commun. Stud. 41 (2), 191–203.

Bugaric, B., Ginsburg, T., 2016. The assault on postcommunist courts. J. Democr. 27 (3), 69–82.

Coman, R., De Waele, J.M., 2007. Judicial Reforms in central and Eastern European Countries. Vanden Broele.

Coppedge, M., Gerring, J., Lindberg, S.I., Skaaning, S.E., Teorell, J., Altman, D., Bernhard, M., Fish, M.S., Glynn, A., Hicken, A., Knutsen, C.H., 2015. V-dem [country-year/country-date] Dataset V5. Varieties of Democracy (V-dem) Project.

Dallara, C., 2014. Democracy and judicial reforms in South-East Europe. In: Between the Eu and the Legacies of the Past.

Doig, A., 1995. Good government and sustainable anti-corruption strategies: a role for independent anti-corruption agencies? Publ. Adm. Dev. 15 (2), 151–165.

Elbasani, A., Sabic, S.S., 2017. Rule of law, corruption and democratic accountability in the course of EU enlargement. J. Eur. Publ. Pol. 1–19.

Ganev, V.I., 2003. The Bulgarian constitutional court, 1991-1997: a success story in context. Eur. Asia Stud. 55 (4), 597–611.

Goldston, J., 2006. Public interest litigation in central and Eastern Europe: roots, prospects, and challenges. Hum. Right Q. 28 (2), 492–527.

Grigorescu, A., 2006. The corruption eruption in East-Central Europe: the increased salience of corruption and the role of intergovernmental organizations. East Eur. Polit. Soc. 20 (3), 516–549.

Hanretty, C., 2014. The Bulgarian Constitutional Court as an additional legislative chamber. East Eur. Polit. Soc. 28 (3), 540–558.

Hardoon, D., Heinrich, F., 2011. Bribe Payers index 2011. Transparency International, Berlin.

Herron, E.S., Randazzo, K.A., 2003. The relationship between independence and judicial review in post-communist courts. J. Polit. 65 (2), 422–438.

Holmes, L., 2003. Political Corruption in central and Eastern Europe. In Corruption in Contemporary Politics. Palgrave Macmillan, London, pp. 193–206.

Holmes, L., 2017. Curbing post-communist corruption: external pressure vs. domestic commitment. In: A Quarter Century of Post-Communism Assessed. Palgrave Macmillan, Cham, pp. 99–126.

Iancu, B., 2019. Quod licet Jovi non licet bovi?: The Venice Commission as Norm Entrepreneur. *Hague Journal on the Rule of Law*, pp. 1-33.

Karklins, R., 2016. The System Made Me Do it: Corruption in Post-communist Societies: Corruption in Post-communist Societies. Routledge.

Kosar, D., 2016. Perils of Judicial Self-government in Transitional Societies. Cambridge University Press.

Kostadinova, T., 2012. Political Corruption in Eastern Europe: Politics after Communism. Lynne Rienner Publishers, Boulder, CO.

Langseth, P., 2001. Value Added of Partnership in the Fight against Corruption. United Nations Office for Drug Control and Crime Prevention, Centre for International Crime Prevention.

Lederman, D., Loayza, N.V., Soares, R.R., 2005. Accountability and corruption: political institutions matter. Econ. Polit. 17 (1), 1–35.

Levitz, P., Pop-Eleches, G., 2010. Why no backsliding? The European Union's impact on democracy and governance before and after accession. Comp. Polit. Stud. 43 (4), 457–485.

Linzer, D.A., Staton, J.K., 2015. A global measure of judicial independence, 1948-2012. J. Law Courts 3 (2), 223–256.

Meagher, P., 2005. Anti-corruption agencies: rhetoric versus reality. J. Pol. Reform 8 (1), 69–103.

Mendelski, M., 2012. EU-driven judicial reforms in Romania: a success story? East Eur. Polit. 28 (1), 23–42.

Mendelski, M., 2015. The EU's pathological power: the failure of external rule of law promotion in South Eastern Europe. SE. Eur. 39 (3), 318-346. Mungiu, A., 2006. Corruption: diagnosis and treatment. J. Democr. 17 (3), 86–99.

Noutcheva, G., Bechev, D., 2008. the successful laggards: Bulgaria and Romania's accession to the EU. East Eur. Polit. Soc. 22 (1), 114–144.

O'Donnell, G.A., 1998. Horizontal accountability in new democracies. J. Democr. 9 (3), 112–126.

Offe, C., Adler, P., 1991. Capitalism by democratic design? Democratic theory facing the triple transition in East Central Europe. Soc. Res. 865-892.

Okov, S., 2017. 'Republic of Macedonia to seize Ex-Premier's Passport amid scandal'. Bloomberg, 4 July. https://www.bloomberg.com/news/articles/2017-0704/republic-of-macedonia-court-rules-to-seize-ex-premier-s-passport. (Accessed 10 June 2018).

Parau, C.E., 2012. The drive for judicial supremacy. In: Judicial Independence in Transition. Springer, Berlin, Heidelberg, pp. 619-665.

Pop-Eleches, G., 2010. Throwing out the bums: protest voting and unorthodox parties after communism. World Polit. 62 (2), 221-260.

Popova, M., 2010. Be careful what you wish for: a cautionary tale of postcommunist judicial empowerment. Demokratizatsiya 18 (1), 56.

Popova, M., 2012. Why Doesn't the Bulgarian judiciary prosecute corruption? Probl. Post-Communism 59 (5), 35-49.

Quah, J.S., 1999. Corruption in Asian countries: can it be minimized? Publ. Adm. Rev. 483-494.

Sajo, A., 1998. Corruption, clientelism, and the future of the constitutional state in Eastern Europe. E. Eur. Const. Rev. 7, 37.

Sandholtz, W., Taagepera, R., 2005. Corruption, culture, and communism. Int. Rev. Sociol. 15 (1), 109-131.

Schedler, A., 1999. Conceptualizing accountability. In: The Self-restraining State: Power and Accountability in New Democracies, 13, p. 17.

Scheppele, K.L., 2005. Democracy by judiciary. Or, why courts can be more democratic than parliaments. Rethink. Rule Law Communism 53-54.

Schönfelder, B., 2005. Judicial independence in Bulgaria: a tale of splendour and misery. Eur. Asia Stud. 57 (1), 61-92.

Schwartz, H., 2000. The Struggle for Constitutional justice in post-communist Europe. University of Chicago Press.

Smithey, S.I., Ishiyama, J., 2002. Judicial activism in post-communist politics. Law Soc. Rev. 36, 719.

Spendzharova, A.B., Vachudova, M.A., 2012. Catching up? Consolidating liberal democracy in Bulgaria and Romania after EU accession. W. Eur. Polit. 35 (1), 39-58.

Tavits, M., 2007. Clarity of responsibility and corruption. Am. J. Polit. Sci. 51 (1), 218-229.

Treisman, D., 2000. The causes of corruption: a cross-national study. J. Publ. Econ. 76 (3), 399-457.

Van Aaken, A., Feld, L.P., Voigt, S., 2010. Do independent prosecutors deter political corruption? An empirical evaluation across seventy-eight countries. Am. Law Econ. Rev. 12 (1), 204–244.

Wilson, S.E., Butler, D.M., 2007. A lot more to do: the sensitivity of time-series cross-section analyses to simple alternative specifications. Polit. Anal. 15 (2), 101–123.

World Bank, 2018. Governance Indicators. http://databank.worldbank.org/data/home.aspx. (Accessed 9 June 2018).

When Civil Engagement is Part of the Problem: Flawed Anti-Corruptionism in Russia and Ukraine

Marina Zaloznaya, William M. Reisinger, Vicki Hesli Claypool
Department of Sociology, The University of Iowa, Iowa City, Iowa, USA,
Department of Political Science, The University of Iowa, Iowa City, Iowa, USA

In developing countries, the fight against corruption entails purges of political and business elites and the restructuring of electoral, financial, and social provision systems, all of which are costly for the incumbents and, therefore, unlikely without sustained pressure from civil society. In the absence of empirical analyses, scholars and practitioners have, therefore, assumes that civil society plays an unequivocally positive role in anti-corruptionism. In this article, we challenge this dominant assumption. Instead, we show that, under certain conditions, an engaged non-governmental community may, in fact, undermine the fight against corruption. Using the data from forty interviews with anticorruption practitioners in Ukraine and Russia, as well as primary documentary sources, we present two models of anti-corruptionism whereby active civil engagement produces suboptimal outcomes. One is faux collaboration, defined as a façade of cooperation between the state and civil society, which hides the reality of one-sided reforms. The other model is that of non-collaborative co-presence, whereby the governance role is shared by the government and non-governmental activists without compromise-based solutions. In both cases, civil engagement helps perpetuate abuses of power and subvert such long-term goals of anti-corruption reforms as democratization and effective governance.

Keywords: Civil society, Corruption, Anti-Corruption, Reform, Russia, Ukraine

In recent decades, the international community has mobilized against a common enemy — corruption (Sampson, 2010; Cole, 2015). Based on abundant research that links corruption to poor economic performance and weak democratic governance (see Lambsdorff,

2007 for an overview), the World Bank has declared corruption "the single greatest obstacle to economic and social development" (Andersson and Heywood, 2012, p. 34). Pressured and incentivized by intergovernmental organizations and domestic constituents, many developing states have vigorously taken up "anti-corruptionism" or systematic reforms to curb the abuses of power.

The success of national anti-corruption reforms, however, has varied greatly. The former Soviet bloc has seen instances of decreased corruption following state-orchestrated reforms, for example, in Georgia (Kupatadze, 2012), as well as instances of selective achievements, like in the Ukrainian criminal justice system (Friesendorf, 2017), and even more numerous cases where purported efforts by national government have not yielded tangible results — in, for instance, Moldova (Transparency International, 2017) and Kyrgyzstan (Ramani, 2015). Scholars attribute these uneven outcomes to cross-national differences in material resources, level of intervention, and variance in political will for earnest reform (Persson et al., 2013; Khan, 2006).

In this article, we focus on one specific characteristic of anti-corruption programs that is widely considered fundamental for their success — the engagement of civil society. Using in-depth interviews with anti-corruption practitioners from Russia and Ukraine, we argue that civil society's participation in anti-corruption reforms does not always increase their effectiveness. Rather, our case studies suggest that a dysfunctional relationship between governmental and non-governmental actors may impede, rather than promote, efforts to eradicate corruption.

In the following two sections, we lay out theoretical arguments for the importance of civil society in promoting genuine anti-corruption reforms and highlight the likely challenges to an effective civil action in this domain. After discussing methodology and justifying our case selection, we describe the two models whereby active engagement of civil society undermines anti-corruption reforms in Russia and Ukraine. First, we focus on the Russian case, where the government subverts the anti-corruptionism by creating a façade of collaboration with civil society and neutralizing the reforms that could challenge the entrenched political corruption. We then turn to Ukraine, where aggressive action by the non-governmental community undermines anti-corruptionism by weakening popular trust in formal institutions, provoking strong opposition from the government, and lowering the legitimacy of ensuing reforms. In conclusion, we discuss the implications of our findings for the dominant consensus that civil society is an unequivocally positive force in the fight against corruption, and raise several questions for further empirical analyses and theorizing.

1. Civil society as a solution to the "orthodox paradox"

For any country, anti-corruption reforms present a paradox. While only national governments hold requisite power and resources to implement large-scale changes in the electoral/campaign financing systems, reorganize social provision, and prosecute those implicated in corruption (Stapenhurst and Langseth, 1997; Ionescu, 2014), anti-corruption initiatives necessarily go against the self-interest of incumbent political elites. For state actors, effective anti-corruption reforms undermine the sources of extra-legal income and carry risks of defamation and prosecution (Abdulai, 2009). It is this internal contradiction embedded in the government-driven anti-corruptionism that Fritzen (2005) calls the "orthodox paradox".[1]

The conditions under which states exhibit genuine political will for reforms have, therefore, become an important focus of policy and academic work on anti-corruptionism. Empirical studies, for instance, suggest that pressure from the international community may help resolve the orthodox paradox (Heineman and Heineman, 2004). Through incentives ranging from recognition to loans,

---

1 While this framing assumes that all the elites share a common level of political will, in our other work, we argue that oftentimes some elites see ways to benefit from the reforms while others do not. Similarly, we argue that civil society actors exhibit different motivations behind, and different degrees of commitment to, anti-corruptionism (Zaloznaya et al., unpublished).

and by threat of economic and diplomatic sanctions, inter-governmental organizations like the International Monetary Fund and the European Union urge developing states to adopt anti-corruption laws and establish independent oversight and criminal justice institutions (Ristei, 2010; Sampson, 2010).

The most widely-recognized solution for the "orthodox paradox", however, is the involvement of active and well-resourced non-governmental groups who are not explicitly engaged in political competition with the incumbents (Kaufmann, 1998; Fritzen, 2005). Domestic and international non-governmental organizations (INGOs) may introduce policy ideas, pressure local governments to turn them into legislation, raise support for their implementation, and monitor the methods used to generate compliance (Mingiu-Pippidi, 2010).

Civil society groups have on multiple occasions helped overcome governmental resistance to genuine anti-corruptionism. For instance, in 1999, the World Bank effectively negotiated the inclusion of civil society in the anti-corruption reforms in Paraguay, which proved to be central to their success (Asis, 2000). Similarly, the anti-corruption surge in post-Suharto Indonesia resulted from consolidated pressure from the civil society (Azra, 2007). By contrast, the reforms carried out by the government of Bolivia without active involvement of non-governmental groups had disappointing results (Asis, 2000). There is also statistical evidence that size and strength of civil society are negatively related to corruption. For instance, Mingiu-Pippidi's (2010, p. 11) analysis of the Corruption Perception and Civil Society Indices shows that "civil society by itself explains 70% of the variation in corruption" in East and Central Europe.

In light of this evidence, it is hardly surprising that "good governance" initiatives of intergovernmental organizations usually support the engagement of civil society in the anti-corruption process. For instance, the United States Agency for International Development (USAID) spends large sums of money on improving the "organizational capacity of [local] Civil Society Organizations to become stronger citizen advocates and government watchdogs", while the European Union made "civil society strengthening" a core of its Neighborhood Anti-Corruption Policy (Martini, 2012).

2. Why doubt the impact of civil engagement?

While it is not surprising that scholars and practitioners put much faith in civil society, we argue that, in the context of anti-corruptionism, the complicated relationship between governmental and non-governmental (NG) actors may undermine the positive impact of civil engagement. For one, when it comes to anti-corruptionism, civil society and the government have fundamentally incompatible goals. State actors tend to approach relevant reforms from the vantage point of self-preservation, promoting a limited vision of restructuring (Fritzen, 2005). NGO actors, by contrast, seek to directly challenge what they see as an unfair advantage of the elites. Moreover, because leaders of domestic anti-corruptionism stand to garner significant material and symbolic rewards from international and domestic publics, governmental and non-governmental actors are likely to compete over its ownership (Sampson, 2012). For instance, incumbent politicians may gain praise from Western counterparts and increase their electoral support while NG actors may obtain grant funding and access to political office vacated through purges (de Sousa et al., 2012).

In this article, we assess how the relationship between governmental and non-governmental actors influences the outcomes of anti-corruption drives. We show that, under certain conditions, an engaged non-governmental community may, in fact, undermine anti-corruption reforms. Using data from Ukraine and Russia, we present two models through which active civil engagement produces suboptimal outcomes. One is faux collaboration, defined as a façade of cooperation that hides the reality of one-sided reforms. The other model is that of non-collaborative co-presence, whereby the governance role is shared without compromise-based solutions. In both cases, civil society may help perpetuate abuses of power and subvert such long-term goals of anti-corruption reforms as democratization and effective governance.

3. Methodology

In the summer and fall of 2015, we collaborated with two local research firms[2] to carry out forty in-depth semi-structured interviews with anti-corruption practitioners in Russia and Ukraine. Initial interviewees were recruited through the professional networks of our local partners; our samples were then filled out through snowball sampling. Half of our sample was employed in governmental agencies in a variety of positions ranging from members of parliament to heads of organizational anti-corruption divisions and deputy ministers. The rest of the respondents worked in non-governmental organizations, ranging from large international NGOs to small citizen activist groups. In Table 1 below we provide a general description of the affiliation and position of our interviewees, crafted to preserve their confidentiality.

In Russia, the respondents were interviewed by a trained local researcher in Moscow, Kazan, Kostroma, and Barnaul; in Ukraine, the first author of this article interviewed nineteen respondents in Kyiv and one respondent over Skype. Some respondents were interviewed in their places of work; others—in a location of their choice, such as the office of our partner research firms or a cafe. Our interviews lasted between forty minutes and two hours. Discussion topics included the history of local anti-corruptionism, specific anti-corruption initiatives, and the relationships among local actors involved in anticorruption efforts, among others.

Our data were later complemented with a survey of NGO reports, policy analyses, and local and Western press coverage of anti-corruptionism in the two countries. These sources provided additional information on the anti-corruption initiatives and their reception by local publics. References to these sources are included at the end of the article.

---

2   Because Russian government has persecuted researchers collaborating with Western universities in the past, we omit the names of our partners.

Table 1. Professional affiliation of interview respondents[3]

N	RUSSIA		UKRAINE	
	Governmental	Non-Governmental	Governmental	Non-Governmental
1	Member of Parliament, minority party	Head, national association of prominent activists	Head, Subcommittee on Interactions with Civil Society, parliamentary anti-corruption committee	Head, Anti-Corruption Expertise Department, investigative thinktank
2	Consultant of the anti-corruption division of human resources office, regional government	Executive head, inter-regional organization focused on corruption in business	Head of a department, General Prosecutor's Office	Senior manager, civil society capacity building donor initiative
3	Specialist in anti-corruption, governing board of a federal transportation agency	Working group member, public chamber of the government of one of Federal Republics	Officer, government agent for anticorruption, Cabinet of Ministers	Group manager for healthcare reform, an NGO coalition
4	Member of Parliament, minority/oppositional party	Legal analyst, an investigative oppositional NGO	Acting head, Sector on Prevention and Detection of Corruption, one of the ministries	Vice head, one of good governance initiatives, USAID
5	Head, anti-corruption committee of the governance board, state-owned corporation	Senior researcher, public chamber, Ministry of Internal Affairs of one of the Federal Republics	Head, Sector on Evaluation and Elimination of Corruption Risks, one of the ministries	Project director, donor-funded educational non-profit
6	Head, human resources office, federal government	President, interregional anticorruption movement	Deputy Minister, one of the ministries	Director, domestic investigative NGO
7	President, governmental anticorruption committee	Head, regional support center for civic initiatives	Head, sub-department, Ministry of Internal Affairs	Head, grassroots anti-corruption movement
8	Secretary, regional committee of a minority party	Vice head, regional anti-corruption committee	Head, Department of Prevention and Combating Corruption, one of the ministries	Analyst for criminal justice reform, an NGO coalition
9	Head, municipal anti-corruption committee	Officer, local chapter of a transnational NGO	An executive, The Anti-Corruption Bureau	Head, local chapter of a transnational NGO
10	Head of regional anti-corruption sector	Head, regional anti-corruption center	High-level official, the Secret Service of Ukraine	Head, independent think-tank

Source: Compiled by the authors

To derive generalizable patterns from our interview and documentary data, we employed a set of analytical principles known as grounded theory. Corbin and Strauss (1990, p. 9) write that this approach aims "to build a theoretical explanation by specifying phenomena in terms of conditions that give rise to them, how they are expressed through action/interaction, the consequences that result from them, and variations of these qualifiers". Grounded theory-

---

[3] For confidentiality purposes, the numbers assigned to respondents in Table 1 do not correspond to numbers in references that follow the quotes, presented in this article.

building combines induction and deduction, and is iterative: typically, a researcher begins with a broad empirical question and derives a preliminary outline of a theory from its systematic analysis; he or she then returns to the data to look for empirical evidence with a goal of confirming and fine-tuning the emerging theory (Corbin and Strauss, 1994).

4. Case selection: Russia and Ukraine

As former Soviet republics, Russia and Ukraine share a legacy of high-level political corruption and widespread in-kind corruption in the public sector, fostered by consumer deficits and pervasive red tape. The two countries have also experienced similar patterns of monetization of informal exchange systems, criminalization of large sectors of respective economies, and state capture during the 1990s. For the last two decades, Russia and Ukraine have received similar rankings on the world's most widely-used corruption indicator, the Transparency International Corruption Perception Index, and have been treated similarly in social science literature on corruption (Rimskii, 2013; Zaloznaya, 2017).

Importantly, in the last five years, both Russia and Ukraine embarked on extensive and highly publicized quests to clean up corruption. Russian government initiated an anti-corruption campaign in the wake of popular protests of 2011–2012. Public discontent with pervasive informal practices in business and politics laid a foundation for the oppositional movement of Alexei Navalny, a young lawyer whose blog documents large-scale corruption at the intersection of state and business affairs. The ruling party, United Russia, chose to deal with Navalny's growing popularity by tackling the issue that mobilized public sentiment—corruption. An anti-corruption campaign, revved up after Putin's reelection in 2012, testifies to the President's determination to signal to the public that ruling elites, rather than opposition, offer the leadership and resources necessary to "fix the country" (Krastev and Inozemtsev, 2013: 9–15).

In Ukraine, an anti-corruption surge followed the Revolution of Dignity in 2014 (also known as Euromaidan), morphing, over time, into an all-encompassing project of societal transformation (Fluri and Badrack, 2016). In the eyes of many Ukrainians and foreign leaders, the country's battle against corruption has become a precondition for its democratization, economic survival, and future as a member of the European community. The infusion of these larger meanings into Ukraine's anti-corruptionism is not incidental. Ukraine's two pro-democracy uprisings in the post-Soviet period, the Orange Revolution and the Revolution of Dignity, both started with popular discontent with widespread corruption, seen as the reason why Ukraine is stuck in the cycle of economic underperformance and subservience to Russia (Editors of Open Democracy, 2017).

5. Russia: involvement of civil society in anti-corruptionism

Our interviews reveal that both governmental and non-governmental actors are actively involved in Russia's fight against corruption. Most commonly-referenced NGOs were public chambers (общественные палаты) — committees made up of civil activists, business representatives, and private lawyers, who oversee the legislative bodies and governmental agencies engaged in anti-corruption work. The main function of these chambers is to identify the "corruption risks" associated with new laws and consult state actors on avoiding these risks. Such chambers exist on different levels of governance — from the Presidential administration to national ministries and municipal governments (Russian Non-Governmental Sector — RNG 3, 5, 9).

Besides public chambers, a number of grassroots citizen groups, like Youth Human Rights Movement (2017) and the musical group of rapper Noize MC (Checkmenova, 2012), are also involved in Russia's anti-corruptionism. Such groups organize outreach, educational, and popular campaigns that promote accountability among low-level officials. One example is a recent campaign to check the identification documents of local police officers (Transparency International, 2013). In addition to concerned citizen groups, Russia hosts multiple professional NGOs that foster relationships between civil society and the business community, such as, Committee for Fighting Corruption (2017), develop legal bases for eradicating corruption in corporate relations, like the Center for Business Ethics and Corporate Governance (2017), and engage in other initiatives. One such organization, the Anti-Corruption Foundation, established by Alexei Navalny, claims to be the only Russia-based NGO that investigates, exposes and fights corruption among high-ranking Russian government officials" (Anti-Corruption Foundation, 2017). Lastly, several branches of INGOs focused on corruption, such as Transparency International and National Endowment for Democracy (2017), also operate in Russia.

5.1. Russia: relationship between the government and NG anti-corruption players

Our data suggest that despite the proliferation of non-governmental "integrity warriors" (Sampson, 2010) of various types, Russia's anti-corruptionism is largely orchestrated by the central government, which dictates the rules of engagement by civil activists and closely monitors their compliance with these rules. Based on our interviews, we argue that in the sphere of anti-corruptionism, the relationship between Russian government and non-governmental actors is best described as "faux cooperation": while the state curates an appearance of collaboration, it also systematically undermines the impact of nongovernmental community.

First, Russia's incumbent elites sabotage the efforts of civil society by strategically selecting which non-governmental entities are allowed to get involved. In July 2012, President Putin signed into law the infamous bill "On Foreign Agents",[4] which imposes strict regulatory requirements on non-commercial organizations that

---

4   In Russian, Федеральный закон РФ "О внесении изМенений в отдельные законодательные акты Российской Федерации в части регулирования деятельности некоММерческих организаций, выполняющих функции иностранного агента".

partake in political activity and receive support from foreign governments. Under this law, any such NGO must register as an agent of a foreign country and open itself to governmental inspections (Russia Today, 2014). Human Rights Watch and other independent monitors have condemned this law for its attempts to "control independent groups by strangling them in kilometers of red tape" and for allowing the authorities to easily dispose of their critics (Checkmenova, 2012). Many anti-corruption organizations in Russia, such as Transparency International, are subject to pressure under the Foreign Agents law (Young, 2015).

Another, less-known but, arguably, even more exclusionary legislation is the 2015 law about "Undesirable Organizations".[5] This law gives Russian government the right to recognize any group as "undesirable" if, based on determination of Prosecutor General, "its activity endangers the security of the Russian state and undermines its constitutional bases" (Rbc.ru, 2015). Any organization proclaimed undesirable can be closed and its employees can be subjected to administrative and criminal punishment. Since the adoption of this law, several NGOs involved in anti-corruptionism have been recognized as undesirable, with a special emphasis on vocal critics of Putin's regime, such as Open Russia, the Institute of Modern Russia, and the Open Russia Civic Movement (MacFarquhar, 2017).

While only a handful of civil society organizations have been closed under these laws, many are controlled through thorough inspections and audits, which supply the state with information on the groups' activity and generate pressure on their members to "walk the line". Here is how one of the leaders of a Russian branch of a global anti-corruption NGO described the experience of his organization: "at any point in time, we have someone auditing us — ROSKOMNADZOR (The Federal Service for Supervision of Communications, Information Technology and Mass Media (2017)), the Ministry of Justice, the Prosecutor's Office, so on. They spend days and nights in our office. It almost never happens that there are no

---

5 In Russian, закон «О нежелательных организациях».

external monitors here, in our office." [RNG 10] He added that inspections become especially rigorous after the publication of cross-national corruption rankings, which are often unfavorable to Russia.

Additionally, these laws have negative reputational consequences for some anti-corruption NGOs, creating schisms that weaken the entire non-governmental sector. For instance, one interviewee contrasted her "patriotic" NGO with others that accept funding from foreign donors: "We won't take a single ruble from any foreigners and we are not going to sell our motherland. [...] members of our committee, we went through a rather earnest Soviet preparation, and through public service [...]. For us, "motherland" is not an empty word, and never in our life will we [...] use the money." [RNG 2] This quote shows that some NG practitioners adopt state-crafted distinctions between "loyal" and "disloyal" groups, turning against their counterparts in civil society. As another interviewee aptly put it, the laws on "undesirable organizations" and "foreign agents" — besides having very tangible consequences for select organizations -- are a part of broader "propaganda campaign" that the government is waging against non-governmental and non-commercial organizations as an attempt to control them [and] make them weaker." [RNG 8]

In addition to controlling entire organizations, Russia's government engages in systematic vetting of their individual members. Our interviews suggest that high-level state officials tend to informally approve the appointment of members of public chambers and anti-corruption committees, especially those in leadership positions [RNG 3,7]. Retention of these positions is also contingent on political loyalty. For instance, one respondent testified to state censorship in the anticorruption commission in the office of the President: "this anti-corruption commission [...], it continues to exist. But first, they got rid of one very honest person, true anti-corruption fighter [...], then they got rid of me, then they got rid of Sholohov, the head of a civil rights protection organization." [RNG 7] Through such selection of members, civil society organizations turns into a shell, filled out with governmental loyalists.

Lastly, Russia's government sets up its own organizations that appear to be based in civil society. One interviewee called such organizations GNGOs or Governmental-Non-Governmental Organizations. GNGOs "approve everything all the time [...] legislators put out a draft of a bill – they approve; presidential administration does this – they approve; ministry does that – they approve [...] All these GNGOs they are very well-financed. While organizations that are independent, the ones that our authorities do not understand, their sources of funding are constantly undermined ..." [RNG 10]

Besides shaping the make-up of the non-governmental field, Russia's political elites also limit the power of civil action by putting restrictions on cases that NG groups are allowed to tackle. Multiple interviewees maintained that most corruption cases, in which non-governmental actors are engaged in any meaningful capacity deal with small-scale, bureaucratic corruption [Russian Government (RG) 5; RNG 4,5,8]. Most civil groups spend their time investigating instances of such corruption, matching complaining citizens with resources, and referring them to law enforcement [RNG 9].

Street-level law enforcement agencies, such as municipal police departments and local prosecutors' offices have emerged as a cornerstone of Russia's anti-corruption drive. Our respondents from the government and civil society alike stressed the punitive emphasis of the anti-corruption measures in local bureaucracies. In the words of one, when it comes to employees of street-level organizations, such as doctors and teachers, "we have a strategy that [...] every person proven guilty – receives the appropriate punishment." [RNG 2] In a system focused on punishing low-level bureaucrats, Russia's civil society provides critical support to the country's under-resourced law-enforcement apparatus. In fact, our non-governmental respondents often mentioned with chagrin that their organizations get bogged down with endless complaints of petty corruption from citizens reluctant to work with law enforcement directly. NG groups spend significant resources to build the cases, which, according to our interviewees, often "die" in the archives of local police offices [RNG 1,3].

At the same time, multiple respondents complained that Russian government forcefully limits civil involvement in cases that deal with large sums of money or implicate political and business elites. As a rule, such limitations come in the form of neglected reports of the abuses of power and stymied investigation and prosecution efforts. For instance, one NGO official told us that her organization's "work with concrete [high-level] instances" of corruption usually does not bear any results: "in cases like this, we have only experienced defeat [...] I have yet to see a single case, where a company that got a contract noncompetitively was removed or that some bosses and directors were actually fired." [RNG 3] Other interviewees corroborated: "we do have effective punishment for corruption but, as a rule, only of those who do not have links to authorities ... Those in the government always get their people out of trouble" [RNG 6]; and: "those who are involved in large-scale corruption [...] they either avoid punishment altogether or get something minimal and symbolic." [RNG 8][6]

As a liaison between ordinary citizens and low-level law enforcement, civil society has little role to play in cases against wealthy, influential and politically-connected individuals. Thus, Russian government's disproportional focus on petty corruption has not only made the entire anti-corruptionism project "safe" for the status quo but allowed the state to avoid genuine collaboration with civil society, circumscribing the latter's impact on the outcome of anti-corruption reforms.

Related is the third way in which the state undermines the power of NG actors in Russia's anti-corruptionism: the government systematically limits the access that these actors have to resources.

---

6 It is important to note that prosecution of high level officials for corruption does happen in present-day Russia. Examples include recent arrests of the Economic Development Minister, Ulyukaev, and the acting head of an anti-graft agency at the Russian interior ministry, Zackharchenko. However, our interviews and previous research suggest that these cases represent selective and politicized justice, often carried out to pressure specific officials and to showcase the coercive power of the state. Thus, only officials who are threatening, disloyal, or otherwise undesirable to the regime run a risk of exposure and punishment. Such singular cases instigate elite loyalty through fear and contribute to the public appearance of a crackdown on corruption (Hartog and Fishman, 2016).

For instance, when asked about the biggest challenge to Russia's anti-corruption NG community, one interviewee singled out the irresponsiveness of state agencies: "the government and the law enforcement ignore [our] opinions, inquiries, and the information that [we] provide." [RNG 4] Other respondents concurred: "the government system is closed" [RNG 5]; "[C]ivil society organizations [...] are ignored [...] or dealt with some formal excuses," [RNG 2] and "[the government] doesn't always hear us." [RNG 10] Some interviewees attributed the government's reluctance to collaborate to Russia's lacking a tradition of civic engagement: "It's alien to them. We understand "civil society" as all the people who care [...] In their understanding, civil society is non-military society, that is, anybody who is not wearing epaulets ..." [RNG 10] Others, however, argued that government-imposed limits on access by civil society is a strategic way of undermining anti-corruptionism. In the words of one respondent, "the opposition from state agencies and officials [...] detracts resources and attention from fighting corruption." [RNG 7]

5.2. Discussion: subversion of anti-corruptionism through civil engagement in Russia

Our data suggest that civil society is active in Russia's fight against corruption. In fact, non-governmental community plays a central role in eradicating the abuses of power by street-level bureaucrats in present-day Russia. Moreover, our interviews reveal that NG activists do work with the country's government, albeit on strict and exclusionary terms, laid out by the state.

Our findings suggest that such limited cooperation between the government and civil society ends up undermining and subverting Russia's fight against corruption. While some autocratic leaders, such as leaders of Belarus and Singapore, sabotage anti-corruption reforms through an outright exclusion of civil society, Russian state's approach is subtler and harder to criticize. As Russia's public has grown more sophisticated through travel and exposure to information, it could be risky for state elites to pretend that civil society has no role to play in raising the accountability of the government. Instead, Putin's government embraced the non-governmental sector while also placing clear and impenetrable boundaries on what its representatives could do in the fight against corruption. Thereby, Russian state created an appearance of a collaborative campaign while also ensuring that none of its outcomes seriously threaten the power of influential incumbents. An important benefit of such pseudo cooperation with civil society was that it offered Russia's leadership a way to appease the country's population and, to a more limited degree, the international community. The appearance of incorporation of nongovernmental actors has, likely, raised the legitimacy of the state and buffered it from popular criticism (especially, on the domestic arena), all the while creating a façade behind which the corrupt activities of the elites continue to go unchallenged.

6. Ukraine: involvement of civil society in anti-corruptionism

In the wake of the Revolution of Dignity - Ukraine's most recent wave of anti-corruption, pro-democracy protests enthusiasm for reform was palatable inside and outside the Ukrainian government. As former president Yanukovich was ousted and the presidency went to a political outsider, Petro Poroshenko, a large number of Euromaidan activists, most without prior experience in politics, gained seats in the country's parliament. Those who remained in the civil society formed a strong coalition, Reanimation Package of Reforms (2017), and numerous other organizations.

International support for Ukraine's anti-corruptionism — a recognized central ingredient for democratization and development - has been unprecedented. In the context of Russia's growing geopolitical power, Ukraine emerged as the West's foothold in the region and the buffer zone between Putin's aggressive and expansionary regime and the European Union. Thus, a wide range of governments and intergovernmental organizations provide funding to domestic civil society groups and chapters of INGOs focused on fighting corruption. United States government is one of the largest contributors via programs of USAID, UNDP, and the World Bank. The support of other Western governments comes primarily through the European Commission and the European Bank for Reconstruction and Development.

Such plethora of funding opportunities gave rise to a dynamic, competitive, and diverse non-governmental sector focused on corruption. A coalition called the Reanimation Package of Reforms (2017) alone brings together eighty NGOs and twenty-two expert groups, working on areas as diverse as judicial accountability, public administration, healthcare, and electoral system. There is also a number of domestic watchdog groups overseeing the implementation of anti-corruption initiatives (Center for Political Studies and Analysis, 2017; Our Money-Nashi Groshi, 2017) or that investigate and publicize abuses of power by high-level officials (Anti-Corruption Action Center, 2017). Distinct from these organizations are international NGOs, such as Transparency International, stand-alone projects funded by Western donors, such as UNITER (2017), and domestic grassroots groups, such as No to Corruption–Ni Habarnitstvu (2017).

6.1. Ukraine: relationship between governmental and NG anti-corruption players

Despite donors' and academics' expectations of productive cooperation between Ukraine's outsider-led government with a strong mandate to fight corruption and a uniquely-active and well-resourced civil society, Ukraine's anti-corruptionism has been characterized by acute competition and mutual undercutting among the involved actors. In this article, we argue that the relationship between Ukraine's governmental and NG anticorruption players can be best described as non-collaborative co-presence, which impedes rather than promotes the goals of anti-corruptionism.

First, our interviews reveal that both types of actors engage in the public questioning of the other side's fitness to carry out the task in question, casting doubt on the purity of each other's motivations, strength of each other's commitment, and each other's expertise.

The most direct criticism comes from the civil society, which vigorously challenges the state's professed will to eradicate corruption. Thus, one of our interviewees, involved in a management capacity in a high-level civil society organization, lamented that "when there is no political will, civil society becomes powerless. Yes, after Maidan, the civil society provides a number of services but it cannot fully replace the government ... than what do you have? State within a state. It is dangerous." [Ukrainian Non-Governmental Sector (UNG) 4] As an example, several respondents invoked reluctance of authorities to enforce the law that limits the size of gifts that officials can receive from their clients. According to our interviewees, activists routinely set up cameras outside medium-level officials' offices around the holidays and document people enter the buildings carrying presents that far exceed the allowed cost and leave the offices without these offerings [UNG 2,8].

In turn, governmental actors question the motivations of NG activists because of their affiliation with foreign governments and international organizations.[7] For instance, shortly after the online asset declaration system for public servants was introduced as an important step towards greater governmental accountability (promoted vigorously by civil activists), lawmakers announced a bill "that would require all organizations receiving foreign funds for anti-corruption work to submit financial disclosures of their own" (Standish and Bateson, 2016). This thinly-veiled attempt at retaliation has, however, cast greater shadow on the will of the Ukrainian government to fight corrupt, provoking unflattering comparisons to Putin's law on "foreign agents." [UNG 8]

Interestingly, even Ukraine's most progressive governmental officials and even some domestic non-governmental groups question the legitimacy of civil activists who accept foreign funding — not because it makes local actors beholden to the interests of other

---

[7] It is important to note that while the Ukrainian government uses these accusations to discredit and weaken civil society, scholars and policy-makers also question the impact that financial dependence on foreign donors has on Ukrainian non-governmental actors involved in anti-corruptionism (Moroff and Schmidt-Pfister, 2010).

governments but because outside powers, allegedly, do not understand what is best for Ukrainians. For instance, one high-level official with a generally-favorable view of civil society told us that "current approach in which a lot of NGOs are making a lot of money through grants is not the best Ukraine. Many donors want to create new agencies, instead of focusing on the ones that already exist. That's wasteful, and that benefits [them], they get to say they accomplished this or that [....] and does little for us." [Ukrainian Government (UG) 1] An interviewee from the Ministry of Internal Affairs corroborated: "I just don't understand why spend millions to make something new and unknown if [...] we already have great human resources. [...] But saying that everybody is bad, let's just get rid of everyone ... We're not that rich to be able to afford that!" [UG 10]

Governmental respondents also suggested that competition for external funding tarnishes the purity of civil society's motivations: "they choose grant-funded initiatives over other ones, even if other ones may be more sensible, because it is prestigious and pays good salaries. They don't think about the people." [UG 2] Another interviewee echoed this sentiment claiming that a high-profile international NGOs speak "really well and know how to appeal to donors and to local community but that what they are doing is just not the best for the country." [UG 8]

Related are governmental actors' attempts to exclude civil society by arguing that NGOs lack experience making or implementing policy. In the words of one governmental interviewee, NGO leaders are "people who [...] had never worked inside the government; their proposals often are quite detached from reality, impossible to implement." [UG 1] Another respondent, a law-enforcement official, insisted that the work of non-governmental activists brings no concrete results in the fight against corruption: "There are all these papers being written, all these new approaches being developed but, really, the effectiveness of it all is pretty dismal." He called civil society activists, "demagogues", "wasting everybody's time." [UG 10] Another interviewee summarized: "What are all these agencies [...] good for? They bring no actual results." [UG 2]

In addition to their adversarial rhetoric, Ukraine's government and civil society, reportedly, erect actual roadblocks to the initiatives promoted by their counterparts. One infamous case of such obstruction involves President Poroshenko's extended refusal to fire the former Prosecutor-General Shokin despite the mounting evidence of Shokin's involvement in the so-called case of Diamond prosecutors.[8] Since our interviews took place during the prolonged impasse in this case, all but one of our NG respondents complained about Poroshenko's reluctance to support the investigation. While civil society activists were demonstrating, writing op-eds, and appealing to their foreign supporters, the President not only refused to fire the Prosecutor General but actually pressured civil society activists to stop criticizing Shokin.

In 2016, local press reported similar government-orchestrated delays in the launch of the e-declarations system which required public officials to publicly report their income and assets. According to *Ukrainska Pravda*, the State Service of Special Communications and Information Protection of Ukraine has "intentionally intervened to prevent the launch of e-declarations" by refusing to issue a security certificate allegedly due to bugs in the software and hardware "for collecting and storing electronic income declarations of Ukrainian state officials filed via the Internet" (Sydorenko, 2016).

In their turn, the governmental respondents complained about the personal attacks that civil society groups launch against high-level politicians, charging that they amount to a "political circus" that "detracts from the real issues" and "undermines" the state's attempts at reform [UG7]. Other interviewees lamented what they saw as a dilution effect of civil engagement on the success of

---

8   The case of Diamond Prosecutors involved the arrest of two high-level law enforcement officials, Volodymyr Shapakin, the head investigator of the prosecutor general's office, and Oleksandr Korniets, the former deputy prosecutor of Kyiv region. Shapakin and Korniets were charged with bribery, extortion, and racketeering after sixty-five diamonds, large sums of cash, and an unregistered weapon were found in their possession. Then Prosecutor-General Shokin pressed for the release of the two men even though the collected evidence of their alleged crimes warranted an investigation and a trial (Allen, 2015).

governmental initiatives: "There are so many different [non-governmental] agencies that work on anti-corruption [...] The more entities work on this problem, the less good they produce. The responsibility gets diffused, divided and spread around. [...] All it does is make it harder for [...] those who really fight corruption [government]." [UG4] Another interviewee, a member of the parliament, corroborated: "The competition with NGOs gets in the way of achieving our [anti-corruption] goals." [UG 1]

Lastly, just as in Russia, Ukraine's anti-corruption players suffer from deliberate limitations on access to reforms; yet, in case of Ukraine, these limitations are not unidirectional but imposed by governmental as well as non-governmental practitioners on each other. Thus, Ukrainian NG activists complain of being excluded from the design of anti-corruption reforms. Such critique, for instance, is leveled in regards to Ukraine's recent police reform. According to one non-governmental interviewee, "nobody listened to our input. After the fact, we were told to evaluate, but it was already too late because these evaluations really don't change much." [UNG 10] Marat (2015) reached the same conclusion: "Civil society activists are only invited to oversee procedures already in place, as opposed to generating ideas for the reform's direction. The vision of change is transmitted directly from the deputy-minister level to specific projects on the ground, bypassing public discussion".

Other interviewees argued that inclusion of civil society into anti-corruption process is superficial and does not permit for genuine collaboration. For instance, our NG interviewees reported participating in debates about policy but not in policy construction: "They invite us [...] to show to Europeans and the Americans that we remember, we invite civil society to participate" and "they often make pronouncements but nothing is done after." [UNG 7] Local and Western press also reports that Ukraine's political elites put undue strain on individual activists and non-governmental groups to exclude them from the anti-corruption reforms (Sambozhuk, 2017; Vitkin, 2017).

On their part, governmental representatives complain about the non-governmental community's alleged attempts to exclude state actors from the anti-corruption process. For instance, political elites argue that recent civil society-led campaign to establish an independent anti-corruption court is motivated by the desire to sideline incumbent leaders and advance political aspirations of NG activists (Apostrophe.ua, 2017) and Western donors' ambition to control Ukraine's political development (RIA Novosti, 2017).

6.2. Discussion: subversion of anti-corruptionism through civil engagement in Ukraine

Our data reveal that, perhaps due to the remarkable volatility of the country's political landscape in the post-Soviet era, active anti-corruption efforts of Ukraine's civil society are perceived by the national government as a threat to incumbents. The resulting governmental approach to their non-governmental counterparts is that of risk management. The government not only seeks to keep civil society out of the anti-corruption sphere (which is a common dynamic in interactions between state and civil society worldwide) but aims to actively undermine it. Faced with such treatment, Ukrainian NG actors intensify their attacks on the government and actively discredit rather than support its anti-corruption initiatives, thereby "fulfilling the prophecy" and closing the vicious circle of mutual undercutting.

The on-going reciprocal attacks by Ukraine's "integrity warriors" inside and outside the state apparatus negatively impact the country's fight against corruption. First, they decrease the legitimacy of anti-corruption actors in both camps and reduce public trust in formal institutions. The results are costly for a society that has been suffering from failed reforms and broken political promises since the early nineties. The Euromaidan uprising of 2014, which set off the most recent round of anticorruption reforms, marked the second time that people of Ukraine put their faith in pro-democracy and anti-corruption elites within a decade. More than once, an in-coming 'revolutionary' government made lofty promises of spurring economic growth while pleading with the public to tolerate austerity measures, high unemployment, and inflation. The unrealized promise of the Orange Revolution of 2004 and the lack of success by Euromaidan reformers make sustained popular mobilization behind the anti-corruption cause less likely. According to recent reports, Ukrainians' patience with "integrity warriors" is thinning, and it is unclear whether they will receive another chance (Wood, 2017). In an interview with Foreign Policy, the International Republican Institute's director for Eurasia, Stephen Nix, claimed that the "government has to realize that the window is closing on this. They have taken some concrete steps but clearly not enough" (Standish and Bateson, 2016).

Besides the direct effects of diminishing public support for the "integrity warriors", lowered trust in institutions also undercuts the project of anti-corruptionism. Since popular support for the government is a source of its strength, continuous attacks from the civil society decrease state capacity to design and oversee effective reforms. Moreover, researchers find that low trust in formal institutions, in and of itself, increases law-breaking (Tyler, 2006). Weakened legitimacy of various political and criminal justice institutions is, therefore, likely to independently raise the rates of corruption (Uslaner, 2008).

The cycle of mutual undercutting also negatively impacts the ability of non-governmental actors to contribute to the anticorruption project. Vociferous attacks from the state decrease their ability to mobilize citizens and foster grass-roots action, diminish their access to resources, and marginalize them on the political arena. More broadly, given the importance of a strong civil society for the maturation of democratic political order, which, as research suggests, decreases corruption in its own right (Montinola and Jackman, 2002), sustained attacks on civil society have baneful long-term consequences.

In addition to the reputational costs to both sides, reciprocal undermining by governmental and NG actors weakens the anti-corruption reforms that are currently underway: it erects obstacles to the passage of legislation, produces delays in its implementation, and incentivizes sabotage by on-the-ground actors. Such direct effects combine with cumulative disadvantage as donors become disappointed with the returns on their investments, decreasing their material and symbolic support for Ukraine's anti-corruption project (Renasch, 2017).

7. Conclusions and unanswered questions

The dominant consensus in academic and policy circles that civil society is an unequivocally positive force in the fight against corruption offers an oversimplified understanding of its impact. While civil society may—and often does—encourage, hasten, and strengthen anti-corruption reforms, we show that it may also undermine the letter and spirit of anti-corruptionism. The Ukrainian and Russian cases present two distinct models of how this may occur. In Russia, incumbent political elites cultivate an appearance of fostering an active civil society and involving it in the anti-corruption efforts while carefully controlling the parameters of this involvement. In this model, civil engagement increases the domestic support for an autocratic regime and shields political and business corruption from detection and prosecution. In Ukraine, an overly-active civil society threatens the government, generating a vicious cycle of mutual undercutting, which leads to stalled reforms, lowered public trust of formal institutions, and decreased support for anti-corruptionism from the domestic and international publics.

Not only do our conclusions suggest that researchers should jettison the assumption that civil society always plays a positive role in fighting corruption, but they raise several important empirical questions. First, due to the unique geopolitical history of Ukraine and Russia, the two models we have identified are unlikely to represent all possible ways, in which civil engagement can be detrimental to anti-corruptionism. What are the other mechanisms whereby civil engagement undermines the fight against corruption? Specification of these models is an important intellectual project as each will have distinct effects on anti-corruptionism and democratization. The awareness of the boundaries between beneficial and pathological civil engagement can, therefore, result in better policies and increase the return on foreign investment in local anti-corruption initiatives.

The second empirical issue arising from our findings concerns the relationship among the different models of civil engagement in anti-corruptionism and, consequently, the scope conditions that give rise to these models. Since many social scientists think about Russia and Ukraine as representing different extents of democratization, it is possible that the two models of civil society involvement in anti-corruptionism, described in this article, represent two points on a continuum between fully representative governments and states that are captured by autocratic elites. Conceivably, at one end of this continuum lies a fully-cooperative relationship between an independent civil society and an open government, and on the other—complete exclusion of civil society from anti-corruptionism by the incumbent state actors. Empirical analyses are necessary to ascertain the existence of such continuum or to identify alternative scope conditions giving rise to distinct models of detrimental civil engagement in anti-corruption reforms.

Another empirical question suggested by our findings concerns the stability of various models of civil engagement in anti-corruptionism. Because all models between the two extremes, described above, allow for some involvement by civil society, they are likely to generate internal impulses for their own transformation into different models. For instance, in Russia, even the limited involvement by civil society may, over time, destabilize the corruption equilibrium, leading to a more meaningful participation of NG community in anti-corruption and other reforms. Similarly, over time, the domestic and international support for Ukraine's over-active civil society may diminish, making it less threatening to the government and leading to a more productive collaboration between the two. Time may, therefore, play an important independent role in moving a country along the democratization continuum, hypothesized earlier. Investigating the temporal dimension of anti-corruptionism, especially in cases where civil engagement exists but does not promote the letter or spirit of the reforms should constitute an important goal of social scientists working on this topic in the former Soviet Union and beyond.

Acknowledgement

This paper is based upon work supported by, or in part by, the U.S. Army Research Laboratory and the U.S. Army Research Office under grant number W911NF-14-1-0541.

References

Abdulai, A., 2009. Political will in combating corruption in developing and transition economies: a comparative study of Singapore, Hong Kong and Ghana. J. Financ. Crime 16 (4), 387-417.

Allen, C., 2015. Ukraine: New Government, Same Corruption. Al Jazeera. Available at: https://www.aljazeera.com/indepth/features/2015/12/ukrainegovernment-corruption-151206133110489.html. (Accessed 29 May 2018).

Andersson, S., Heywood, P., 2012. Anti-corruption as a risk to democracy. In: de Sousa, L., Larmour, P., Hindess, B. (Eds.), Governments, NGOs, and Anticorruption: the New Integrity Warriors. Routledge, New York, pp. 33-51.

Anti-Corruption Action Center, 2017. [online]. Available at: https://antac.org.ua/en/pro-nas/[Accessed 29 December 2017].

Anti-Corruption Foundation. (2017). About Us, [online]. Available at: https://fbk.info/english/[Accessed 29 May 2018].

Apostrophe.ua, 2017. Суд По "Посадке" Топ-Чиновников: Стало Известно, Чего Боятся Власти Украины. Available at: https://apostrophe.ua/news/society/ accidents/2017-10-05/sud-po-posadke-top-chinovnikov-stalo-izvestno-chego-boyatsya-vlasti-ukrainyi/109351. (Accessed 29 May 2018).

Asis, M., 2000. Coalition-building to Fight Corruption. Anti-corruption Summit. World-Bank Institute. Available at: http://unpan1.un.org/intradoc/groups/public/documents/un-dpadm/unpan044605.pdf. (Accessed 29 December 2017).

Azra, A., 2007. Religious-based civil society and anti-corruption campaign. In: James, H. (Ed.), Civil Society, Religion and Global Governance: Paradigms of Power and Persuasion. Routledge, New York, pp. 288-300.

Center for Business Ethics and Corporate Governance. 2017. [online]. Available at: http://www.ethicsrussia.org/index.php [Accessed 29 May 2018].

Centre for Political Studies and Analysis. 2017. About Us, [online]. Available at: http://cpsa.org.ua/en/[Accessed 29 December 2017].

Checkmenova, M., 2012. Russia's Civil Society. Fordham Political Review. Available at: http://fordhampoliticalreview.org/russia%e2%80%99s-civil-society/ (Accessed 29 December 2017).

Cole, W., 2015. Institutionalizing a global anti-corruption regime: perverse effects on country outcomes, 1984e2012. Int. J. Comp. Sociol. 56 (1), 53-80.

Committee for Fighting Corruption. 2017. [online]. Available at: http://www.againstcorruption.eu/articles/russian-ngo-launches-anti-corruptionprogram/ (Accessed 29 December 2017).

Corbin, J., Strauss, A., 1990. Grounded theory research: procedures, canons, and evaluative criteria. Qual. Sociol. 13 (1), 3-21.

De Sousa, L., Hindess, B., Larmour, P, 2012. Introduction. In: de Sousa, L., Larmour, P., Hindess, B. (Eds.), Governments, NGOs, and Anti-corruption: the New Integrity Warriors. Routledge, New York, pp. 1-15.

Editors of Open Democracy, 2017. Is the Anti-corruption Agenda All that It's Cracked Up to Be? Opendemocracy.net. Available at: https://www.opendemocracy.net/od-russia/editors-of-opendemocracy-russia/is-anti-corruption-agenda-all-that-it-s-cracked-up-to-be (Accessed 29 December 2017).

Fluri, P., Badrack, V., 2016. Anti-corruption Measures in Ukraine after the Revolution of Dignity. Center for Army, Conversion and Disarmament Studies, Kyiv.

Friesendorf, C., 2017. Police reform in Ukraine as institutional bricolage. Probl. Post-Communist., 1–13.

Fritzen, S., 2005. Beyond "political will": how institutional context shapes the implementation of anti-corruption policies. Pol. Soc. 24 (3), 79–96.

Groshi, Nashi, 2017 [online]. Available at: http://nashigroshi.org (Accessed 29 December 2017).

Habarnitstvu, Ni, 2017 [online]. Available at: http://nihabarnyctvu.org.ua (Accessed 29 December 2017).

Hartog, E., Fishman, M., 2016. The Loyalty of Fear: Putin Sends a Message to the Elites with the Arrest of Russia's Economic Development Minister. The Moscow Times. Available at: https://themoscowtimes.com/articles/the-loyalty-of-fear-56159. (Accessed 29 December 2017).

Heineman, B., Heimann, F., 2006. The long war against corruption. Foreign Aff. 85 (3), 75–86.

Ionescu, L., 2014. The role of government auditing in curbing corruption. Econ. Manag. Financ. Market. 9 (3), 122-149.

Kaufmann, D., 1998. Challenges in the Next Stage of Anti-corruption. New Perspectives on Combating Corruption. The World Bank, pp. 139--164. Available at: http://siteresources.worldbank.org/INTWBIGO VANTCOR/Resources/challenges.pdf (Accessed 29 December 2017).

Khan, M., 2006. Governance and anti-corruption reforms in developing countries: policies, evidence, and ways forward. United nations conference on trade and development. In: G24 Discuss. Pap. Ser, 42. Available at: http://eprints.soas.ac.uk/9920/1/UNCTAD_GDS_M DPB_G24_2006_4.pdf (Accessed 29 December 2017).

Krastev, I., Inozemtsev, V., 2013. Putin's self-destruction. Foreign Aff. 915. Available at: http://cddrl.fsi.stanford.edu/sites/default/files/krast tev_and_ inozemtsev_putins_self-destruction.pdf (Accessed 30 May 2018).

Kupatadze, A., 2012. Explaining Georgia's anti-corruption drive. Eur. Secur. 21 (1), 16–36.

Lambsdorff, J., 2007. Causes and consequences of corruption: what do we know from a cross-section of countries? In: Rose-Ackerman, S. (Ed.), International Handbook on the Economics of Corruption. Edward Elgar Publishing Ltd., UK, pp. 3–52.

MacFarquhar, N., 2017. Russia Bans Group Led by Kremlin Critic as More Protests Loom. N. Y. Times. Available at: https://www.nytimes. com/2017/04/26/world/europe/open-russia-khodorkovsky-putin -opponent-protests.html (Accessed 29 December 2017).

Marat, E., 2015. The problem with Ukrainian police reform. Foreign Pol. Available at: http://foreignpolicy.com/2015/12/29/the-problem-with-ukrainianpolice-reform-ukraine/(Accessed 1 January 2018).

Martini, M., 2012. European Union Strategies to Support Anti-corruption Measures in Neighboring Countries. U4 Expert Number. Anti-Corruption Resource Center. Available at: https://www.transparen cy.org/files/content/corruptionqas/345_EU_strategies_to_support _AC_measures_in_neighbouring_ countries.pdf (Accessed 29 December 2017).

Montinola, G., Jackman, R., 2002. Sources of corruption: a cross-country study. Br. J. Polit. Sci. 32 (1), 147–170.

Moroff, H., Schmidt-Pfister, D., 2010. Anti-corruption movements, mechanisms, and machines—an introduction. Global Crime 11 (2), 89–98.

Mungiu-Pippidi, A., 2015. The Quest for Good Governance: How Societies Develop Control of Corruption. Cambridge University Press, Cambridge.

National Endowment for Democracy. (2017). [online]. Available at: https://www.ned.org/ (Accessed 29 December 2017).

RIA Novosti, 2017. Антикоррупционный Суд и Борьба С Кастой Неприкасаемых. Available at: https://rian.com.ua/country/20171 103/1029099625/antikorrupcionnyy-sud-ukrania.html (Accessed 29 December 2017).

Persson, A., Rothstein, B., Teorell, J., 2013. Why anticorruption reforms faildsystemic corruption as a collective action oroblem. Governance 26 (3), 449-471.

Ramani, S., 2015. Kyrgyzstan's Anti-corruption Failure. The Diplomat. Available at: https://thediplomat.com/2015/10/kyrgyzstans-anti-corruption-failure/ (Accessed 29 December 2017).

Rb.ru, 2015. Путин Подписал Закон О нежелательных Иностранных Организациях. Available at: http://www.rbc.ru/politics/23/05/2015/55609f719a794774b30bd2a7 (Accessed 29 December 2017).

Reanimation Package of Reforms. 2017. [online]. Available at: http://rpr.org.ua/en/ (Accessed. 29 December 2017).

Rensch, S., 2017. Ukraine to step up anti-corruption efforts amid international concerns. Publ. Finance Int. Available at: http://www.public financeinternational.org/news/2017/12/ukraine-step-anti-corrupti on-efforts-amid-international-concerns (Accessed 2 January 2018).

Rimskii, V., 2013. Bribery as a norm for citizens settling problems in government and budget-funded organizations. Russ. Polit. Law 51 (4), 8-24.

Ristei, M., 2010. The politics of corruption: political will and the rule of law in post-communist Romania. J. Commun. Stud. Transit. Polit. 26 (3), 341-362.

Russia Today, 2014. Федеральный Закон 121 "Об Иностранных Агентах". Available at: https://ria.ru/spravka/20140616/1011656413.html (Accessed 29 December 2017).

Sambozhuk, N., 2017. Сотрудничество или Борьба? Новые Тенденции Антикоррупционной Политики. Ukrainskaya Pravda. Available at: http://www.pravda.com.ua/rus/columns/2017/10/2/7156966/. (Accessed 29 December 2017).

Sampson, S., 2010. The anti-corruption industry: from movement to institution. Global Crime 11 (2), 261-278.

Sampson, S., 2012. Corruption and anti-corruption in southeast Europe. In: de Sousa, L., Larmour, P., Hindess, B. (Eds.), Governments, NGOs, and Anticorruption: the New Integrity Warriors. Routledge, New York, pp. 168-186.

Standish, R., Bateson, I., 2016. Ukraine has opened Pandora's database of corruption. Foreign Pol. Available at: http://foreignpolicy.com/2016/11/04/ukrainecorruption-declaration-poroshenko-clinton-trump-russia-oligarch/ (Accessed 29 December 2017).

Stapenhurst, F., Langseth, P., 1997. The role of the public administration in fighting corruption. Int. J. Public Sect. Manag. 10 (5), 311-330.

Sydorenko, S., 2016. Who Scuppered the Launch of Digital Income Declarations? Ukrayinska Pravda. Available at: http://www.pravda.com.ua/eng/articles/2016/08/14/7117707/ (Accessed 29 December 2017).

The Federal Service for Supervision of Communications, Information Technology and Mass Media. 2017. [online]. Available at: http://rkn.gov.ru/eng/ (Accessed 29 December 2017).

Transparency International, 2013. Two Sides of Fighting Corruption in Russia. Available at: https://www.transparency.org/news/feature/two_sides_of_ fighting_corruption_in_russia (Accessed 29 December 2017).

Transparency International, 2015. The State of Corruption: Armenia, Azerbaijan, Georgia, Moldova, and Ukraine. Available at: https://www.transparency.org/whatwedo/publication/the_state_of_corruption_armenia_azerbaijan_georgia_moldova_and_ukraine (Accessed 29 December 2017).

Tyler, T., 2006. Why People Obey the Law. Princeton University Press, Princeton.

UNITER. 2017. [online]. Available at: https://uniter.org.ua/(Accessed 29 December 2017).

USAID, 2017. Ukraine. Available at: https://www.usaid.gov/ukraine (Accessed 29 December 2017).

Uslaner, E., 2008. Corruption, Inequality, and the Rule of Law: the Bulging Pocket Makes the Easy Life. Cambridge University Press, New York.

Vitkin, B., 2017. Борьба С Коррупцией На Украине Наталкивается На Противодействие.

Wood, T., 2017. Ukraine's Anti-corruption Promise Fades by the Day. Washington Post. Available at: https://www.washingtontimes.com/news/2017/nov/30/ukraines-anti-corruption-promise-fades-by-the-day/ (Accessed 2 January 2017).

Young, J., 2015. Russia Pressures Anti-corruption Group. Voanews.com. Available at: https://www.voanews.com/a/russia-pressures-anti-corruption-group/2654840.html (Accessed 29 December 2017).

Youth Human Rights Movement. 2017. [online]. Available at: http://yhrm.org/ (Accessed 29 December 2017).

Zaloznaya, M., 2017. The Politics of Bureaucratic Corruption in Post-Transitional Eastern Europe. Cambridge University Press, New York.

Zaloznaya, M., Reisinger, W., and V. Claypool. Mechanisms of Decoupling: Local Contestation of International Anti-corruptionism in Russia and Ukraine (unpublished).

Constitutional Values and Civil Servant Recruitment: The Principles for Filling Revenue Service Positions in Poland

Kaja Gadowska
Jagiellonian University, Krakow, Poland

The functioning of public administration should be consistent with the general interest, common to all citizens, and independent from the particularized interests of changing political forces. A condition for the proper functioning of administration is the selection of appropriate personnel to perform the duties defined by the state. According to the premises of this paper, the recruitment of personnel based upon objective criteria is of fundamental importance for the effective realization of the administration's mission. This article analyzes the weaknesses of personnel policy in fiscal administration in Poland after 1989 against the background of the broader process of creating a Polish civil service. The study aims at determining the extent to which the actual relations between politics and administration reflect legal regulations. The article focuses on personnel policy with regard to senior positions in fiscal administration, whose occupants have leverage over decision-making processes and human resources policy in various agencies. It turns out that after every parliamentary election there is major turnover in the personnel occupying senior positions in the fiscal administration offices, that is, the persons associated with the previous governing team are replaced with individuals enjoying the confidence of those who have just come to power. In light of these findings one can infer that, contrary to the constitutional principles guiding the functioning of the government administration in Poland, its politicians have deliberately designed legal regulations in such a manner as to enable them to assume control over fiscal administration.

Keywords: Tax administration, Filling positions, Civil service, The common good

1. Introduction

The principle of the "common good"[1] — found, among other places, in article 1 of the Polish Constitution of 2 April 1997 — comprises the *raison d'être* for public administration. After all, in executing state functions, such an administration should serve the welfare and well-being of the citizens. By the same token this guiding principle points to a model for the way a government should operate: the role of an administration executing the functions of the state is to realize the common good.

A government administration comprises the entire set of organs, offices, and central or territorial institutions which perform public tasks on behalf of the individual citizens and collective subjects (Zieliński, 2001: 14). According to article 153, paragraph 1 of the Polish Constitution — in order to assure professional, honest, impartial, and politically neutral performance of state duties — a corps of civil servants is employed in the offices of the administration. As the Constitutional Tribunal (*Trybunał Konstytucyjny*, TK) has indicated,

> The essential significance of civil service is related to the pursuit of ensuring a desired mode of operation for the public administration, and, therefore, should be read in conjunction with a profile of the state as the common good of all its citizens (article 1, Constitution) [...]. The functioning of the state administration — seen in this broader systemic context — should be concordant with a properly understood general interest, common to all citizens, and free of particularized interests as perceived through the prism of the effects of changing political forces (TK, 14 June 2011).

A condition for the proper functioning of an administration is the selection of appropriate personnel to perform the duties of the state. As Polish scientists Antoni and Bartłomiej Kamiński (2004: 235-270) aptly demonstrate, the assurance of a high moral and intellectual level in the civil service requires the formation of a

---

[1] The focus of this article does not permit delving deeper into the issue of the "common good." Its beginnings date back to Plato and Aristotle, but it is also one of the fundamental principles of social life in the social teachings of the Roman Catholic Church. A broader discussion of the common good as a constitutional principle can be found in Piechowiak (2012), Zubik (2007), Sokolewicz and Zubik (2016).

competitive recruitment system (based upon meritocratic criteria), appropriate remuneration, stable employment, and guarantees of the solemnity and sovereignty of the institution, that is, limiting to an absolute minimum the possibilities for politicians and other outside interest groups to gain special advantages or profits. These conditions are especially crucial in the case of fiscal administration which constitutes a key link in the system for accrual of public revenues.

The fiscal administration[2] is a component of a non-combined territorial government administration, subordinated to the minister governing public finance (Zieliński, 2001; Sawczuk, 2011a, 2011b).[3] With respect to numbers, operatives of the fiscal administration comprise the largest of all groups encompassed by the civil service. In 2017, the civil service employed 119,382 persons among whom 47,179 (39.52%) were employees of tax chambers, tax offices, and tax audit offices (Sprawozdanie Szefa, 2018[4]: 20 attachment 1).

The state is, naturally, financed by taxes and other public contributions. In 2017, tax revenues in Poland amounted to 315, 257, 413 PLN, which constituted 90% of the state budget revenues (Sprawozdanie z wykonania, 2018: 32–33). The percentage which tax revenues present in the structure of the state budget income has remained at about the same level for the past two decades. Therefore, the goal of the fiscal administration is the gaining of such revenues in the most effective, efficient, and fair manner, under conditions of a uniformly applied tax law.

The tax system in Poland, however, displays much instability and opacity (Brzeziński and Nykiel, 2011; Uszyński, 2010;

---

2 The terms "fiscal" or "tax" administration are applied alternately in the literature, partly due to a lack of precise legal definitions. Nonetheless, the first of these is of historical lineage, appearing in descriptions of the interwar period in Poland (Teszner, 2012: 55–63).
3 On another note, the title of the minister responsible for public finance tends to vary; in presentday Poland, it is the Minister of Economic Development and Finance.
4 Because versions in other languages are not available, Polish document titles will not be translated herein; however, to facilitate comprehension translation of selected titles is provided in the list of references.

Ruśkowski, 2006; NIK, 2014). Altogether it encompasses a sum total of 303 acts of legislation, that is, 11 laws and 292 ordinances by the minister of finance. As the findings of research by Grant Thornton (2017) illustrate, regulations governing personal income tax currently number 2689 pages, those governing excise tax amount to 991 pages, while those pertaining to the VAT amount to 890 pages. Yet a key problem in Polish tax law is, in addition to the voluminous provisions, their high level of changeability. The personal income tax law of 1991 has been amended 56 times; if, however, we count the corrections introduced by amendments to other laws, the total is 269 times. The 1993 act on taxation of goods and services—along with the 2004 law which superseded it—has been revised 47 times over the course of 23 years and changed a total of 99 times. Additionally, the law on corporate income tax, from the time it was instituted in 1992, has been amended to a crucial degree some 36 times; the sum total of its alterations is 187 (Grant Thornton, 2017; LEX).

Testifying to the lack of clarity and abundance of complexity in the tax law is the increasing number of requests for formal interpretations to be issued by organs of the tax administration. Whereas in 2008, there were 22,478 individual interpretations, in 2015 this number had risen to 38,159 (Grant Thornton, 2017). In the face of the great changeability in Polish tax law, its breadth, complexity, and low quality, it is difficult to interpret its provisions, and yet a consequence of a revenue office's erroneous decision can be damaging to the taxpayer. Furthermore, considering the constant political pressure to increase tax revenues needed to finance mounting budget expenses in order to cover social welfare costs, the question of how to ensure high meritocratic and moral competencies among fiscal administration employees is pivotal.

The aim of this article is to analyze weaknesses in the fiscal administration system in Poland—especially those which impact the shaping of a professional workforce of civil servants therein. According to the premises of this paper, the recruitment of personnel based upon objective criteria is of fundamental significance to the efficient realization of the tax administration's mission. Special attention is paid here to the filling of positions at a senior level — the posts of the directors and vice directors of tax chambers, heads of tax offices and their deputies, of the directors and vice directors of tax audit offices; considering the current legal state of affairs, investigated, too, will be the directors and vice directors of tax administration chambers. The quality of the functioning of these offices depends upon the competencies of the individuals who occupy these positions. Appointments to these managerial positions is, in turn, connected with control over the employment policy reigning in subordinate units of this administration. In line with the assumed hypothesis, the greater the influence of political factors (rather than impartial, merit-based criteria) on the process by which positions are filled, and the weaker the guarantees of stable employment, the more difficult it is for employees to resist political pressure, and the more they are apt to succumb to suggestions/demands made by political patrons.

This inquiry seeks to determine how, in practice, from the beginning of transformation in Poland, a division was constructed between the political and administrative spheres, and to determine the extent to which the actual relations between politics and administration reflect the legal regulations.

The first section describes the research design and methodology used in the study on which this paper is based. The subsequent section briefly outlines the process of creating a civil service in Poland after 1989. The main part of the paper discusses the legal principles for and the real practices of filling senior positions in the tax administration in Poland. The final section provides summary and short discussion of the research findings.

2. Research methodology

Applied in this article will be the results of a broader research conducted in the course of a Polish Ministry of Science and Higher Education project no. N116 029 31/3130 directed by the author in the years 2006–2009 and entitled "Law in Action: The Question of Political-Administrative Relations in Poland after 1989 in Light of

Civil Service Reforms"; supplementary material stems from research projects the author conducted under the auspices of the Institute of Sociology at the Jagiellonian University in the years 2009-2018. In addition to an analysis of the changing legal principles for the filling of positions in the government administration, specifically in the tax administration, of reports from the Supreme Audit Office (*Najwyższa Izba Kontroli*, NIK), of interpellations and questions posed by members of parliament (alongside responses thereto), and, finally, of articles in the press, 55 in-depth interviews with the personnel of the tax administrative offices were conducted.[5]

3. The process of creating a civil service in Poland after 1989

The fiscal administration is a component of a non-combined territorial government administration, and as such has been and continues to be the subject of successive civil service acts currently in effect. In concentrating, like other countries of East-Central Europe,[6] on economic and political reforms in the 1990's, Poland neglected reform of the public administration and the process of creating a modern civil service. Basing on the results of comparative studies, political sociologist Eva Etzioni-Halevy (1999) demonstrates that when the political parties manage to gain a strong position in the governing structures before public administration achieves a sufficient degree of autonomy needed to define its competence and strategic interests, as was the case of Poland, the result is permanent direct interference of political and partisan interests in administrative decisions.

---

[5] In the course of research in total 198 individual in-depth interviews were conducted with selected members of the civil service employed in the Chancellery of the Prime Minister, in ministries and central administrative offices, provincial administrative offices, and combined and non-combined territorial government administrative offices, as well as with experts on the civil service, politicians and businesspeople. Furthermore, three focussed interview with selected respondents were carried out.

[6] Except Hungary which adopted an Act on civil service in 1992.

The specific experience of Poland and other countries of the former communist bloc called for the selection of the most suitable model of political-administrative relations. The growing complexity of the environment and globalisation processes, accompanied by increased scope of tasks performed by modern public administration, imposed new challenges on contemporary states. They resulted in a transition from the classical 19th century model of bureaucratic careers in which roles in administration are based on experience and expertise and gradual promotion is the norm (Weber 1978, 1998), to a new public management model based on competition and opened at higher levels to managers hired for specific tasks (Hausner, 2007; Bossaert and Demmke, 2003: 27–30).[7] Some experts warned, however, that an adoption of the latter model might result in the strengthening of the political influence in administration (Izdebski and Kulesza, 2004: 275–280). Although, undoubtedly, the open recruitment system allows a greater elasticity in the search for candidates with sufficient qualifications, the disadvantages of this model are the weak connection of the civil service servants with the office and susceptibility to external factors, which are not always meant to be beneficial to the state. While designing new institutions one shall take into account the cultural and historical context in which they are to function. The creation of an effective and impartial civil service in a country in which for almost half a century an administration was totally dependent on the communist party and the qualifications of the personnel were low seemed to call for a hybrid system closer to the traditional career model than to the model based on positions.

A premise underlying the formation of the civil service in Poland, enshrined in the Constitution of the Republic of Poland of 2 April 1997, was that it would be professional, competent, inde-

---

7   A critical evaluation of the application of the new public management in public administration in Central and Eastern Europe is discussed by Drechsler (2005). He based his claims on the results of international research, and he found out that this model is particularly unfavorable for countries undergoing systemic transformation, contributing, among others, to politicization of the civil service and erosion of its ethos. Detailed analysis of civil service systems in East-Central European countries were also discussed by Verheijen (1999); Meyer-Sahling (2004, 2009); and Bossaert and Demmke (2003).

pendent, impartial, and politically neutral. It was assumed that personnel would be selected by way of open and competitive procedures, and that it would perform its duties, in the name of the state and its citizens, free of any influence due to changing political configurations.[8] In Poland, however, it is evident that political parties are striving to limit the autonomy of the administration, subordinating it to their interests. In practice, the human resource policies in public administration lead to a changeover of officials holding senior positions; their substitution by persons who are supported by the political party which has just taken power. This occurs despite the principle that decisions regarding employment and advancement in public administration should be made on the basis of skills and competencies, not political loyalties. Naturally, the politicizing of senior civil service positions carries the danger that there will be escalated manipulation of personnel at the lower levels (Gadowska, 2009, 2015, 2018).

After the 1989 change of the political system, the first civil service act was passed only in 1996 during the first coalition government of the Democratic Left Alliance (*Sojusz Lewicy Demokratycznej*, SLD) and Polish Peasant Party (*Polskie Stronnictwo Ludowe*, PSL). The law drew a division between the political and administrative spheres. At the beginning, the majority of employees in the public administration were to be hired on the previous principles and legal bases. Later, gradually, after passing the qual-

---

[8] Consideration shall be given, however, to the fact that although the concept of a politically neutral, professional, merit-based civil service is commonly perceived as a feature of good governance, current trends bring challenges to it. B. Guy Peters points out that „there is a need for civil servants to respond both to political leaders and their policy preferences but also to the wants of ordinary citizens", while the demands for neutrality and responsiveness potentially conflict with one another (Peters, 2018: 13–14). In the discussion on the desirability of separating politics and administration, the question is also raised of threats resulting from an excessive autonomy of the administration, whereby civil servants, subjected to weaker social control than politicians, can in practice control the government actions by selecting information and managing its flow (see Peters, 2001: 221–259). Political leaders who have mandate from their elections to create and implement certain policies point that their mandate should not be thwarted by permanent and unelected civil servants. It is also argued that politicization of civil service may enhance its accountability (Peters, 2018).

ifying procedures, the employees would be nominated to one of four categories of civil servants in the civil service corps. However, the new condition that candidates for the highest category of administrative positions had to have a minimum of seven years' work experience, including four years in a managerial or independent position, made it impossible in practice for persons connected with the Polish Solidarity to apply. This condition also privileged administrative personnel associated with the communist system. Both the opposition and the PSL pointed out that the majority of the newly-appointed directors general who claimed to be politically non-aligned, were in fact persons who were previously associated with the Polish United Workers' Party (*Polska Zjednoczona Partia Robotnicza*, PZPR) (Derdziuk et al., 1998: 5-12; Stawowiak, 1997: 10-12).

After new parliamentary elections, the outcomes of such qualifying procedures were considered by the political victors to have been politically motivated and unreliable, and as a result, a large part of the directors general were removed from their positions (Rydlewski, 2001: 35; Dostatni, 2011: 97). Therefore, by the end of 1998, during the rule of the coalition cabinet of Solidarity Electoral Action (*Akcja Wyborcza Solidarność*, AWS) and Freedom Union (*Unia Wolności*, UW), for reasons that were both objective and political, the 1996 civil service law was replaced by another act, which was later amended numerous times. Members of the civil service corps were divided into two categories: employees of the civil service, who were hired on the basis of an employment contract, and civil servants, hired by nomination. One of the conditions for being eligible for nomination—in addition to preparatory service and having worked for at least two years in the civil service—was to pass a qualifying procedure conducted by the Head of Civil Service. The provisions of the law ensured greater work security for nominated civil servants in comparison with other members of the corps. The act introduced an open, transparent, and competitive system of recruitment for the civil service. However, it did not set forth either the manner or the mode of selecting the best candidates, and as a result directors general could conduct recruitment according to criteria freely formulated by themselves. The basic mechanism of recruitment to senior positions in the civil service, that is, the positions of directors general, and directors of departments and their deputies in ministries and in central and provincial offices, was supposed to be a competition, conducted by the Head of Civil Service with the aid of specially established competition panels, open to nominated civil servants. The introduction of transparent competition procedures to choose the best candidates on the basis of merit was supposed to contribute to limiting political clientelism in public administration. But from the beginning, various loopholes were used to bypass it. In addition to the competition, temporary or parallel measures were introduced which allowed for senior positions to be filled with persons from the ruling parties' political base. During the period of Prime Minister Leszek Miller's government (the second rule of the coalition of the post-communist SLD and PSL parties) a transitional provision was introduced, enabling persons from outside the corps to hold senior positions in the civil service without the preservation of competition procedures. As a result, employment in these positions on an acting appointment basis (*pełniący obowiązki*, p.o.) became widespread. It led to the undermining of the principle of the civil service's apolitical nature, and opened the gate for the politicized filling of senior positions in government offices with persons lacking the appropriate qualifications (NIK, 2005; Sprawozdanie Szefa, 2003: 4, 20). In December 2002, the Constitutional Tribunal ruled that the provision was incompatible with the Basic Law as allowing the appointment of persons from outside the corps to senior civil service positions, while bypassing the competition procedures risked the politicization of the government administration and could lead to undermining the civil service institution itself (TK, 12 December 2002).

At the same time, a whole range of means was used to avoid holding competitions and instead to hire a preferred person for a given position, or, if a competition was won contrary to the hopes of a given political superior, to not appoint the unacceptable winner to the position. At the request of a minister or a governor of a province, a director general of an office might refrain from reporting a vacant position, in order to fill it with a person acting in a stand-in capacity (p.o.), and thus preventing the Head of Civil Service from announcing a competition for the position. In cases where directors general reported vacancies, the Head of Civil Service for many months was often unable to determine with a political superior the requirements that the candidate for a given position was supposed to fulfill—which was a condition for holding the competition. Even the successful conduct of a competition did not guarantee the filling of the position, as a political superior could express objections to the selected candidate. The process of recruitment to the civil service was also not free of irregularities. There were numerous cases in which, due to the pressure from superiors, recruitment was conducted in a non-objective manner, so that it ended with the selection of the favoured candidate, even if this meant rejecting candidates who clearly met the requirements to a greater extent (NIK, 2005: 36–51; Sprawozdanie Szefa, 2001: 5–7; Sprawozdanie Szefa, 2003: 4–20; Sprawozdanie Szefa, 2004: 4, attachment 16; Sprawozdanie Szefa, 2005: 14, attachment 14).

After the Law and Justice (*Prawo i Sprawiedliwość*, PiS) party's victory in the parliamentary elections of 2005, activities were undertaken at once to facilitate a return to the discretionary selection of civil service personnel. For this purpose, the acts on the civil service, on local self-government employees, and on the Supreme Audit Office were amended to allow positions in offices falling under the provisions of the civil service act to be occupied by persons transferred (bypassing the qualifying procedures) from local self-governments or the Supreme Audit Office. At the same time, employees hired on an acting appointment basis (p.o.) during the rule of the previous coalition were dismissed on the grounds that they lacked the necessary qualifications, because they were filling their positions as political nominees.

After the change of Prime Minister, when Jarosław Kaczyński became the new head of government, two substantively interrelated acts were passed: the new civil service act, replacing the act of 1998, and the act on state reserve of human resources and high-ranking state positions. In essence, these brought about the relinquishment of the basic institutions and procedures that had previously been in force in the civil service. One major change introduced on the basis of the new provisions was removal of senior positions in the civil service from under the civil service act and to bring them under the provisions of the act on state reserve of human resources and high-ranking state positions. By relinquishing competitions, and introducing in exchange the principle of appointing persons enjoying the political support and confidence of the ruling party to high state positions from the state reserve of human resources, the PiS openly questioned the value of the political neutrality of civil servants. To justify the changes, the politicians of the PiS indicated that their aim was to provide for effective cooperation between the administrative apparatus and the political sphere, ensuring not only the competence of civil servants, but also their political loyalty. The regulations of 2006 met with general criticism. It was argued that excluding senior positions from the civil service corps led to depriving that group of political neutrality, thus making it a threat to the realization of the basic constitutional aim of the civil service. In the view of experts, the legislative measure adopted in 2006 made it possible to introduce, in place of independent, professional, and apolitical civil servants, persons serving those in power, inclined in the performance of their duties to be directed by the interests of the party to which they owe their position (Uhlig, 2006; Heywood and Meyer-Sahling, 2008: 45–47). The pressure connected with the possible loss of position – under the provisions of the act on state reserve of human resources directors general, department directors and deputy directors could be dismissed at any time – additionally weakened people's ability to defend their own opinions, and increases their dependence on their political promoters.

In late autumn 2007, after early parliamentary elections, a government was formed by the Civic Platform (*Platforma Obywatelska*, PO) and the PSL. As might have been expected, the new government quickly made use of the provisions in force for the purpose of dismissing civil servants appointed during the period of Law and Justice's rule and replacing them with its own trusted personnel. In November 2008, in accordance with Civic Platform's electoral campaign promises, a new civil service act was passed. The new law reinstated the main legal measures of the act of 1998, in particular it again included senior civil service positions in the civil service corps, and reintroduced the principle of open and competitive recruitment to them.

In contrast to the civil service act of 1998, which introduced a centralized system for conducting competitions for senior positions in the civil service, the act of 2008 decentralized the procedure. In the case of recruitment for the position of a director general of an office, recruitment was conducted by a panel established by the Head of Civil Service, while in the case of recruitment for the position of a department director and his deputy, recruitment was by a panel established by the director general of the office. The possibility of the recruitment panel's selecting two candidates, from which the head of the office (in the case of recruitment to the position of a director general) or the director general (in the case of recruitment to the remaining senior positions) would make a choice according to his or her own judgment, suggested the risk of a possible politicization of decisions (Drobny et al., 2010: 273; Radwan, 2012). Reservations were also expressed in regard to the legislators' formulation of the requirements to be met by candidates for senior positions in the civil service. Under the provisions, persons applying for such positions did not need to be civil servants, or even members of the civil service corps. Adoption of this measure has brought the Polish model of the civil service closer to the position model, while in the native cultural context, it would seem more advantageous to base the principle of the corps' personnel policy on the career model (Działocha, 2008: 59).

The act allowed for exceptions to the necessity of conducting open and competitive recruitment for senior positions. Filling positions of department's deputy director could occur by means of the transfer of a member of the civil service corps, that is, a so-called internal advancement. In addition, under the provisions of the act, senior positions in offices, with the exception of the position of a director general, could be occupied by persons delegated, on the basis of separate provisions, to perform tasks outside the organizational unit in which they were hired. Although the overriding statutory rule for filling senior positions in the civil service is the procedure of open and competitive recruitment, the most often practised method of filling deputy department director positions—as might have been expected—was the transfer method (Sprawozdanie Szefa, 2011: 19; Sprawozdanie Szefa, 2012: 23). The provisions of the act also provided for the possibility of transferring a member of the corps occupying a senior position to another civil servant position, if the office or interest of the civil service justifiably requires it. The adoption of this measure, which serves the so-called vacating of positions, weakens the stability of employment necessary for maintaining political independence in senior positions in the civil service (Liszcz, 2010: 49).

From the moment when the civil service act of 2008 entered into force, has been noted that the problem of not observing the statutory rule of filling senior positions without delay still existed. Arrangements between the Head of Civil Service and office directors in regard to the requirements that should be included in descriptions of director general positions and in announcements of recruitment have been subject to excessive deferment. In addition, situations have occurred where, in spite of the selection of candidates for the position of department director, the director general failed to make the decision to appoint one of them to the position. A practice of repeating competitions when the selected candidates did not suit a minister, central office head, or province governor also emerged. Competitions being tailored to a person indicated by a political superior were still occurring. Given the statutory prohibition against staffing senior positions on an acting appointment basis (p.o.), a measure consisting of a general director's functions being performed by a person serving "in substitution" was exercised (Sprawozdanie Szefa, 2012: 44; NIK, 2012: 16–18; Góra-Ojczyk, 2010; Radwan, 2011).

In December 2015, soon after a new government of Law and Justice was formed, a substantial amendment to the 2008 civil service act was passed, consisting in the relinquishment of competitions for senior positions and the introduction, in exchange, of the discretionary mode of their filling by way of appointment by entitled authorities, which opened the possibility of taking political control over the corps. In addition, the requirements to be met by candidates for senior positions in the civil service have been reduced. The demand of having professional experience, including experience in a managerial position, in the public finance sector, while applying for the position of director general of the office, and director and deputy director of department was removed.

The draft, hastily enforced by parliament, was submitted by a group of MPs of the governing party to avoid public consultations obligatory in case of government initiatives. The critical opinions of experts, including the Civil Service Council, the Prosecutor General, the Polish Bar Council, National Council of Attorneys at Law, the Supreme Court, NGOs, and the opposition indicating that the draft breached the Constitution, were ignored (Gadowska, 2018).

In tune with the amendment, work contracts of senior civil servants expired 30 days after the new law came into force if they did not receive or did not accept new employment or remuneration conditions before that date. Nominated civil servants whose work contracts could not expire under provisions in force, could be transferred to other positions in the same or another office. It seems that these legal measures were aimed at massive replacement in senior civil service positions to suit the political needs of the current cabinet and the parliamentary majority (Izdebski, 2015). In the opinion of the Ombudsmen (*Rzecznik Praw Obywatelskich*, RPO), the adopted mechanism of dissolution of labour relations violates the principle of stable employment, which is an important guarantor of the political neutrality and professional character of the civil service (RPO, 2016). New provisions are contrary to basic constitutional principles of the professional, competent, impartial, and politically neutral performance of the state's obligations by officials of the government administration. Moreover, they limit the citizens' constitutional right of access to the public service based on the principle of equality. For these reasons, the Ombudsman (as well as the Civic Platform MPs) appealed to the Constitutional Tribunal to examine the new regulation's conformity with the Constitution (*ibidem*; Grupa Posłów, 2016).

According to a poll carried out by "Gazeta Prawna" in the first year of the legislation being in force, in many offices there were significant changes in the senior civil service positions. The lack of proper verification of candidates has adversely affected the functioning of the offices, causing the necessity of dismissing persons appointed from outside the civil service corps who lacked the requisite professional qualifications (Radwan, 2017). The Report by the Head of the Civil Service shows that during the statutory transitional period, out of 1580 persons occupying senior positions in civil service, 293 (19%) were transferred to other positions in the civil service, and upon the end of this period the labor contracts of 212 (13%) senior civil servants expired (Sprawozdanie Szefa, 2017: 29–30).

The analysis of the changing legal bases for the functioning of the civil service in Poland demonstrates that the introduction of legal framework makes only a limited contribution to the stabilization of the civil service. Research results show that regulations drafted as instruments to ensure the effectiveness of the system were used partially in accord with the official intentions of the legislators, but also partially contrary to those intentions—as a tool for the politicization of the civil service. Civil service legislation, particularly the provisions that regulated the rules for filling senior positions in the civil service, has been largely subjugated to the political interest of the moment, and not to the long-term interest of the state. That the political system should repeatedly conduct personnel purges in the civil service—either through the use of legal instruments intended to serve other aims, or by means of temporary changes to the civil service act—bears witness to the fact that the real relation of the political system to the civil service differs from the official attitude.

As B. Guy Peters aptly noticed, "By injecting political appointees into public organizations political leaders may be able to control those organizations more effectively. The question remaining, of course, is whether that accountability is being exercised in the pursuit of the public interest or whether it is being used just to pursue the interest of a political party" (Peters, 2018).

4. The legal principles for and the real practices of filling senior positions in the tax administration

The fiscal administration in Poland currently encompasses 16 tax administration chambers, 400 tax offices, and 16 tax and customs offices, with 45 branch offices and 143 customs houses. So, until 28 February 2017, the structure of the territorial fiscal administration was organized by the tax administration (encompassing 16 tax chambers and 400 tax offices), plus the tax control administration (16 tax audit offices and 8 branch offices), as well as the customs service (16 customs chambers, 45 customs offices, and 143 customs houses). These entities, as has already been mentioned, have been and continue to be the subject of four successive civil service laws currently in effect (1996, 1998, 2006 and 2008).

As it was demonstrated, despite the civil service in Poland was established with the intention to ensure that the public administration performed its duties in a professional and impartial manner, unhindered by political interests, political parties make attempts to limit the autonomy of the administration and to subordinate it to their interests. This phenomenon is especially clear in the fiscal administration. Due to the fact that taxes are the primary source of state revenues which permit the funding of state programs, senior positions in the fiscal administration are an object of permanent interest for parties in power.

Until 26 February 2017, the positions of directors and vice directors in tax chambers, the heads and their deputies in tax offices, as well as the directors and vice directors in tax audit offices belonged to the intermediate level of management in the civil service. However, as of 27 February 2017, on the basis of statutes introducing a new law on the National Tax Administration (*Krajowa Administracja Skarbowa*, KAS), the positions of the director of the National Tax Information (*Krajowa Informacja Skarbowa*, KIS), the directors and vice directors of tax administration chambers, as well as the heads and deputy heads of both tax offices and tax and customs offices have been brought under senior management in the civil service. Nevertheless, the actual filling of these positions continues to be on the basis of separate and distinct laws from the rest of the civil administration corps.

The legal foundations for the functioning of the fiscal administration in Poland, including the bases upon which the just mentioned positions were filled, were delineated in a specific law on tax offices and tax chambers passed on 21 June 1996 during the first government of the SLD and the PSL. This law came into force as of 1 January 1997 pursuant to the introductory regulations to the statutes reforming how the state economy and public administration functioned. On the basis of these legal provisions, the minister of finance possessed the power to appoint and dismiss the director of the tax chamber; further, upon a request by that director, the minister appointed and dismissed the vice director of the tax chamber or the head of a tax office. The law did not, however, outline the precise procedures for this. The deputy head of the tax office was hired and fired by the director of the tax chamber upon the request of the head of the tax office.

It was not until 1 September 2003, during the second SLD-PSL government, that rules were introduced regarding open competition for selection of directors of tax chambers and heads of tax offices. This was on the basis of a law of 27 June 2003 regarding the creation of Provincial Tax Colleges, but which also changed certain laws regulating the duties and competencies of specific organs as well as the organization of units subordinate to the minister in charge of public finance. In light of the new laws, candidates for these positions would be chosen on the basis of a competition among current employees who had worked for a minimum of four years in offices and organs subject to the minister of finance. The procedure included an examination in the course of which knowledge indispensable to the execution of the duties of the position was tested; also investigated were general predispositions and competencies as well as the managerial abilities of the candidates. To conduct and oversee this process the minister of finance appointed a commission. The process, including the conducting of the competition for directors of tax chambers and heads of tax offices, was precisely described in a minister of finance ordinance dated 29 October 2003.

At the same time, the provisions of the law stated that, until such positions were filled via these competitive hiring procedures, the minister of finance would assign a person to temporarily act in a stand-in capacity (p.o.) of the director of tax chamber or head of tax office. Still, the law did not indicate time limit for such temporary management. Moreover, the minister of finance could also refuse to appoint a tax chamber director or tax office head who had been selected according to procedures if, in the opinion of that minister, none of the candidates guaranteed objective fulfillment of the duties relevant to their position. Additionally, in a case whereby two successive competitions had not sifted out a fitting candidate or one the minister assessed as guaranteeing objective execution of duties, the minister of finance was empowered by law to call up an individual to fill the position of the director of a tax chamber or the head of a tax office without resorting to open competition within the tax administration.

Analogous principles were in force with respect to the filling of positions of directors of tax audit offices. Originally, on the basis of the provisions of a law dated 28 September 1991 on tax audits, the director of this office was appointed by the minister of finance from among tax audit inspectors and upon the request of the general inspector of tax audits. The latter, in his turn, was appointed and dismissed by the prime minister upon a request from the minister of finance. The law did not describe, however, the specific procedures for appointment.

The rules regulating the competition for selection of directors of tax audit offices were introduced on 1 September 2003 on the basis of the earlier mentioned law of 27 June 2003. The provisions stipulated that directors of tax audit offices are appointed, as well as dismissed, from amidst the candidates selected by way of an open competition, by the minister of finance upon the request of the general inspector of tax audits. To enter the competition, individuals had to have been employed in tax auditing units and to have worked for at least five years in the tax administration or had at least three years of practice in tax auditing units. Candidates also needed to pass a qualifying examination for the position of inspector before a commission called up by the general inspector of tax audits or have already been on the list of tax consultants. Hence the competition relied upon the conducting of an examination which would test knowledge requisite for performance of the tasks of the director of a tax audit office, the general predispositions and competencies, as well as managerial skills. The examination was to be organized and overseen by a special commission brought into existence by the general inspector who, fundamentally, was the hierarchical supervisor of all directors of tax audit offices. A competition would be held only if at least two candidates presented themselves. The precise rules and regulations for this competition were found in the provisions of ordinances issued by the minister of finance on 20 November 2003 on the issue of competitions for the position of director of a tax audit office.

Until the director of a tax audit office was appointed by way of an open, competitive call, the minister of finance, upon a request from the general inspector of tax audits, designated an acting director (p.o.). In cases where the open call did not draw the minimum number of candidates or if none of the candidates received a positive recommendation from the general inspector, then the minister (again upon a request from the general inspector) appointed a director for the tax audit office, bypassing the competition.

This was different from the case of the law on tax chambers and offices. This legislation did not specify the conditions an individual should meet in order for the minister of finance to provisionally bestow upon him or her the duties of a director of a tax chamber or head of a tax office (p.o.), or to simply be assigned permanently to this position without competition. The law on tax auditing, however, did stipulate precisely that a person acting in stand-in capacity (p.o.) or who has been appointed director of a tax audit office must meet the very same conditions as a candidate competing for the position. Nonetheless, in practice, despite the introduction of a mandatory competition, the positions of directors and heads of various offices were filled by persons assigned by the minister of finance as acting directors (p.o.).

In discussing the laws which shape the principles underlying how managerial positions in the state fiscal administration are filled, a bill was presented on 14 May 2007 by the Law and Justice coalition government for a statute on the KAS, together with a bill proposing laws for the introduction of the new provisions regarding this institution. On the basis of these projects, it was planned to establish a new and consolidated tax administration, distinct from the civil service. As of 1 January 2008, this law was to have liquidated tax chambers and offices as well as customs chambers and offices; in their lieu there would be tax administration chambers and tax administration offices. The legislative proposal foresaw the lifting of the 2003 obligatory competitions for filling managerial positions in tax chambers, tax offices, and tax audit offices. In order to relieve the government from competitive calls, a fiscal reserve of human resources was to be established, modeled after the state reserve of human resources (*państwowy zasób kadrowy*, PZK) in existence since 2006. This new body would encompass employees of the finance ministry, tax chambers and offices, as well as some members of the PZK. The proposed statute also anticipated the expiration of all employment contracts and appointments of persons working heretofore in the tax administration within three months of the effective date of the law on the KAS. An exception would be persons who were offered, and who accepted, new contracts for further employment. Ultimately, because that government collapsed, this bill did not pass.

Yet concurrently—and despite the 2003 law in force which mandated obligatory calls and competitions for the directors of tax chambers, heads of tax offices, and the directors of tax audit offices—during the roughly two years of the first PiS government, there was mass replacement of persons specifically holding these positions, paying little heed to the legal procedures for their selection. In order to be able to maintain a semblance of legitimacy, provisos were applied which granted the minister of finance permission to assign person acting in a stand-in capacity (p.o.) of directors and heads until such time as competitions could be held. Tax offices witnessed the supplanting of their top officials (including recognized and respected experts) on a grand scale—their seats taken by individuals advertised as being from "outside the system."[9] Usually the directors of tax chambers would be replaced, and then the heads of tax offices.

The case of the Świętokrzyskie Province serves as an apt illustration. Between 2006 and 2007, after the director of the tax chamber was recalled, 15 out of 15 heads of tax offices were replaced (including three offices in which the head was replaced twice); 10 deputy heads were also swapped out. Within the first month of assuming his duties, the acting director (p.o.) of the tax chamber in Kielce (the provincial capital) requested replacements for five heads of tax offices (Odpowiedź na zapytanie nr 2501, 2008). His first personnel decision was to dismiss the vice director of the tax chamber and install a sister of a PiS senator in this position (Interpelacja nr 2507, 2008; Jak, 2008).

In March of 2006, the directors of the tax chambers in Łódź, Kielce, and Szczecin were called to Warsaw for a meeting to discuss the provisions of the tax statute with the then vice minister of finance, Marian Banaś. Upon their arrival, they were handed their dismissals, signed by minister of finance Zyta Gilowska (Kowalewska, 2006; Kowalewska et al., 2006). All in all, during this brief two-year period, PiS managed to replace nearly 90% of the top officials in the tax chambers and tax audit offices. Additionally,

---

9 *Spoza układu*; the word *układ* (system) is seen as negative and pejorative in postcommunist Poland.

239 out of 401 heads of tax offices (60%) were given notice. In some instances, as courts subsequently confirmed, the dismissal was executed by breaching the law (Skwirowski, 2008a). Vice minister Banaś argued that "the dismissals were provoked by critical reviews of the work performed by the recalled individuals—their poor management of these institutions and their substandard effects according to supervisors" (Glapiak, 2007), but observers discerned the purely political nature of these dismissals. According to a former vice minister of finance, Stanisław Stec (a Left and Democrats, *Lewica i Demokraci*, LiD deputy), "These [officials] had worked there for years; they knew their craft. PiS has not exchanged them for better [people], but for their own. This is all the more clear since this has happened without the announcement of even a single competition" (*ibidem*). Here it should be noted that the supplanting of persons in managerial positions naturally leads to staff changes in more subordinate positions.

Just after the elections towards the end of 2007, the incoming PO and PSL coalition government declared a desire to regulate the human resources situation in the fiscal civil service. Yet the tempo taken to satisfy this promise was highly disappointing. By April of 2008, so many acting directors and heads (p.o. who had never undergone a competitive open call) were still in place that an MP from the left made this the topic of an interpellation directed to the minister of finance (Interpelacja nr 2507, 2008). In response, vice minister Andrzej Parafianowicz admitted that acting directors still led 14 out of 16 tax chambers and acting heads still led 201 out of 401 tax offices; the average term among the former was 22 months whereas the average among the latter was 16 months (Odpowiedź na interpelację nr 2507, 2008). A segment of the persons acting in a stand-in capacity (p.o.) were assigned to their positions under the auspices of the new coalition (Glapiak, 2007).

Nonetheless, in September 2008, a PiS MP posed a question addressed to the minister of finance, pointing to political motivations behind the appointments of five heads of tax offices in spite of the proclaimed notion that the new government would be rooted in professionalism (Zapytanie nr 2501, 2008). In his rejoinder,

Andrzej Parafianowicz reminded one and all about the 15 heads of tax offices who had been dismissed after the replacement of the director of the tax chamber in Kielce during the rule of the political party represented by the MP (Odpowiedź na zapytanie nr 2501, 2008).

In August of 2008 a new minister of finance ordinance (dated 14 July 2008) came into effect; it pertained to the manner in which an examining commission would be convened and how competitions for the positions of directors of tax chambers and heads of tax offices would be conducted. Answering the ministry's call for candidates to fill 201 (approximately 50%) positions as heads of tax offices were 618 individuals (Skwirowski, 2008b; Skwirowski, 2008a]). The recruitment process was made up of two parts: the first was a test of specialized knowledge; the second was the assessment of general predispositions and competencies as well as managerial skills. Ultimately, in March and April of 2009, 540 individuals continued, but, after the second part, only 173 applicants remained. In due course, after both parts of the procedure, only 139 participants achieved the mandatory number of points. This was not quite 26% of the original pool of candidates, and meant that 69 of the competitions ended in failure (Konderak, 2009).

Furthermore, with reference to 11 (of the 139) candidates, the minister of finance decided not to appoint a candidate who had qualified, having come to the conclusion that the individual did not guarantee objective performance of duties; in one case the minister appointed a person who had won a competition for head of a different tax office. Concurrently, in seven cases, candidates who had not achieved the minimum points in the first round allowing them to continue to the second, were assigned as acting heads of tax offices (Odpowiedź na interpelację nr 12972, 2009). This set of circumstances became grounds for an interpellation directed to the prime minister by PiS members of parliament. The latter discerned abuse of the provisions of the law aimed at eliminating persons who had passed both parts but whom the minister of finance did not trust for reasons other than objective questions of merit (Interpelacja nr 12972, 2009; Interpelacja nr 11252, 2009; Interpelacja nr 11252, renewed, 2009).

Another round of competition took place in October and November 2009 for 110 positions as heads of tax offices. This time 71 qualified candidates passed both parts; the minister of finance appointed 53 to permanent positions (Odpowiedź na interpelację nr 12972, second response, 2010). PiS MPs returned again to their interpellation (Interpelacja nr 12972, renewed, 2010).

The findings of a NIK audit depicts the state of affairs as of 1 January 2011. Out of 400 heads of tax offices, 263 were filled by persons selected by way of open competitions and transparent procedures; 59 persons were appointed on the basis of the provisions of a 16 September 1982 law on employees of state offices; 9 were appointed on the basis of the provisions of the statute on tax chambers and offices which permit appointments without a competition if either no qualified candidate guarantees (in the view of the minister) objective fulfillment of duties or two consecutive competitions do not yield a suitable candidate. Another 69 individuals were assigned by the minister of finance as acting heads on the basis of the statute on tax chambers and offices; however, 53 of these individuals (76.8%) had already been operating in this capacity for over 12 months. That said, the NIK did remark that, compared to the situation on 1 January 2009, the number of provisional, temporary appointees had been reduced by 138 (66.7%). In other words, the number had been reduced to 69 positions and, as of that 2011 audit, only 17% of the heads of tax offices needed to be filled by competition; by 30 June 2011, the numbers had fallen to 46 and 11.5% respectively (NIK, 2012: 26–27, 42).

Simultaneously, the NIK audit of 1 January 2011 showed that of the 16 directors of tax chambers, 2 persons had been nominated on the basis of provisions of the law on employees of state offices, while 14 had been assigned as acting directors by the minister of finance on the basis of the law on tax chambers and offices. Of the latter group,11 (78.6%) had been in their provisional positions for over 12 months. Compared to the state of affairs on 1 January 2009, the number of temporary directors had not changed at all because the minister of finance had not announced a single call for candidates to fill these positions (NIK, 2012: 26). Notwithstanding promises made by the PO-PSL coalition at the beginning of their first term, the minister of finance had not resolved the problem of vacancies in the tax administration and it had thus not met its legal obligations to appoint directors via open calls.

Responding to the audit charges, the minister of finance sent an explanation to the NIK. The minister clarified that its decision to conduct, in first order, competitions for heads of tax offices was justified because of the high number of provisional heads, as well as the fact that these offices comprise the first level in tax revenue cases and are directly responsible for the consistency and regularity of operational services provided to taxpayers. Yet this does not seem a convincing argument. In the opinion of the NIK, the decision to forsake selection of directors of tax chambers could be vindicated neither by the structural percentage of persons employed without undergoing competitive procedures at both these two levels, nor by their real essentiality within the system. The directors of tax chambers, as an organ of second instantiation, supervised subordinate tax offices (NIK, 2012: 26–27).

Regrettably, by February of 2013, 15 of the 16 directors of tax chambers were still assigned to act in a stand-in capacity (p.o.) by the minister of finance. Additionally, 42 heads of tax offices were also provisional appointees (Leśniak, 2014). Nevertheless, towards the end of its second term, in May 2015, PO's minister of finance announced a competition to fill the positions of 62 heads of tax offices in order to complete the appointments prior to the parliamentary elections which were drawing near. At the same time, the government was preparing a proposal for a new statute on tax administration, one which was to introduce a change in the functioning of the tax chambers and offices.

In light of the provisions of the statute of 10 July 2015, the filling of the posts of the director and vice director of a tax chamber, the head of a tax office, and the director and vice director of the National Bureau of Tax Information (*Biuro Krajowej Informacji Podatkowej*, BKIP) was to take place via an open, competitive recruitment. Candidates for director or vice director of tax chambers and the director and vice director of the BKIP had to have five years of job seniority in an office under the auspices of the finance minister, or in one subordinated or supervised by this minister, including three years of experience at a managerial post with a clean reputation. The post of the head of a tax office could be occupied by a person with at least three years of work experience in an office serving the minister of finance, or in one subordinated or supervised thereby; additionally, the candidate needed to be in good standing and have two years of job experience at a managerial position. In the case of deputy heads of tax offices, a minimum of two years of job experience at an office falling in some way under the minister of finance was required. There was also a minimum of one year's experience at a managerial level with an unblemished reputation. The procedures here encompassed a test of knowledge as well as an evaluation of managerial competencies and an interview.

Recruitment was to be conducted by a team called up by the Chief of Tax Administration (*Szef Administracji Podatkowej*, SAP) which would include at least five members of the civil service corps. This team was to cull no more than two candidates per position. On the basis of a request originating with the SAP, the minister of finance was to appoint a person chosen from among candidates gleaned during the recruitment process to fill the position of a director of a tax chamber, the BKIP director, or head of a tax office. In turn, upon the request of a director of a tax chamber or the director of the BKIP, the minister filled the positions of the vice director of a tax chamber or of the BKIP. The finance minister was also the competent organ for dismissals from these positions. Statute provisions contained optional powers for the minister of finance to issue orders with reference to the organization of recruitment competitions.

At the same time, the law introduced the possibility of appointing a vice director of a tax chamber or the vice director of the BKIP without recruitment procedure from the civil service corps members already employed in offices serving, subordinated by, or supervised by the minister of finance. Mandatory was a positive, recent work review (no older than two years), achieving one of the two highest levels foreseen on the evaluation scale. Moreover, in specifically justified cases, the minister of finance—upon a request by the SAP and with the approval of the individual in mind—could appoint a director or vice director of a tax chamber, or the head of a tax office to take up an equivalent position elsewhere. The law also allowed for the possibility of the SAP to select persons occupying the position of vice director of a tax chamber, or vice director of the BIKP, or the deputy head of a tax office to execute the duties of director of tax chamber, director of BIKP or head of tax office—until such positions were appointed by way of an open, competitive call—for a period of six months with the option to extend for an additional six months. Additionally, if two successive recruitments had not yielded a fitting candidate, then the minister of finance could (without open competition) call up a member of the civil service corps to assume the position of the director of a tax chamber or of the BKIP, as well as their vice directors or the position of the head of a tax office.

The law just discussed was originally to come into full force on 1 January 2016—a date after the parliamentary elections which brought a victory for PiS. As a consequence, that date was postponed thrice until, as of 1 March 2017, the law on tax administration became null and void due to provisions which were transitioning in the statute dealing with the KAS. As of 1 March 2017, the law on tax chambers and offices, the law on tax audits as well as the law on the tax and customs service also expired.

Had the new law on tax administration entered into force on 1 January 2016, it would have placed PiS in a troublesome situation. For instance, were PiS to dismiss a director of a tax chamber or a head of a tax office, the party's hands would be tied: in light of the new statute's provisions, replacements of the acting in a stand-in capacity (p.o.) could only be current vice directors or deputy heads—but this meant promotion of individuals who had been appointed to their positions under the previous, PO government. Besides this, the compulsory, open recruitment required the meeting of more prerequisites than the earlier legal state of affairs. Thus the postponement of the new law's effective date facilitated the implementation of personnel changes on the basis of the preexisting, much less rigorous laws. Unsurprisingly, by mid-December 2015, 9 out of the 16 directors of tax chambers had been dismissed (Wójcik and Rochowicz, 2015). This predictably led to exchanges of the heads of tax offices. A case in point is that, after the director of the tax chamber in Kielce was replaced, the heads of 10 (out of 15) subordinate tax offices were also replaced in the brief period between 2 February 2016 and 8 April 2016 (Święcicka, 2016).

The justification for the proposed law on the KAS pointed out that consolidation of the tax, tax auditing, and customs service administrations would restrict the possibility and reduce the scale of tax fraud, increase the effectiveness of tax and customs duty collection, lower the costs of fiscal administration operation, and contribute to the development of a professional personnel corps (Druk sejmowy nr 826, 2016). On the basis of statutes transitioning in the law regarding the KAS, tax chambers became tax administration chambers; these were conjoined with the customs chambers and tax audit offices located in the same province. Customs offices were abolished along with their subordinate branches; established in their stead were tax and customs offices, the KIS as well as the Informatics Center for the National Tax Administration (*Centrum Informatyki Krajowej Administracji Skarbowej*, CIKAS). Also liquidated were the general inspector for tax audits, the head of the customs service, the directors of tax chambers, the directors of customs chambers, the directors of tax audit offices, as well as the heads of customs offices. Appearing in lieu of these were established new organs of the KAS: the chief of the KAS, the director of the KIS, the director of the tax administration chamber, as well as the head of the tax and customs office. Heads of tax offices became organs of the KAS.

The law passed on 16 November 2016 regarding the KAS eliminated the need for competitive recruitment procedures. The chief of the KAS and his deputies (no more than three) — now possessing the status of, respectively, a cabinet secretary and undersecretaries — are appointed by the prime minister on the basis of a request by the minister in charge of public finance. The director of KIS (5 year term, maximum 2 terms) is called up by the minister of finance on the basis of a request by the chief of the KAS. The vice director of KIS is appointed by the chief of the KAS on the basis of the director's request. The director of the tax administration chamber is appointed by the minister of finance upon request by the chief of the KAS; the vice director of the tax administration chamber is appointed directly by the chief of the KAS upon the director's request. The head of a tax office is likewise appointed by the chief of the KAS upon request by the director of the tax administration chamber; the deputy head of a tax office is appointed by that director of the tax administration chamber upon a request by the head of the relevant tax office. The head of a tax and customs office is called up by the chief of the KAS upon a request of the director of the tax administration chamber; the deputy head of a tax and customs office is called up by the director of the tax administration chamber upon request by the head of the relevant tax and customs office.

It is manifest that abandonment of competitive procedures for the selection of people to fill managerial positions in the KAS has caused their appointment to be dependent upon the will and whim of persons holding higher positions in the hierarchy. Such a solution stands in clear contradiction with a need to warranty transparent principles for hiring, advancing as well as dismissing civil service employees; a consequence is a lack of motivation for them to develop professionally and, therefore, an overall lack of professionalization in the fiscal administration. In the opinion of experts from the Center for Analyses and Taxation Studies at the Warsaw School of Economics, "this model not only maintains the level of politicization found heretofore in fiscal institutions, but it also sanctions it legally" (Skwirowski, 2016). Based upon the provisions of the statute on the KAS, just between 1 March and 19 June 2017, five changes have been made regarding directors of tax administration chambers and 25 changes have been made at the level of heads of tax offices (Odpowiedź na interpelację nr 13839, 2017; Odpowiedź na interpelację nr 13647, 2017). It is worth keeping in mind, however, that substitutions at the level of directors and their vice director, heads and their deputy heads were already carried out in various institutions of the fiscal administration system right after the PiS victory in the parliamentary elections.

Over and above this, in line with the provisions of the laws introducing the KAS statute, the labor contracts of persons working in tax administration chambers who had not, by 31 May 2017, received a written proposition delineating the new conditions of their employment or service, automatically expired as of 31 August 2017. A similar solution had been applied beforehand, under the provisions of a statute from 30 December 2015 regarding changes in the law on civil service and specifically with regards to senior positions therein. The presentation of a proposed employment contract — or not — was left in the hands of the superordinate organ. Crucial, too, is the fact that rules and regulations do not foresee any possibility for verification or control of these decisions by higher administrative bodies.

Worth noting is that among the 2664 persons who were not, in fact, offered a new employment contract, 1313 were persons who, by 31 August 2017, had reached or were imminently close to retirement age (60 for women, 65 for men). Nevertheless, these were civil servants possessing great knowledge and experience; among them were individuals who had earlier held managerial positions. In addition, 192 persons, who had reached retirement age but were still offered a new employment proposal, signed a declaration that they would leave the KAS within a year's time (or some other unambiguous date). Such tactics could be recognized as symptoms of age discrimination. Moreover, they strongly counteracted a social campaign announced in May 2017 by the country's president, alongside the minister of family, labor, and social policy: "Dignified Choice" ("*Godny wybór*") was aimed precisely at encouraging Poles who had attained retirement age to work longer. Furthermore, other employees and functionaries were forced to accept new employment contracts at lower positions and at lower pay; others were assigned to new workplaces, even a few hundred kilometers from their place of residence (Interpelacja nr 14265, 2017; Odpowiedź na interpelację nr 14265, 2017; Kwaśniewski, 2017).

5. Summary and findings

Overall, several hundred managerial and other senior bureaucratic positions in the fiscal administration have been statutorily disengaged from the rest. Formally, and in light of the law, the people who hold these positions are part and parcel of the civil service corps. In practice, however—because distinctly different principles and proceedings are being applied for hiring by the minister of finance—these people appear to be functioning outside the system. This is a crucial breach in the congruity and integrity of the Polish model of civil service. The statutes, rules, and regulations discussed herein are, in fact, granting unlimited powers to the minister of finance with regards to upper management personnel in the fiscal administration; attesting to this reality are opinions, verdicts, and decisions handed down by administrative courts in Poland.

As the Supreme Administrative Court of the Republic of Poland (*Naczelny Sąd Administracyjny*, NSA) has indicated, the provisions of the 1996 law on tax chambers and offices anticipate, "the mandate of the minister responsible for issues concerning public finance to appoint persons who will act in a stand-in capacity of a director of a tax chamber (until such time as a director of this agency is not selected via competitive recruitment) does not contain any limitations pertaining to the competencies of such an individual" (NSA, 26 November 2009). Furthermore, "the winning of a competition for the position of director of a tax chamber or head of a tax office does not engender any obligation on the part of the minister of finance to appoint persons who have won such competitions because this organ has the authority to render an assessment with regards to the objective fulfillment of duties by the candidate" (NSA, 21 March 2012). At the same time, the NSA determined that, "The principle of unrestricted appointment to civil service positions in public administration is organically incongruous with the principles of a professional, politically neutral, and stable civil service corps in the state administration" (NSA, 7 July 2016).

The filling of senior, managerial positions in a fiscal administration on the basis of provisional, temporary assignment or by overstepping competitive recruitment procedures is in dissonance with the fundamental principle which guided the establishment of a civil service corps: a guarantee of steadiness and stability in the functioning of the state administration, regardless of political changes ensuing after parliamentary elections. The "solutions," put into operation in 21st, century Poland enable the placement of individuals who will work at the disposal of superordinate authorities, inclined in the performance of their tasks to favor not the common good, but political group interests (thanks to which he or she is retained). Pressures associated with the possibility of job termination further strengthen dependencies upon political promotors; when considering a fiscal administration, this can have grave consequences for citizens. Political pressures to increase the budget income can result in more rigorous treatment of taxpayers; in cases where doubts arise, interpretations can be to the detriment of the ordinary citizen.

Additionally, imprecise laws cause difficulties in correct application. Attesting to this is the rising number of taxpayer appeals with reference to decisions made by revenue service organs and the high percentage of overruled decisions made by lower level, first instantiation organs of taxation. Increasingly more frequent are pointers found in the verdicts delivered by administrative courts (at the provincial as well as national levels) which are disadvantageous for the Polish revenue service. The NIK has many a time drawn attention to faulty bureaucratic decisions, the poor quality of legal statutes, and the incongruity of the tax code with Community law and the Constitution (NIK, 2010; NIK, 2011;

NIK, 2014; NIK, 2015). Of influence here, too, are staff shortages and, hence, excess work burdening the civil servant (NIK, 2014).

In the first half of 2013, taxpayers submitted appeals to the directors of tax chambers with respect to roughly 30% of the decisions or interpretations rendered in first order. The percentage of decisions changed at the second instantiation as a consequence of appeals and reconsideration was 34.4% (NIK, 2014). Over the course of that same year, provincial administrative courts overrode 25.8% of the contested assessment decisions by directors of tax chambers, while the NSA issued verdicts against those directors in 29.7% of all cases (NIK, 2015). In comparison, in 2015, in provincial administrative courts and the Supreme Administrative Court, 32% of all fiscal administration decisions which were subsequently appealed by taxpayers were overturned (Grant Thornton, 2017).

Going further, in the opinion of the Center of Tax Documentation & Studies (*Centrum Dokumentacji i Studiów Podatkowych*, CDiSP) in Łódź,

> Observable is a certain curbed objectivism in the content of interpretations, something which is made manifest in relatively frequent elucidations (pertaining to doubts with regards to the meaning of the tax law) to the disadvantage of the taxpayer, and even forcing a position which is clearly erroneous. The latter usually pertains to situations in which a correct interpretation of the law would (to a vital degree) limit tax revenues on which the tax administration is counting on gaining (Brzeziński and Nykiel, 2011: 74).

This diagnosis seems to be confirmed by the significant number of complaints and appeals filed with administrative courts against individual interpretations of tax law. Whereas in the year 2011, 55.4% of the 2109 interpretations taken to provincial administrative courts were overruled, in 2012 and the first half of 2013, those same courts reviewed 3867 complaints against individual interpretations — 56.2% were overridden (NIK, 2014).

In this context there is an especially evident need to constantly work on raising the level of administrative professionalism and organizational efficiency in the tax administration; there is a need to increase the expert competencies of its employees and functionaries. Requisite for the correct functioning of a fiscal administration is, indubitably, the proper recruitment of candidates for managerial, senior positions in these institutions: the process must be open, competitive, transparent, and anchored in relevant criteria which are impartially evaluated. Poland's experiences heretofore indicate that this is a difficult, but viable endeavor.

References

Bossaert, D., Demmke, Ch, 2003. Civil Services in the Accession States: New Trends and the Impact of the Integration Process. EIPA, Maastricht.

Brzeziński, B., Nykiel, W., 2011. Stan prawa podatkowego w Polsce. Raport 2010. Kwart. Prawa Podatkowego 1, 61–83.

Derdziuk, Z., Gintowt-Jankowicz, M., Stępień, J., Kochanowski, J., Warakomski, J., 1998. Raport z przeprowadzonej analizy i oceny tworzenia służby cywilnej (sierpień 1996 – wrzesień 1997). Biul. Służby Cywilnej 4 (10), 5–12.

Dostatni, G., 2011. Koncepcja służby cywilnej a realizacja konstytucyjnego celu jej działania. Wolters Kluwer, Warszawa.

Drechsler, W., 2005. The Re-Emergence of 'Weberian' Public Administration after the Fall of New Public Management: The Central and Eastern European Perspective. Halduskultuur 6, 94–108.

Drobny, W., Mazuryk, M., Zuzankiewicz, P., 2010. Ustawa o służbie cywilnej. Komentarz. Wolters Kluwer, Warszawa.

Druk sejmowy nr 826, 3 March 2016. Poselski projekt ustawy o Krajowej Administracji Skarbowej. http://www.sejm.gov.pl/sejm8.nsf/druk.xsp?nr¼826 (retrieved: 1.06.2017).

Działocha, K., 2008. Opinia o projekcie ustawy o zmianie ustawy o służbie cywilnej oraz o zmianie niektórych innych ustaw (Druk Sejmowy Nr 595). Biuro Analiz Sejmowych, Warszawa.

Etzioni-Halevy, E., 1999. Exchanging Material Benefits for Political Support: A Comparative Analysis. In: Heidenheimer, A.J., Johnston, M., LeVine, V.T. (Eds.), Political Corruption: A Handbook. Transaction Publishers, New Brunswick – London, pp. 287–304.

Gadowska, K., 2009. Działania pozorne. Problem upolitycznienia procesu obsady wyższych stanowisk w służbie cywilnej w Polsce. Przegląd Socjol. LVIII (1), 51–90.

Gadowska, K., 2015. Dysfunkcje administracji. Służba cywilna w perspektywie neoinstytucjonalnej. Wydawnictwo UJ, Kraków.

Gadowska, K., 2018. The Process of Creating Civil Service in Poland in the Perspective of the New Institutionalism. In: Itrich-Drabarek, J., Mazur, S., Wiśniewska-Grzelak, J. (Eds.), The Transformation of the Civil Service in Poland in Comparison with International Experience. Peter Lang, Berlin—Bern—Bruxelles—New York—Oxford—Warszawa—Wien, pp. 77–108.

Glapiak, E., 2007. Odnowiona skarbówka. Rzeczpospolita, 23 November.

Góra-Ojczyk, J., 2010. Etat w urzędzie tylko z politycznym poparciem. Gazeta Prawna, 24 March.

Grant Thornton, 2017. Raport. Podatki w Polsce. Grant Thornton, Warszawa.

Grupa Posłów na Sejm VIII kadencji, 2016. Wniosek Grupy Posłów na Sejm VIII kadencji do Trybunału Konstytucyjnego (Appeal of a Group of Members of Parliament of the 8th Term to the Constitutional Tribunal). File reference number K 6/16. Warszawa, 22 January.

Hausner, J., 2007. Od idealnej biurokracji do zarządzania publicznego. In: Marody, M. (Ed.), Wymiary życia społecznego. Polska na przełomie XX i XXI wieku. Wydawnictwo Naukowe Scholar, Warszawa, pp. 492–515.

Heywood, P., Meyer-Sahling, J.-H., 2008. Corruption Risks and the Management of the Ministerial Bureaucracy in Poland. Raport. Ernst and Young, Program Sprawne Państwo, Warszawa. http://www.meyer-sahling.eu/papers/Heywood-Meyer-Sahling-Corruption-Risks-in-Poland.pdf (retrieved: 1.06.2017).

Interpelacja nr 2507—do Ministra Finansów—w sprawie wielomiesięcznego utrzymywania na stanowiskach naczelników urzędów skarbowych i dyrektorów izb skarbowych osób nie powołanych w drodze konkursów, a jedynie pełniących obowiązki, oraz ważności wydawanych przez takie osoby decyzji administracyjnych, 8 April 2008. Warszawa.

Interpelacja nr 11252—do Prezesa Rady Ministrów—w sprawie braku przejrzystości procedury konkursowej podczas wyłaniania kandydatów do objęcia stanowisk naczelników urzędów skarbowych, 21 August 2009. Warszawa.

Interpelacja nr 11252—do Ministra Finansów—w sprawie braku przejrzystości procedury konkursowej podczas wyłaniania kandydatów do objęcia stanowisk naczelników urzędów skarbowych—ponowna, renewed, 20 October 2009. Warszawa.

Interpelacja nr 12972 – do Prezesa Rady Ministrów – w sprawie bulwersujących praktyk przy obsadzaniu stanowisk naczelników urzędów skarbowych, 19 November 2009. Warszawa.

Interpelacja nr 12972 – do Prezesa Rady Ministrów – w sprawie bulwersujących praktyk przy obsadzaniu stanowisk naczelników urzędów skarbowych – ponowna, renewed, 25 January 2010. Warszawa.

Interpelacja nr 14265 – do Ministra Finansów – w sprawie procesu wdrażania oraz obecnego funkcjonowania Krajowej Administracji Skarbowej, 13 June 2017. Warszawa.

Izdebski, H., 2015. Opinia prawna na zlecenie Fundacji im. Stefana Batorego w sprawie projektu nowelizacji ustawy o służbie cywilnej oraz niektórych innych ustaw (druk nr 119). Warszawa, 21 December.

Izdebski, H., Kulesza, M., 2004. Administracja publiczna. Zagadnienia ogólne. Wydawnictwo LIBER, Warszawa.

Jak, 2008. P.o. Dyrektorzy i naczelnicy w skarbówce. Gazeta Wyborcza, 8 April.

Kamiński, A.Z., Kamiński, B., 2004. Korupcja rządów. Państwa pokomunistyczne wobec globalizacji. Wydawnictwo Trio, ISP PAN, Warszawa.

Konderak, E., 2009. Tylko 26 proc. osób zdało egzamin na naczelnika. Gazeta Prawna, 5 June.

Kowalewska, J., 2006. Wymiatanie dyrektorów służb celnych i podatkowych. Gazeta Wyborcza, 23 March.

Kowalewska, J., Drabikowska, A., Geront, J., 2006. Czystka w skarbówkach i urzędach celnych. Gazeta Wyborcza, 24 March.

Kwaśniewski, T., 2017. Nieprzydatni. Gazeta Wyborcza (Duży Format), 21 August.

Leśniak, G., 2014. Administracja skarbowa w rękach osób pełniących obowiązki. To próba obchodzenia prawa. Gazeta Prawna, 14 February.

LEX System Informacji Prawnej (Legal Information System) http://www.lex.pl (retrieved: 30.10.2017).

Liszcz, T. (Ed.), 2010. Prawo urzędnicze. Oficyna Wydawnicza Verba, Lublin.

Meyer-Sahling, J.-H., 2004. Civil Service Reform in Post-Communist Europe. The Bumpy Road to Depoliticisation. Int. Rev. Adm. Sci. 75 (3), 509–528.

Meyer-Sahling, J.-H., 2009. Varieties of Legacies. A Critical Review of Legacy Explanations of Public Administration Reform in East Central Europe. W. Eur. Polit. 27 (1), 71–103.

NIK (Supreme Audit Office), 2005. Informacja o wynikach kontroli organizacji i funkcjonowania służby cywilnej, No. 14/2005/P04001/KAP.

NIK (Supreme Audit Office), 2010. Pobór podatku dochodowego od osób fizycznych, No. 18/2010/P09024/KBF.

NIK (Supreme Audit Office), 2011. Prawidłowość postępowań kontrolnych i podatkowych prowadzonych przez organy podatkowe i organy kontroli skarbowej, No. 46/2011/P10024/KBF.

NIK (Supreme Audit Office), 2012. Informacja o wynikach kontroli funkcjonowania służby cywilnej w ramach obowiązujących regulacji prawnych, No. 14/ 2012/P/11/004/KAP.

NIK (Supreme Audit Office), 2014. Przestrzeganie praw podatników przez wybrane urzędy skarbowe i izby skarbowe, No. 26/2014/P/13/039/KBF.

NIK (Supreme Audit Office), 2015. Wykonywanie wyroków wojewódzkich sądów administracyjnych i Naczelnego Sądu Administracyjnego przez urzędy skarbowe i izby celne, No. 22/2015/P/14/016/KBF.

NSA, Opinia Naczelnego Sądu Administracyjnego w Warszawie z dnia 7 lipca 2016 r. (Opinion of the Supreme Administrative Court of the Republic of Poland of 7 July 2016). File reference number BSAIII-021-269-270/16.

NSA, Postanowienie Naczelnego Sądu Administracyjnego w Warszawie z dnia 21 marca 2012 r. (Order of the Supreme Administrative Court of the Republic of Poland of 21 March 2012). File reference number I OSK 322/11.

NSA, Wyrok Naczelnego Sądu Administracyjnego w Warszawie z dnia 26 listopada 2009 r. (Judgment of the Supreme Administrative Court of the Republic of Poland of 26 November 2009). File reference number II FSK 951/08.

Odpowiedź podsekretarza stanu w Ministerstwie Finansów — z upoważnienia Ministra — na interpelację nr 2507 w sprawie wielomiesięcznego utrzymywania na stanowiskach naczelników urzędów skarbowych i dyrektorów izb skarbowych osób nie powołanych w drodze konkursów, a jedynie pełniących obowiązki, oraz ważności wydawanych przez takie osoby decyzji administracyjnych, 7 May 2008. Warszawa.

Odpowiedź sekretarza stanu w Ministerstwie Finansów – z upoważnienia Prezesa Rady Ministrów – na interpelację nr 12972 w sprawie bulwersujących praktyk przy obsadzaniu stanowisk naczelników urzędów skarbowych, 21 December 2009. Warszawa.

Odpowiedź podsekretarza stanu w Ministerstwie Finansów – z upoważnienia Prezesa Rady Ministrów – na ponowną interpelację nr 12972 w sprawie bulwersujących praktyk przy obsadzaniu stanowisk naczelników urzędów skarbowych, second response, 26 February, 2010. Warszawa.

Odpowiedź sekretarza stanu w Ministerstwie Finansów na interpelację nr 13647 w sprawie zwolnień pracowników administracji skarbowej, kontroli skarbowej i służby celnej w kontekście reformy powołującej Krajową Administrację Skarbową, 17 July 2017. Warszawa.

Odpowiedź podsekretarza stanu w Ministerstwie Finansów – z upoważnienia Ministra Rozwoju i Finansów – na interpelację nr 13839 w sprawie struktury zatrudnienia w Krajowej Administracji Skarbowej przed i po reformie, 27 July 2017. Warszawa.

Odpowiedź podsekretarza stanu w Ministerstwie Finansów – z upoważnienia Ministra Rozwoju i Finansów – na interpelację nr 14265 – do Ministra Finansów – w sprawie procesu wdrażania oraz obecnego funkcjonowania Krajowej Administracji Skarbowej, 8 August 2017. Warszawa.

Odpowiedź podsekretarza stanu w Ministerstwie Finansów – z upoważnienia Ministra – na zapytanie nr 2501 w sprawie daleko idących zmian kadrowych w świętokrzyskich organach skarbowych, czego jaskrawym przykładem jest powołanie T. D. na stanowisko zastępcy naczelnika I urzędu skarbowego w Kielcach przez podległego Ministrowi Finansów dyrektora Izby Skarbowej w Kielcach, 16 October 2008. Warszawa.

Piechowiak, M., 2012. Dobro wspólne jako fundament polskiego porządku konstytucyjnego. Biuro Trybunału Konstytucyjnego, Warszawa.

Peters, B.G., 2001. The Politics of Bureaucracy. Routledge, London – New York. Chapter 6. The Politics of Bureaucracy, pp. 219–259.

Peters, B.G., 2018. The Civil Service and Political Influence: Balancing Neutral and Responsive Competence. In: Itrich-Drabarek, J., Mazur, S., Wiśniewska-Grzelak, J. (Eds.), The Transformation of the Civil Service in Poland in Comparison with International Experience. Peter Lang, Berlin – Bern – Bruxelles – New York – Oxford – Warszawa – Wien, pp. 13–24.

Radwan, A., 2011. W urzędach naginają przepisy. Urzędnik może być p.o. nawet przez kilka lat. Gazeta Prawna, 10 November.

Radwan, A., 2012. Konkursy w urzędach to formalność. Kierownicy ustawiają kryteria naboru. Gazeta Prawna, 3 August.

Radwan, A., 2017. Urzędy: Powoływanie szefów bez konkursów, częste zmiany — to destabilizuje pracę. Gazeta Prawna, 10 January.

Ruśkowski, E., 2006. Kontrola stosowania prawa podatkowego. In: Etel, L. (Ed.), Kontrola tworzenia i stosowania prawa podatkowego pod rządami Konstytucji RP. Wolters Kluwer, Warszawa, pp. 81–145.

Rydlewski, G., 2001. Służba Cywilna w Polsce. Przegląd rozwiązań na tle doświadczeń innych państw i podstawowe akty prawne. Wydawnictwo Naukowe Scholar, Warszawa.

RPO, 2016. Wniosek Rzecznika Praw Obywatelskich do Trybunału Konstytucyjnego (Appeal of the Ombudsman to the Constitutional Tribunal). File reference number K 8/16. Warszawa, 1 February.

Sawczuk, P., 2011a. Niezespolona administracja skarbowa. In: Czuryk, M., Karpiuk, M., Kostrubiec, J. (Eds.), Niezespolona administracja rządowa. Wydawnictwo Difin, Warszawa, pp. 56–82.

Sawczuk, P., 2011b. Niezespolona administracja kontroli skarbowej. In: Czuryk, M., Karpiuk, M., Kostrubiec, J. (Eds.), Niezespolona administracja rządowa. Wydawnictwo Difin, Warszawa, pp. 83–96.

Skwirowski, P., 2008a. Megakonkurs w skarbówce. Gazeta Wyborcza, 2 November.

Skwirowski, P., 2008b. Naczelnicy z konkursu, a nie z nominacji. Gazeta Wyborcza, 3 November.

Skwirowski, P., 2016. Ryzykowna rewolucja w administracji skarbowej. Gazeta Wyborcza, 23 October.

Sokolewicz, W., Zubik, M., 2016. Artykuł 1. In: Garlicki, L., Zubik, M. (Eds.), Konstytucja Rzeczypospolitej Polskiej. Komentarz, vol. I. Wydawnictwo Sejmowe, Warszawa, pp. 53–93.

Sprawozdanie Szefa Służby Cywilnej za 2000 r., za 2001 r., za 2002 r., za 2003 r., za 2004 r., za 2005 r. (Report of the Head of Civil Service for 2000, 2001, 2002, 2003, 2004, 2005), 2001, 2002, 2003, 2004, 2005, 2006. https://www.usc.gov.pl/ (retrieved:15.04.2006).

Sprawozdanie Szefa Służby Cywilnej o stanie służby cywilnej i o realizacji zadań tej służby w 2010 r., w 2011 r., w 2016 r., w 2017 r. (Report of the Head of Civil Service on the state of the Civil Service and realization of its tasks in 2010, 2011, 2016, 2017), 2011, 2012, 2017, 2018. https://dsc.kprm.gov.pl/ sprawozdania-szefa-sluzby-cywilnej-0 (retrieved:15.06.2018).

Sprawozdanie z wykonania budżetu państwa za okres od 1 stycznia do 31 grudnia 2017 r. Omówienie (Report on the execution of the state budget for the period from 1 January to 31 December 2017. Discussion), 2018. Rada Ministrow, Warszawa. https://www.mf.gov.pl/documents/764034/6401579/20180601_Omowienieþspraw ozdaniaþzaþ2017þr.pdf (retrieved:15.06.2018).

Stawowiak, Z., 1997. Działalność komisji kwalifikacyjnej do służby cywilnej. Biul. Służby Cywilnej 5–6, 10–12.

Święcicka, E., 2016. Czystka w świętokrzyskich urzędach skarbowych. Odwołano już większość naczelników. Echo Dnia, 12 April.

Teszner, K., 2012. Administracja podatkowa i kontrola skarbowa w Polsce. Wolters Kluwer, Warszawa.

TK, Wyrok Trybunału Konstytucyjnego z dnia 12 grudnia 2002 r. (Judgment of the Constitutional Tribunal of 12 December 2002). File reference number K 9/ 02 (Journal of Laws 2002 No. 238, item 2025).

TK, Wyrok Trybunału Konstytucyjnego z dnia 14 czerwca 2011 r. (Judgment of the Constitutional Tribunal of 14 June 2011). File reference number kp 1/11 (Official Gazette of the Republic of Poland Monitor Polski 2012 No 57, item 577).

Uhlig, D., 2006. Eksperci: Propozycje PiS godzą w neutralność służby cywilnej. Gazeta Wyborcza, 18 July.

Uszyński, D., 2010. Niejasne przepisy, legislacyjne pułapki i luki w systemie prawa podatkowego. In: Kołosowska, B., Prewysz-Kwinto, P. (Eds.), W świecie finansów i prawa finansowego. Działalność dydaktyczna profesora Jana Głuchowskiego. Wyższa Szkoła Bankowa, Toruń, pp. 143–160.

Verheijen, T.J.G., 1999. Civil Service Systems in Central and Eastern Europe. Edward Elgar, Cheltenham.

Weber, M., 1978. Economy and Society: An Outline of Interpretive Sociology, vol. 2. University of California Press, Berkeley. Chapter XI. Bureaucracy, pp. 956–1005.

Weber, M., 1998. Polityka jako zawód i powołanie. Społeczny Instytut Wydawniczy Znak, Fundacja im. Stefana Batorego, Kraków.

Wójcik, K., Rochowicz, P., 2015. Kadrowa czystka w izbach skarbowych, PiS zmienia zasady naboru w administracji skarbowej. Rzeczpospolita, 14 December.

Zapytanie nr 2501 — do Ministra Finansów — w sprawie daleko idących zmian kadrowych w świętokrzyskich organach skarbowych, czego jaskrawym przykładem jest powołanie T. D. na stanowisko zastępcy naczelnika I Urzędu Skarbowego w Kielcach przez podległego ministrowi finansów dyrektora Izby Skarbowej w Kielcach, 22 September 2008. Warszawa.

Zubik, M., 2007. Refleksje nad "dobrem wspólnym" jako pojęciem konstytucyjnym. In: Zubik, M. (Ed.), Prawo a polityka. Materiały z konferencji Wydziału Prawa i Administracji Uniwersytetu Warszawskiego, która odbyła się 24 lutego 2006 roku. Wydawnictwo Liber, Warszawa, pp. 389–404.

Zieliński, E., 2001. Administracja rządowa w Polsce. Dom Wydawniczy Elipsa, Warszawa.

Selected legal acts

Personal income tax law of 26 July 1991 (Journal of Laws 1991 No. 80, item 350 as amended).

The Act of 28 September 1991 on tax control (Journal of Laws 1991 No. 100, item 442 as amended).

Corporate income tax law of 15 February 1992 (Journal of Laws 1992 No. 21, item 86 as amended).

The Act of 8 January 1993 on taxation of goods and services (Journal of Laws 1993 No. 11, item 50 as amended).

The Act of 21 June 1996 on the office of the minister of finance, and on tax offices and tax chambers (Journal of Laws 1996 No. 106, item 489 as amended).

The Act of 5 July 1996 on civil service (Journal of Laws 1996 No. 89, item 402 as amended).

The Constitution of the Republic of Poland of 2 April 1997 (Journal of Laws 1997 No. 78, item 483).

The Act of 18 December 1998 on civil service (Journal of Laws 1999 No. 49, item 483 as amended).

The Act of 27 July 2001 amending the act on public finances, the act on the organization and mode of operation of the council of ministers and the scope of ministers' operation, the act on branches of the government administration and the act on civil service (Journal of Laws 2001 No. 102, item 1116).

The Act of 27 June 2003 on creation of Provincial Tax Colleges and on the amendment of some acts regulating the duties and competences of organs and the organization of units subordinate to the minister in charge of public finance (Journal of Laws 2003 No. 137, item 1302 as amended).

The Act of 11 March 2004 on taxation of goods and services (Journal of Laws 2004 No. 54, item 535 as amended).

The Act of 10 March 2006 amending the act on local self-government employees, the act on the Supreme Audit Office and the act on civil service (Journal of Laws 2006 No. 79, item 549).

The Act of 24 August 2006 on the state reserve of human resources and high-ranking state positions (Journal of Laws 2006 No. 170, item 1217 as amended).

The Act of 24 August 2006 on civil service (Journal of Laws 2006 No. 170, item 1218 as amended).

The Act of 21 November 2008 on civil service (Journal of Laws 2008 No. 227, item 1505 as amended).

The Act of 10 July 2015 on tax administration (Journal of Laws 2015 No. 0, item 1269).

The Act of 30 December 2015 amending the act on civil service and some other acts (Journal of Laws 2015 No. 0, item 34).

The Act of 16 November 2016 on the National Tax Administration (Journal of Laws 2016 No. 0, item 1947).

The Act of 16 November 2016 — Introductory regulations to the act on the National Tax Administration (Journal of Laws 2016 No. 0, item 1948).

The Minister of Finance ordinance of 29 October 2003 regarding appointment of the commission and the conducting of the competition for the position of director of tax chamber and head of tax office (Journal of Laws 2003 No. 187, item 1826).

The Minister of Finance ordinance of 20 November 2003 regarding the competition for the position of director of a tax audit office (Journal of Laws 2003 No. 210, item 2043 as amended).

The Minister of Finance ordinance of 14 July 2008 regarding appointment of the commission and the conducting of the competition for the position of director of tax chamber and head of tax office (Journal of Laws 2008 No. 133, item 844).

The Minister of Finance ordinance of 30 March 2015 regarding the competition for the position of director of tax chambers and head of tax offices (Journal of Laws 2015 No. 0, item 523).

Obtaining Redress for Abuse of Office in Russia: The Soviet Legacy and the Long Road to Administrative Justice

Elena Bogdanova
University of Eastern Finland, Department of Social Science and Business Studies,
European University at St. Petersburg, RANEPA, Russia

This article examines the options for redressing abuse of office available to citizens in Soviet and post-Soviet Russia. I consider the courts, the procuracy, and the complaint mechanism as sites for citizens to lodge claims against abuse of office in late-Soviet and post-Soviet times. After the collapse of the Soviet system there was an attempt to overcome the Soviet legacy, to strengthen legal institutions and establish administrative justice. Analysis of Soviet and post-Soviet normative documents and statistical data allows us to argue that opportunities for Russian citizens to combat service crimes in the courts have improved substantially. However, the system for coping with abuse of office remains imperfect, and retains features of the Soviet legacy despite vague legislation about administrative justice and dual ways of coping with abuse through legal and quasi-legal mechanisms. The re-establishment of the complaint mechanism in the conditions of contemporary Russia exacerbates this imperfection. Overall, the complaint mechanism occupies a significant place in people's options for making claims against officials, especially claims against high-ranking officials.

Keywords: Abuse of office, Complaint mechanism, Administrative justice, Soviet legacy

1. Introduction

During a recent teleconference (2017) with President Vladimir Putin, several families from Izhevsk called in to complain about poor living conditions. The president promised to visit them later. After that, a house in Izhevsk, the capital city of the Udmurt Republic, became the subject of close attention by local officials, the procuracy, and the investigative committee. It had been lightly renovated, and the courtyard around the house had been paved. At the end of June 2017 the President visited the house, and spoke with the acting head of Udmurtia right in front of the house:

> *President Putin (P):* How many families have to be resettled? How many families need new housing?
> *Mayor (M):* Eleven.
> *P:* They must be resettled within this neighborhood.
> *M:* We have a new apartment building in this area. It is not ready yet, but we plan to complete it in a year.
> *P:* Do you have enough available apartments there?
> *M:* At the moment we have one or two apartments available in the building.
> *P:* So, by the end of this year all eleven families must be resettled in the new building.
> *M:* I'm not sure. We will do our best to make the right decision.
> *P:* Try to do that.
> *M:* Yes. We will do our best. We will discuss each and every situation personally.

The President gets millions of calls from citizens during his teleconferences. A special office of the President's administration registers about a million of submitted complaints annually. Some problems articulated in the complaints, like the one mentioned above, have no clear legal solution. It is a challenging task to provide eleven apartments in a new building when only one or two are available and all the others are sold out. It is unclear at present if the local official's promise has been executed or not, but it is obvious that this order of the president can hardly be executed without bending legal rules or procedures — a form of abuse of office.

The problem of abuse of office belongs to the sphere of law; specifically, administrative justice. Yet the mainstream literature on democratic regime survival has almost entirely ignored legal institutions (Reenock et al., 2013, p. 503). In the case of Russia, when studying problems of abuse of office it is not enough to consider anti-corruption measures only within the framework of the law enforcement system, because in Russia legal institutions have never been the only ones who dealt with problems in this sphere.

In spite of the long road towards administrative justice, and certain achievements in this field, the mechanism of complaints to the authorities remains an important path to obtaining redress for abuse of office in Russia. At the same time, the complaint mechanism remains even more marginal among researchers than legal institutions, which is quite a serious omission.

Over the centuries this mechanism has influenced understandings of abuse of office by the state and society, the means of addressing the problem, and the role of the law and the legal system in processing claims against maleficence in office. For Russia, where the level of corruption is consistently one of the highest in the world, it is especially important to understand how abuse of office is comprehended and how these types of violations have been regulated not only today, but in previous eras. The purpose of this article is to consider the different methods for coping with abuse of office in the late-socialist and post-socialist periods, and to identify the role of the complaint mechanism among them.

The article is based on analysis of normative documents regulating the fight against abuse of office in the Soviet and post-Soviet periods; analysis of court statistics; and official data presenting the number and topic of complaints addressed to the Russian President. The first part of the article describes the Soviet definition of the notion "abuse of office." The second part presents an analytical review of late-Soviet options for claims against abuse of office to the legal, supervisory, and administrative bodies. Then, in the third part the article addresses the contemporary period, analyzing particular features of coping with abuses in today's Russia. The closing section debates post-socialist transformation to claims against officials.

2. "Abuse of office" versus "corruption": The Soviet understanding of crimes by officials

The term "abuse of office" is connected directly with the category of "corruption." Both notions may be similarly defined as the illegal, unethical, or immoral use of power for private gain. The concepts are very similar in meaning, and the differences between them are vague. No theory gives a universal explanation of the differences between these two terms. Positioning corruption as the key offense, Western scholars are concerned with the definition, and argue about the constituent elements of corruption. The most common characteristics which are usually used to classify an offense as corruption concern the abuse of public office. This definition of corruption is commonly used by the World Bank and Transparency International, and also in Western academic debates (Andersson and Heywood, 2009, pp. 746–767). Joseph S. Nye classifies as corruption acts such as bribery, nepotism, and misappropriation (Nye, 1967, p. 419), emphasizing material interest as the core of this type of offense.

The category "abuse of office" is of secondary importance in Western debates. As seen from the previous paragraph, it is considered a primary characteristic of corruption rather than a separate phenomenon. No precise definition is available: the dictionary says only that "to abuse" means "to misuse" or "to commit wrongful acts",[1] and the meanings of "misuse" and "wrongful" are as vague as that of abuse. Canadian political scientist Kenneth Gibbons suggests a number of actions which could be labeled "abuse of office": nepotism, patronage (for instance, giving priority to political party supporters), legislative conflicts of interest, and bureaucratic conflicts of interest (Gibbons, 1989, p. 778). In comparison with corruption, in the Western debate abuse of office seems to be a more general definition, covering lesser violations which do not have an immediate connection to material profit, and may not include crimes such as bribery (Gibbons, 1989; Nye, 1967; Andersson and Heywood, 2009.).

The definition of corruption used by Transparency International is vulnerable to criticism even in the context of Western style

---

1   Abuse of Office" TheLaw.Com Dictionary. Available at: https://dictionary.thelaw.com/abuse-of-power/.

liberal democracies. As the British Law Commission stated, corruption constitutes "a common law offense (with) no exhaustive definition. As a result the boundaries of the offense are uncertain" (Mendilow and Peleg, 2014, p. 4). The possibility of applying this understanding of corruption to other types of societies is equally doubtful. Some governments do not have formal rules about official conduct, and in some nations it may be taken for granted that elected officials and bureaucrats will mix their official duties and private business affairs. In other words, the "normal duties" of an official in one country may include accepting gifts or making a decision even if it involves a conflict of interest (Gardiner, 2017 [2002], p. 39). Kate Gillespie of the University of Texas at Austin, and Gwenn Okrahlik of the University of Arkansas argue that it is problematic to apply the Western conception of corruption, based on a Western model of authority constrained by the principles of transparency and accountability, in societies where patrimonial authority prevails (Gillespie and Okrahlik, 1991, p. 83). Sino- American political scientist Yan Sun, considering corruption in Russia and China, argues that multiple factors influence the ways, depth, and severity of the corruptness of officials. The structure of government institutions and political processes are important determinants of levels of corruption because weak governments that do not control their agencies experience high levels of corruption (Sun, 1999, p. 6). Obviously, the ways of defining, regulating, and coping with this type of offense also crucial.

The Soviet approach, features of which are reproduced in Russia today, gives us a very different comprehension of the connection between the notions of "corruption" and "abuse of office". In Soviet legislation the abuse of office was understood as a broad "umbrella" term referring to a number of managerial and official practices—from insults or failure to deliver benefits to citizens, to serious matters such as taking or giving bribes. They include, other than those mentioned, a variety of phenomena: for example, deceiving the state about the results of an organization's activities; appropriating state property; deceiving customers; dismissing people for reasons of personal hostility; giving unauthorized special rewards to favored employees; and engaging in illicit exchange with the managers of other organizations (Lampert, 1985, p. 2).

Moreover, the concept "official" is much wider in Soviet criminal law than in the Western legal system, since it includes not only state officials, but also the managerial staff of enterprises. It was used even more broadly in the 1930s, when rank-and- file workers (especially kolkhoz farmers) were held to be "officials" (Van den Berg, 1985, p. 60).

The Soviet leadership seemed to be faced with a major dilemma. In order to secure effective political control, the Soviet rulers needed law and legality—stable rules and clearly specified rights and duties for individuals and organizations. Yet the Soviet form of political management itself helped to create an environment in which illegal practices flourished.

The requirements of the ever-looming plan confront Soviet managers with a struggle for survival that cannot be fought without regular breaches of law. For example, sending gifts and bribes to suppliers and higher officials, the illicit use of enterprise funds for entertaining, setting aside scarce goods for 'important' people who will be useful to the organization, barter exchange between enterprises, private contracts for construction work—all these can be seen as measures that help to create the necessary conditions of success, that help to overcome a series of ever-present constraints (Lampert, 1985, p. 24).

Office holders were often forced to use their powers not for private gain but rather to secure the successful completion of production cycles, or to fulfill plans and orders—which in conditions of centralized economy and constant shortage of primary products and components, lack of means of transportation, and so on, would be impossible. This strategy could actually support production, although in the eyes of controlling agencies it was still a violation.

The very structure of the socialist system created multiple possibilities for abuse of office. Since managerial and official practices were surrounded by so many laws and regulations, abuse of office was supported by the law itself. Deeper causes included: 1. an ineffective planned economy and shortage of goods; 2. the centralized character of management; 3. denial of private property. Anybody with authority in any recognized organization in the Soviet Union was considered a "servant of the state," even if the organization (say, a trade union) was not officially regarded as a "state organization." Any holder of office was responsible to the political authority and his or her obligations to the state were defined by criminal law as well as administrative rules.

Abuse of office in the context of Soviet society had a specific meaning. It combined a wide variety of offenses by officials, from light misconduct to serious crimes. In the conditions of the Soviet system hardly any official could avoid violations, which turned the legislation on abuse of office into a strong arm of control and management and a tool of personnel policy. The unification of such diverse offenses under one umbrella concept contributed to an erosion of concern about the severity of the violations, and also facilitated the easy reclassification of particular violations as lighter — or vice versa, as more severe.

3. The Soviet choice to struggle against the abuse of office beyond the judiciary

In 1918 the State Control Committee (Goskontrol') drafted a structure for a special Committee to examine complaints against the actions of officials. The draft was considered at a special meeting which, however, found the establishment of an administrative court untimely and too complicated, and made a decision to replace it with the Complaint Bureaus. They were the special bodies, established by the People's Commissariat of the State Control, charged with the task of receiving applications for abuse and misconduct of officials. Great attention was paid to the formation of the complaint mechanism in the first years after the Revolution. The mechanism was transformed throughout the whole Soviet period, but the basic principles and rules of its operation were laid in the first decade of Soviet power. The Resolution "On the Strict Observance of Laws" of November 8, 1918 established the legal duty of all officials and institutions of the RSFSR to receive and process complaints from the citizens (S'ezdy, 1935, pp. 103–104). Thus, the protection of citizens' interests was proclaimed as the duty of the authorities.

In 1919 a branch of the bureau of complaints was established in almost all provincial cities, uyezds and even a number of *volosts*[2] of the RSFSR. In 1934 the bureaus were abolished and the function of processing complaints was passed to the party-state apparatus (Postanovlenie VTsIK, 1934), which remained the most powerful addressee of citizens' complaints until the end of the Soviet period.

In part of supervisory authority in 1922 a key Tsarist institution the procuracy was restored. In addition to its prosecutorial functions, the Bolsheviks revived its earlier power to supervise the activities of administrative officials, agencies, and citizens—including the order of consideration of complaints addressed to the authorities (Boim and Morgan, 1978). Since its restoration, the procuracy was involved in working with complaints at various levels,[3] monitoring both the legality of the actions of those who had been accused by complainants and the legality of the actions of those who processed the complaints.

In the 1920s—the years of New Economic Policy—there were lawyers who "classified insurance councils, land, housing and other commissions, the complaint bureaus and the procuracy in the category of administrative justice bodies" (Pravilova, 2000, p. 145). Thus, an avenue was established for claims against abuse of office outside of the court system in accordance with the rules of the so-called administrative way of resolving issues. Renowned expert in socialist law and post-socialist transformations Inga Markovits argues that such a cleavage was typical of the Soviet system (Markovits, 1995). In Russian, the two different meanings of "administrative" raised confusion between two ways of resolving problems

---

2   Before the administrative reform of 1923–1929 *volost'* was a small rural area, subordinated to the city. The union of several *volosts* (including the city or village as a center) formed an *uyezd*.
3   The Circular Resolution (1930) ordered the procuracy to pay special attention to work with complaints of peasants and Red Army soldiers.

of abuse. The first one was an administrative way of resolving issues concerned with justice claims, managed by the forces of administrative bodies, by the rules of handling complaints. The second involved the prosecution of officials for administrative violations, and was realized by the courts. These two ways coexisted during the whole Soviet period, compensating for the lack of institutions of administrative justice. Both dealt with the problems of abuse of office, and the jurisdictional division of problems was nebulous, remaining unclear until the end of the Soviet period. Serious criminal cases were considered by the courts or procuracy. An insignificant segment of crimes by officials was considered by the courts as part of civil justice. Relatively light misconduct could be managed through complaints. There were also offenses in the middle for which claims could be made simultaneously to the courts, the administrative bodies, or the procuracy.

3.1. Practice of combatting abuse of office in late-Soviet period

Service crimes such as negligence or bribery seem to have been the typical offenses of the Stalinist period. In the 1920s, and especially in the 1930s, their prosecution was widespread, which however was partly due to the circumstance that embezzlement by officials was classified as crimes by officials (Van den Berg, 1985, p. 60). There was a sudden decrease in the prosecution of service crimes in the first years of Brezhnev's leadership. In the late Soviet years statistics showed relatively stable figures of service crimes: in the beginning of the 1970s the most frequently prosecuted service crimes constituted about 5% of all criminal cases (Van den Berg, 1985, pp. 60–61). The most frequently prosecuted was negligence (*khalatnost'*, Article 172 RSFSR of Criminal Code of 1960), which made up more than 45% of all service crimes. The second group of violations involved bribery, making up 13% of all service crimes, or about 0,2% of all crimes. The third group combined all the other types of abuse of official position, making up one third of all registered service crimes (Zdravomyslov, 1975, p. 124).

Criminological characterizations of typical service crimes in the Soviet Union were noteworthy. The vast majority (up to 95%)

of prosecuted officials were representatives of the medium and lower levels of the administrative apparatus. Among them, first place was taken by "low-ranking workers who have the direct financial liability of property entrusted to them—sellers, cashiers, store holders. Employees of the administrative apparatus seldom appear in the role of subjects of the considered service crimes" (Kriminologiia, 1976).

Appropriation, embezzlement, and other abuses of official position fell within the scope of Article 92 of the RSFSR Criminal Code. From 1980 to 1986 the number of these crimes increased annually for the USSR as a whole, a result attributable to active law enforcement measures, and declined from 1987 to 1989, as well as bribery, represented in a separate statistical graph (Butler, 1992, p. 153). Soviet specialists, however, believed the real incidence of these crimes had increased, and that the statistical decrease merely meant that a greater number of incidents went unprosecuted.

In 1989 cases of abuse totaled 47 623, or 3% of all crimes (Alekseeva et al., 1992, p. 110). Likewise, the cases of high officials are hidden in the statistical classification of offenders. According to statistics, offenders belonged to the social groups of workers (42,5%), employees (52,4%), collective farmers (4,1%), and students (0,1%) (Alekseeva et al., 1992, pp. 114–115). From 1987 to 1991, the adjudication of punishment by the courts in the form of deprivation of the right to occupy certain positions or engage in certain activities decreased from 50,2% to 40%. A significant reduction in convictions for crimes in the sphere of the economy — official embezzlement fell by a factor of 2,7, and bribery by a factor of 5,6 — was also noteworthy in this period (Alekseeva et al., 1992, pp. 114–115). The statistics of the 1980s suggest that the possibility of claimants going to court to challenge the illegal actions of high- and even middle-ranking officials was for the most part absent.

The low number of service crimes among the total statistics is not only a result of the high number of unreported crimes, but also of the lenient approach of the procuracy to these matters and the availability of several other sanctions (exaction of the damage, public censure, disciplinary action, party sanctions). According to a poll within the procuracy, criminal sanctions were only applied in one third of all cases (Alekseeva et al., 1992, p. 122).

Researchers call the Soviet procuracy a substitute for administrative justice (Smith, 2007), or compare its functions with those of the Ombudsman (Gellhorn, 1967). From its very beginnings the procuracy occupied a central position in the administration of justice. This position was derived not only from its hierarchical and centralized organisational structure, but also from the wide range of functions it performed. The procurator was involved at every stage in the criminal process (Smith, 1997, p. 350).

Complaints against improper actions of officials could be submitted to the authorities and to the procuracy. However, complaints addressed to the procuracy should have been sustained through legal norms. The filing of complaints to the authorities did not require legal justification and more often appealed to the norms of socialist morality. Gradually, the procuracy took over the function of considering certain types of offense, mainly but not only criminal.

Legislative initiatives of the final Soviet decade allow us to talk about yet another attempt to create the appearance of administrative justice outside the judicial system. Changes which affected the procuracy and the complaint mechanism addressed to the authorities should be considered precisely. In the 1977 Constitution, "complaint" was removed from the list of habitual forms of appeals to the authorities. Article 49 legitimated appeals to officials in the forms of petitions (*zaiavleniia*) and proposals (*predlozheniia*). Complaint as a form of appeal to the authorities was covered by Article 58 and made equal to the administrative legal instrument of coping with abuse of office: "Citizens of the USSR have the right to appeal against actions committed by officials as well as state and public bodies .... The actions committed by officials in breach of the law that relate to abuse of office and infringe upon citizens' rights can be lodged with the courts in accordance with procedure established by law" (Article 58). Peter Solomon recalls that "in the 1970s Soviet legal scholars had already begun discussing the expansion of the scope of judicial review of administrative acts and in 1977 succeeded in securing an entry for this subject in the 1977 Constitution of the USSR" (Solomon, 2004, p. 555; Sharlet, 1978, pp. 94–95; Barry, 1978; Chechot, 1973; Salishcheva, 1970).

The connection of the complaint mechanism with the procuracy was strengthened by the amendments of 1980, which introduced certain changes into the main regulator of the complaint mechanism, the Decree of the Presidium of the Supreme Soviet of the USSR "Concerning the Procedure for Consideration of Proposals, Petitions and Complaints" of April 12, 1968. The procuracy was designated the main supervising authority regarding public complaints. According to the amendment, the Prosecutor General of the USSR and his subordinate prosecutors were responsible for superintendence of accurate and uniform compliance with the Soviet legislation by all institutions that considered citizens' proposals, petitions, and complaints. The procuracy had the authority to conduct inspections and to provoke proceedings. However, it remained unclear which agency should, in turn, check the work of the procuracy.

The next important event was the enactment of the Code of RSFSR for Administrative Offenses on June 20, 1984. This was the first attempt in Soviet—indeed, the whole of Russian—history to codify administrative offenses. The Code introduced the concept of administrative offenses, provided their classification, and determined various types of administrative penalties. The powers to apply the Code when considering administrative offenses, meting out punishments, or taking preventive measures were vested in the local Councils of People's Deputies and their executive committees (Article 6). These structures became central in the design of the general complaint mechanism by the final decade of the Soviet Union. The Code stipulated the transfer of cases to comrades' courts, public organizations, or labor collectives (Articles 21, 31, 32, 40). Thus, it determined the final structure of the instances responsible for addressing administrative offenses, which was virtually excluded from the judicial system.

According to the Code of Administrative Offenses, the Councils of People's Deputies were responsible for considering administrative offenses and taking administrative proceedings. The Code granted the Councils an unprecedented right to "establish the rules which violation is administratively punishable" (Article 6) under several articles of the Code (Articles 85, 101, 144, 149). Thus, the Councils and their executive committees became more than regular enforcers of legal norms, empowered to determine, adjust, and interpret administrative norms. The 1987 law "On the procedure for appealing to the court illegal acts " emphasized the importance of the complaint mechanisms internal to government agencies, and strengthened continuity between those, and court system, requiring that the complainant must exhaust all such administrative remedies before turning to the courts (Barry, 1978).

The results of the work of the complaint mechanism have never been considered systematically alongside judicial statistics, though episodic studies conducted in the late Soviet years indicated that the number was huge. In the 1960s and 1970s, the mechanism attained its highest level of use. As Stephen White documents, Communist Party organizations received more than 500 000 appeals annually during the 1970s. The stream of letters to the central press reached sixty to seventy million per year (White, 1983, pp. 202-207). Another analysis estimates that in 1966-1967 the newspaper *Komsomol'skaia Pravda* received 900-1000 letters daily, or 300 000 annually (Grushin, 2003, p. 178). Stephen White (1983) gives even more impressive figures, arguing that all the Soviet national newspapers together received sixty to seventy million letters a year. The biggest circulation national dailies — *Pravda, Izvestiia, Trud* — got about half a million letters annually (Table 1):

Table 1: Complaints to the central Party newspapers.

	Pravda	Izvestiia	Trud
1974	456000		
1975		467858	548174
1977		520000	
1981	514000		415417

Source: Various Soviet publications. (White, 1983, p. 52)

The Communist Party Central Committee was also a very popular and influential addressee of citizens' complaints. According to the Central Committee statement, during the period between the 25th and 26th Party Congresses (1976-1981), the Central Committee received nearly three million letters and nearly one million visitors. Meanwhile local party organs received fifteen million written and oral submissions (Pravda, 1981) (Table 2):

Table 2:   Complaints to the CPSU central committee.

Number of complaints	
1976	693260
1977	657360
1978	558740
1979	570880
1980	671600

Source: Spravochnik partiinogo rabotnika, 1981.

Statistical information about the number of complaints addressed by citizens to the executive committees in the last Soviet decade is not available. According to Theodore Friedgut, "in the first four months of 1962 the Kirov district Soviet executive committee in Moscow received 11 803 applications and complaints" (Friedgut, 1978, p. 466). Simple calculations give the result about half million of applications only in Moscow annually.

Not all the letters addressed to the different power bodies were complaints, and not all informed about abuse of office. Many of the letters expressed concerns about the supply of consumer goods and services, housing problems, or conditions of work. No statistics are available about the number of the complaints devoted to problems of abuse.[4] However, the accusation of officials of abuse

---

[4]   A much earlier study by Inkeles and Geiger (1968) threw some light on this point in a survey of letters to the press in the late Stalinist period, based on 270 critical letters to 8 Soviet newspapers in 1947. Some of 64 of the letter-writers were acting in an 'occupational' capacity, and 127 'organisational relationships between critics and targets of criticism' were identied in the 64 letters. There were only 12 cases where critics focused criticism of the work of their own organizations.

of official powers became a familiar way of argumentation, attaching importance to the complaint, determining its legitimacy and loyalty, and became a marker of the genre (Fitzpatrick, 1996, p. 79; Orlova, 2004; Pecherskaya, 2012). At all stages of the Soviet period, complaints about salespersons, shopkeepers, shop directors, heads of public services, directors of sanatoriums and hospitals, and managers of restaurant and taxi parks, took the leading positions in the general statistics of complaints (Markovits, 1986; Bogdanova, 2014). Officials were accused of rudeness, cruelty, deliberate restriction of access to goods and services, refusal to provide a book of complaints, and other forms of abuse of office. This set of problems is very similar to the complaints processed by the courts and procuracy.

The work of the complaint mechanism was never perfect. The number of complaints always exceeded the capabilities of the complaint mechanism apparatus. It always experienced problems with resources, personnel, and norms. Researchers of the Soviet complaint mechanism unanimously note that the complaint mechanism could never cope with the flow of complaints in a procedurally correct way, and was distinguished by its ingenuity in evading full-fledged consideration of violations (Fitzpatrick, 2001; Friedgut, 1978; White, 1983; Bogdanova, 2006).

Throughout the Soviet period, the court and quasi-judicial methods of resolving violations related to abuse of office operated in parallel. Statistics show that the number of cases of abuse of authority considered in the courts decreased, and the severity of punishments were weakened. The late Soviet approach to justice contributes to the fact that the consequent articles of the Criminal Code were applied mainly to the officials of middle and lower levels. High-ranking officials were largely protected from accusations of abuse of power.

In the last decade of the Soviet period, quasi-judicial ways of making claims against abuse of office were supported by the state. The newly adopted legislative documents gave to the administrative apparatus involved in the proceedings of such cases certain features of the administrative judiciary, supervised by the procuracy.

The practice of addressing abuse of office was attended by all the disadvantages and peculiarities of the complaint mechanism functioning — lack of regularity, chronic overload, blurred rules, as well as the almost total elimination of legal premises and their substitution with socialist moral norms. State and party bodies, press editors, and public activists were entrusted with addressing (and sometimes classifying) the corresponding violations. The mass of complaints, including specific complaints concerning abuse of office, had a very low rate of decision enforcement. Although, for many citizens the complaints mechanisms represented the main path to satisfaction.

4. Abuse of office during the post-socialist period: a new duality

Since 1990, the People's Control (*Narodnyi Kontrol'*), to which the mechanism of complaints was subordinated, lost its power almost entirely. On May 16, 1991, the fifth session of the Supreme Soviet of the USSR adopted the law "On the Control Chamber of the USSR," which replaced the People's Control. Examining citizens' appeals and complaints was excluded from its functions. For the first time in several centuries of Russian history, the mechanism of complaint was without state support (Kabashov, 2011). Shortly thereafter, on August 1, 1991, Yeltsin's decree prohibited the activities of the CPSU. Difficult times came for the Party publication. The most important addressees of citizens' complaints either ceased to exist, or entered a period of crisis. The media, in conditions of the competitive market and freedom of speech, ceased to be the mouthpiece of the governing structures. Executive authorities survived, and continued to work with complaints, but the officials were not obliged to consider complaints any more. There are no statistics on the number of complaints sent to the authorities in the early post-socialist period; however, there is a collection of complaints addressed to Boris Yeltsin during 1990–1991, numbering about 12 000 letters, in the State Archives of the Russian Federation (Kollektsiia pisem B.N. Yeltsinu, 1991). The people's habit of complaining faced

THE LONG ROAD TO ADMINISTRATIVE JUSTICE 313

institutional collapse, and was looking for some new legitimate addressees.

After that, the complaint mechanism began to gradually lose its importance, influence, and priority in dealing with cases involving abuse of office. Most of the Soviet laws regulating the operation of the complaint mechanism had not been abolished; however, the sociopolitical context had radically changed. Judicial reform and priority of the rule of law left to the mechanism of complaint the role of a marginal, weakly effective administrative way of solving problems.

A bit later, in 1999, the Constitutional Court of the Russian Federation determined the court's priority over the complaint mechanism in resolving administrative issues and the order of supervision over the decisions taken by administrative bodies: "legislation on administrative offenses defines, that courts (judges) ... control the legality and validity of decisions on imposition of administrative penalties imposed by other commissioners of the administrative bodies (officials)" (Postanovlenie Konstitutsionnogo, 1999).

Post-socialist judicial reforms were launched which aimed to restructure the entire Soviet judiciary on the model of European justice. In the opinion of Peter Solomon and Todd Foglesong, 2000, in the first 10 years the reform achieved significant results. The initial plan of the post-socialist legal reform was supposed to strengthen judicial institutions. Particularly, some felt that the procuracy needed to be weakened in order to permit the court and the Ministry of Justice to assume dominance in the evolving legal system; that "as long as the procuracy retained the powers it enjoyed during the communist era, the courts will never gain supremacy" (Smith, 2007, p. 2).

A system of administrative courts was not established in post-socialist Russia. As in the late-socialist period, the bet was made on "judicial procedure for the settlement of administrative disputes in the jurisdictional bodies" (Zelentsov, 2009, p. 82–83). The legislative instruments for judging the offenses of officials were improved. After a serious revision of Soviet legislation, two primary articles on the relevant crimes were included into the Criminal Code (1996): Article

285 "Abuse of official authority" (*zloupotreblenie dolzhnostnymi polnomochiiami*), and Article 286 "Excess of official authority" (*prevyshenie dolzhnostnykh polnomochii*). These articles prescribe punishments such as fines, forced labor, or imprisonment up to 10 years (Bannikov, 2016). Violation of the rights of citizens is mentioned in both articles only as an indirect consequence.

In April 1993 the Law of the Russian Federation "On Appealing to the Court Actions and Decisions Violating the Rights and Freedoms of Citizens" was adopted, replacing two earlier laws on administrative justice from 1987 to 1989. The new law dramatically extended the right of citizens to bring claims to courts about the illegal actions of officials, even when taken in the name of a collective body, covering virtually any action by any official, whether normative or non-normative, that violated the rights and freedoms of citizens. Then, in 1995, the target of potential complaints was expanded from "officials", or persons in responsible positions, to any and all government employees (*sluzhashchie*) (Khamaneva, 1997, pp. 100–115; Federal Law "On amending the law 'On appealing to the court of wrongful acts.'" 1995). These laws established a full fledged administrative justice and gave the courts a significant role in handling citizen's claims against officials.

The number of lawsuits against officials began to grow rapidly from the very beginning of the 1990s. Russians found much to complain about, and the number of suits against officials rose steadily — from 4 944 in 1990, to 20 326 in 1994, to 56 659 in 1997, to approximately 160 000 in 2000 (Solomon and Foglesong, 2000, pp. 68–71; Verkhovnyi Sud, 2000, pp. 54–57).

The success rate of citizens' suits was high. The overall rate of satisfaction for these lawsuits, according to official statistics from 1999, was 82,8%. The figures for 1996 and for 1997 were similar: 74,4% and 83,4% respectively (Khamaneva and Salishcheva, 2001, p. 36; Verkhovnyi Sud, 1998, pp. 55–58, 1999, pp. 51–53).

In the field of administrative proceedings, one major event occurred, namely: the adoption of the "Code of the Russian Federation on Administrative Offenses" (CRFAO). Work on the Code began in 2001, and on July 1, 2002, it was put into effect, abolishing the then-existing Code of RSFSR for Administrative Offenses. The legislative base of the administrative judiciary is still in the process of formation. The Code of the Russian Federation on Administrative Offenses went through a long period of revisions. The Code of Administrative Court Proceedings was enacted on 15 September 2015. Among other things, it defines the jurisdiction of administrative cases to courts and administrative bodies (Articles 17–27). Recent amendments were introduced to the CRFAO in 2018. It covers a great variety of offenses made by officials which have no criminal component but are serious enough to be considered in the courts (at the level of Justices of the Peace, and ordinary courts of the lower level), or by bodies of executive power. Among them are Article 14.24 "Violation of the legislation on organized tenders," Article 7.32 "Violation of the procedure for concluding, changing the contract," Article 14.7 "Deception of consumers," or Article 14.51 "On violation of the legislation of the Russian Federation on tourist activities." In general, the Code contains about 50 articles regulating crimes by officials, assuming lesser forms of punishment such as warnings, fines, or forced labor. The Code of Administrative Court Proceedings (2015) also includes procedures for administrative justice cases (Chapters 21 and 22).

At the moment, there are particular practices associated with claims against abuse of office. Consideration of the different forms of abuse is allowed by criminal, civil, administrative, and arbitration judiciaries. It remains possible to make complaints against the abuse of office to the procuracy. In the last 10–12 years the opportunity to address complaints to the authorities, including the President of the Russian Federation, has also become available.

In the sector of criminal justice claims against the abuse of office are usually considered on the grounds of Articles 285 and 286 (abuse of office), 287 (refusal to provide information), 291 (bribery), 292 (forgery), and 293 (negligence). In 2015, 10 664 cases were launched using these charges, which is 1,1% of the total number of criminal cases. As is traditional for the Russian criminal justice system, there is a high rate of conviction (91,5%) and a low rate of acquittal (1,3%). In 2016 the number of cases was similar: 10 023 (1%

of all criminal cases), and the rate of convictions was a bit lower (86,2%), presumably because of reconciliation (Otchet, 2015a, 2015b).

Under Putin the procuracy became more involved in the investigation of high profile cases and accidents, and contributed to the criminal prosecution of oligarchs Mikhail Khodorkovskii, Vladimir Gusinskii, and Boris Berezovskii. The involvement of the procuracy in these cases reinforced its image as a heavily politicized institution—"the eye of the tsar" (*oko tsaria*)—that has been utilized by Putin to further his own agenda (Smith, 2007, p. 6–7). Officially the procuracy does not belong to any of the three branches of power. In most legal settings, the procuracy functions in all three: executive, legislative, and judicial (Smith, 2007, p. 6–7). In these ways, Putin has created the prerequisites for a new strengthening of the procuracy and its supervisory function, to involve it in criminal proceedings, and to improve his own ability to influence the work of the procuracy.

An essential part of the work of the procuracy is also connected with the consideration of statements, complaints and other applications from citizens. The order of response of the procuracy is regulated by the federal law No. 59-FZ "On the Procedure for Consideration of Citizens' Applications in the Russian Federation," which also regulates the order of processing of complaints by administrative bodies and officials. The statistical data show that in 2017 the procuracy satisfied 1 251 762 requests "On issues of supervision over the implementation of laws and the legality of legal acts." This figure had increased by 8% since 2012 (Statisticheskie dannye, 2017).

In the sector of civil justice, the elements of the abuse of office are covered by a large number of legal acts related to labor law, electoral rights, environmental pollution, as well as the laws related to administrative justice. In the statistics, this category of offenses are shown in a graph titled "Complaints against illegal actions (inaction) of officials, state and municipal employees, public authorities, bodies of local self-government" (Otchet, 2015a, 2015b).

In 2015 judges handled 105 966 complaints on illegal actions by officials, or about 0,9% of all civil cases. The percentage was exactly the same in 2016. In the statistics for 2015, this category of cases is divided into violations committed by the state and municipal officials, and those committed by the state and local self-government bodies. Of these 28 067 (26,4%) were satisfied, and 46 509 (43,9%) refused. The number of complaints about unlawful actions by state and local self-government bodies was 42 762. Among them 18 825 (44%) were satisfied, and 14 023 (32,7%) were refused. In total, only 31,5% of civil complaints on abuse were satisfied. In 2017 the proportion of satisfied complaints was higher (50,9%), but in comparison with the criminal statistics, the win rate is relatively low, and officials are more protected from accusations of abuse of office in comparison with power bodies (Otchet, 2015a, 2015b).

In the realm of administrative offenses, the bulk of offenses by officials are considered on the basis of Chapter 22 of the Code of Administrative Court Proceedings, "Proceedings in administrative cases disputing the decisions, actions, or omissions of a state authority, local authority, other body, organization vested with specific state or other public powers, official, or state or municipal public servant."

In 2016 157 297 claims were considered based on Chapter 22, which is 3,8% of all administrative cases received by the courts of general jurisdiction in that year. Statistics for 2016 also give the number of administrative claims provoked by an individual plaintiff, and namely, a citizen of the Russian Federation, as 211 571 (5,1% of all administrative appeals). The overall rate of satisfaction for the complainants, according to official statistics in 2016, was 62%, and 23,8% were not satisfied. In total, 98,7% of administrative cases were completed (Otchet, 2016). It is interesting that the statistics also provide data on cases in which the administrative plaintiffs were the state authorities or other state bodies. The aggregate number of such appeals amounted to 3 121 833 in 2016, or 75,6% of the total number of administrative cases. Of these, 97,2% were satisfied, while only 1,2% were not satisfied. More than 100% of cases provoked by the power bodies were completed when we take into account cases carried over from the previous year (ibid).

In sum, the courts consider cases related to misconduct of officials on the basis of criminal, civil, and administrative legislation. All in all, in 2015-2017 the criminal, civil, and administrative segments of the judiciary considered about 1,3-1,5% of cases involving abuse of authority each year. The average success rate for claims against abuse of office in all three segments is about 63%. At the same time, the level of satisfaction of claims against abuse is higher in the criminal sphere than in the civil and administrative sectors. The percentage of individual complaints against officials in the administrative sector is higher than in criminal and civil practice. It gives us reason to note the process of improvement of the practice of administrative justice, although the rate of individual claims against the state remains very low.

4.1. Complaining to Putin about abuse of office

The adoption of the 2006 Law No. 59-FZ "On the Procedure for Consideration of Citizens' Applications in the Russian Federation" provided new impetus for improving the work with citizens' appeals at all levels of executive authority. According to this law, each citizen of the Russian Federation has a right to submit suggestions, appeals, and complaints to a state authority or local government representative, and the range of issues that may be raised in the appeals is without restriction.

Having entered into force, the Law superseded all the normative documents regulating the work with complaints, and those in force since Soviet times. Article 17 of the Law abolished the Decree of the Presidium of the Supreme Council of 1968, the amendment of 1980, as well as all other laws and decrees that were not abolished after the collapse of the Soviet system and formally remained in force until 2006. In fact, Law No. 59 displayed considerable continuity with its Soviet precursor, while creating new mechanisms.

While Law No. 59 made complaints a formal element of the modern national legal system, the bureaucracy that processes these complaints remains outside of the judiciary. Complaints may be submitted to specially designated administrative offices, including those of the president.[5] In the law a complaint is defined as "a citizen's request for the restoration or protection of her violated rights, freedoms, or legitimate interests, or rights, freedoms, or legitimate interests of others" (Article 4.4), and it has much in common with the definition of a lawsuit. The difference between them is that the grounds for filing a lawsuit are limited to violations of the law, while the grounds for complaint may be found in a large variety of circumstances which are subjectively felt by the addresser to be unjust. So, in fact, the Soviet configuration of the recipients of claims against abuse of power has been recreated.

The opportunity to send direct applications to the president is available, legitimized, and widely used. The personal involvement of the president in the processing of complaints is built into the contemporary mechanism of complaint. All agencies of the executive and governing party branches receiving and processing complaints are structured hierarchically and supervised directly or indirectly by the president. Bureaucratic structures providing complaints to the president are constructed in a similar way. They are interchangeable, which demonstrates the significance of the president as the addressee of citizens' complaints. The Administrative Office of the President registers all the complaints addressed to the President. According to figures kept by the Office, the number of complaints in recent years has been about a million annually (Table 3):

---

[5] See the Decree of the President of the Russian Federation No. 201 On Administrative Office of the President of the RF on Work with Applications of Citizens and Organizations of February 17, 2010.

Table 3: Number of complaints registered by the Administrative Office of the President of the RF on work with applications of citizens and organizations, 2009–2017.[6]

2009	2010	2011	2012	2014	2015	2016	2017
683 841	832 734	960 326	835 941	987775	1103605	930683	889714

Source: Website of the Administrative Office of the President of the RF on Work with Applications of Citizens and Organizations (http://www.letters.kremlin.ru)

Complaints addressed to the authorities begin to duplicate the function of administrative justice insofar as they discipline the actions or inactions of officials and local governments. Detailed statistics available on the website of the Administrative Office of the President indicate that a significant proportion of complaints addressed to the President are devoted to the problems of abuse of office. An overview of the data gives the following figures (Table 4):

6　Only complaints are taken into account here. The general number of correspondence, registered by the administrative office is more extended. In different years the complaints consisted from 25% to 75% of all the messgases, involving also requests for information, suggestions, or thanks.

Table 4: Number of complaints about officials, addressed to the President, 2015-2017.[7]

	2015	2016	017
The work of the prosecutor's office	19764	21491	34819
Activities of bailiffs	16267	19286	21044
Activities of internal affairs bodies	10649	12692	13668
Activities of local governmental bodies and its leaders	4208	5212	5593
The work of the executive bodies of the subjects of the Russian Federation	3675	4126	5434
Activities of state bodies and local self-government bodies in the field of land relations	1526	2708	3753
The work of ministries and other federal executive bodies	1872	2366	3711
State traffic police of the Russian Federation (GIBDD)	2700	3341	3416
Local government officials	1465	1488	1657
Execution of official duties by state civil servants of the subjects of the Russian Federation	251	167	1172
Activities of deputies, committees of the State Duma Apparatus	525	669	1119
Activities of the Government of the Russian Federation	463	853	1054
Activities of Investigative Committee of the Russian Federation	527	598	808
Penitentiary authorities	288	349	565
The activities of the welfare bodies and their officials	330	497	559
Execution of official powers and duties	199	501	509
Facts of unlawful behavior of employees of the Federal Bailiff Service of the Russian Federation	102	68	204
Activities of members of the Council of Federation	23	35	112
Activities of bodies of judicial community	50	97	100
Administration of the President of the Russian Federation	91	84	98
Supreme Court of the Russian Federation	20	21	49
Total number of complaints against officials	64 995 (5,9%)	76 649 (8,2%)	99 444 (11,2%)
Total number of complaints addressed to the Number of complaints, addressed to the president	1103605	930683	889714

Source: Website of the Administrative Office of the President of the RF on Work with Applications of Citizens and Organizations (http://www.letters.kremlin.ru)

Complaints about abuse of office authorized by a wide variety of officials are included in the standard classification of general statistics on complaints. Out of the total number of complaints addressed to the president, the number of complaints related to abuse of office

---

[7] In comparison with the table published in the article: Bogdanova E. 2018. Obtaining redress for abuse of office in Russia: The Soviet legacy and the long road to administrative justice. *Communist and Post-Communist Studies*. 51(3), 273-284 the data has been updated, clarified and reclassified (May 14, 2019).

is not so high; however the proportion of such complaints—absolute and relative—has been steadily growing over the past three years.

According to the review of complaints and the results of discussions published by the president, complaints are usually resolved by the executive authorities. The statistics show that in 2017 measures were taken at the federal level in 86,9% of all cases, at the regional level in 56%ofcases, and at the local level in 53,4%. The highest rate of measures taken at the federal level were taken by the federal ministries, at 93,3%.

Legislation contains particular tools for each group of offenders identified in the complaints. However, the statistics show that the complaint mechanism and, in particular, the opportunity for direct application to the president, is considered by Russian citizens to be a significant alternative. The contemporary mechanism of complaint co-exists with legal institutions, and creates a new situation of a substantial duality of tools and sources of justice. It is important to note that the top lines in the ranking of complaints are occupied by complaints against the activities of the procuracy, the Ministry of Internal Affairs, judicial and security bodies, and high-ranking officials. This may, first of all, speak to the excessive involvement of the presidential office into the problems of abuse of office committed by representatives of these bodies. Another interpretation, which does not exclude the first one, is that the formation of an exclusive oversight function for the figure of the president corrects the functioning of all the institutions in the country.

5. Conclusion

Seeking redress for wrongful actions of officials was a challenging task in Soviet society. There was no single system of administrative justice, single addressee, or single legislative framework regulating the issues of abuse. Soviet courts considered mainly criminal cases. The offenses which did not have any criminal component were almost completely covered by quasi-judicial structures: the procuracy and complaint mechanism, and administrative justice was narrow and limited. In the judicial practice of the late-Soviet years, cases of abuse were marginalized and their number was small. This says something, however, not about the small number of violations, but about the specifics of the context, which provoked concealment and the granting of priority to quasi-judicial tools. Complaints submitted to the authorities were also marginalized due to the weakness and imperfection of the complaint mechanism itself. This whole situation has formed a certain attitude towards this type of violation, when the punishment is not inevitable, and level of punishment may be not equivalent to the legal norm.

Post-Soviet efforts for introduction of administrative justice tools in the courts of general jurisdiction brought certain results. The segment of malfeasance in criminal practice is shrinking, but the overall number of administrative cases considered by the courts especially suits by citizens against officials is growing. At the same time, a situation wherein the courts cease to be the only (and primary) addressee of claims against abuse of authority has been fully restored under Putin. In particular, the mechanism of complaint, which is hierarchically arranged under the President, has been recreated. The process of politicization of the procuracy and the control over it is intensifying. This does not contribute to a strengthening of the judicial system, but rather the contrary.

Statistics on the complaints addressed to the president and their processing reproduce the supremacy of the executive bodies. The figure of the president appears as the main supervisory authority that oversees, among other things, the work of the procuracy and high officials. According to Gelman appeal to the legacy is "for the most part, a social construct created and supported by ruling groups in order to maximize their own power" (Gel'man, 2016, p. 18).

This study has argued that, together with the complaint mechanism, particular attitudes towards abuse of office have been revived. Analogous to the Soviet experience, they divide more serious cases—those that hurt the interests of the state and require criminal prosecution—from less serious ones that affect the interests of citizens and can be considered both in the courts and through administrative means. This means that the interests of citizens suffering due to abuse of office are marginalized again. It can be assumed that, by analogy with the Soviet experience, the duality of ways of coping affects the perception of problems of abuse of office as minor or insoluble, and that in Putin's Russia informal as opposed to formal legal approaches to correcting official misconduct still dominate.

References

Alekseeva, M., Gagarskii, A., Ignatov, L. (Eds.), 1992. Prestupnost' i pravonarusheniia. Statisticheskii Sbornik. Finansy i statistika, Moscow.

Andersson, S., Heywood, P., 2009. The politics of perception: use and abuse of transparency International's approach to measuring corruption. Polit. Stud. 57, 746 767.

Bannikov, G.N., 2016. Praktika rassmotreniia ugolovnykh del o prestupleniiakh so zloupotrebleniem i prevysheniem dolzhnostnymi polnomochiiami (stat'i 285 i 286 UK RF. Available at: http://www.oblsud.penza.ru/item/a/1170/.

Barry, D.D., 1978. Administrative justice and judicial review in Soviet Administrative Law. In: Barry, D., Ginsburg, G., Maggs, R.B. (Eds.), Soviet Law after Stalin. Part I: Social Engineering through Law. A. W. Sijthoff, Alphen aan den Rijn, the Netherlands.

Bogdanova, E., 2006. Obrashcheniia grazhdan v organy vlasti kak opyt otstaivaniia svoikh interesov v usloviiakh pozdnesovetskogo obshchestva (1960-e 1970-e gg.). In: Avtoreferat na soiskanie uchenoi stepeni kandidata sotsiologicheskikh nauk. Norma, Saint Petersburg.

Bogdanova, E., 2014. Religious justifications of complaints, addressed to the president in contemporary Russia. Lab. Russ. Rev. Soc. Res. 3, 55 79.

Boim, L., Morgan, G.G. (Eds.), 1978. The Soviet Procuracy Protests: 1937-1973; a Collection of Translations. A. W. Sijthoff, Alphen aan den Rijn, the Netherlands.

Butler, W.E., 1992. Crime in the Soviet Union: early glimpses of the true story. Br. J. Criminol. 32 (2).

Chechot, D.M., 1973. Administrativnaia Iustitsiia. Izdatelstvo LGU, Leningrad.

Fitzpatrick, Sh, 1996. Supplicants and citizens: public letter-writing in Soviet Russia in the 1930s. Slav. Rev. 55 (1), 78–105.

Fitzpatrick, Sh, 2001. Stalinskie krest'iane: Sotsial'naia istoriia Sovetskoi Rossii v. 30-e gody: Derevnia. ROSSPEN, Moscow.

Friedgut, T.H., 1978. Political Participation in the USSR. Princeton University Press, Princeton, NJ.

Gardiner, J., 2017. [2002]. Defining corruption. In: Heidenheimer, A.J., Johnston, M. (Eds.), Political Corruption: Concepts and Contexts. Routledge, Abingdon, New York.

Gellhorn, W., 1967. Ombudsmen and Others. Harvard University Press, Cambridge, Mass.

Gel'man, V., 2016. Politicheskie osnovaniia "nedostoinogo pravleniia" v postsovetskoi Evrazii: nabroski k issledovatel'skoi povestke dnia. Izdatel'stvo Evropeiskogo Universiteta v Sankt-Peterburge, SPb.

Gibbons, K.M., 1989. [1985]. Variations in attitudes towards corruption in Canada. In: Hedenheimer, A.J., Johnston, M., LeVine, V.T. (Eds.), Political Corruption: a Handbook. Transaction Publishers, New Brunswick.

Gillespie, K., Okruhlik, G., 1991. The political dimensions of corruption cleanups: a framework for analysis. Comp. Polit. 1 (24), 77 95.

Grushin, B., 2003. Chetyre zhizni Rossii v zerkale oprosov obshchestvennogo mneniia: epokha Brezhneva. Progress-Traditsiia, Moscow.

Kabashov, S., 2011. Organizatsiia raboty s obrashcheniiami grazhdan v istorii Rossii. Flint, Moscow.

Khamaneva, N., 1997. Zashchita prav grazhdan v sfere ispolnitelnoi vlasti. IGPRAN, Moscow.

Kollektsiia pisem B.N. Yeltsinu, 1991. Gosudarstavennyi Arkhiv Rossiiskoi Federatsii (GARF). F. A - 664, op. 1, doc. 48.

Kriminologiia, 1976. Moscow.

Lampert, N., 1985. Whistle-Blowing in the Soviet Union Complaints and Abuses under State Socialism. Palgrave McMillan, UK.

Markovits, I., 1986. Pursuing One's rights under socialism. Stanford Law Rev. 3 (38), 689 761.

Markovits, I., 1995. Imperfect Justice: an East-West German Diary. Oxford University Press, Oxford.

Mendilow, J., Peleg, I., 2014. Introduction: Edmund Burke's concept of corruption and beyond. In: Mendilow, J., Peleg, I. (Eds.), Corruption in the Contemporary World: Theory, Practice, and Hotspots. Lexington Books, Lanham, Boulder, New York, London.

Nye, J.S., 1967. Corruption and political development: a cost-benefit analysis. Am. Polit. Sci. Rev. 2 (61), 417 427.

Orlova, G., 2004. Rossiiskii donos i ego metamorfozy: zametki o poetike politicheskoi kommunikatsii. POLIS Polit. Issled. 2, 133 145.

Otchet o rabote sudov obshchei iurisdiktsii po rassmotreniiu ugolovnykh del po pervoi instantsii. Available at: http://www.cdep.ru/index.ph php? id=79&item=3417.

Otchet o rabote sudov obshchei iurisdiktsii po rassmotreniiu grazhdanskikh, administrativnykh del po pervoi instantsii. Available at: http://www.cdep.ru/ index.php?id=79&item=341 .

Otchet o rabote sudov obshchei iurisdiktsii po rassmotreniiu grazhdanskikh, administrativnykh del po pervoi instantsii. Available at: http://www.cdep.ru/ index.php?id=79&item=3832.

Pecherskaya, N., 2012. Looking for justice: the everyday meaning of justice in Late Soviet Russia. Anthropol. East Eur. Rev. 30 (2), 20 38. Pravda, 4 April 1981, p. 1.

Pravilova, E., 2000. Zakonnost' i prava lichnosti: administrativnaia iustitsiia v Rossii (vtoraia polovina XIX v. - oktiabr' 1927 g.). Institut Rossiiskoi Istorii RAN, St. Petersburg.

Reenock, C., Staton, J.K., Redean, M., 2013. Legal institutions and democratic survival. J. Polit. 2 (75), 491–505. April.

Salishcheva, N.G., 1970. Grazhdanin i admnistrativnaia iurisdiktsiia v SSSR. Nauka, Moscow.

Sharlet, R., 1978. The New Soviet Constitution of 1977: Analysis and Text. King's Court Communications, Brunswick, OH.

Smith, G.B., 1997. The struggle over the procuracy. In: Solomon Jr., P.H. (Ed.), Reforming Justice in Russia, 1864–1996. M E Sharpe, New York.

Smith, G.B., 2007. The procuracy, Putin, and the rule of law in Russia. In: Feldbrugge, F. (Ed.), Russia, Europe, and the Rule of Law. Brill, Leiden.

Solomon Jr., P.H., 2004. Judicial power in Russia: through the prism of administrative justice. Law Soc. Rev. 3 (38), 549–582.

Solomon Jr., P.H., Foglesong, T.S., 2000. Courts and Transition in Russia: the Challenge of Judicial Reform. Routledge.

Spravochnik partiinogo pabotnika, Vyp. 21, 1981, pp. 503–504. Moscow.

Statisticheskie dannye ob osnovnykh pokazateliakh deiatel'nosti prokuratury RF za ianvar'-dekabr'. 2017 g. Available at: https://gen proc.gov.ru/stat/data/1336134/.

Sun, Y., 1999. Reform, state, and corruption: is corruption less destructive in China than in Russia? Comp. Polit. 32 (1), 1–20.

S'ezdy Sovetov Vserossiiskie i Soiuza SSR v postanovleniiakh i rezoliutsiiakh, 1935. Moscow.

Van den Berg, G.P., 1985. The Soviet System of Justice: Figures and Policy. Martinus Nijhoff Publishers, Dordrecht, Boston, Lancaster.

Verkhovnyi Sud, R.F., 1998. Rabota raionnykh sudov obshchei iurisdiktsii v. 1997 g. Ross. iustitsiia 7, 55–58.

Verkhovnyi Sud, R.F., 1999. Rabota raionnykh sudov obshchei iurisdiktsii v. 1998 g. Ross. iustitsiia 9, 51–53.

Verkhovnyi Sud, R.F., 2000. Rabota raionnykh sudov obshchei iurisdiktsii v pervom polugodii 2000 g. Ross. iustitsiia 12, 54–57.

White, S., 1983. Political communications in the USSR: letters to party, state and press. Polit. Stud. 31 (1), 43–60.

Zdravomyslov, B., 1975. Dolzhnostnye prestupleniia. poniatie i klassifikatsiis, Moscow.

Zelentsov, A.V., 2009. Administrativnaia iustitsiia. Rossiiskii Universitet Druzhby Narodov. Moscow.

Normative Documents

Dekret "O distsiplinarnykh vzyskaniiakh za narushenie sluzhebnoi distsipliny v sovetskikh uchrezhdeniiakh" [Decree "On Distiplinary Penalties for Violation of Service Discipline in the Soviet Institutions"]. January 27. Available at: http://www.consultant.ru/cons/cgi/online.cgi?req=doc&base=ESU&n=9467&rnd=E1CB8E44A90433FE7135F1A230170A07#07219252600676547.

Doklad General'nogo sekretariia TsK KPSS M. S,1988. Gorbachev na XIX Vsesoiuznoi konferentsii KPSS 28 iuniia 1988 g. [Report of the General Secretary of the CPSU Central Committee M. S. Gorbachev at the XIX All-Union Conference of the CPSU 28 June 1988]. In: Izvestiia. June 29, col. 1.

Federal'nyi zakon "O poriadke rassmotreniia obrashchenii grazhdan Rossiiskoi Federatsii" [Federal Law "On the Procedure for Consideration of Citizens' Applications in the Russian Federation"] No. 59-FZ. May 2. Available at: http://www.consultant.ru/cons/cgi/online.cgi?req=doc&ts=56845078202006210516992326&caheid=6341A834A0DF5BBDFF43BE44B12D34E5&mode=splus&base=LAW&n=283578&rn=E1CB8E44A90433FE7135F1A230170A07#09858153796272937.

Kodeks administrativnogo sudoproizvodstva Rossiiskoi Federatsii [Code of Administrative Court Proceedings] No. 21-FZ, 2015. March 8. Available at: http://www.consultant.ru/document/cons_doc_LAW_176147/.

Kodeks RSFSR ob administrativnykh pravonarusheniiakh [Code of RSFSR for Administrative Offenses], 1984. June 20. Available at: http://www.consultant.ru/ document/cons_doc_LAW_2318/.

Kodeks Rossiiskoi Federatsii ob administrativnykh pravonurusheniiakh No 195-FZ [Code of Russian Federation for Administrative Offenses], 2001. December 30. Available at: http://www.consultant.ru/ document/cons_doc_LAW_34661/.

Konstitutsiia (osnovnoi zakon) Soiuza Sovetskikh Sotsialisticheskikh Respublik [Constitution of USSR],1977. Moscow. Available at: http://www.constitution. garant.ru/DOC_1449448.htm.

Konstitutsiia (osnovnoi zakon) Soiuza Sovetskikh Sotsialisticheskikh Respublik [Constitution of USSR],1936. Moscow. Available at: http://www.constitution. garant.ru/DOC_1449448.htm.

Postanovlenie Konstitutsionnogo Suda RF po delu o proverke konstitutsionnosti chasti vtoroi stat'i 266 i punkta 3 chasti pervoi stat'i 267 kodeksa RSFSR ob administrativnykh pravonarusheniiakh v sviazi s zhalobami grazhdan E.A. Arbuzovoi, O.B. Kolegova, A.D. Kutyreva, P.T. Nasibulina i V.I. Tkachuka [Resolution of Constitutional Court of the Russian Federation Concerning Verification of the Constitutionality of Article 266 Part Two, and Article 267 Part One Paragraph Tree of the Code of RSFSR for Administrative Offenses in connection with complaints of citizens E.A. Arbuzova, O.B. Kolegov, A.D. Kutyrev, P.T. Nasibulin i V.I. Tkachuk"] No. 9-P, 1999. May 28. Available at: http://www.consultant.ru/document/cons_doc_LAW_196 00/92d969e26a4326c5d02fa79b8f9cf4994ee5633b/.

Postanovlenie VTsIK "Ob utverzhdenii polozheniia o distsiplinarnoi otvetstvennosti v poriadke podchinionnosti" [Resolution of the All-Russian Central Executive Committee "On Approval of the Provision on Disciplinary Liability in Accordance with the Order of Subordination"], 1927. July 4. Available at: http://www.consultant.ru/cons /cgi/online.cgi?req=doc;base=ESU;n=43717#032258229386488124.

Postanovlenie VTsIK "Ob uporiadochenii dela rassmotreniia i razresheniia zhalob" [Resolution of the All-Russian Central Executive Committee "On Streamlining the Consideration and Resolution of Complaints"], 1934. July 1.

Postanovlenie VTsIK SNK "O distsiplinarnoi otvetstvennosti v poriadke podchinionnosti" [Resolution of the All-Russian Central Executive Committee of the Council of People's Commissars "On Disciplinary Liability in Accordance with the Order of Subordination"], 1932. March 20. Available at: http://www.consultant.ru/cons/cgi/online. cgi?req=doc;base=ESU;n=1904#09658107330654313.

Tsirkuliarnoe postanovlenie Presidiuma Vserossiiskogo Tsentral'nogo Komiteta o meropriiatiiakh po rassmotreniiu krest'ianskikh zhalob [Circular Resolution of the Presidium of the All-Russia Central Executive Committee on Measures to Review Peasant Complaints] No. 130, 1930. April 20.

Ugolovnyi kodeks RSFSR [Criminal Code of RSFSR], 1922. Available at: http://www.consultant.ru/cons/cgi/online.cgi?req=doc&base=ESU&n=3006#02329189944766851.

Ugolovnyi kodeks RSFSR [Criminal Code of RSFSR], 1926. Available at: http://www.consultant.ru/cons/cgi/online.cgi?req=doc&ts=39327 8705789128357467577&cacheid=DFCA20D6D70CF9C518315827B660 D1C0&mode=splus&base=ESU&n=44458&rnd=0.7541976983375034 #06237323093016762.

Ugolovnyi kodeks RSFSR [Criminal Code of RSFSR], 1960. Available at: http://www.consultant.ru/document/cons_doc_LAW_2950/.

Ugolovnyi kodeks Rossiiskoi Federatsii [Criminal Code of Russian Federation] No 63-FZ, 1996. June 13. Available at: http://www.consultant.ru/document/cons_doc_LAW_10699/.

Ukaz Prezidenta RF, 2010. "Ob upravlenii Prezidenta Rossiiskoi Federatsii po rabote s obrashcheniiami grazhdan i organizatsii" [Decree of the President of the Russian Federation No. 201 On Administrative Office of the President of the RF on Work with Applications of Citizens and Organizations] No. 201. February 17. Available at: http://www.consultant.ru/document/cons_doc_LAW_97691/.

Ukaz Presidiuma Verkhovnogo Soveta SSSR "O poriadke rassmotreniia predlozhenii, 1968. zaiavlenii i zhalob grazhdan" [Decree of the Presidium of the Supreme Soviet of the USSR "On the Procedure for Consideration of Proposals, Petitions and Complaints of Citizens"] No. 2534-VII. Gazette of the Supreme Soviet of the USSR 17.

Zakon o sudoustroistve RSFSR [Law on Judiciary of the RSFSR], 1981. July 8. Available at: http://www.consultant.ru/document/cons_doc_LAW_913/.

Zakon, R.F., 1993. "Ob obzhalovanii v sud deistvii i reshenii, narushaiushchikh prava i svobody grazhdan" [Federal Law "On Appealing to the Court Actions and Decisions Violating the Rights and Freedoms of Citizens"]. April 27. Available at: http://www.consultant.ru/document/cons_doc_LAW_1889/.

Zakon, R.F., 1995. "O vnesenii izmenenii i dopolnenii v zakon Rossiiskoi Federatsii 'Ob obzhalovanii v sud deistvii i reshenii, narushaiushchikh prava i svobody grazhdan' [Federal Law On Amending the Law 'On Appealing to the Court Actions and Decisions Violating the Rights and Freedoms of Citizens' "] No. 193-FZ. December 14. Available at: http://www.consultant.ru/document/cons_doc_LAW_8595/.

Zakon, S.S.S.R., 1987. "O poriadke obzhalovaniia v sud nepravomernykh deistvii dolzhnostnykh lits, ushchemliaiushchikh prava grazhdan" [The Law of the USSR "On the Procedure for Appealing Unlawful Acts of Officials Infringing the Rights of Citizens"]. Vedomosti Verkhovnogo Soveta SSSR 26, st. 388; 42, st. 764.

Zakon, S.S.S.R., 1989. O poriadke obzhalovaniia v sud nepravomernykh deistvii organov gosudarstvennogo upravleniia i dolzhnostnykh lits, ushchemliaiushchikh prava grazhdan [The Law of the USSR On the Procedure for Appealing Unlawful Acts of Officials Infringing the Rights of Citizens]. Vedomosti Verkhovnogo Soveta SSSR 22, st. 416.

SOVIET AND POST-SOVIET POLITICS AND SOCIETY
Edited by Dr. Andreas Umland | ISSN 1614-3515

1 Андреас Умланд (ред.) | Воплощение Европейской конвенции по правам человека в России. Философские, юридические и эмпирические исследования | ISBN 3-89821-387-0

2 Christian Wipperfürth | Russland – ein vertrauenswürdiger Partner? Grundlagen, Hintergründe und Praxis gegenwärtiger russischer Außenpolitik | Mit einem Vorwort von Heinz Timmermann | ISBN 3-89821-401-X

3 Manja Hussner | Die Übernahme internationalen Rechts in die russische und deutsche Rechtsordnung. Eine vergleichende Analyse zur Völkerrechtsfreundlichkeit der Verfassungen der Russländischen Föderation und der Bundesrepublik Deutschland | Mit einem Vorwort von Rainer Arnold | ISBN 3-89821-438-9

4 Matthew Tejada | Bulgaria's Democratic Consolidation and the Kozloduy Nuclear Power Plant (KNPP). The Unattainability of Closure | With a foreword by Richard J. Crampton | ISBN 3-89821-439-7

5 Марк Григорьевич Меерович | Квадратные метры, определяющие сознание. Государственная жилищная политика в СССР. 1921 – 1941 гг | ISBN 3-89821-474-5

6 Andrei P. Tsygankov, Pavel A. Tsygankov (Eds.) | New Directions in Russian International Studies | ISBN 3-89821-422-2

7 Марк Григорьевич Меерович | Как власть народ к труду приучала. Жилище в СССР – средство управления людьми. 1917 – 1941 гг. | С предисловием Елены Осокиной | ISBN 3-89821-495-8

8 David J. Galbreath | Nation-Building and Minority Politics in Post-Socialist States. Interests, Influence and Identities in Estonia and Latvia | With a foreword by David J. Smith | ISBN 3-89821-467-2

9 Алексей Юрьевич Безугольный | Народы Кавказа в Вооруженных силах СССР в годы Великой Отечественной войны 1941-1945 гг. | С предисловием Николая Бугая | ISBN 3-89821-475-3

10 Вячеслав Лихачев и Владимир Прибыловский (ред.) | Русское Национальное Единство, 1990-2000. В 2-х томах | ISBN 3-89821-523-7

11 Николай Бугай (ред.) | Народы стран Балтии в условиях сталинизма (1940-е – 1950-е годы). Документированная история | ISBN 3-89821-525-3

12 Ingmar Bredies (Hrsg.) | Zur Anatomie der Orange Revolution in der Ukraine. Wechsel des Elitenregimes oder Triumph des Parlamentarismus?| ISBN 3-89821-524-5

13 Anastasia V. Mitrofanova | The Politicization of Russian Orthodoxy. Actors and Ideas | With a foreword by William C. Gay | ISBN 3-89821-481-8

14 Nathan D. Larson | Alexander Solzhenitsyn and the Russo-Jewish Question | ISBN 3-89821-483-4

15 Guido Houben | Kulturpolitik und Ethnizität. Staatliche Kunstförderung im Russland der neunziger Jahre | Mit einem Vorwort von Gert Weisskirchen | ISBN 3-89821-542-3

16 Leonid Luks | Der russische „Sonderweg"? Aufsätze zur neuesten Geschichte Russlands im europäischen Kontext | ISBN 3-89821-496-6

17 Евгений Мороз | История «Мёртвой воды» – от страшной сказки к большой политике. Политическое неоязычество в постсоветской России | ISBN 3-89821-551-2

18 Александр Верховский и Галина Кожевникова (ред.) | Этническая и религиозная интолерантность в российских СМИ. Результаты мониторинга 2001-2004 гг. | ISBN 3-89821-569-5

19 Christian Ganzer | Sowjetisches Erbe und ukrainische Nation. Das Museum der Geschichte des Zaporoger Kosakentums auf der Insel Chortycja | Mit einem Vorwort von Frank Golczewski | ISBN 3-89821-504-0

20 Эльза-Баир Гучинова | Помнить нельзя забыть. Антропология депортационной травмы калмыков | С предисловием Кэролайн Хамфри | ISBN 3-89821-506-7

21 Юлия Лидерман | Мотивы «проверки» и «испытания» в постсоветской культуре. Советское прошлое в российском кинематографе 1990-х годов | С предисловием Евгения Марголита | ISBN 3-89821-511-3

22 Tanya Lokshina, Ray Thomas, Mary Mayer (Eds.) | The Imposition of a Fake Political Settlement in the Northern Caucasus. The 2003 Chechen Presidential Election | ISBN 3-89821-436-2

23 Timothy McCajor Hall, Rosie Read (Eds.) | Changes in the Heart of Europe. Recent Ethnographies of Czechs, Slovaks, Roma, and Sorbs | With an afterword by Zdeněk Salzmann | ISBN 3-89821-606-3

24 *Christian Autengruber* | Die politischen Parteien in Bulgarien und Rumänien. Eine vergleichende Analyse seit Beginn der 90er Jahre | Mit einem Vorwort von Dorothée de Nève | ISBN 3-89821-476-1

25 *Annette Freyberg-Inan with Radu Cristescu* | The Ghosts in Our Classrooms, or: John Dewey Meets Ceauşescu. The Promise and the Failures of Civic Education in Romania | ISBN 3-89821-416-8

26 *John B. Dunlop* | The 2002 Dubrovka and 2004 Beslan Hostage Crises. A Critique of Russian Counter-Terrorism | With a foreword by Donald N. Jensen | ISBN 3-89821-608-X

27 *Peter Koller* | Das touristische Potenzial von Kam"janec'–Podil's'kyj. Eine fremdenverkehrsgeographische Untersuchung der Zukunftsperspektiven und Maßnahmenplanung zur Destinationsentwicklung des „ukrainischen Rothenburg" | Mit einem Vorwort von Kristiane Klemm | ISBN 3-89821-640-3

28 *Françoise Daucé, Elisabeth Sieca-Kozlowski (Eds.)* | Dedovshchina in the Post-Soviet Military. Hazing of Russian Army Conscripts in a Comparative Perspective | With a foreword by Dale Herspring | ISBN 3-89821-616-0

29 *Florian Strasser* | Zivilgesellschaftliche Einflüsse auf die Orange Revolution. Die gewaltlose Massenbewegung und die ukrainische Wahlkrise 2004 | Mit einem Vorwort von Egbert Jahn | ISBN 3-89821-648-9

30 *Rebecca S. Katz* | The Georgian Regime Crisis of 2003-2004. A Case Study in Post-Soviet Media Representation of Politics, Crime and Corruption | ISBN 3-89821-413-3

31 *Vladimir Kantor* | Willkür oder Freiheit. Beiträge zur russischen Geschichtsphilosophie | Ediert von Dagmar Herrmann sowie mit einem Vorwort versehen von Leonid Luks | ISBN 3-89821-589-X

32 *Laura A. Victoir* | The Russian Land Estate Today. A Case Study of Cultural Politics in Post-Soviet Russia | With a foreword by Priscilla Roosevelt | ISBN 3-89821-426-5

33 *Ivan Katchanovski* | Cleft Countries. Regional Political Divisions and Cultures in Post-Soviet Ukraine and Moldova| With a foreword by Francis Fukuyama | ISBN 3-89821-558-X

34 *Florian Mühlfried* | Postsowjetische Feiern. Das Georgische Bankett im Wandel | Mit einem Vorwort von Kevin Tuite | ISBN 3-89821-601-2

35 *Roger Griffin, Werner Loh, Andreas Umland (Eds.)* | Fascism Past and Present, West and East. An International Debate on Concepts and Cases in the Comparative Study of the Extreme Right | With an afterword by Walter Laqueur | ISBN 3-89821-674-8

36 *Sebastian Schlegel* | Der „Weiße Archipel". Sowjetische Atomstädte 1945-1991 | Mit einem Geleitwort von Thomas Bohn | ISBN 3-89821-679-9

37 *Vyacheslav Likhachev* | Political Anti-Semitism in Post-Soviet Russia. Actors and Ideas in 1991-2003 | Edited and translated from Russian by Eugene Veklerov | ISBN 3-89821-529-6

38 *Josette Baer (Ed.)* | Preparing Liberty in Central Europe. Political Texts from the Spring of Nations 1848 to the Spring of Prague 1968 | With a foreword by Zdeněk V. David | ISBN 3-89821-546-6

39 *Михаил Лукьянов* | Российский консерватизм и реформа, 1907-1914 | С предисловием Марка Д. Стейнберга | ISBN 3-89821-503-2

40 *Nicola Melloni* | Market Without Economy. The 1998 Russian Financial Crisis | With a foreword by Eiji Furukawa | ISBN 3-89821-407-9

41 *Dmitrij Chmelnizki* | Die Architektur Stalins | Bd. 1: Studien zu Ideologie und Stil | Bd. 2: Bilddokumentation | Mit einem Vorwort von Bruno Flierl | ISBN 3-89821-515-6

42 *Katja Yafimava* | Post-Soviet Russian-Belarussian Relationships. The Role of Gas Transit Pipelines | With a foreword by Jonathan P. Stern | ISBN 3-89821-655-1

43 *Boris Chavkin* | Verflechtungen der deutschen und russischen Zeitgeschichte. Aufsätze und Archivfunde zu den Beziehungen Deutschlands und der Sowjetunion von 1917 bis 1991 | Ediert von Markus Edlinger sowie mit einem Vorwort versehen von Leonid Luks | ISBN 3-89821-756-6

44 *Anastasija Grynenko in Zusammenarbeit mit Claudia Dathe* | Die Terminologie des Gerichtswesens der Ukraine und Deutschlands im Vergleich. Eine übersetzungswissenschaftliche Analyse juristischer Fachbegriffe im Deutschen, Ukrainischen und Russischen | Mit einem Vorwort von Ulrich Hartmann | ISBN 3-89821-691-8

45 *Anton Burkov* | The Impact of the European Convention on Human Rights on Russian Law. Legislation and Application in 1996-2006 | With a foreword by Françoise Hampson | ISBN 978-3-89821-639-5

46 *Stina Torjesen, Indra Overland (Eds.)* | International Election Observers in Post-Soviet Azerbaijan. Geopolitical Pawns or Agents of Change? | ISBN 978-3-89821-743-9

47 *Taras Kuzio* | Ukraine – Crimea – Russia. Triangle of Conflict | ISBN 978-3-89821-761-3

48 *Claudia Šabić* | "Ich erinnere mich nicht, aber L'viv!" Zur Funktion kultureller Faktoren für die Institutionalisierung und Entwicklung einer ukrainischen Region | Mit einem Vorwort von Melanie Tatur | ISBN 978-3-89821-752-1

49 *Marlies Bilz* | Tatarstan in der Transformation. Nationaler Diskurs und Politische Praxis 1988-1994 | Mit einem Vorwort von Frank Golczewski | ISBN 978-3-89821-722-4

50 *Марлен Ларюэль (ред.)* | Современные интерпретации русского национализма | ISBN 978-3-89821-795-8

51 *Sonja Schüler* | Die ethnische Dimension der Armut. Roma im postsozialistischen Rumänien | Mit einem Vorwort von Anton Sterbling | ISBN 978-3-89821-776-7

52 *Галина Кожевникова* | Радикальный национализм в России и противодействие ему. Сборник докладов Центра «Сова» за 2004-2007 гг. | С предисловием Александра Верховского | ISBN 978-3-89821-721-7

53 *Галина Кожевникова и Владимир Прибыловский* | Российская власть в биографиях I. Высшие должностные лица РФ в 2004 г. | ISBN 978-3-89821-796-5

54 *Галина Кожевникова и Владимир Прибыловский* | Российская власть в биографиях II. Члены Правительства РФ в 2004 г. | ISBN 978-3-89821-797-2

55 *Галина Кожевникова и Владимир Прибыловский* | Российская власть в биографиях III. Руководители федеральных служб и агентств РФ в 2004 г.| ISBN 978-3-89821-798-9

56 *Ileana Petroniu* | Privatisierung in Transformationsökonomien. Determinanten der Restrukturierungs-Bereitschaft am Beispiel Polens, Rumäniens und der Ukraine | Mit einem Vorwort von Rainer W. Schäfer | ISBN 978-3-89821-790-3

57 *Christian Wipperfürth* | Russland und seine GUS-Nachbarn. Hintergründe, aktuelle Entwicklungen und Konflikte in einer ressourcenreichen Region| ISBN 978-3-89821-801-6

58 *Togzhan Kassenova* | From Antagonism to Partnership. The Uneasy Path of the U.S.-Russian Cooperative Threat Reduction | With a foreword by Christoph Bluth | ISBN 978-3-89821-707-1

59 *Alexander Höllwerth* | Das sakrale eurasische Imperium des Aleksandr Dugin. Eine Diskursanalyse zum postsowjetischen russischen Rechtsextremismus | Mit einem Vorwort von Dirk Uffelmann | ISBN 978-3-89821-813-9

60 *Олег Рябов* | «Россия-Матушка». Национализм, гендер и война в России XX века | С предисловием Елены Гощило | ISBN 978-3-89821-487-2

61 *Ivan Maistrenko* | Borot'bism. A Chapter in the History of the Ukrainian Revolution | With a new Introduction by Chris Ford | Translated by George S. N. Luckyj with the assistance of Ivan L. Rudnytsky | Second, Revised and Expanded Edition ISBN 978-3-8382-1107-7

62 *Maryna Romanets* | Anamorphosic Texts and Reconfigured Visions. Improvised Traditions in Contemporary Ukrainian and Irish Literature | ISBN 978-3-89821-576-3

63 *Paul D'Anieri and Taras Kuzio (Eds.)* | Aspects of the Orange Revolution I. Democratization and Elections in Post-Communist Ukraine | ISBN 978-3-89821-698-2

64 *Bohdan Harasymiw in collaboration with Oleh S. Ilnytzkyj (Eds.)* | Aspects of the Orange Revolution II. Information and Manipulation Strategies in the 2004 Ukrainian Presidential Elections | ISBN 978-3-89821-699-9

65 *Ingmar Bredies, Andreas Umland and Valentin Yakushik (Eds.)* | Aspects of the Orange Revolution III. The Context and Dynamics of the 2004 Ukrainian Presidential Elections | ISBN 978-3-89821-803-0

66 *Ingmar Bredies, Andreas Umland and Valentin Yakushik (Eds.)* | Aspects of the Orange Revolution IV. Foreign Assistance and Civic Action in the 2004 Ukrainian Presidential Elections | ISBN 978-3-89821-808-5

67 *Ingmar Bredies, Andreas Umland and Valentin Yakushik (Eds.)* | Aspects of the Orange Revolution V. Institutional Observation Reports on the 2004 Ukrainian Presidential Elections | ISBN 978-3-89821-809-2

68 *Taras Kuzio (Ed.)* | Aspects of the Orange Revolution VI. Post-Communist Democratic Revolutions in Comparative Perspective | ISBN 978-3-89821-820-7

69 *Tim Bohse* | Autoritarismus statt Selbstverwaltung. Die Transformation der kommunalen Politik in der Stadt Kaliningrad 1990-2005 | Mit einem Geleitwort von Stefan Troebst | ISBN 978-3-89821-782-8

70 *David Rupp* | Die Rußländische Föderation und die russischsprachige Minderheit in Lettland. Eine Fallstudie zur Anwaltspolitik Moskaus gegenüber den russophonen Minderheiten im „Nahen Ausland" von 1991 bis 2002 | Mit einem Vorwort von Helmut Wagner | ISBN 978-3-89821-778-1

71 *Taras Kuzio* | Theoretical and Comparative Perspectives on Nationalism. New Directions in Cross-Cultural and Post-Communist Studies | With a foreword by Paul Robert Magocsi | ISBN 978-3-89821-815-3

72 *Christine Teichmann* | Die Hochschultransformation im heutigen Osteuropa. Kontinuität und Wandel bei der Entwicklung des postkommunistischen Universitätswesens | Mit einem Vorwort von Oskar Anweiler | ISBN 978-3-89821-842-9

73 *Julia Kusznir* | Der politische Einfluss von Wirtschaftseliten in russischen Regionen. Eine Analyse am Beispiel der Erdöl- und Erdgasindustrie, 1992-2005 | Mit einem Vorwort von Wolfgang Eichwede | ISBN 978-3-89821-821-4

74 Alena Vysotskaya | Russland, Belarus und die EU-Osterweiterung. Zur Minderheitenfrage und zum Problem der Freizügigkeit des Personenverkehrs | Mit einem Vorwort von Katlijn Malfliet | ISBN 978-3-89821-822-1

75 Heiko Pleines (Hrsg.) | Corporate Governance in post-sozialistischen Volkswirtschaften | ISBN 978-3-89821-766-8

76 Stefan Ihrig | Wer sind die Moldawier? Rumänismus versus Moldowanismus in Historiographie und Schulbüchern der Republik Moldova, 1991-2006 | Mit einem Vorwort von Holm Sundhaussen | ISBN 978-3-89821-466-7

77 Galina Kozhevnikova in collaboration with Alexander Verkhovsky and Eugene Veklerov | Ultra-Nationalism and Hate Crimes in Contemporary Russia. The 2004-2006 Annual Reports of Moscow's SOVA Center | With a foreword by Stephen D. Shenfield | ISBN 978-3-89821-868-9

78 Florian Küchler | The Role of the European Union in Moldova's Transnistria Conflict | With a foreword by Christopher Hill | ISBN 978-3-89821-850-4

79 Bernd Rechel | The Long Way Back to Europe. Minority Protection in Bulgaria | With a foreword by Richard Crampton | ISBN 978-3-89821-863-4

80 Peter W. Rodgers | Nation, Region and History in Post-Communist Transitions. Identity Politics in Ukraine, 1991-2006 | With a foreword by Vera Tolz | ISBN 978-3-89821-903-7

81 Stephanie Solywoda | The Life and Work of Semen L. Frank. A Study of Russian Religious Philosophy | With a foreword by Philip Walters | ISBN 978-3-89821-457-5

82 Vera Sokolova | Cultural Politics of Ethnicity. Discourses on Roma in Communist Czechoslovakia | ISBN 978-3-89821-864-1

83 Natalya Shevchik Ketenci | Kazakhstani Enterprises in Transition. The Role of Historical Regional Development in Kazakhstan's Post-Soviet Economic Transformation | ISBN 978-3-89821-831-3

84 Martin Malek, Anna Schor-Tschudnowskaja (Hgg.) | Europa im Tschetschenienkrieg. Zwischen politischer Ohnmacht und Gleichgültigkeit | Mit einem Vorwort von Lipchan Basajewa | ISBN 978-3-89821-676-0

85 Stefan Meister | Das postsowjetische Universitätswesen zwischen nationalem und internationalem Wandel. Die Entwicklung der regionalen Hochschule in Russland als Gradmesser der Systemtransformation | Mit einem Vorwort von Joan DeBardeleben | ISBN 978-3-89821-891-7

86 Konstantin Sheiko in collaboration with Stephen Brown | Nationalist Imaginings of the Russian Past. Anatolii Fomenko and the Rise of Alternative History in Post-Communist Russia | With a foreword by Donald Ostrowski | ISBN 978-3-89821-915-0

87 Sabine Jenni | Wie stark ist das „Einige Russland"? Zur Parteibindung der Eliten und zum Wahlerfolg der Machtpartei im Dezember 2007 | Mit einem Vorwort von Klaus Armingeon | ISBN 978-3-89821-961-7

88 Thomas Borén | Meeting-Places of Transformation. Urban Identity, Spatial Representations and Local Politics in Post-Soviet St Petersburg | ISBN 978-3-89821-739-2

89 Aygul Ashirova | Stalinismus und Stalin-Kult in Zentralasien. Turkmenistan 1924-1953 | Mit einem Vorwort von Leonid Luks | ISBN 978-3-89821-987-7

90 Leonid Luks | Freiheit oder imperiale Größe? Essays zu einem russischen Dilemma | ISBN 978-3-8382-0011-8

91 Christopher Gilley | The 'Change of Signposts' in the Ukrainian Emigration. A Contribution to the History of Sovietophilism in the 1920s | With a foreword by Frank Golczewski | ISBN 978-3-89821-965-5

92 Philipp Casula, Jeronim Perovic (Eds.) | Identities and Politics During the Putin Presidency. The Discursive Foundations of Russia's Stability | With a foreword by Heiko Haumann | ISBN 978-3-8382-0015-6

93 Marcel Viëtor | Europa und die Frage nach seinen Grenzen im Osten. Zur Konstruktion ‚europäischer Identität' in Geschichte und Gegenwart | Mit einem Vorwort von Albrecht Lehmann | ISBN 978-3-8382-0045-3

94 Ben Hellman, Andrei Rogachevskii | Filming the Unfilmable. Casper Wrede's 'One Day in the Life of Ivan Denisovich' | Second, Revised and Expanded Edition | ISBN 978-3-8382-0044-6

95 Eva Fuchslocher | Vaterland, Sprache, Glaube. Orthodoxie und Nationenbildung am Beispiel Georgiens | Mit einem Vorwort von Christina von Braun | ISBN 978-3-89821-884-9

96 Vladimir Kantor | Das Westlertum und der Weg Russlands. Zur Entwicklung der russischen Literatur und Philosophie | Ediert von Dagmar Herrmann | Mit einem Beitrag von Nikolaus Lobkowicz | ISBN 978-3-8382-0102-3

97 Kamran Musayev | Die postsowjetische Transformation im Baltikum und Südkaukasus. Eine vergleichende Untersuchung der politischen Entwicklung Lettlands und Aserbaidschans 1985-2009 | Mit einem Vorwort von Leonid Luks | Ediert von Sandro Henschel | ISBN 978-3-8382-0103-0

98 Tatiana Zhurzhenko | Borderlands into Bordered Lands. Geopolitics of Identity in Post-Soviet Ukraine | With a foreword by Dieter Segert | ISBN 978-3-8382-0042-2

99 Кирилл Галушко, Лидия Смола (ред.) | Пределы падения – варианты украинского будущего. Аналитико-прогностические исследования | ISBN 978-3-8382-0148-1

100 Michael Minkenberg (Ed.) | Historical Legacies and the Radical Right in Post-Cold War Central and Eastern Europe | With an afterword by Sabrina P. Ramet | ISBN 978-3-8382-0124-5

101 David-Emil Wickström | Rocking St. Petersburg. Transcultural Flows and Identity Politics in the St. Petersburg Popular Music Scene | With a foreword by Yngvar B. Steinholt | Second, Revised and Expanded Edition | ISBN 978-3-8382-0100-9

102 Eva Zabka | Eine neue „Zeit der Wirren"? Der spät- und postsowjetische Systemwandel 1985-2000 im Spiegel russischer gesellschaftspolitischer Diskurse | Mit einem Vorwort von Margareta Mommsen | ISBN 978-3-8382-0161-0

103 Ulrike Ziemer | Ethnic Belonging, Gender and Cultural Practices. Youth Identitites in Contemporary Russia | With a foreword by Anoop Nayak | ISBN 978-3-8382-0152-8

104 Ksenia Chepikova | ‚Einiges Russland' - eine zweite KPdSU? Aspekte der Identitätskonstruktion einer postsowjetischen „Partei der Macht" | Mit einem Vorwort von Torsten Oppelland | ISBN 978-3-8382-0311-9

105 Леонид Люкс | Западничество или евразийство? Демократия или идеократия? Сборник статей об исторических дилеммах России | С предисловием Владимира Кантора | ISBN 978-3-8382-0211-2

106 Anna Dost | Das russische Verfassungsrecht auf dem Weg zum Föderalismus und zurück. Zum Konflikt von Rechtsnormen und -wirklichkeit in der Russländischen Föderation von 1991 bis 2009 | Mit einem Vorwort von Alexander Blankenagel | ISBN 978-3-8382-0292-1

107 Philipp Herzog | Sozialistische Völkerfreundschaft, nationaler Widerstand oder harmloser Zeitvertreib? Zur politischen Funktion der Volkskunst im sowjetischen Estland | Mit einem Vorwort von Andreas Kappeler | ISBN 978-3-8382-0216-7

108 Marlène Laruelle (Ed.) | Russian Nationalism, Foreign Policy, and Identity Debates in Putin's Russia. New Ideological Patterns after the Orange Revolution | ISBN 978-3-8382-0325-6

109 Michail Logvinov | Russlands Kampf gegen den internationalen Terrorismus. Eine kritische Bestandsaufnahme des Bekämpfungsansatzes | Mit einem Geleitwort von Hans-Henning Schröder und einem Vorwort von Eckhard Jesse | ISBN 978-3-8382-0329-4

110 John B. Dunlop | The Moscow Bombings of September 1999. Examinations of Russian Terrorist Attacks at the Onset of Vladimir Putin's Rule | Second, Revised and Expanded Edition | ISBN 978-3-8382-0388-1

111 Андрей А. Ковалёв | Свидетельство из-за кулис российской политики I. Можно ли делать добро из зла? (Воспоминания и размышления о последних советских и первых послесоветских годах) | With a foreword by Peter Reddaway | ISBN 978-3-8382-0302-7

112 Андрей А. Ковалёв | Свидетельство из-за кулис российской политики II. Угроза для себя и окружающих (Наблюдения и предостережения относительно происходящего после 2000 г.) | ISBN 978-3-8382-0303-4

113 Bernd Kappenberg | Zeichen setzen für Europa. Der Gebrauch europäischer lateinischer Sonderzeichen in der deutschen Öffentlichkeit | Mit einem Vorwort von Peter Schlobinski | ISBN 978-3-89821-749-1

114 Ivo Mijnssen | The Quest for an Ideal Youth in Putin's Russia I. Back to Our Future! History, Modernity, and Patriotism according to Nashi, 2005-2013 | With a foreword by Jeronim Perović | Second, Revised and Expanded Edition | ISBN 978-3-8382-0368-3

115 Jussi Lassila | The Quest for an Ideal Youth in Putin's Russia II. The Search for Distinctive Conformism in the Political Communication of Nashi, 2005-2009 | With a foreword by Kirill Postoutenko | Second, Revised and Expanded Edition | ISBN 978-3-8382-0415-4

116 Valerio Trabandt | Neue Nachbarn, gute Nachbarschaft? Die EU als internationaler Akteur am Beispiel ihrer Demokratieförderung in Belarus und der Ukraine 2004-2009 | Mit einem Vorwort von Jutta Joachim | ISBN 978-3-8382-0437-6

117 Fabian Pfeiffer | Estlands Außen- und Sicherheitspolitik I. Der estnische Atlantizismus nach der wiedererlangten Unabhängigkeit 1991-2004 | Mit einem Vorwort von Helmut Hubel | ISBN 978-3-8382-0127-6

118 Jana Podßuweit | Estlands Außen- und Sicherheitspolitik II. Handlungsoptionen eines Kleinstaates im Rahmen seiner EU-Mitgliedschaft (2004-2008) | Mit einem Vorwort von Helmut Hubel | ISBN 978-3-8382-0440-6

119 Karin Pointner | Estlands Außen- und Sicherheitspolitik III. Eine gedächtnispolitische Analyse estnischer Entwicklungskooperation 2006-2010 | Mit einem Vorwort von Karin Liebhart | ISBN 978-3-8382-0435-2

120 Ruslana Vovk | Die Offenheit der ukrainischen Verfassung für das Völkerrecht und die europäische Integration | Mit einem Vorwort von Alexander Blankenagel | ISBN 978-3-8382-0481-9

121 Mykhaylo Banakh | Die Relevanz der Zivilgesellschaft bei den postkommunistischen Transformationsprozessen in mittel- und osteuropäischen Ländern. Das Beispiel der spät- und postsowjetischen Ukraine 1986-2009 | Mit einem Vorwort von Gerhard Simon | ISBN 978-3-8382-0499-4

122 Michael Moser | Language Policy and the Discourse on Languages in Ukraine under President Viktor Yanukovych (25 February 2010–28 October 2012) | ISBN 978-3-8382-0497-0 (Paperback edition) | ISBN 978-3-8382-0507-6 (Hardcover edition)

123 Nicole Krome | Russischer Netzwerkkapitalismus Restrukturierungsprozesse in der Russischen Föderation am Beispiel des Luftfahrtunternehmens "Aviastar" | Mit einem Vorwort von Petra Stykow | ISBN 978-3-8382-0534-2

124 David R. Marples | 'Our Glorious Past'. Lukashenka's Belarus and the Great Patriotic War | ISBN 978-3-8382-0574-8 (Paperback edition) | ISBN 978-3-8382-0675-2 (Hardcover edition)

125 Ulf Walther | Russlands "neuer Adel". Die Macht des Geheimdienstes von Gorbatschow bis Putin | Mit einem Vorwort von Hans-Georg Wieck | ISBN 978-3-8382-0584-7

126 Simon Geissbühler (Hrsg.) | Kiew – Revolution 3.0. Der Euromaidan 2013/14 und die Zukunftsperspektiven der Ukraine | ISBN 978-3-8382-0581-6 (Paperback edition) | ISBN 978-3-8382-0681-3 (Hardcover edition)

127 Andrey Makarychev | Russia and the EU in a Multipolar World. Discourses, Identities, Norms | With a foreword by Klaus Segbers | ISBN 978-3-8382-0629-5

128 Roland Scharff | Kasachstan als postsowjetischer Wohlfahrtsstaat. Die Transformation des sozialen Schutzsystems | Mit einem Vorwort von Joachim Ahrens | ISBN 978-3-8382-0622-6

129 Katja Grupp | Bild Lücke Deutschland. Kaliningrader Studierende sprechen über Deutschland | Mit einem Vorwort von Martin Schulz | ISBN 978-3-8382-0552-6

130 Konstantin Sheiko, Stephen Brown | History as Therapy. Alternative History and Nationalist Imaginings in Russia, 1991-2014 | ISBN 978-3-8382-0665-3

131 Elisa Kriza | Alexander Solzhenitsyn: Cold War Icon, Gulag Author, Russian Nationalist? A Study of the Western Reception of his Literary Writings, Historical Interpretations, and Political Ideas | With a foreword by Andrei Rogatchevski | ISBN 978-3-8382-0589-2 (Paperback edition) | ISBN 978-3-8382-0690-5 (Hardcover edition)

132 Serghei Golunov | The Elephant in the Room. Corruption and Cheating in Russian Universities | ISBN 978-3-8382-0570-0

133 Manja Hussner, Rainer Arnold (Hgg.) | Verfassungsgerichtsbarkeit in Zentralasien I. Sammlung von Verfassungstexten | ISBN 978-3-8382-0595-3

134 Nikolay Mitrokhin | Die "Russische Partei". Die Bewegung der russischen Nationalisten in der UdSSR 1953-1985 | Aus dem Russischen übertragen von einem Übersetzerteam unter der Leitung von Larisa Schippel | ISBN 978-3-8382-0024-8

135 Manja Hussner, Rainer Arnold (Hgg.) | Verfassungsgerichtsbarkeit in Zentralasien II. Sammlung von Verfassungstexten | ISBN 978-3-8382-0597-7

136 Manfred Zeller | Das sowjetische Fieber. Fußballfans im poststalinistischen Vielvölkerreich | Mit einem Vorwort von Nikolaus Katzer | ISBN 978-3-8382-0757-5

137 Kristin Schreiter | Stellung und Entwicklungspotential zivilgesellschaftlicher Gruppen in Russland. Menschenrechtsorganisationen im Vergleich | ISBN 978-3-8382-0673-8

138 David R. Marples, Frederick V. Mills (Eds.) | Ukraine's Euromaidan. Analyses of a Civil Revolution | ISBN 978-3-8382-0660-8

139 Bernd Kappenberg | Setting Signs for Europe. Why Diacritics Matter for European Integration | With a foreword by Peter Schlobinski | ISBN 978-3-8382-0663-9

140 René Lenz | Internationalisierung, Kooperation und Transfer. Externe bildungspolitische Akteure in der Russischen Föderation | Mit einem Vorwort von Frank Ettrich | ISBN 978-3-8382-0751-3

141 Juri Plusnin, Yana Zausaeva, Natalia Zhidkevich, Artemy Pozanenko | Wandering Workers. Mores, Behavior, Way of Life, and Political Status of Domestic Russian Labor Migrants | Translated by Julia Kazantseva | ISBN 978-3-8382-0653-0

142 David J. Smith (Eds.) | Latvia – A Work in Progress? 100 Years of State- and Nation-Building | ISBN 978-3-8382-0648-6

143 Инна Чувычкина (ред.) | Экспортные нефте- и газопроводы на постсоветском пространстве. Анализ трубопроводной политики в свете теории международных отношений | ISBN 978-3-8382-0822-0

144 *Johann Zajaczkowski* | Russland – eine pragmatische Großmacht? Eine rollentheoretische Untersuchung russischer Außenpolitik am Beispiel der Zusammenarbeit mit den USA nach 9/11 und des Georgienkrieges von 2008 | Mit einem Vorwort von Siegfried Schieder | ISBN 978-3-8382-0837-4

145 *Boris Popivanov* | Changing Images of the Left in Bulgaria. The Challenge of Post-Communism in the Early 21st Century | ISBN 978-3-8382-0667-7

146 *Lenka Krátká* | A History of the Czechoslovak Ocean Shipping Company 1948-1989. How a Small, Landlocked Country Ran Maritime Business During the Cold War | ISBN 978-3-8382-0666-0

147 *Alexander Sergunin* | Explaining Russian Foreign Policy Behavior. Theory and Practice | ISBN 978-3-8382-0752-0

148 *Darya Malyutina* | Migrant Friendships in a Super-Diverse City. Russian-Speakers and their Social Relationships in London in the 21st Century | With a foreword by Claire Dwyer | ISBN 978-3-8382-0652-3

149 *Alexander Sergunin, Valery Konyshev* | Russia in the Arctic. Hard or Soft Power? | ISBN 978-3-8382-0753-7

150 *John J. Maresca* | Helsinki Revisited. A Key U.S. Negotiator's Memoirs on the Development of the CSCE into the OSCE | With a foreword by Hafiz Pashayev | ISBN 978-3-8382-0852-7

151 *Jardar Østbø* | The New Third Rome. Readings of a Russian Nationalist Myth | With a foreword by Pål Kolstø | ISBN 978-3-8382-0870-1

152 *Simon Kordonsky* | Socio-Economic Foundations of the Russian Post-Soviet Regime. The Resource-Based Economy and Estate-Based Social Structure of Contemporary Russia | With a foreword by Svetlana Barsukova | ISBN 978-3-8382-0775-9

153 *Duncan Leitch* | Assisting Reform in Post-Communist Ukraine 2000–2012. The Illusions of Donors and the Disillusion of Beneficiaries | With a foreword by Kataryna Wolczuk | ISBN 978-3-8382-0844-2

154 *Abel Polese* | Limits of a Post-Soviet State. How Informality Replaces, Renegotiates, and Reshapes Governance in Contemporary Ukraine | With a foreword by Colin Williams | ISBN 978-3-8382-0845-9

155 *Mikhail Suslov (Ed.)* | Digital Orthodoxy in the Post-Soviet World. The Russian Orthodox Church and Web 2.0 | With a foreword by Father Cyril Hovorun | ISBN 978-3-8382-0871-8

156 *Leonid Luks* | Zwei „Sonderwege"? Russisch-deutsche Parallelen und Kontraste (1917-2014). Vergleichende Essays | ISBN 978-3-8382-0823-7

157 *Vladimir V. Karacharovskiy, Ovsey I. Shkaratan, Gordey A. Yastrebov* | Towards a New Russian Work Culture. Can Western Companies and Expatriates Change Russian Society? | With a foreword by Elena N. Danilova | Translated by Julia Kazantseva | ISBN 978-3-8382-0902-9

158 *Edmund Griffiths* | Aleksandr Prokhanov and Post-Soviet Esotericism | ISBN 978-3-8382-0903-6

159 *Timm Beichelt, Susann Worschech (Eds.)* | Transnational Ukraine? Networks and Ties that Influence(d) Contemporary Ukraine | ISBN 978-3-8382-0944-9

160 *Mieste Hotopp-Riecke* | Die Tataren der Krim zwischen Assimilation und Selbstbehauptung. Der Aufbau des krimtatarischen Bildungswesens nach Deportation und Heimkehr (1990-2005) | Mit einem Vorwort von Swetlana Czerwonnaja | ISBN 978-3-89821-940-2

161 *Olga Bertelsen (Ed.)* | Revolution and War in Contemporary Ukraine. The Challenge of Change | ISBN 978-3-8382-1016-2

162 *Natalya Ryabinska* | Ukraine's Post-Communist Mass Media. Between Capture and Commercialization | With a foreword by Marta Dyczok | ISBN 978-3-8382-1011-7

163 *Alexandra Cotofana, James M. Nyce (Eds.)* | Religion and Magic in Socialist and Post-Socialist Contexts. Historic and Ethnographic Case Studies of Orthodoxy, Heterodoxy, and Alternative Spirituality | With a foreword by Patrick L. Michelson | ISBN 978-3-8382-0989-0

164 *Nozima Akhrarkhodjaeva* | The Instrumentalisation of Mass Media in Electoral Authoritarian Regimes. Evidence from Russia's Presidential Election Campaigns of 2000 and 2008 | ISBN 978-3-8382-1013-1

165 *Yulia Krasheninnikova* | Informal Healthcare in Contemporary Russia. Sociographic Essays on the Post-Soviet Infrastructure for Alternative Healing Practices | ISBN 978-3-8382-0970-8

166 *Peter Kaiser* | Das Schachbrett der Macht. Die Handlungsspielräume eines sowjetischen Funktionärs unter Stalin am Beispiel des Generalsekretärs des Komsomol Aleksandr Kosarev (1929-1938) | Mit einem Vorwort von Dietmar Neutatz | ISBN 978-3-8382-1052-0

167 *Oksana Kim* | The Effects and Implications of Kazakhstan's Adoption of International Financial Reporting Standards. A Resource Dependence Perspective | With a foreword by Svetlana Vlady | ISBN 978-3-8382-0987-6

168 Anna Sanina | Patriotic Education in Contemporary Russia. Sociological Studies in the Making of the Post-Soviet Citizen | With a foreword by Anna Oldfield | ISBN 978-3-8382-0993-7

169 Rudolf Wolters | Spezialist in Sibirien Faksimile der 1933 erschienenen ersten Ausgabe | Mit einem Vorwort von Dmitrij Chmelnizki | ISBN 978-3-8382-0515-1

170 Michal Vít, Magdalena M. Baran (Eds.) | Transregional versus National Perspectives on Contemporary Central European History. Studies on the Building of Nation-States and Their Cooperation in the 20th and 21st Century | With a foreword by Petr Vágner | ISBN 978-3-8382-1015-5

171 Philip Gamaghelyan | Conflict Resolution Beyond the International Relations Paradigm. Evolving Designs as a Transformative Practice in Nagorno-Karabakh and Syria | With a foreword by Susan Allen | ISBN 978-3-8382-1057-5

172 Maria Shagina | Joining a Prestigious Club. Cooperation with Europarties and Its Impact on Party Development in Georgia, Moldova, and Ukraine 2004–2015 | With a foreword by Kataryna Wolczuk | ISBN 978-3-8382-1084-1

173 Alexandra Cotofana, James M. Nyce (Eds.) | Religion and Magic in Socialist and Post-Socialist Contexts II. Baltic, Eastern European, and Post-USSR Case Studies | With a foreword by Anita Stasulane | ISBN 978-3-8382-0990-6

174 Barbara Kunz | Kind Words, Cruise Missiles, and Everything in Between. The Use of Power Resources in U.S. Policies towards Poland, Ukraine, and Belarus 1989–2008 | With a foreword by William Hill | ISBN 978-3-8382-1065-0

175 Eduard Klein | Bildungskorruption in Russland und der Ukraine. Eine komparative Analyse der Performanz staatlicher Antikorruptionsmaßnahmen im Hochschulsektor am Beispiel universitärer Aufnahmeprüfungen | Mit einem Vorwort von Heiko Pleines | ISBN 978-3-8382-0995-1

176 Markus Soldner | Politischer Kapitalismus im postsowjetischen Russland. Die politische, wirtschaftliche und mediale Transformation in den 1990er Jahren | Mit einem Vorwort von Wolfgang Ismayr | ISBN 978-3-8382-1222-7

177 Anton Oleinik | Building Ukraine from Within. A Sociological, Institutional, and Economic Analysis of a Nation-State in the Making | ISBN 978-3-8382-1150-3

178 Peter Rollberg, Marlene Laruelle (Eds.) | Mass Media in the Post-Soviet World. Market Forces, State Actors, and Political Manipulation in the Informational Environment after Communism | ISBN 978-3-8382-1116-9

179 Mikhail Minakov | Development and Dystopia Studies in Post-Soviet Ukraine and Eastern Europe | With a foreword by Alexander Etkind | ISBN 978-3-8382-1112-1

180 Aijan Sharshenova | The European Union's Democracy Promotion in Central Asia A Study of Political Interests, Influence, and Development in Kazakhstan and Kyrgyzstan in 2007–2013 | With a foreword by Gordon Crawford | ISBN 978-3-8382-1151-0

181 Andrey Makarychev, Alexandra Yatsyk (Eds.) | Boris Nemtsov and Russian Politics. Power and Resistance | With a foreword by Zhanna Nemtsova | ISBN 978-3-8382-1122-0

182 Sophie Falsini | The Euromaidan's Effect on Civil Society. Why and How Ukrainian Social Capital Increased after the Revolution of Dignity | With a foreword by Susann Worschech | ISBN 978-3-8382-1131-2

183 Andreas Umland (Ed.) | Ukraine's Decentralization. Challenges and Implications of the Local Governance Reform after the Euromaidan Revolution | ISBN 978-3-8382-1162-6

184 Leonid Luks | A Fateful Triangle. Essays on Contemporary Russian, German and Polish History | ISBN 978-3-8382-1143-5

185 John B. Dunlop | The February 2015 Assassination of Boris Nemtsov and the Flawed Trial of his Alleged Killers. An Exploration of Russia's "Crime of the 21st Century" | ISBN 978-3-8382-1188-6

186 Vasile Rotaru | Russia, the EU, and the Eastern Partnership. Building Bridges or Digging Trenches? | ISBN 978-3-8382-1134-3

187 Marina Lebedeva | Russian Studies of International Relations. From the Soviet Past to the Post-Cold-War Present | With a foreword by Andrei P. Tsygankov | ISBN 978-3-8382-0851-0

188 Tomasz Stępniewski, George Soroka (Eds.) | Ukraine after Maidan. Revisiting Domestic and Regional Security | ISBN 978-3-8382-1075-9

189 Petar Cholakov | Ethnic Entrepreneurs Unmasked. Political Institutions and Ethnic Conflicts in Contemporary Bulgaria | ISBN 978-3-8382-1189-3

190 A. Salem, G. Hazeldine, D. Morgan (Eds.) | Higher Education in Post-Communist States. Comparative and Sociological Perspectives | ISBN 978-3-8382-1183-1

191 Igor Torbakov | After Empire. Nationalist Imagination and Symbolic Politics in Russia and Eurasia in the Twentieth and Twenty-First Century | With a foreword by Serhii Plokhy | ISBN 978-3-8382-1217-3

192 *Aleksandr Burakovskiy* | Jewish-Ukrainian Relations in Late and Post-Soviet Ukraine. Articles, Lectures and Essays from 1986 to 2016 | ISBN 978-3-8382-1210-4

193 *Natalia Shapovalova, Olga Burlyuk (Eds.)* | Civil Society in Post-Euromaidan Ukraine. From Revolution to Consolidation | With a foreword by Richard Youngs | ISBN 978-3-8382-1216-6

194 *Franz Preissler* | Positionsverteidigung, Imperialismus oder Irredentismus? Russland und die „Russischsprachigen", 1991–2015 | ISBN 978-3-8382-1262-3

195 *Marian Madeła* | Der Reformprozess in der Ukraine 2014-2017. Eine Fallstudie zur Reform der öffentlichen Verwaltung | Mit einem Vorwort von Martin Malek | ISBN 978-3-8382-1266-1

196 *Anke Giesen* | „Wie kann denn der Sieger ein Verbrecher sein?" Eine diskursanalytische Untersuchung der russlandweiten Debatte über Konzept und Verstaatlichungsprozess der Lagergedenkstätte „Perm'-36" im Ural | ISBN 978-3-8382-1284-5

197 *Alla Leukavets* | The Integration Policies of Belarus and Ukraine vis-à-vis the EU and Russia. A Comparative Case Study Through the Prism of a Two-Level Game Approach | ISBN 978-3-8382-1247-0

198 *Oksana Kim* | The Development and Challenges of Russian Corporate Governance I. The Roles and Functions of Boards of Directors | With a foreword by Sheila M. Puffer | ISBN 978-3-8382-1287-6

199 *Thomas D. Grant* | International Law and the Post-Soviet Space I. Essays on Chechnya and the Baltic States | With a foreword by Stephen M. Schwebel | ISBN 978-3-8382-1279-1

200 *Thomas D. Grant* | International Law and the Post-Soviet Space II. Essays on Ukraine, Intervention, and Non-Proliferation | ISBN 978-3-8382-1280-7

201 *Slavomír Michálek, Michal Štefansky* | The Age of Fear. The Cold War and Its Influence on Czechoslovakia 1945–1968 | ISBN 978-3-8382-1285-2

202 *Iulia-Sabina Joja* | Romania's Strategic Culture 1990–2014. Continuity and Change in a Post-Communist Country's Evolution of National Interests and Security Policies | With a foreword by Heiko Biehl | ISBN 978-3-8382-1286-9

203 *Andrei Rogatchevski, Yngvar B. Steinholt, Arve Hansen, David-Emil Wickström* | War of Songs. Popular Music and Recent Russia-Ukraine Relations | With a foreword by Artemy Troitsky | ISBN 978-3-8382-1173-2

204 *Maria Lipman (ed.)* | Russian Voices on Post-Crimea Russia. An Almanac of Counterpoint Essays from 2015–2018 | ISBN 978-3-8382-1251-7

205 *Ksenia Maksimovtsova* | Language Conflicts in Contemporary Estonia, Latvia, and Ukraine. A Comparative Exploration of Discourses in Post-Soviet Russian-Language Digital Media | With a foreword by Ammon Cheskin | ISBN 978-3-8382-1282-1

206 *Michal Vít* | The EU's Impact on Identity Formation in East-Central Europe between 2004 and 2013. Perceptions of the Nation and Europe in Political Parties of the Czech Republic, Poland, and Slovakia | With a foreword by Andrea Pető | ISBN 978-3-8382-1275-3

207 *Per A. Rudling* | Tarnished Heroes. The Organization of Ukrainian Nationalists in the Memory Politics of Post-Soviet Ukraine | ISBN 978-3-8382-0999-9

208 *Peter H. Solomon Jr., Kaja Gadowska (Eds.)* | Legal Change in Post-Communist States. Progress, Reversions, Explanations | ISBN 978-3-8382-1312-5

209 *Pawel Kowal, Georges Mink, Iwona Reichardt (Eds.)* | Three Revolutions: Mobilization and Change in Contemporary Ukraine I. Theoretical Aspects and Analyses on Religion, Memory, and Identity | ISBN 978-3-8382-1321-7

210 *Pawel Kowal, Georges Mink, Adam Reichardt, Iwona Reichardt (Eds.)* | Three Revolutions: Mobilization and Change in Contemporary Ukraine II. An Oral History of the Revolution on Granite, Orange Revolution, and Revolution of Dignity | ISBN 978-3-8382-1323-1

211 *Li Bennich-Björkman, Sergiy Kurbatov (Eds.)* | When the Future Came: The Collapse of the USSR and the Emergence of National Memory in Post-Soviet History Textbooks | ISBN 978-3-8382-1335-4

212 *Olga R. Gulina* | Migration as a (Geo-)Political Challenge in the Post-Soviet Space. Border Regimes, Policy Choices, Visa Agendas | With a foreword by Nils Muižnieks | ISBN 978-3-8382-1338-5

ibidem.eu